The Maoist Insurgency in Nepal

The book deals with the dynamics and growth of a violent twenty-first century communist rebellion initiated in Nepal by the Communist Party of Nepal (Maoist) – CPN(M). It contextualizes and explains why and how a violent Maoist insurgency grew in Nepal after the end of the Cold War, in contrast to the decline of other radical communist movements in most parts of the world.

Scholars from diverse disciplinary backgrounds employ a wide variety of approaches and methods to unravel different aspects of the rebellion. Individual chapters analyse the different causes of the insurgency, factors that contributed to its growth, the organization, agency, ideology and strategies employed by the rebels and the state, and the consequences of the insurgency.

New issues are analysed in conjunction with the insurgency, such as the role of the Maoist student organization, Maoist cultural troupes, the organization and strategies of the People's Army and the Royal Nepal Army, indoctrination and recruitment of rebels, and international factors. While reviewing economic aspects, the book's contributors also look at land issues and their contribution to the growth of the insurgency. Based on original fieldwork and a thorough analysis of empirical data, this book fills an existing gap in academic analyses of the insurgency in Nepal.

Mahendra Lawoti teaches at Western Michigan University and is president of the Association for Nepal and Himalayan Studies, Associate Fellow at Asia Society and a columnist for *The Kathmandu Post.*

Anup K. Pahari received his MA from the George Washington University and PhD in Sociology from the University of Wisconsin-Madison. He is currently an independent contractor with the US Government and specializes in language, culture and politics of South Asia.

Routledge Contemporary South Asia Series

The Maoist Insurgency in Nepal

Revolution in the twenty-first century

**Edited by
Mahendra Lawoti and
Anup K. Pahari**

 Routledge
Taylor & Francis Group

LONDON AND NEW YORK

First published 2010
by Routledge
2 Park Square, Milton Park, Abingdon, Oxon OX14 4RN

Simultaneously published in the USA and Canada
by Routledge
270 Madison Ave, New York, NY 10016

Routledge is an imprint of the Taylor & Francis Group, an Informa business

Typeset in by Times New Roman by Swales & Willis Ltd, Exeter, Devon

British Library Cataloguing in Publication Data
A catalogue record for this book is available
from the British Library

Library of Congress Cataloging in Publication Data
  The Maoist insurgency in Nepal : revolution in the twenty-first century /
  edited by Mahendra Lawoti and Anup K. Pahari.
  p. cm.—(Routledge contemporary South Asia series ; 20)
  Includes bibliographical references and index.
  1. Communism—Nepal. 2. Insurgency—Nepal.
  3. Nepal—Politics and government—1990-
  I. Lawoti, Mahendra, 1965- II. Pahari, Anup K.
  HX385.9.A6M37 2009
  954.96—dc22
  2009013237

ISBN10: 0–415–77717–8 (hbk)
ISBN10: 0–203–86939–0 (ebk)

ISBN13: 978–0–415–77717–9 (hbk)
ISBN13: 978–0–203–86939–0 (ebk)

Mahendra dedicates the book to his loving sons
Sajjan Lawoti and Sumbon Lawoti
and peace, democracy and social justice for the future
generation
Anup dedicates the book to his loving wife and precious
daughters
Lilly KC, Aria Pahari and Savarna Pahari
and to Nepalis who yearn for early, positive and lasting
changes in Nepal

Contents

Illustrations

Figures

Tables

Boxes

Acknowledgements

In the preparation of this volume, we have incurred a lot of debt. Mahendra would like to thank the Faculty Research and Creative Activities Support Fund and the Department of Political Science at Western Michigan University for supporting field work in summer 2006 and 2008 respectively. Mahendra would also like to thank Sanjaya Serchan and J. B. Pun Magar for support during the field work. He would like to thank all people who shared their experience, views and opinions during the field work in Kathmandu, Rolpa, Banke, Panchather and Sunsari districts. He would especially like to thank Kumar Fudung, Arun Neupane, Anup K. Pahari, Ashok Sayenju, Laxmi Prasad Tumbahamphe and anonymous Nepal Army readers for commenting on drafts of various papers. At the Department of Political Science, Western Michigan University, Mahendra would like to thank his colleagues, especially Jim Butterfield, Kevin Corder and Sybil Rhodes, for support in developing and carrying out the project. Mahendra also benefited from feedback he received when he presented different papers at different conferences.

Finally he would like to thank his loving wife Geeta, sons Sajjan and Sumbon, parents (P. S. Lawoti and V. S. Lawoti), sisters and brothers and their spouses (Gurans and Anek Gurung; Dovan and Mohan Subba; Surendra Lawoti and Sagun and Babina Lawoti) for supporting the research in Nepal and the USA and accommodating peculiar demands that research and writing entails.

Anup is grateful to Mahendra Lawoti for valuable comments on earlier drafts of the chapter included in this book. He is also thankful to Alok Bohara and Prakash Adhikari of the Nepal Studies Center at the University of New Mexico-Albuquerque for comments, advice and research assistance. Anup owes a special debt to his parents Sachey and Sabi Pahari who have supported him in every venture in life, including this one. His brother Anil, sister-in-law Sabina, and nephews Kirtijai and Virajit have helped in many seen and unseen ways. His 90-year-old father-in- law, Lt Col. Tej Bahadur Khatri, a veretan of World War II, is a source of daily inspiration. Anup's young daughters, wise beyond their years, have supported by fully understanding the importance of this project, and by often resisting the urge to recruit their father for alternative uses. Finally, Anup would like to mention his dear and patient wife, Lilly KC, as the person whose logistical and emotional support made the greatest difference in his completing this project.

Both Mahendra and Anup would like to thank the two reviewers for helpful suggestions, Bal Krishna Mabuhang for allowing us to reprint the caste/ethnographic map of Nepal and Milan Shrestha for preparing a topographic map, and Dorothea Schaefter and Suzanne Richardson at Routledge for showing an interest in the project and pushing it through speedily. They would also like to thank all contributors for preparing the chapters in time and accommodating various comments and suggestions.

Mahendra Lawoti, Kalamazoo, Michigan
Anup K. Pahari, Manassas, Virginia
March 2009

List of abbreviations

AINUS	All India Nepali Unity Society
ANCCC	All Nepal Communist Coordination Committee
ANNISU-R	All Nepal National Independent Student Union-Revolutionary
APF	Armed Police Force
BJP	Bharatiya Janata Party
CoAS	Chief of Army Staff
CBNUPN	Chure Bhawar National Unity Party Nepal
CBS	Central Bureau of Statistics
CCM	Central Committee Member
CCOMPOSA	Coordination Committee of Maoist Parties and Organizations of South Asia
CMPP	Common Minimum Policy and Program
CPA	Comprehensive Peace Agreement
CPI-M	Communist Party of India-Maoist
CPI-ML	Communist Party of India-Marxist Leninist
CPM	Communist Party of India (Marxist)
CPN	Communist Party of Nepal
CPN-J	Communist Party of Nepal-Joint
CPN-M	Communist Party of Nepal-Maoist
CPN-ML	Communist Party of Nepal-Marxist Leninist
CPN-U	Communist Party of Nepal-United
CPN-UC	Communist Party of Nepal-Unity Centre
CPN-UML	Communist Party of Nepal-United Marxist Leninist
CRZ	Compact Revolutionary Zone
DHQ	District Headquarter
DNP	Dalit Nationalities Party
FDI	Foreign Direct Investment
FDNF	Federal Democratic National Forum
FUG	Forest User Groups
GDP	Gross Domestic Product
GNP	Gross National Product
HDI	Human Development Index
HEI	Human Empowerment Index

HOR	House of Representatives
HPI	Human Poverty Index
HRW	Human Rights Watch
ICG	International Crisis Group
ICJ	International Commission of Jurists
ICRC	International Committee of the Red Cross
IG	Indigenous Groups
IISDP	Integrated Internal Security and Development Program
INBCGSI	India-Nepal Bilateral Consultative Group on Security Issues
LTTE	Liberation Tigers of Tamil Eelam
MCC	Maoist Communist Centre
MNLF	Madhesi National Liberation Front
MPRF	Madhesi People's Rights Forum
MRD	Movement for the restoration of democracy
NDC	National Defence Council
NDP	National Democratic Party
NDP-N	National Democratic Party-Nepal
NDSP	Nepal Democratic Socialist Party
NEFIN	Nepal Federation of Indigenous Nationalities
NFP	Nepal Family Party
NGP	Nepal Goodwill Party
NGP-A	Nepal Goodwill Party-Anandi
NHDR	Nepal Human Development Report
NHRC	National Human Rights Commission
NLSS	Nepal Living Standard Survey
NNP	Nepa: National Party
NPF	National Peoples Front
NPLP	National People's Liberation Party
NPP	Nepal People's Party
NPPP	National People Power Party
NWPP	Nepal Workers and Peasants Party
OHCHR	Office of the High Commissioner for Human Rights
PFN	People's Front Nepal
PLA	People's Liberation Army
PPP	Purchasing Power Parity
PWG	People's War Group
RAW	Research and Analysis Wing
RIM	Revolutionary Internationalist Movement
RNA	Royal Nepal Army
RTLF	Republican Tarai Liberation Front
RTLF-J	Republican Tarai Liberation Front-Jwala Singh
SAARC	South Asian Association for Regional Cooperation
SATP	South Asia Terrorism Portal
SF	Security Forces
SPA-M	Seven Party Alliance and the Maoists

TMDP	Tarai-Madhesh Democratic Party
TPU	12-Point Understanding
UCD	Uppsala Conflict Database
ULF	United Left Front
UMDF	United Madhesi Democratic Front
UNDP	United Nations Development Project
UNMIN	United Nations Mission in Nepal
UPFN	United People's Front Nepal
URPC	United Revolutionary People's Council
VDC	Village Development Committee
WPRM	World Peoples Resistance Movement
YCL	Young Communist League

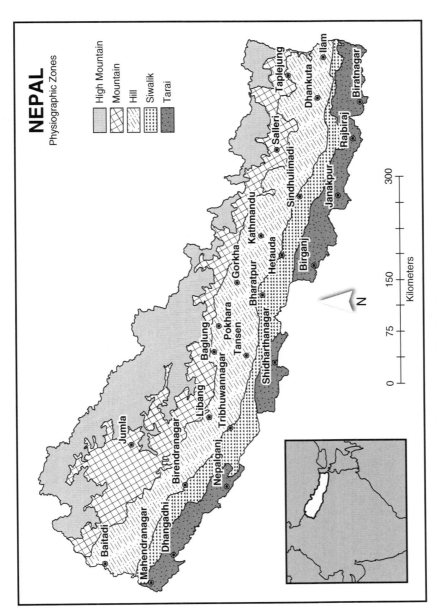

Figure 0.1 Topographic Map of Nepal. Prepared by Milan Shrestha

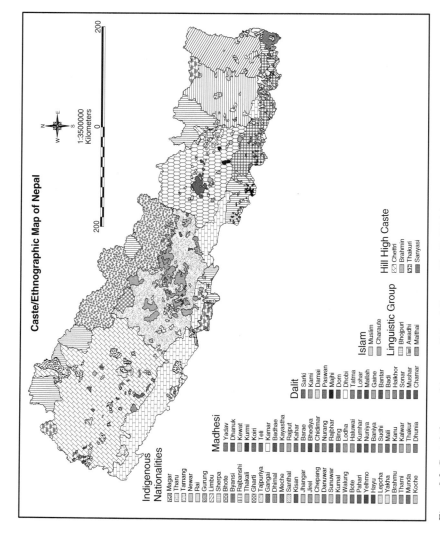

Figure 0.2 Caste/ethnographic map of Nepal. Prepared by Bal Krishna Mabuhang

Part I
Introduction

1 Evolution and growth of the Maoist insurgency in Nepal

Mahendra Lawoti[1]

Introduction

The growth of the Maoist insurgency in Nepal around the turn of the century confounded the world by defying several layers of conventional wisdom about politics and society.[2] The Communist Party of Nepal-Maoist (CPN-M) controlled a large swath of territory within a decade of launching an insurgency. The armed conflict led to the death of more than 13,000 people, in addition to many other costs of civil war such as destruction, displacement and gross human rights abuses (see chapter 15 for discussion of consequences of the conflict). Eventually, the Maoists successfully negotiated a peace settlement in their favor and went on to win the postwar election.

The first challenge to the prevalent understanding comes from the rise of a violent communist rebellion in the 21st century even as communist regimes fell one after another around the world. The communist insurgency expanded rapidly in Nepal despite the declaration of an end of ideology after the end of Cold War (see Fukuyama 1993) and despite lack of significant external support. In fact, the Maoist insurgency grew despite an adverse international climate, including the US-led War on Terror after Al Qaida's 9/11 attacks.

Second, Nepal had restored democracy in 1990 and democracy is supposed to defuse violence by transforming such tendencies into non-violent conflicts through electoral politics and non-violent protests (Ward and Gleditsch 1998; Hegre et al. 2001). However, the CPN-M launched the insurgency in February 1996 after taking part briefly in the fledgling democracy – it regularly engaged in petitioning and public protests in early 1990s and competed in the 1991 general and 1992 local elections. The predecessor of the CPN-M, in fact, had emerged as the third largest parliamentary party after the 1991 election. The launch and rapid growth of the insurgency challenged the notion that democracy could settle conflicts peacefully and that it was the only acceptable game in town (see Diamond 1999).

Third, the insurgency gained momentum even though Nepal was witnessing reasonable economic growth, expansion of development, and improvement in human development index (HDI) in the 1990s, including in the Maoist strongholds of the mid-western hills. The average real GDP (gross domestic product) for 1987–88 to 1994–95 was 4.1 percent compared to 3 percent during 1976–77 to 1986–87

(Sharma 2006: 1242).[3] The HDI had increased in 2001 compared to 1996 in most districts (UNDP 2004; NESAC 1998). Roads, schools, health facilities, universities, banks and other development infrastructure and service sectors expanded in the 1990s (Mahat 2005; Khanal 2007). Class-based rebellions are said to ignite when economic conditions worsen but the Maoist People's War was launched and gained momentum when national economic and development indicators demonstrated positive trends in Nepal.

Fourth, the escalation of violence surprised many because Nepal was considered a peaceful country. More than a hundred countries had endorsed the zone of peace initiative of King Birendra by 1990. Hence, it shocked many people when the country regarded as a 'Shangrila' turned into a bloody battlefield.

The growth of the insurgency in Nepal thus raises many interesting questions. How did a violent Maoist movement grow and succeed in the post-Cold War adverse global environment? Why did a party that had participated in a democratic election launch a violent movement and receive significant support? Why did people support the rebellion when economic and development indicators were showing improvements? Does the success of the Maoists in Nepal indicate resurgence of radical communism globally? The objective of the book is to contextualize and explain the growth of a violent communist rebellion. It will fill an existing void in academic analyses of the insurgency and connect the Nepali case to a broader literature on rebellions.

The chapters analyze factors that contributed to the insurgency's growth, strategies employed by the rebels and the state, and the consequences of the insurgency. The chapters cover issues that have not been explicated or analyzed thoroughly yet: indoctrination and recruitment of rebels, the role of the Maoist student organization and cultural troupe, organization, mobilization, and strategies of the rebels and the state, including the People's Liberation Army (PLA) and Royal Nepal Army's (RNA), ethnic dimension of the class-based rebellion, external factors, revolutionary governance, and the role of electoral democracy and liberal market economy.[4] The chapters also build onto existing analyses and review and retest the role of economy, geography, incentives of leaders and recruits, ideology, literacy, road density and so on.

We have brought together scholars working in different fields employing a variety of approaches and methods to unravel different aspects of the insurgency. Scholars from multiple disciplinary backgrounds – anthropologists, economists, political scientists, sociologists, and conflict experts – with particular disciplinary expertise have tackled different questions and gleaned valuable insights. The chapters are based on original fieldwork as well as analyses of secondary data and the contributors have employed both qualitative and quantitative methods. Fieldwork-based chapters have marshaled rare ethnographic data of the conflict and provide rich, thick descriptions and analyses while chapters employing sophisticated econometric tools have identified causes of the insurgency based on available quantitative data. Chapters that have studied the rebellion from a comparative perspective, on the other hand, have produced valuable insights through rigorous analyses and filled an important methodological gap (among few exceptions are Marks and Palmer 2005; Bownas 2003; Ramirez 2004; Nickson 1992).

History of the communist movement in Nepal

The communist movement arrived in Nepal via its southern democratic neighbor India, and not, in fact, directly via communist China, the northern neighbor. The Communist Party of Nepal (CPN) was established in 1949 in Calcutta, India, with the active assistance of Indian communists. The party was banned from 1952 to 1956 during the interim democratic period. The communists tied with the People's Council to win the most seats – six out of 18 – in the first adult franchise-based election for Kathmandu municipality in 1953 but won only four seats out of 109 in the first election to the Parliament in 1959 (KC 1999).

The communist movement spread clandestinely during the Panchayat period (1960–90) when the regime was more focused on tackling the overt challenges from the Nepali Congress, whose two-thirds majority government King Mahendra had dissolved in 1960. The common strident nationalist agenda between the communists and the palace sometimes brought them closer. Many communist cadres, especially the more radical ones, however, were jailed or killed during the period.

The communist movement in Nepal has faced a chronic problem of factionalism and frequent splits. There have been around a dozen communist parties and factions in the country at any one time since the 1960s (KC 1999; Khadka 1995; Maharjan 2000; Rawal 2047 v.s. (1991)). The splits began when King Mahendra seized power in 1960 and banned the political parties. The 'Russian communists' or those that were closer to the USSR were supportive of the royal action whereas the 'Chinese communists' or the group that followed the Beijing line remained aloof. Both the CPN factions split numerous times. The splits and factionalism often occurred over minor differences in interpretations of policies and strategies or personality clashes among the leaders. In 1974 the more extremist leaders of the mainstream communist movement – notably Nirmal Lama and Mohan Bikram Singh – established the Nepal Communist Party (Fourth Congress). The top Maoist leadership hails from this group (Maharjan 2000; Thapa and Sijapati 2003).

The Nepali communists launched a violent movement for the first time in 1971. Influenced by the violent Naxalite Maoist movement in West Bengal, a group of young communists killed several 'class enemies' in Jhapa district in east Nepal. The campaign was brutally crushed by the state. Nevertheless, the group went on to form the Communist Party of Nepal-Marxist Leninist (CPN-ML) in 1978 and became the largest communist faction by 1990. It merged with CPN-Marxist, a party with well-known leaders but a weak mass base, to become the CPN-United Marxist Leninist (CPN-UML) in 1990 and emerged as the major opposition party after the 1991 general election. It formed the first democratically elected communist government (minority) in the world after the mid-term election in 1994 but lasted for only a year

The communist movement had grown considerably by the 1990s, even though it was split into numerous factions. The utopian ideals and wide-ranging promises to

Table 1.1 Votes and seats received by communist and non-communist parties in parliament

Political parties	1959		1991		1994		1999		2008	
	Vote %	Seats	Vote %	Seats	Vote %	Seats	Vote %	Seats	Vote %	Seats
Communists	7.2	4	36.26	82	33.15	87	39.51	75	56.98	353
Non-communists	76.48	101	53.79	120	54.8	106	52.74	128	40.48	222

end all forms of inequalities and injustices have attracted the poor, youth and marginalized groups into the communist fold. The communist movement has also received considerable support among the clerical government workers, labor unions and public school teachers.

The political parties that call themselves communist range from the radical Maoists to moderate groups like the CPN-UML. Nepali communists are highly nationalist, unlike the international communist movement. Many moderate communist parties also do not uphold many other elements of the communist ideology anymore. Many accepted the constitutional monarchy and multiparty parliamentary democracy after 1990. Likewise, since 1990 many communists have adopted market-friendly policies.

The communists collectively received 36, 33 and 39 percent of votes in 1991, 1994 and 1999 respectively (see table 1.1). Collectively they received more votes than the Nepali Congress, the largest party, only in 1999. The communists finally obtained more votes than all the non-communist parties in 2008. The brief history of the communist movement shows that by early 1990, communists had firmly established themselves as a major political force in Nepal despite the fact that the world was headed towards a post-communist global order.

Evolution of the Maoists

The Maoists were a small communist faction among a number of extremist communist parties before 1996. Scholars identify the origin of the Maoists with the establishment of the CPN-Fourth Congress in 1974 under Nirmal Lama and Mohan Bikram Singh. After a number of splits, some of the persons and groups involved in the CPN-Fourth Congress, except Mohan Bikram Singh and the CPN-Masal he led, formed the CPN-Unity Center (CPN-UC) on 23 November 1990.[5] The CPN-UC was made up of the CPN-Fourth Congress led by Nirmal Lama, CPN-Mashal led by Prachanda aka Puspa Kamal Dahal who had replaced Kiran, and the breakaway faction of the CPN-Masal led by Baburam Bhattarai, the Maoist ideologue. The CPN-UC established a political front headed by Baburam Bhattarai – the United People's Front Nepal (UPFN) – to participate in the elections (Maharjan 1993).

Before the 1994 mid-term elections, the CPN-UC and the UPFN split and the faction led by Prachanda and Baburam Bhattarai boycotted the elections partly because their front was not recognized by the Election Commission. In 1995,

Prachanda-led CPN-UC held its Third Plenum during which the party renamed itself as CPN-Maoist and decided to begin an armed insurgency (Thapa and Sijapati 2003).[6] On 4 February 1996, the UPFN led by Baburam Bhattarai submitted a list of 40 demands on nationalism, people's democracy and livelihood with an ultimatum to initiate insurgency if they were not met.[7] The demands included a range from genuine concerns (land rights to tenants, secular state) to wishful issues (employment guarantee to all). A majority of the nine demands on nationalism related to Nepal's relations with India. The people's democracy subsection included demands concerning indigenous nationalities, women and Dalit. Some others points were ideological and questionable in terms of democratic credentials, such as restricting the activities of NGOs. One demand called for the abolishment of royal privileges but did not call for a republican state, which became a major issue during different phases of the insurgency. The list included a demand for a new Constitution to be drawn by people's representatives. Four days before the ultimatum expired, the Maoists launched the insurgency on 13 February 1996 by attacking rural police posts in three districts – two in the mid-western and one in the central region (Maharjan 2000). The insurgency grew rapidly. The next section discusses major factors that contributed to the initiation and growth of the insurgency.

Conditions for rebellion

Poverty and economic inequality

Poverty and inequality, and how they are perceived – relative deprivation or the gap between expected and achieved well-being – can increase alienation and push groups towards violent conflict (Muller and Seligson 1987; Gurr 1968). A lot of work has focused on poverty and economic inequality and their contribution to the initiation and growth of the Maoist insurgency in Nepal.

Economic indicators, however, as discussed earlier, showed improvement during the 1990s. Infrastructure and service sector also expanded more rapidly in the 1990s. The total road length increased from 7,036 km in 1989/90 to 15,308 km in 1999/2000. The number of commercial banks increased to 17 in 2004 from five in 1990. Internal air traffic saw a growth from 228,000 a year in 1989/90 to 1,209,000 in 2002/03. The primary, lower secondary and secondary schools increased by 45, 83 and 122 percent in a decade. Private education expanded in primary, secondary, university, vocational and technical education (Mahat 2005). The 1990s witnessed print and media booms and the communication network expanded rapidly: telephone connection per thousand increased from 3.1 in 1990 to 13.1 in 2001 (World Bank 2006, cited in Khanal 2007). Do these data contradict the poverty, inequality and relative deprivation theories? A closer look at the data shows that the theories are relevant.

First, Nepal remained mired in extreme poverty despite the growth and progress in the 1990s. Nepal is one of the poorest countries in the world. Its GNI (gross national income) per capita was US$290 in 2006, the lowest in South Asia except for Afghanistan. Even the better off in Nepal were poor. For instance, "over

40 percent of medium and large landowners in the hills were classified as 'poor' in 1996" (Deraniyagala 2005). Thus, in many parts of the country, especially in the hills and mountains, poverty affected a large proportion of the population. Poverty intensified and expanded owing to an increase in population and decrease in land productivity in the 1990s: "unlike in previous generations, it is no longer possible, for a significant proportion of the poor, to cultivate new public land and ameliorate poverty at the household level . . . the size of intergenerational transfer of agricultural land has become progressively smaller" (Mishra 2004: 22). The intensified poverty had direct consequences on people's basic daily needs. Macfarlane's (2001) ethnographic study provides a vivid picture of everyday ramifications of increasing poverty: in a hill village in central Nepal, where he has frequently returned, a wage earner could buy a chicken with a day's wage in the late 1960s whereas in the mid-1990s it took eight days of wages.

Second, the absolute number of poor increased in Nepal. Government statistics show around 40 percent of the people as poor – people unable to access basic human needs, including a minimum defined basket of food. Even though this proportion remained constant in the decades from the 1970s to the 1990s, the absolute number of poor increased in huge numbers. For instance, between 1977 and 1996 "the absolute number of the absolutely poor persons nearly *doubled*" (Mishra 2004: 22; NESAC 1998).

Third, expansion of infrastructure and services benefited more people than before; but with an increase in the absolute number of people owing to a population boom, access to the benefits of development and services may have continued to elude large segments of the population. Further, many of the development projects, infrastructure and services such as expansion of banking and air transportation benefited the better-off section of society living in and around urban areas.

Fourth, findings of econometric analyses, which demonstrate that rugged terrain (hill), road density and so on explain intensity of conflict (Bohara et al. 2006) also indirectly support the inequality and poverty theses. The rugged hill regions have fewer roads, are deprived of infrastructure and many other services, and are generally poorer (see Tiwari; Acharya, this volume).

Finally, inequality increased in Nepal despite improved national economic indicators. Nepal had become the most unequal country in South Asia in the 1990s with the highest Gini Index of 0.426.[8] The growth in a few select areas and stagnation in others led to this ironic situation. Inequality in Nepal existed among different sectors: geographic regions (mountain and hills and Tarai, and east to west), rural and urban areas, and gender, ethnic and caste groups (Murshed and Gates 2005).

The improvements in GDP, growth in output, and exports and international reserve brought about by the deregulation of the market since the mid-1980s occurred through an expansion of the urban-based modern sector and did not close the inequality gap. Poverty levels are significantly higher in rural areas (44 percent) than in urban areas (20 percent). The nominal income of the people living in urban areas increased by 16 percent per annum (from US$126 to US$285) during 1988–96 compared to only 4 percent for the rural population (from US$95 to US$125). Large parts of the rural areas stagnated while the urban centers, especially the Kathmandu valley, developed into pockets of wealth and consumption. Sharma (2006: 1242–43) argues that "[w]hen the average annual rate of inflation is taken into consideration, the growth in rural income is in fact negative. This not only increased poverty in the rural areas but also increased rural–urban inequality." The growth in urban areas and stagnation in the rural areas widened the perception of inequality further among rural residents (Deraniyagala 2005).

Poverty is also more widespread in the mountains, where its incidence is 56 percent, compared with around 40 percent in the hills and plains. The incidence of poverty in the central (67 percent) and mid- and far-western (72 percent) hills/mountains also far outstrips that in eastern (28 percent) and western (40 percent) regions (Deraniyagala 2005). The Maoist stronghold districts had relatively low human development indicators (Bray et al. 2003; UNDP 2004).

The stagnation of rural regions during the 1970s through the neglect of the periphery, the increasing pressure on limited land in the hills, and the erosion of traditional jobs and sources of income was portrayed vividly by, among others, *Nepal in Crisis* (Blaikie et al. 1980). Economic and demographic indicators demonstrate the continued neglect of rural regions. This neglect contributed to the rising inequality. Poverty levels were 33 percent in 1976–77 but rose to 42 percent by 1995–96. The "income share of the top 10 percent of the people increased from 21 percent in the mid-1980s to 35 percent by the mid-1990s, while the share of the bottom 40 percent shrank from 24 percent to 15 percent by the mid 1990s" (Sharma 2006).

Poverty and economic stagnation had a more detrimental impact on the rural residents (87 percent in 2001) because they were dependent upon the stagnating agriculture. Annual growth rates of agricultural output (major crops) declined from 1961–62 to 1991–93. The growth rate was a negative 0.07 percent for all crops in Nepal during the period while other South Asian countries witnessed an increase. The stagnation was due to the government policy of import substitution industrialization – the government invested in industrialization in urban areas at the cost of peasants and rural areas. Sharma (2006: 1241–42) writes that agriculture, the major source of employment and income for 80 percent of the people, "has not received more than 26 percent of development expenditure in any development plan since the mid 1950s . . . Nepal, which had the highest agriculture yield (per hectare) in South Asia in the early 1960s fell significantly behind other countries by early 1990s."

Land ownership patterns also contributed to poverty and inequality. Despite the relatively small size of land ownership in general, land ownership reflects the persistence of the feudal system: "44 percent of households in the country are marginal landowners [0–0.5 hectare], but this group only accounts for 14 percent of total privately owned agricultural land. In contrast, the 5 percent of agricultural households who own plots greater than 3 h[ectare] account for around 27 percent of total agricultural land."[9] Land and land-based resources such as forests and water are very valuable in an agricultural society like Nepal and their unequal distribution has contributed to conflicts (Upreti 2004). Land scarcity contributed to environmental degradation as people and animals attacked forests and exploited less fertile land.

Environmental degradation in turn decreased productivity and increased poverty and inequality (Bhurtel and Ali, unpublished paper).[10]

Socio-cultural inequality

Nepal not only faced class inequality, but extreme socio-cultural inequality also existed among numerous linguistic, ethnic, religious, racial, caste and regional groups.[11] The Caste Hill Hindu Hill Elite Males (CHHEM) monopolized the political, economic, social and cultural power. Bahun, Chhetri, Newar and Tarai 'high caste' have better access to material resources while Dalit, indigenous nationalities, mid-level Madhesi caste, and Muslims are generally worse off. The HDI of Brahmin was 135 in 1996 compared to national index of 100 while the indigenous nationalities, Dalit, Madhesi and Muslim, had 92.21, 73.62, 96.28 and 73.67 respectively (NESAC 1998). Not only are groups like Dalit, indigenous nationalities and Muslim poorer, but even the decrease in the incidence of poverty among them is slower compared to Bahun, Chhetri and Newar. While between 1995–96 and 2003–4 poverty declined by 46 percent among Brahmin and Chhetri, it declined only by 6, 10 and 21 percent respectively for Muslims, hill indigenous nationalities and Dalit (Tiwari 2008). Within all groups, women generally face discrimination but the incidence is higher among Muslims and 'high caste' Hindus.

Only Bahun and Chhetri are among the effective executive head in Nepal.[12] They are politically dominant to such an extent that even ideological opponents hail from the same group. Neupane (2000) found that the CHHE overwhelmingly dominated 12 influential sectors in 1999: the executive, judiciary, Constitutional Councils, civil administration, parliament, political party leadership, local government heads, and leadership of industrial and commercial, academic, professional, cultural, science and technology, and civil society associations. In fact, presence of the indigenous nationalities decreased in some institutions during the post-1990 democratic era compared to the Panchayat and the first parliamentary democratic (1959–60) periods (NESAC 1998; Neupane 2000; Lawoti 2005). The gap between the dominant and other groups further widened in the bureaucracy. In 2001/2002, the CHHE made up nearly 90 percent of civil service exam graduates. The extent of domination can be conveyed by the case of the Dalit. Not a single Dalit was inducted into the cabinet and only one Dalit was elected to the House of Representative in the entire 13 years from 1990 to 2002 (Lawoti 2008).

CHHE domination in the mainstream civil society sector was/is overwhelming as well. The CHHE and Newar dominated around 90 percent of the top positions in prominent Nepali NGOs and human rights groups in 1999 (Neupane 2000). Onta and Parajuli (2058 v.s. (2001–2)) found that CHHE made up 80 percent of media elite (editors, publishers and columnists). This shows that most power, both at the state and civil society, was effectively enjoyed by CHHE.[13]

In addition to this political, social and economic domination, the marginalized groups face cultural discrimination, perhaps the most important feature because it was the foundation of discrimination in other realms. Even socio-economically well-off groups like Newar, Thakali and Tarai Brahmin face socio-cultural discrimination, formally as well as informally. The state was declared Hindu, discriminating against other indigenous and non-indigenous religions. Khas-Nepali enjoyed special privileges compared to other native languages. Citizenship discrimination occurred based on racial markers. The government-formed Citizenship Commission stated that in the 1990s more than 3 million adult Nepalis, mostly Madhesi but Dalit and indigenous nationalities as well, were denied citizenship (Upadhaya 2052 (1995)); the state awarded citizenship certificates only after the 2006 political transformation. Cultural imperialism, or the imposition of the dominant group's language, religion and values on the rest of the society, was a consequence as well as cause of ethnic domination. The CHHE performed better in schools taught in their native language and their social standings were enhanced because their culture and values were projected as superior by the communal state (Maddox 2003; Lawoti 2005). On the other hand, free residential education in Sanskrit up to PhD, fully supported by the state, provided social mobility opportunities to CHHEM while comparable opportunities did not exist for others.

Modernization, social change and fluidity

Many of the inequalities had existed for a long time but unequal societies can be stable, as Nepal was before the 1990s. Modernization that began in the 1950s and 1960s, however, began to create conditions for conflict by changing societal conditions and introducing uncertainty and fluidity. The spread of education challenged traditional norms and practices and lessened respect for the older order based on reinforcing hierarchies of class, ethnicity, caste, gender and age. Education also enabled dissatisfied groups to form alternate collective imaginations, including a revolutionary one (Fujikura 2003). Penetration of markets eroded traditional professions, for instance by making available cheaper clothes and shoes – resulting in loss of work for the artisan Dalit. Globalization and the communication revolution enabled educated but unemployed youth to be aware of opportunities in other societies through television, cable, radio and internet while remaining deprived of opportunities locally. On the other hand, specific state policies contributed to the marginalization of some groups. For instance, land reform policies took away the community-owned land of indigenous peoples by mandating individual land ownership. The displacement eroded their identity, which was intertwined with the land, increased poverty and destabilized their communities (Joshi and Mason 2007; Guneratne 2002; Caplan 2000, revised edition).

These multi-level changes eroded the old order, created fluidity and destabilized society. Groups in fluid conditions are prone to mobilization and often support forces that recognize them (Davidheiser 1992). The Maoists recognized the plight of the fluid groups like the marginalized indigenous nationalities, women, unemployed youth, de-skilled Dalit and others, and mobilized and incorporated many among them into the armed insurgency. For instance, youths who could not get jobs, afford college education or residence in urban centers, nor receive recognition from the age-based social hierarchy in rural areas, joined the insurgency, where they received recognition and reward (Pettigrew 2003).

Agency, ideology and strategy of the Maoists

Conducive conditions for rebellion, such as poverty and inequality, had been present in Nepal for a long time; hence, the existence of fertile conditions alone does not explain the rise of the Maoist rebellion. Unless a committed group exploits favorable conditions to build an organization and engage in large scale mobilization, a successful rebellion may not occur. The role of professionals in rebellions – an educated middle class that wants to change the society – is very important (Migdal 1975). The professionals adopt or construct ideology, create awareness, form organizations, train cadres, develop networks and mobilize people, including the poor and the peasants. To date, scholarship in Nepali rebellion has paid less attention to the agency, ideology and organization side of the People's War (the few exceptions are Khanal 2007; Mishra 2004; Graham 2007). This volume will help to fill the gap.

Leadership and ideology

The role of Maoist leadership in developing and refining a 'correct' ideology, building and expanding organization, mobilizing people, exploiting available conditions and developing strategies to outsmart a more resourceful enemy was very significant in the growth of the rebellion. The leadership began with a long preparation for the People's War. Mishra (2004: 10), a close left-movement observer in Nepal, notes that "The CPN-UC engaged in an intense five year intra-party struggle to develop and sharpen a 'correct' ideological line, 'purge' the 'minority faction' and eventually transform the 'majority faction' of the CPN-UC into CPN-M in 1995." The Maoist leaders claim that before launching the insurgency they thoroughly analyzed why the communists were successful globally in attaining power but not in retaining it.[14]

The Maoists organized awareness and training programs in their strongholds to prepare cadres and supporters for the People's War. They developed a collective political imagination for social justice and a better Nepal among their cadres that helped to overcome the initial costs of engaging in a dangerous violent conflict. The long ideological preparation benefited them significantly in the long run. Scholars have argued that rebel outfits that take time to indoctrinate their cadre ideologically end up with a disciplined cadre base that does not plunder, harass and kill indiscriminately during the war. On the other hand, if the rebel leadership takes the easy route and recruits cadres by distributing resources, the process could be easy in the short run but problematic later on. The undisciplined cadres could undermine rebellions through rapacious actions and haphazard violence (Weinstein 2007). The absence of lootable natural resources, which has been identified by some as a cause of civil wars (Collier and Hoeffler 2004), turned out to be a blessing for the Maoists.

The Maoist built a well-oiled party organization and established an army – the PLA – and a United Front – the United Revolutionary People's Council Nepal (see ICG 2005). They formed many sister organizations and fronts to assist the party and the PLA. They were often instrumental in recruiting and providing initial exposure to the party and its programs (see Eck; Mottin; and Snellinger, this volume). The party's numerous organizations and fronts, which often operated in a decentralized manner, were coordinated to achieve the common objectives. For instance, the PLA was used to attack and raid targets identified by the party, and the party and sister organizations aided the PLA during the raids. On the other hand, when the party and PLA were unable to launch attacks, the sister organizations – the student front, trade unions or ethnic fronts – organized street protests and strikes and/or blockaded towns, district headquarters and the capital. These activities filled gaps when the party and PLA were facing setbacks and generated huge psychological dividends by bewildering the state and boosting the morale of cadres. The PLA deputy chief credited the synergy between war and political struggles in the success of the rebellion.[15]

The role of leadership in the growth of the insurgency also becomes clear through their success in avoiding the 'break-up disease' that the communists in Nepal and Maoists in India were afflicted with. Some commentators point out that Prachanda, the top leader, is skilled in balancing different factions and leaders, for instance, through incorporation of issues raised by others into the official party line. Many commentators consider that the line following which they joined the multi-party system was originally propounded by Baburam Bhattarai; Prachanda co-opted it as the party line and prevented break-up of the party in the Chunwang plenary in 2005. Likewise, in late 2007 Prachanda co-opted the line of hardliners who were supported by many cadres in the national conference in Kathmandu.[16]

Mishra (2004) argues that the ideology of the rebels contributed to preventing splits within the party. The argument is plausible because before the party adopted the Maoist ideology and changed name, the predecessor party had frequently split; however, once the party adopted the Maoist ideology and launched the insurgency, the party avoided splits despite major disagreements and debates within the party – leaders gave up positions and personal advantages and were committed to a clearly articulated ideology and the goal of establishing communism.

The party followed Mao's strategy of guerrilla warfare and mass political mobilization in pursuit of a communist republic (Spence 1999). Initially they adopted Mao's three-stage strategy for people's revolution that had worked in China: strategic defense, strategic balance and strategic offence. Accordingly, they first mobilized the peasants and the poor in rural areas. The goal was to surround the center with rural peasant mobilization in the classic Mao mould. It was a good strategy because it allowed the Maoists to expand organization and build support away from the center's reach in early and weaker years.

Once the insurgency got going, a large pool of communist cadres and voters facilitated the rapid spread of the Maoists. First, converting communist sympathizers, who were familiar with ideology and political culture, into Maoist supporters/cadres was much easier than indoctrinating non-communists into Maoist cadres. Second, hardcore communists, who were frustrated with parties like the CPN-UML that had begun to demonstrate ambivalence towards the core communist ideology by the mid-1990s, were attracted to the Maoists. The discourse on revolution had been initiated in the 1970s and it had created cadres who looked forward to it. Third, after the CPN-UML split in late 1990s and the factions began harassing supporters of the other side, many disillusioned cadres joined the Maoists, among others, for security reasons.

The Maoists had also been flexible and adaptive in their approaches, strategies and ideology. Once the Maoists realized that rural mobilization was not sufficient to pressure the center, they revised their strategy and complemented it with urban mobilization – subsuming the dual rural–urban mobilization strategy within Prachanda Path or Prachanda Line. Second, despite being a primarily a class-based insurgency, the Maoist recognized the salience of identity issues in Nepal. It may have come from the recognition that the Dalit, indigenous nationalities, and women – at a later phase the Madhesi – offered potential recruitment and mobilization opportunities owing to the groups' marginalization by the state controlled by the dominant group. Nevertheless, this was a significant leap ideologically, and the mobilization produced rich rewards, especially because the mainstream political parties were either lukewarm or hostile towards identity issues. The Maoists formed many ethnic fronts, established autonomous ethnic regions, and raised ethnic and caste issues to mobilize the Dalit and indigenous nationalities. The inability of ethnic parties and movements, who raised the issues vociferously, to get concessions from the state, helped the Maoists because it alienated marginalized groups from the mainstream political process and ethnic movements that did not appear as effective vehicles for change.

The indigenous nationalities, Dalit and women (as well as the Madhesi in later years) participated in the Maoist insurgency in significant numbers. Their participation here was much wider than it was in the mainstream political parties and the state (Lawoti 2003a). The Dalit and indigenous nationalities, especially the Kham-Magars, filled the ranks of the PLA and provided recruits for the party and numerous sister organizations and fronts.

Selective deployment of violence

Violence and its threat is probably the most potent power of rebels, but if it is not used judiciously it can backfire. In Peru the indigenous peasants initially supported the Shining Path, but after the rebels began employing violence indiscriminately against the civilian population, the communities formed civil defense groups and pushed back the rebels (see chapter 7) and contributed in the decline of the movement. In Nepal, to a large extent the Maoists used violence judiciously to push the state away from rural areas, eliminate enemies, control rural areas, collect resources and implement their policies. The Maoists in Nepal faced reactions against extreme brutalities and extortions in some regions – notably in Dailekh (Shah 2008) – but it was not widespread and the Maoists were quick to diffuse strong community reactions through apologies and withdrawal of strong reaction-generating activities. They killed many innocent people, but they did not use violence indiscriminately and hence avoided large scale resistance.

The Maoists used violence and its threat selectively to expand their organizations. In new areas the Maoist had begun to infiltrate, they would post anonymous notices in public places such as schools and government offices prohibiting certain activities and threatening actions against those who did not conform. When after their activities increased the Maoists still did not feel safe in an area, anonymous threat letters would be sent to individuals whom the Maoists perceived as 'enemies' or potential donors. In regions under their control, a few or a large group of Maoists would make personal visits to threaten individuals if they were perceived to be working against their interest (Shneiderman and Turin 2003). In new areas, the Maoists visited during the night to beat people who resisted their dictates. The members of these violent teams were often unknown to the victims to avoid future retaliations in new areas (de Sales 2003). The activities were quite effective without much repercussion for the Maoists. People followed the Maoist dictates because of fear – the mobile Maoist army or militia could visit any time to take 'actions,' which could include minor punishment, public humiliation through garlanding with shoes and the shaving of heads, torture or even death.

The level of fear was quite widespread in rural areas, as anthropologists have pointed out (Pettigrew 2003a, 2003b). The Maoists deliberately created fear to control the population: "For the Maoists, the spreading of fear functioned as an exceptionally powerful means of control" (Graham 2007: 238). They often killed village elite to gain wider publicity. They also engaged in public demonstrations of torture and killings and often advertised such actions in newspapers, newsletters and cultural programs to demonstrate their strength (Fujikura 2003). The fear spread through threat and intimidation, real or implied, and backed up by mobile PLA and militia that could cover a wide area, enabled the Maoists to control large swathes of rural areas with limited cadres (Lecomte-Tilouine, this volume).

The Maoists also used coercion in recruitment. In some regions, they adopted a policy of "one person for PLA from one house." The Maoists abducted teachers, school children and political opponents and took the abductees around their rallies and programs for initial exposure to the Maoist ideologies (Eck, this volume). Some of the abducted children became political cadres, PLA foot soldiers, porters and medical assistants. The Human Rights Watch (2007) estimated 3,500 to 4,500 child soldiers to be part of the Maoist fighting force.

Another important function of violence was the displacement of the state and its agencies and opposition political cadres from rural areas. As the rebels attacked police posts and government offices and looted arms, ammunition and cash, the state agencies were shifted to more secure areas. This created voids in rural areas, and the Maoists filled them without much resistance from the local population. With the lack of protection from the state, villagers and cadres of other political parties were unable to resist the Maoists. People who were considered an enemy by the Maoists were harassed and many were expelled while others migrated out of fear.

The deployment of violence against local elite and state agencies in rural areas enabled the Maoists to win support from poor peasants. The Maoists had not been able to gain the support of the poor and disadvantaged groups before the insurgency, as is demonstrated by their inability to garner votes during elections, despite raising their issues, because the poor peasants were under the patronage of the local elite. The peasants voted as dictated by their patrons and against their class interest. Once the Maoists broke down the patron–client network with violence against the local elite, the former 'clients' became free to support the Maoists (Joshi and Mason 2007). Alternatively, a slightly different mechanism may have been set in motion, but with the very same results; namely, with the breakdown of the old order and the inability of former patrons to protect or constrain, poor peasants supported the Maoists who emerged as the new masters with violent capabilities. The Maoist patronage, however, was perceived as progressive by many and probably was less harmful to supporters because it was not strongly rooted, as village chiefs and party cadres were frequently transferred.

Revolutionary governance and provision of public goods

Guerrilla warfare cannot sustain without the support and compliance of the people. "Civilians are strategic actors, and as such they have the capacity to provide or withhold their participation and support" (Weinstein 2007: 163). Rebels have to win the hearts of the people while at the same time obtaining supplies. The Maoists attempted to win support in villages by providing different "public goods."

One of the better-known and successfully advertised public goods by the Maoists was actions against unpopular village elites, money lenders and 'slack' public school teachers. They confiscated the property of their opponents and distributed it among their supporters and the poor in some regions. The Maoists prohibited public sale of liquor in many areas and punished men engaged in domestic violence. The actions against untouchability, ethnic prejudice and sexism created a pro-people image for the Maoists and attracted committed cadres to the Maoist fold. Many people, especially those who were targeted from these actions, were offended but often were not able to resist owing to the breakdown of the state support system. The Maoists attempted to increase the legitimacy of their governance by holding elections in base areas and appointing Dalit, indigenous nationalities and women, who were rarely nominated or elected to public offices, as heads of different levels of people's governments.

The Maoists also engaged in the building of infrastructures, such as roads and bridges. Road-building was quite widespread in the hilly areas, even though many of the roads were never completed and vehicles never plied along them. Even though the Maoists mostly used 'voluntary' labor for construction projects, the people were not totally against such development initiatives.

A successful governance tool innovated by the Maoists and that affected more people was the People's Court, which adjudicated conflicts in villages and punished Maoist opponents. The courts often addressed the immediate needs of the rural people because the formal conflict resolution mechanism – the district court system – was far away, slow, costly and often corrupt. Many people were relieved when minor conflicts were settled quickly in villages at much lower cost.[17]

The Maoists governed the areas under their control with some level of "consensus." In many instances, they listened to the common people, who had rarely been asked for opinions before by "big people" (Shneiderman and Turin 2003). The Maoists levied "revolutionary" taxes,[18] collected food, took goods from shops on "credit," forced "voluntary" labor for "development" projects, restricted people's travel to district headquarters in some regions, and exerted local power in other ways. But in most cases their activities did not reach intolerable levels. For instance, they did not collect food without leaving any for villagers. They often presented their claims and demands on the people as a necessity for waging a war to better the lives of people. This attempt at "consensus" governance prevented strong reactions from the villagers even though they may not have been happy with forced contributions. When the policies of the Maoists generated strong and wide reaction and resistance, they were quick to defuse this through modification or withdrawal of policies, forming investigation committees and offering public apologies.

Exploiting contradictions and creating opportunities

The Nepali Maoists brilliantly exploited contradictions at all levels – at the family, household, local, national and international levels – to their benefit. The Maoists often used binary oppositions such as oppressed–oppressor, proletariat–feudal, reactionary–revolutionary, just and unjust wars (Lecomte-Tilouine 2006) to exploit the contradictions for recruiting and mobilizing people. If there was conflict in the family, they would take one side. Likewise, the Maoists often took sides in village disputes. Taking sides in a conflict allowed them to gain a foothold in villages and provided access to information about villagers and local political dynamics (de Sales 2003; Pettigrew 2003a).

To compete with other political parties, the Maoists successfully projected an image of a party that most vociferously raised the issues of the poor and the oppressed. Likewise, in addition to class issues, as discussed earlier, they exploited identity and socio-cultural contradictions to attract the marginalized indigenous nationalities, Dalit and women. As the ethnic and caste claims were largely against the state controlled by the dominant group, oppositional positions of the marginalized groups and the Maoists vis-à-vis the state converged.

At the political level, the Maoists effectively played on the fault lines and divisions among establishment political forces. For the first half of the insurgency, while their movement was still weak, they deliberately avoided antagonizing the Royal Nepal Army. The Maoists have publicly said that they had some sort of understanding with late King Birendra, who refused to deploy the army against "its own people." Without the well-equipped and trained army breathing behind their back, the Maoists established an army, trained them, equipped them with looted arms and ammunition, gained fighting experience in conflicts with the less prepared police and established base areas (see Mehta and Lawoti, this volume). The Maoists selectively attacked the cadres of the ruling Nepali Congress at the beginning while calling for unity among leftist and nationalist forces. The moderate communist factions and rightist groups were unmoved – if not pleased – by attacks against their arch political opponent which they felt was abusing state powers to undermine them politically. When the moderate left formed the government, the Maoists began attacking their cadres. This turn of events pleased Nepali Congress and the royalists. When the Maoists targeted the rightist cadres, the NC and

CPN-UML seemed to be least bothered. The Maoists began to highlight the republican demand after King Gyanendra began intervening in politics. The mainstream political parties were allowed by the Maoists to operate more freely in rural areas after that. By mostly attacking the cadres of the ruling party, the Maoists did not provide grounds for all establishment parties to form a joint coalition against them. The Maoists brilliantly exploited the lust for power and conflicts of interests among the mainstream political forces (the king and different political parties).

At the international level also, the Maoists changed their positions and tactics for attaining strategic goals. For instance, they raised anti-India rhetoric initially to attract nationalist support among the educated elite and middle class. When the Maoist leadership had to take shelter in India, the rhetoric took a backseat. They raised the specter of Indian expansionism again and even dug trenches to allegedly resist the invading Indian forces after the Indian government captured some Maoist leaders in India after the turn of the century. Eventually, they reached an agreement with the seven parliamentary parties in India under the supervision of Indian officials after King Gyanendra irked the Indians (see Upreti, this volume). This brief discussion shows that the Maoists brilliantly exploited contradiction and opportunities in pursuit of their goals.

Exclusionary democracy and the weak state

A fertile environment and committed insurgents are important and necessary conditions but not sufficient for the success of rebellions. Rebellions are launched against a state and their success and failure are dependent to a considerable extent on the capability, coherence and responsiveness of the state (Skocpol 1979; Goodwin and Skocpol 1989; Davidheiser 1992; Gurr 1968). An effective state can improve societal conditions so that insurgency-favorable conditions no longer remain, or are lessened. Capable states can also successfully repress rebellions. Rebellions have been repressed in many countries such as Peru, Malaya, Bolivia, Sri Lanka (Maoist rebellion) and India (1960s Naxalite uprising).[19] On the other hand, Goodwin and Skocpol (1989: 505) argue that narrow, incompetent and corrupt regimes are vulnerable to revolutionary takeover: "Revolutionary coalitions have formed and expanded in countries in which one finds . . . political exclusion and severe and indiscriminate (while not overwhelming) repression." Cuba, Vietnam and China are examples of successful revolutions. Despite the important role of the state in rebellions, the nature of the democratic state in Nepal and its role in the growth of the Maoist rebellion has not received thorough attention (a few exceptions are Lawoti 2003b, 2007b; Khanal 2007; Hachhethu 2004).

With the restoration of democracy in 1990 and universal adult franchise, the Nepali state appeared to have become more inclusive than before. Extremist communist groups like the CPN-UC (predecessor of the Maoists), in fact, participated in elections in the early 1990s before launching the insurgency. The question is why did the Maoists abandon the electoral path (only to eventually return to it)? What was the role of the state in the growth of the rebellion?

Exclusionary democracy

Scholars have pointed out that majoritarian democracies with the first-past-the-post (FPTP) electoral method and unitary structure are more prone to violent conflicts than power-sharing democracies with federal system and proportional representative electoral method (Cohen 1997; Saideman et al. 2002; Horowitz 1994; Lijphart 1977). Others have pointed out that new democracies in fact could incite violence by exacerbating tensions through competition for power, especially if the yet to be consolidated rules of the game are not perceived as fair (Gurr 2000; Snyder 2000; Jarstad and Sisk 2008). Nepal had the formal trappings of a democracy, such as regular elections and parliament; but Nepal's state institutions and democracy were exclusionary. The winner-take-all majoritarian democracy Nepal adopted in 1990 alienated ideological and cultural minorities through denial of political space in governance. It was instrumental in pushing a party that participated in the 1991 general and 1992 local elections to an insurgency (Lawoti 2005).[20]

Democracy was defined very narrowly during the 1990s in Nepal. The prevalent notion was that the party that won a majority of seats in the Parliament had the right to rule in whatever way it pleased. The state structure and political culture gave little role to the opposition in governance, while the ruling party often abused the state machinery and resources to undermine and harass opposition parties. The FPTP electoral method and the unitary system facilitated the concentration of power in a narrow majority. Further, the parliamentary committee system was weak, because of which opposition had no significant role in making legislations and holding the government accountable. As a result the non-ruling political party actors, including the Maoists, and citizens, felt excluded from the governance processes (Lawoti 2007b).

The Maoists raised issues with different governments in the early 1990s and called many strikes to attract the attention of the government. The 40-point demands submitted to the Sher Bahadur Deuba government before launching the insurgency was the final list – they expanded the demands over the years as they petitioned successive governments. The various governments from 1991 to 1996 were not responsive to these demands.

The Maoists also suffered from the extreme partisan governance. To have an upper hand in the local political conflicts, the Nepali Congress government at the center used the local administration under it to imprison, torture and implicate cadres of its competitor – the CPN-UC – in false cases in Rolpa and Rukum in the western hills (INSEC 1999). During the initial counter-insurgency activities in the Maoist heartland of the mid-western hill districts, the police burned houses of Maoist suspects and villagers, looted cash and other goods, raped women and arrested hundreds of people, and thrashed common people and Maoist sympathizers. Operation Romeo, launched in 1995 prior to the insurgency, and Operation Kilo Sera-2, launched in 1998, have been cited as very brutal and repressive actions that pushed the common people into the Maoist fold (INSEC 1999). Often, the would-be Maoists instigated the conflicts by beating cadres of other political forces but the administration usually targeted only the Maoists for harassment (Gersony 2003). Even the Maoist-elected local government officials were not spared. Owing to the issuance of warrants for arrests and repression, many Maoists went underground (incognito).

The repression was capped by the non-recognition of the Maoist faction by the Election Commission in 1994. When the UPFN, the political front of the CPN-UC split, the Election Commission recognized the UPFN allied to Nirmal Lama and did not recognize the outfit led by Baburam Bhattarai. Stung by non-recognition, the UPFN led by Baburam Bhattarai boycotted the 1994 mid-term election. Would the Maoists have launched the insurgency if they had won seats in the Parliament in 1994? It is hard to know whether electoral victory could have worked against launching the insurgency. Perhaps they would have continued to utilize the electoral opportunities if the political environment had not been turned against them (Thapa and Sijapati 2003; Lawoti 2005).

As the repression continued and conflict escalated, the Maoists launched the insurgency. Regan and Norton (2005: 324) write: "As state increases repression, more people will mobilize around the rebel cause to avoid the abuse at the hands of the state," especially if they are suspected by the state of being rebel sympathizers. Many victims of the police brutality joined the Maoists for protection if not for revenge.

The highly majoritarian and centralized democracy excluded more than two thirds of the marginalized Dalit, indigenous nationalities and Madhesi from governance, as discussed earlier. A state that is weak owing to exclusion can endure if there are no challenges, but if a challenge emerges it could dismantle rapidly, especially if the rebel forces mobilize the excluded people. The exclusion in Nepal did not manifest into political ramification in pre-1990 years because radical groups could not mobilize owing to restrictions on political rights and civil liberties. The continued exclusion in the post-1990 open polity, however, meant that the Maoists had opportunities to exploit the situation, which they did rather effectively. The increase in awareness of inequality, exclusion and discrimination among the marginalized groups, on the other hand, made the Maoist task easier.

While the majoritarian democracy excluded and pushed the Maoists towards the insurgency, it also provided the Maoists with basic rights that allowed them to organize and prepare for the People's War. The Maoists could openly organize political activities and expand party organization and mobilize people after 1990. The intelligentsia was sympathetic and the free media covered the insurgency extensively. The due process and habeas corpus guaranteed by the 1990 Constitution protected Maoist cadres' rights to some degree through release from arbitrary detentions. The Maoists benefited from these limited rights because the restored democracy, however flawed, guaranteed basic political rights and civil liberties.

In addition, once the Maoists launched the People's War, the government could not repress it as brutally as in pre-1990 years. The government was constrained to some degree by the free press, human rights groups and the norms of a democratic regime. Thus, unlike in 1971, when the state successfully repressed a violent communist movement in east Nepal, the government in the 1990s was tied because of the nature of the regime.

Weak state and divided establishment

Democracy may constrain unrestrained repression, but as states have legal monopoly over the use of violence, capable and strong states can and do repress rebellions. The Nepali state, however, was weak, incoherent and detached. It not only could not repress but, in fact, contributed to the growth of the Maoists by neither formulating substantive reforms to address problems, nor developing a coherent and comprehensive policy towards the rebels.

The Nepali state had not effectively penetrated the countryside and hence did not reach a vast segment of population. The health sector and physical infrastructure provide some examples of shortages of services: in the mid-1990s, 11 out of 75 districts did not have public hospitals; there was one doctor for nearly 14,000 people in 1993/94; and only 754 health posts and 117 primary health centers were operating by 1997 (NESAC 1998: 61). Likewise, black-topped roads per 10,000 persons stood at 2 km and only five persons out of 1,000 had telephone connections (NESAC 1998: 16). Kathmandu's HDI in the 1990s was above 0.6 while 21 rural districts' HDI ranged between 0.2 and 0.3, and another three districts had lower than 0.2 (NESAC 1998: 42). As the state had not done much for the people, a large segment of the population demonstrated ambivalence towards the state when the Maoists emerged to challenge it.

The historic apathy continued in the 1990s because of the continuation of extractive policy and absence of substantive reforms. The restoration of democracy in 1990 had raised high hopes among many people but the state failed to meet the aspirations. Substantive reforms with regard to land distribution, devolution and citizenship were not introduced. The CPN-UML minority government introduced some reforms in 1994 but they were minimal.

The centralization of power in Kathmandu and within the executive at the center rendered the parliament and other agencies of the state ineffective. They had no power to formulate and execute public policies. On the other hand, concentration of power in the executive meant that its scope was wide and made it impossible to focus on priority issues. When the executive failed to deliver, the overall state failed because other branches and agencies lacked authority to deliver (Lawoti 2007b; Huntington 1968). The local governments were weak despite the 1999 decentralization act because they were not empowered with fiscal and political authority. Likewise, the police and civil administration was still controlled by the central government. The weak local governments also could not provide services or protect the people.

The centralized but ineffective and unresponsive state contributed to governance crises in the 1990s and eroded the performance legitimacy of the state (Riaz and Basu 2007). Power abuse, corruption and a culture of impunity became widespread and administration was politicized for partisan purposes. Absence of effective accountability mechanism further fuelled power abuse and corruption. The crises increased dissatisfaction among common citizens. As the political parties, especially the ruling party, abused state power and administration to influence electoral outcomes, elections in particular and democracy in general began to lose legitimacy, the more so because the open polity allowed the articulation of dissatisfaction (Lawoti 2007b).

The state not only failed to repress the insurgency, but its counter-insurgency activities, as discussed earlier, fuelled the insurgency because of the haphazard deployment of force. Further, the Maoist rebellion grew rapidly owing to the irresponsible response of the state. When the Maoists began attacking rural police posts and government offices, the state agencies were withdrawn to district centers and other safe areas. For instance, between 2052 v.s. (1996) and the second restoration of democracy in 2063 v.s. (April 2006), 1,271 police units out of nearly two thousand total units (around 65 percent) were removed from rural areas and merged with units in secure towns and district headquarters (Lawoti, forthcoming, 2009). The aim may have been to prevent overrunning of the units and looting of weapons by the Maoists but it allowed the Maoists to occupy the vacated space and consolidate their hold in the rural regions. Even locals who opposed Maoist ideology could not resist because the state failed to provide them with security.

Once the insurgency got going, the state failed to come up with a coherent and comprehensive policy to deal with the rebellion. One reason for failure was probably the state's denial of potential armed conflicts in Nepal. The state and its military did not envision any internal threat, as the absence of RNA's preparation to deal with the internal threat suggests (Mehta and Lawoti, this volume). The government's projection of Nepal as a peaceful society and its attempts to declare Nepal as a zone of peace, despite many small scale conflicts (Lawoti 2007a; Dastider 2000), may have created a 'mental block.' The state may have begun to believe in the myths it had manufactured, and this denial undermined not only its preparedness but also its ability to recognize the depth of the problem and to respond accordingly.

The divisions and factionalism in the establishment side also contributed to the polity's ineffectiveness. First, as discussed earlier, the RNA was deployed late because of mistrust between the king and the political parties as well as suspicion between the political parties and the RNA. Second, frequent government changes meant that attitudes, strategies and policies towards the Maoists kept on changing. There were 11 governments during the decade-long insurgency. The division and infighting within the establishment side allowed the Maoists to grow without effective resistance from the establishment. The mainstream political parties led by leaders who confined themselves in the capital did not launch an effective joint resistance against the Maoists even when their cadres were harassed, displaced or killed. The infighting among and within political parties was primarily driven by clientelistic politics. Politicians needed to distribute resources to expand and maintain support among cadres as well as voters. Because of centralization, resources could be had only if one was in the government.

The divisions among the establishment finally dropped victory into the Maoists' lap. With King Gyanendra's February 2005 coup, the division sharpened and the state became isolated. The parliamentary political parties reached an understanding with the Maoists while most international actors opposed the move and suspended aid to the government. India, the main arms and ammunition supplier to the RNA, conducted a volte-face and facilitated the understanding between the parliamentary parties and the Maoists. This new development resulted in the successful mass movement of April 2006 that forced the royal regime into capitulation and facilitated the Maoists' ascension to state power.

External factors

External conditions affect revolutions through influence on local conditions, institutions and actors. Military competition and war, intrusion from abroad, international support to rebels or the establishment side, and transnational economic conditions could create revolutionary political conditions by affecting economic development and administrative and military coherence or breakdown (Skocpol 1979). The Maoists themselves have pointed to international factors as structural causes of the rebellion in Nepal. They have alleged that "capitalist imperialism" and "Indian expansionism" have caused underdevelopment in Nepal characterized by "semi-colonialism" and "semi-feudalism" (Bhattarai 2003). Scholars have found in other contexts that "historically developing transnational economic relations have always strongly (and differentially) influenced national economic development" (Skocpol 1979: 20), which is true for Nepal as well. The Nepali market has been flooded with cheaper Indian goods and this has had a detrimental impact on traditional goods produced by artisans as well as on manufacturing industries.

The global economy has affected the insurgency indirectly through remittance economy, which is a large contributor to the income of many Nepali households, particularly outside Kathmandu. With their 'donation' networks spread across the country, the Maoists tapped into remittance earnings in a significant way. The majority of those who go abroad for work are from villages and the Maoists taxed people who returned for holidays as well as when they sent money home to their families. The seasonal and longer migration, especially that to India facilitated by an open border and working rights, which had worked as a safety valve to diffuse revolutionary potential for decades by allowing poor villagers to earn and pay their debts and meet other household monetary needs, were tapped by the Maoists for collecting resources in an otherwise resource-scarce society. The Maoists also received funds from the large Nepali diaspora in India organized by the All India Nepali Unity Society (AINUS). The Maoists also benefited from INGO development projects, either directly taxing them or taxing people who worked in such projects. Projects like road construction circulated cash in rural areas and this enabled the Maoists to collect donations.

The amount of funds collected by the Maoists from remittances, INGO projects and AINUS is not known. Likewise, transnational economic relations' affect on the insurgency has not been analyzed. Of the few scholarly works that have analyzed the impact of external factors on the Nepali insurgency, some have pointed to India's attempt to exploit the Maoist insurgency by allowing the Maoists free movement in India for possible leverage to extract concessions from Nepal (Shah 2004; Mishra 2004). Others have shown that India aided the Nepali state by providing large amounts of arms, ammunition and training to the RNA (Mehta 2005).

With the end of the Cold War, the Nepali Maoists did not receive significant material support from their brethren, unlike during the Cold War years when the global communist powers encouraged and aided communist movements with arms, ammunition and other resources. In contrast, in the post-Cold War and post-9/11 environment democratic countries like India, the US and the UK considered the rise of the Maoists as a threat. The US and India labeled the Maoists as terrorists and provided equipment, training and other support to the state army. Upreti's chapter discusses the role of different external actors in the Maoist insurgency and how change in India's attitude after February 2005 became detrimental to the monarchy and benefited the Maoists.

Overall, perhaps apart from transnational economic relations affect on the Nepali society and indirect fund collection from development projects and the remittance economy, other international factors did not directly aid the Maoists. In fact, the external environment was adverse. Thus, it may be safe to conclude that non-external factors were more salient in the growth of the Maoist insurgency.

Chapter plan

Part II includes chapters on agency, ideology, organization and support. In chapter 2, Eck discusses the importance of agency in rebellions through an analysis of the Maoist recruitment drive. In chapter 3, Mottin provides a rich ethnographic analysis of a Maoist cultural troupe's contribution to the insurgency and Cultural Revolution via its artistic representations and programs. Snellinger in chapter 4 argues that the motivation of the Maoists – students in her study – came from their notion of being involved in a struggle for societal transformation. In chapter 5, Joshi argues that failings of the electoral democracy and liberal market economy alienated rural people and the aggrieved population supported the Maoists.

Part III consists of chapter 6, where Lecomte-Tilouine provides a rare glimpse of revolutionary governance in a Maoist base area. Part IV consists of two chapters that look at the ethnic dimension of the insurgency. In chapter 7, Lawoti shows that, based on a comparative study of Nepal, India and Peru, higher ethnic participation contributed to differential trajectories of the three rebellions. In chapter 8 Kantha points to the contradiction between the Maoist positions and Madhesi aspirations and how it pitched the two forces against each other and impeded the Maoist infiltration among the Madhesi.

Part V is composed of two chapters on the state and military. In chapter 9 Mehta and Lawoti point out the reasons behind the failure of the well-equipped, trained and bigger state army to contain the rebel army. Pahari, in chapter 10 argues that inferior organization of the Naxalites in West Bengal in the 1960s and 1970s led to its suppression by the state while superior organization of the Nepali Maoists contributed to it success. In chapter 11 of Part VI, Upreti analyzes the role of external actors in the armed conflict as escalators, mediators and insurgency supporters.

In chapter 12 of Part VII Tiwari analyzes the role of various structural variables in the conflict with two dependent variables while Acharya in chapter 13 adds political economy variables such ideology and political activism to identify the causes of the conflict.

Part VIII contains two chapters on the post-conflict trajectory of the Maoist movement. In chapter 14, Lawoti argues that the Maoists obtained electoral victory not only because people aspired to change; intimidation and threat by the Maoists also contributed to their victory. In the last chapter, Lawoti and Pahari assess the revolutionary impact of the Maoist rebellion and project possible trajectories of the Maoists and the Nepali polity.

Notes

1 A few sections of the chapter draw liberally from Lawoti (2005, 2007a; forthcoming (2009)) and chapter 28 from Malik et al. (2008).
2 We will interchangeably use the terms insurgency, rebellion, People's War, armed conflict and civil war in this volume to describe the armed mobilization of the CPN-M from 1996 to 2006.
3 Deraniyagala (2005: 54) found GDP real growth at 1985 prices for 1981–85, 1986–90, 1991–95 and 1996–2000 as 5.0, 4.8, 5.0 and 5.0 percent respectively. Growth rates were less than 3 percent in the preceding one-and-half decades.
4 We failed to get chapters on gender and Dalit dimensions. See Manchanda (2004) and Pettigrew and Shneiderman (2004) for analyses of women's participation in the armed conflict.
5 The CPN-Fourth Congress split in 1983 into CPN-Masal led by Mohan Bikram Singh and CPN-Fourth Congress led by Nirmal Lama. The CPN-Masal broke into two in 1985: CPN-Masal led by Mohan Bikram Singh and CPN-Mashal led by Mohan Baidya aka Kiran. See Thapa and Sijapati (2003) and Rawal (2047 v.s. (1991)) for a detailed history of the breakups.
6 The CPN-Fourth Congress had adopted a proposal for an agrarian revolution in 1979 (Thapa and Sijapati 2003: 25).
7 See appendix A for the 40-point demand. It was divided into Nationalism, People's Democracy, and Livelihood sections which included 9, 17 and 14 points respectively.
8 Inequality, as measured by the Gini Index, was less in the 1980s in Nepal (0.300) than in India (0.312), Sri Lanka (0.341) and Pakistan (0.326) (Wagle 2007).
9 The analyses of the Nepali insurgency have not engaged on the ongoing debate in the third world revolution literature on whether smallholder peasants or property-less laborers and sharecroppers are revolutionary. Some argue that property-holding peasants have material and organizational advantages to offer collective resistance (Wolf 1969), while others claim that smallholding peasants are normally conservative and quiescent (Paige 1975).
10 Despite his earlier prediction of environmental degradation from the population boom in a hill village in central west Nepal, Macfarlane (2001) found that outward migration had taken off the pressure on land and forests. Likewise, community forestry that had begun since the 1970s and expanded rapidly in the 1980s and 1990s also contributed to the protection of the environment to some degree (Agrawal and Ostrom 2001; Varughese 2000).
11 Nepal has four religious groups (Hindu, Buddhist, Muslim and Kiranti) with more than 3 percent population, more than 100 linguistic groups and numerous caste and sub-caste groups, and the government has recognized 59 nationalities. The groups can be broadly categorized as Caste Hill Hindu Elite (CHHE), Dalit ('untouchable' caste, according to Hindu tradition), indigenous nationalities and Madhesi (plain dwellers) of North Indian origin. Muslims are counted as Madhesi. They number approximately 31, 15, 37 and 17 percent respectively. The Madhesi population would become 32 percent if Tarai indigenous nationalities and Dalit are included in the count.

12 Monarchs are considered as the effective executive head during the Panchayat in this count.
13 Some of the larger ethnic groups are less marginalized or even dominant in areas of their origin but once they come into contact with the centre or its representatives at district levels they become marginalized. Studies have shown that local CHHE use their caste network at district and national levels to enhance their economic, political and social positions (Caplan 2000, revised edition; Holmberg 2006).
14 Interviews, Maoist leaders, summer 2006 and 2008.
15 Interview, August 2008.
16 Subsequently the Maoist quit the government and launched street protests demanding postponement of the Constituent Assembly election and an end to monarchy.
17 In many instances the people's court delivered controversial and partisan judgments but the point is that they provided useful service to the people as well.
18 In one hill village in east Nepal I visited in summer 2006, the Maoists had collected 'taxes' at least once from everyone, including the poorest. The lowest amount was a day's wage, at the time 25 rupees.
19 The states were successful in counter-insurgency not only because of repressive capability but because they introduced reforms to improve societal conditions.
20 The Maoists claimed that they had participated in the election to expose the parliamentary system but such rhetoric is common among communists. In fact, another extremist faction – CPN-Masal led by Mohan Bikram Singh – boycotted the 1991 election but did not launch a violent rebellion. It has participated in subsequent elections. Likewise, even the CPN-UML was initially very critical of the 1990 Constitution.

Bibliography

Agrawal, Arun, and Elinor Ostrom. 2001. Collective Action, Property Rights, and Decentralization in Resource Use in India and Nepal. *Politics and Society* 29 (4):485–514.
Bhattarai, Babu Ram. 2003. The Political Economy of People's War. In *The People's War: Left Perspectives*, edited by A. Karki and D. Seddon. Delhi: Adroit Publishers.
Bhurtel, Jugal, and Saleem H. Ali. Unpublished paper (2009). Green Roots of Red Rebellion: Environmental Degradation as the Ultimate Cause of Social Vulnerability and Militancy in Nepal.
Blaikie, Piers, John Cameron, and David Seddon. 1980. *Nepal in Crisis: Growth and Stagnation at the Periphery*. Delhi: Oxford.
Bohara, Alok K., Neil J. Mitchell, and Mani Nepal. 2006. Opportunity, Democracy and the Exchange of Political Violence. *Journal of Conflict Resolution* 50 (1):108–28.
Bownas, Richard. 2003. The Nepalese Movement in Comparative Perspective: Learning from the History of Naxalism in India. *Himalaya: The Journal of the Association for Nepal and Himalayan Studies* 23 (1):31–37.
Bray, John, Leiv Lunde, and S. Mansoob Murshed. 2003. Economic Drivers in Nepal's Maoist Insurgency. In *Political Economy of Armed Conflict: Beyond Greed and Grievance*, edited by K. Ballentine and K. Sherman. Boulder, CO: Lynne Rienner.
Caplan, Lionel. 2000, revised edition. *Land and Social Change in East Nepal*. Kathmandu: Himal Books.
Cohen, Frank S. 1997. Proportional Versus Majoritarian Ethnic Conflict Management in Democracies. *Comparative Political Studies* 30 (5):607–30.
Collier, Paul, and Anke Hoeffler. 2004. Greed and Grievances in Civil War. *Oxford Economic Papers* 56:563–95.
Dastider, Mollica. 2000. Muslim Mobilization and the State in Nepal, 1951–95. *European Bulletin of Himalayan Research* 18:20–35.

Davidheiser, Evenly B. 1992. Strong States, Weak States: The Role of the State in Revolution. *Comparative Politics* 24 (4):463–75.

de Sales, Anne. 2003. The Kham Magar Country: Between Ethnic Claims and Maoism. In *Resistance and the Nepalese State*, edited by D. N. Gellner. New Delhi: Social Science Press.

Deraniyagala, Sonali. 2005. The Political Economy of Civil Conflict in Nepal. *Oxford Development Studies* 33 (1):47–62.

Diamond, Larry. 1999. *Developing Democracy: Towards Consolidation*. Baltimore and London: Johns Hopkins University Press.

Election Commission, Nepal. 2008. *Constituent Assembly Election 2064*. Election Commision, Nepal 2008 [cited April 2008 2008]. Available from http://www.election.gov.np/EN/.

Fujikura, Tatsuro. 2003. The Role of Collective Imagination in the Maoist Conflict in Nepal. *Himalaya: The Journal of the Association for Nepal and Himalayan Studies* XXIII (1):21–30.

Fukuyama, Francis. 1993. *The End of History and the Last Man.* New York: Harper Perennial.

Gersony, Robert. 2003. Sowing the Wind . . .: History and Dynamics of the Maoist Revolt in Nepal's Rapti Hills: Mercy Corps International.

Goodwin, Jeff, and Theda Skocpol. 1989. Explaining Revolutions in the Contemporary Third World. *Politics & Society* 17 (4):489–509.

Graham, George. 2007. People's War? Self-Interest, Coercion and Ideology in Nepal's Maoist Insurgency. *Small Wars and Insurgencies* 18 (2):231–48.

Guneratne, Arjun. 2002. *Many Tongues, One People: The Making of Tharu Identity in Nepal*. Ithaca and London: Cornell University Press.

Gurr, Ted Robert. 1968. A Causal Model of Civil Strife: A Comparative Analysis Using New Indices. *The American Political Science Review* 62 (4):1104–24.

———. 2000. *Peoples Versus States: Minorities at Risk in the New Century*. Washington, D.C.: United Institute of Peace Press.

Hachhethu, Krishna. 2004. The Nepali State and the Maoist Insurgency, 1996–2001. In *Himalayan People's War*, edited by M. Hutt. Bloomington and Indianpolis: Indiana University Press.

Hegre, Havard, Tanja Ellingsen, Scott Gates, and Nils P. Gleditsch. 2001. Toward a Democratic Civil Peace? Democracy, Political Change, and Civil War, 1816–1992. *American Political Science Review* 95 (1):33–47.

Holmberg, David. 2006. Violence, Non-violence, Sacrifice, Rebellion and the State. *Studies in Nepali History and Society* 11 (1):31–64.

Horowitz, Donald. 1994. Democracy in Divided Socities. In *Nationalism, Ethnic Conflict, and Democracy*, edited by L. Diamond and M. F. Plattner. Baltimore: Johns Hopkins University.

Human Rights Watch. 2007. Children in the Ranks: The Maoists' Use of Child Soldiers in Nepal. New York: Human Rights Watch.

Huntington, Samuel P. 1968. *Political Order in Changing Societies*. New Haven: Yale University Press.

ICG. 2005. Nepal's Maoists: Thier Arms, Structure and Strategy. Kathmandu/Brussels: International Crisis Group.

INSEC. 1999. Maoist Activities and the Treatment of the Government, Annex 3. In *Nepal Human Rights Year Book*. Kathmandu: INSEC.

Jarstad, Anna K., and Timothy D. Sisk, eds. 2008. *From War to Democracy: Dilemmas of Peacebuilding*. Cambridge: Cambridge University Press.

Joshi, Madhav, and David T. Mason. 2007. Land Tenure, Democracy, and Insurgency in Nepal. *Asian Survey* 47 (3):393–414.

KC, Surendra. 1999. *Nepalma Communist Andolanko Itihas (The History of Communist Movement in Nepal)*. Kathmandu: Vidhyarthi Pustak Bhandar.

Khadka, Narayan. 1995. Factionalism in the Communist Movement in Nepal. *Pacific Affairs* 68 (1):55–76.

Khanal, Shishir. 2007. Committed Insurgents, Divided State and the Maoist Insurgency in Nepal. In *Contentious Politics and Democratization in Nepal*, edited by M. Lawoti. Los Angeles, London and New Delhi: Sage Publications.

Lawoti, Mahendra. 2003a. Maoists and Minorities: Overlap of Interests or the case of Exploitation? *Studies in Nepali History and Society* 8 (1):67–97.

———. 2003b. Centralized Politics and the Growth of the Maoist Insurgency in Nepal. *Himalaya: The Journal of the Association for Nepal and Himalayan Studies* 23:49–58.

———. 2005. *Towards a Democratic Nepal: Inclusive Political Institutions for a Multicultural Society*. New Delhi, London, and Thousand Oaks: Sage Publications.

———. ed. 2007a. *Contentious Politics and Democratization in Nepal*. Los Angeles, London, New Delhi and Singapore: Sage Publications.

———. 2007b. *Looking Back, Looking Forward: Centralization, Multiple Conflicts and Democratic State Building in Nepal*. Washington, D.C.: East-West Center.

———. 2008. Exclusionary Democratization in Nepal, 1990–2002. *Democratization* 15 (2):363–85.

———. Forthcoming (2009). Nepal. In *Encyclopedia of Human Rights*, edited by D. P. Forsythe. New York: Oxford University Press.

Lecomte-Tilouine, Marie. 2006. "Kill One, He Becomes One Hundred": Martydom as Generative Sacrifice in the Nepal People's War. *Social Analysis* 50 (1):51–72.

Lijphart, Arend. 1977. *Democracy in Plural Societies: A Comparative Exploration*. New Haven and London: Yale University Press.

Macfarlane, Alan. 2001. Sliding Down Hill: Some reflections on thirty years of change in a Himalayan Village. *European Bulletin of Himalayan Research* 20 (1 (double)):105–24.

Maddox, Bryan. 2003. Language Policy, Modernist Ambivalence and Social Exclusion: A Case Study of Rupendehi District in Nepal's Tarai. *Studies in Nepali History and Society* 8 (2):205–24.

Maharjan, Pancha N. 2000. The Maoist Insurgency and the Crises of Governability in Nepal. In *Domestic Conflict and Crises of Governability in Nepal*, edited by D. Kumar. Kathmandu: CNAS.

———. 1993. Role of the Extra-Parliamentary Political Party in Multi-Party Democracy: A Study of CPN-Unity Center. *Contributions to Nepalese Studies* 20 (2):221–30.

Mahat, Ram Sharan. 2005. *In Defense of Democracy: Dynamics and Fault Lines of Nepal's Political Economy*. New Delhi: Adroit Publishers.

Malik, Yogendra K., Charles H. Kennedy, Robert C. Oberst, Ashok Kapur, Mahendra Lawoti, and Syedur Rahman. 2008. *Government and Politics in South Asia*. Sixth ed. Boulder, CO: Westview Press.

Manchanda, Rita. 2004. Maoist Insurgency in Nepal: Radicalizing Gendered Narratives *Cultural Dynamics* 16 (2/3):237–58.

Marks, Thomas A., and David Scott Palmer. 2005. Radical Maoist Insurgents and Terrorist Tactics: Comparing Peru and Nepal. *Low Intensity Conflict & Law Enforcement* 13 (2):91–116.

Mehta, Ashok K. 2005. *The Royal Nepal Army: Meeting the Maoist Challenge*. New Delhi: Rupa and Co.

Migdal, Joel S. 1975. *Peasants, politics, and revolution; pressures toward political and social change in the third world.* Princeton: Princeton University Press.

Mishra, Chaitanya. 2004. Locating the "Causes" of the Maoist Struggel. *Studies in Nepali History and Society* 9 (1):3–56.

Mishra, Rabindra 2004. India's Role in Nepal's Maoist Insurgency. *Asian Survey* 44 (5):627–46.

Muller, Edward N., and Mitchell A. Seligson. 1987. Inequality and Insurgency. *The American Political Science Review* 81 (2):425–51.

Murshed, Mansoob S., and Scott Gates. 2005. Spatial-Horizontal Inequality and the Maoist Insurgency in Nepal. *Review of Development Economics* 9 (1):121–34.

NESAC. 1998. *Nepal Human Development Report 1998.* Kathmandu: NESAC.

Neupane, Govinda. 2000. *Nepalko Jatiya Prashna: Samajik Banot ra Sajhedariko Sambhawana (Nepal's National Question: Social Composition and Possibilities of Accommodation).* Kathmandu: Center for Development Studies.

Nickson, Andrew R. 1992. Democratization and the Growth of Communism in Nepal: A Peruvian Scenario in the Making? *Journal of Commonwealth and Comparative Politics* 30 (3).

Onta, Praytoush, and Shekhar Parajuli, eds. 2058 v.s. (2001–2). *Nepali Mediama Dalit ra Janajati.* Kathmandu: Ekta Books.

Paige, Jeffery M. 1975. *Agrarian Revolution.* New York: The Press Press.

Pettigrew, Judith. 2003a. Guns, Kinship, and Fear: Maoists among the Tamu-mai (Gurungs). In *Resistance and the State: Nepalese Experience,* edited by D. Gellner. New Delhi: Social Science Press.

——. 2003b. Living Between the Maoists and the Army in Rural Nepal. *Himalaya: The Journal of the Association for Nepal and Himalayan Studies* 23 (1):9–20.

Pettigrew, Judith, and Sara Shneiderman. 2004. Women and Maobaadi: Ideology and Agency in Nepal's Maoist Movement. *Himal South Asian.*

Ramirez, Philippe. 2004. Maoism in Nepal: Towards a Comparative Perspective. In *Himalayan People's War: Nepal's Maoist Rebellion,* edited by M. Hutt. Bloomington and Indianapolis Indiana University Press.

Rawal, Bhim. 2047 v.s. (1991). *Nepalma Samyabadi Andolanko: Adbhav ra Bikash (Communist Movement in Nepal: Rise and Development).* Kathmandu: Pairavi Prakashan.

Regan, Patrick M., and Daniel Norton. 2005. Greed, Grievance, and Molibilzation in Civil Wars. *Journal of Conflict Resolution* 49 (3):319–36.

Riaz, Ali, and Subho Basu. 2007. *Paradise Lost? State Failure in Nepal.* Lanham, MD: Lexington Books.

Saideman, Stephen M., David Lanoue, Michael Campenni, and Samuel Stanton. 2002. Democratization, Political Institutions, and Ethnic Conflict: A Pooled Time-Series Analysis, 1985–98. *Comparative Political Studies* 35 (1):103–29.

Shah, Saubhagya. 2004. A Himalayan Red Herring? Maoist Revolution in the Shadow of the Legacy Raj. In *Himalayan People's War: Nepal's Maoist Rebellion,* edited by M. Hutt. Bloomington: Indiana University Press.

——. 2008. Revolution and reaction in the Himalayas: Cultural resistance and the Maoist "new regime" in western Nepal. *American Ethnologist* 35 (3):481–99.

Sharma, Kishor. 2006. The Political Economy of Civil War in Nepal. *World Development* 34 (7):1237–53.

Shneiderman, Sara, and Mark Turin. 2003. The Path to Jan Sarkar in Dolakha District: towards an ethnography of the Maoist movement. In *Himalayan People's War: Nepal's Maoist Rebellion,* edited by M. Hutt. London: Hurst & Co.

Skocpol, Theda. 1979. *States and Social Revolutions: A Comparative Analysis of France, Russia, and China.* Cambridge: Cambridge University Press.

Snyder, Jack L. 2000. *From Voting to Violence: Democratization and Nationalist Conflict.* New York: W.W. Norton and Company.

Spence, Jonathan. 1999. *Mao.* London: Phoenix.

Thapa, Deepak, and Bandita Sijapati. 2003. *A Kingdom Under Siege: Nepal's Maoist Insurgency, 1996 to 2003.* Kathmandu: The Printhouse.

Tiwari, Bishwa. 2008. Horizontal Inequality and Conflict in Nepal, March 23–25, at Sri Lanka.

UNDP. 2004. *Nepal Human Development Report 2004: Empowerment and Poverty Reduction.* Kathmandu: UNDP.

Upadhaya, Dhanpati. 2052 (1995). Report of the High Level Citizenship Commission-2051. Kathmandu: HMG Nepal.

Upreti, Bishnu Raj. 2004. *The Price of Neglect: From Resource Conflict to Maoist Insurgency in the Himalayan Kingdom.* Kathmandu: Bhrikuti Academic Publications.

Varughese, George. 2000. Population and Forest Dynamics in the Hills of Nepal: Institutional Remedies by Rural Communities. In *People and Forests: Communities, Institutions and Governance*, edited by C. Gibson, M. A. McKean and E. Ostrom. Cambridge, MA: The MIT Press.

Wagle, Udaya. 2007. Are Economic Liberalization and Equality Compatible? Evidence from South Asia. *World Development* 35 (11):1836–57.

Ward, Michael D., and Kristian S. Gleditsch. 1998. Democratizing for Peace. *American Political Science Review* 92 (March):51–62.

Weinstein, Jeremy. 2007. *Inside Rebellion: The Politics of Insurgent Violence.* New York: Cambridge University Press.

Wolf, Eric. 1969. *Peasant Wars of the Twentieth Century.* Norman, OK: University of Oklahoma Press.

Part II

Agency, ideology, organization, and support

2 Recruiting rebels

Indoctrination and political education in Nepal

*Kristine Eck**

Introduction

The Communist Party of Nepal-Maoist (CPN-M) developed from having only a few dozen fighters in 1996, to having an estimated 30,000 fighters by the signing of the Comprehensive Peace Agreement (CPA) in November 2006.[1] How was the CPN-M able to successfully recruit fighters to its organization? This question is relevant to understanding the development of the conflict in Nepal, since a rebel group's ability to recruit and motivate soldiers is essential not only to the growth of the organization, but also to its very existence.

The field of civil war studies has seen a burgeoning interest in the processes of rebel recruitment. Recruitment is vital to the study of civil war for the very reason that a rebel group's ability to force concessions is contingent on its success in recruiting and retaining its troops. The recruitment literature has had two primary focal points. The first examines the motivations of individuals and why they opt to join rebellion. Building on collective action and social movement literature (Olson 1965; Popkin 1979; Lichbach 1998), this line of reasoning has of late dichotomized into a discussion of whether the incentives that motivate an individual to choose rebellion are primarily loot-seeking in nature or whether they are better explained by grievances (cf. Collier and Hoeffler 2001; Regan and Norton 2005). The second focus has concentrated on conditions that increase the likelihood for successful recruitment. Factors like geography, ethnicity, and whether the group is ideologically-oriented are argued to play an important role in shaping recruitment opportunities (cf. Gates 2002; Fearon and Laitin 2003).

In empirical studies using these approaches, the variables employed to measure recruitment possibilities are all structural in nature; for example, the presence of natural resources, percent of mountainous terrain, ethnic composition of the country, GDP per capita, etc. This raises the question of what agency the rebel group itself has in facilitating recruitment. What scope is there for rebel groups to adopt particular recruitment strategies? Given the economic, ethnic, and geographical context in which a rebel group finds itself, can it develop strategies that increase its effectiveness in recruiting supporters and fighters? The aim of this chapter is to move from the structural level to the agent level[2] in discussing rebel recruitment by focusing specifically on rebel recruitment strategies. In doing so, I focus on one key strategy that rebels in Nepal, and indeed the world over have employed in recruitment: indoctrination and related forms of political education.

This chapter first gives a brief overview of previous research on rebel recruitment. It then turns to Nepal and a discussion of the structural factors commonly cited in explaining the growth of the Maoist organization. This is followed by a discussion of the CPN-M's use of indoctrination and other forms of political education as a key strategy to recruit followers.[3] I argue that while structural variables provided an important context in which the Maoists operated, the primary mechanism for the CPN-M's successful recruitment strategy lay in this focus on indoctrination and political education. By linking villagers' dissatisfaction with their daily lives to larger problems in the political system, the CPN-M was able to exploit grievances for the purpose of rebel recruitment.[4] The importance of indoctrination was central to the CPN-M strategy and reportedly superseded even military training and arms acquisition in its efforts to expand the organization. This chapter thus seeks to provide a more nuanced understanding of the Nepalese conflict that goes beyond commonly cited structural causes and incorporates Maoist agency more explicitly into the causal story.

Previous research on rebel recruitment

Virtually all literature on rebel recruitment departs from the collective action problem: rebel groups fight for public goods but individuals involved in rebellion pay private costs and face enormous risks. Moreover, all potential benefits are highly uncertain and distributed in the future, creating strong incentives for rational individuals to abstain from participation and instead opt to free-ride (Olson 1965). The rationalist solution to the free-rider problem is selective incentives, which are private gains distributed only to those individuals that participate in rebellion (Popkin 1979; Olson 1965). This literature argues that grievances, the ostensible *raison d'être* of rebellion, are in and of themselves insufficient to motivate rational individuals to accept the private costs rebellion entails; private benefits are necessary as well. In more recent formulations, it is these selective incentives, in the form of material benefits, which are seen as the motivating force behind rebellion (Collier 2000). Natural resources and other forms of financial gain are argued to be the primary aim of greedy rebels who seek to profit from the opportunities for exploitation and illegal trade that war creates.

Within the rationalist paradigm, a number of critiques have arisen concerning the relevance of the collective action framework for understanding armed conflict. Kalyvas and Kocher refute the assumption of the collective action literature that non-participation is relatively costless in insurgency (Kalyvas and Kocher 2007). They argue that in fact, non-participation in rebellion can be as risky as or even more risky than participation: civilian populations are regularly victimized by one or both warring parties in insurgencies. Rebels, on the other hand, have access to skills and networks that often help them avoid victimization. For this reason, rational individuals should participate in rebellion "not in spite of risk but in order to better manage it," effectively eliminating the collective action problem (Kalyvas and Kocher 2007: 183).[5] Another line of critique argues that the collective actions framework is inappropriate in the context of rebellion, since it focuses on horizontal interaction of agents, while the dynamics of civil war has a much heavier component of vertical interaction between leaders and followers (Elster 2006).[6]

Other explanations for rebel recruitment move beyond the rationalist paradigm embodied in the collective action literature. In this literature, incentives are seen in a broader sense, such as social benefits from group belonging (Petersen 2001). Rebel leaders appeal to ethnic, religious, ideological, or other social bonds within aggrieved groups, drawing on individuals' loyalties to the group. This can be related to the promise of future benefits, in which common norms within the group increase cooperation and reciprocity and make leaders promises about the distribution of benefits in the future more credible (Weinstein 2007). But joining the movement can also be explained as a good in itself; it is part of "the pleasure of agency" (Wood 2003). Recent research also emphasizes the distinction between using economic endowments and social endowments as incentives to attract rebels. These different strategies are argued to have implications for the type of rebels which join a group: individuals who join groups that offer economic incentives tend to be opportunistic "consumers" who are motivated primarily by private gains, while those who join movements characterized by social endowments are more committed "investors" who demonstrate higher levels of loyalty to the group (Weinstein 2007).[7]

Finally, a number of empirically-oriented studies focus on conditions that increase the likelihood of successful recruitment. Factors like geography, ethnicity, and whether the group is ideologically-oriented are argued to play an important role in shaping recruitment opportunities. In all of the systematic empirical evaluations of the recruitment literature, the variables which are employed to measure recruitment possibilities are structural in nature. These variables are meant to capture either the structural constraints on rebellion or the individual opportunity costs involved in joining a rebellion.

Despite the advances of recent research, many gaps remain. In particular, the focus on structural variables has resulted in a lack of attention to the rebel group itself as an agent. The extent to which rebel strategies for recruitment can affect a group's success in attracting individuals has been largely overlooked in previous literature. Given the structural context in which it finds itself, what agency does the rebel group have in employing recruitment strategies? Shifting the level of analysis to the rebel group and its recruitment strategies may provide clues to why some rebellions generate more recruits than others. In this chapter I focus on one recruitment strategy, indoctrination, and explore how it works to facilitate rebel recruitment. This is meant to complement previous literature, as I agree that structural variables are fundamental to understanding recruitment. To set the stage, therefore, I first turn to an overview of the Nepalese context.

Structural factors affecting recruitment possibilities

There are a number of factors which have contributed to the rise and continuation of the armed conflict in Nepal. Above all, the issues of social and economic inequality, geographic disparities, poor governance, and repressive behavior by the state apparatus are raised by most observers of the conflict. The Maoists themselves also highlight many of these factors as key justifications for their war on the Nepalese state (CPN-M 1996/2003). These factors are central in the existing literature and dominate most analyses of the armed conflict in Nepal.

Nepal is characterized by multiple overlapping identities based on ethnicity, caste, class, and geography. Many groups are characterized by relative inequalities and are effectively excluded from political power. Indigenous nationalities, which constitute around 35 percent of the population, have long-standing grievances based on their historical exclusion from power (Thapa 2001).[8] Under-representation in policy-making, exclusionary language laws, and Hindu chauvinism are some of the concerns expressed by various groups. The marginalization of lower castes and ethnic groups has been largely dismissed by successive governments who have done little to address this grievance, leaving these groups under-represented at the policy-making level (Lawoti 2005; Subba 2006; Thapa 2002). Likewise, indigenous nationalities experience higher levels of poverty. Seeking to take advantage of this situation, the Maoist leadership deliberately targeted indigenous nationalities, hoping to capitalize on their discontent.[9] The CPN-M listed amongst its 40 demands that indigenous nationalities should be allowed to form autonomous regions and that mother-tongue education should be guaranteed in an effort to stop racial exploitation (CPN-M 1996/2003). Similar disparities exist between the different castes in the Hindu system: lower-caste individuals have a higher incidence of poverty and have traditionally had little access to power. Caste-based discrimination has led to frustration over the lack of opportunities for lower castes. Recent research has found that caste disparities indeed are a crucial dimension in explaining the genesis of the conflict (Gates and Murshed 2005). The Maoists also sought to appeal to these individuals by demanding that Nepal be proclaimed a secular state and the system of untouchability eliminated.

The ethnic and caste facets of social inequality are overlaid by class issues, which are favored in Maoist rhetoric (cf. Prachanda 1999/2003; Bhattarai 2003). Lower classes (which often overlap with certain ethnic or caste backgrounds) are characterized by extreme poverty. Nepal is one of the poorest countries in the world; the small industrial sector, landlocked location, proclivity to natural disasters, disadvantageous trade treaties, and lack of technology have all hindered economic progress. But more important in this context is not the absolute level of poverty, but how economic resources are distributed. With the vast majority of the labor force engaged in agriculture, access to land is a key economic issue. There is an unequal distribution of land that in many areas has resulted in the majority of the land being consolidated under the ownership of few individuals, leaving the majority of the population landless or semi-landless; over 37 percent of the land is in the hands of 5 percent of the population (UNDP 2004).[10] The failure of the state to rectify or substantively address these economic grievances is commonly cited as a grievance which fueled the armed conflict (Hutt 2004; Macours 2006; Gates and Murshed 2005). Poverty makes rebellion more attractive and less costly for individuals, leading some to conclude that poverty-stricken areas see higher levels of violence because rebels are better able to recruit amongst the populace (Bohara, Mitchell, and Nepal 2006).[11]

Geographic issues are also woven into the fabric of social and economic inequalities in Nepal. The hilly terrain of the mid-western part of Nepal was host to the birth of the Maoist movement, purportedly because the people there are more oppressed by the ruling classes than elsewhere, that the government is largely absent, and that the region suffers from historical underdevelopment (Prachanda 2000/2003). Indeed, the mid-western heartland regions of Nepal where the conflict originated have very poor scores on economic and health indicators (Singh et al. 2005). The terrain of this region is also advantageous for rebellion: violence tends to increase with rugged terrain since mountains minimize the government's ability to control territory and facilitate rebel insurgency operations (Bohara et al. 2006). It is, however, the general distinction between urban and rural areas that is most often mentioned in the literature on the war in Nepal (ICG 2005; Hutt 2004; Rose 2001). The relationship between Kathmandu and the rest of the country is characterized by an income gap that is indicative of the regional disparities between urban and rural life prevalent across Nepal. Kathmandu's average GDP is almost four times that of some rural districts, and research has found that the larger this gap between any given district and Kathmandu, the more likely was the district to experience increased civil conflict (Kumar 2003; Gates and Murshed 2005). The differences are not only economic, however, but also relate to governance issues: the state has little presence in the countryside due to weak local and district governance structures. The effect is a governance vacuum that further alienates rural areas from the central government, and has led to a tendency amongst the regions to reject Kathmandu's authority (Ramirez 2004).

Indeed, at the heart of the matter are the patterns of weak democratic governance. The high expectations for the new democratic system after the 1990 People's Movement were met with a corrupt and marginally functioning state throughout the 1990s. Political power was centralized in Kathmandu leading to a neglect of the periphery, power abuse and corruption were rife, politicians avoided accountability, and parties focused on infighting rather than coalition-building (Hachhethu 2000; Onta 2004). The state apparatus became associated with rent-seeking politicians and political exclusion, and the political parties continued to be dominated by upper caste Hindus. Moreover, political parties were run undemocratically and characterized by constant bickering both between and within parties. Parties in power systematically used the state machinery against opponents, resulting in government institutions being colored by personal antagonisms. Instead of policies linked to citizen preferences, the Nepalese people were faced with severe factionalism, corruption, and inefficiency. As a result, the general populace tired of party politics and lost faith in democratic governance as it was practiced in Kathmandu, creating conducive environment for the growth of the CPN-M (Lawoti 2005; Kumar 2000). Because of party differences, the various organs of the state found it difficult to muster a coordinated response to the Maoist threat and went so far as to try to use the insurgency as a means of consolidating power. This prompted one noted columnist to retort, "the political mainstream has to realize that insurgency is a dangerous tool for scoring points over each other" (Lal 2001: 46). The Maoists were able to capitalize on this situation in a number of ways. First, the rampant corruption, party factionalism, weak state institutions, centralization of power, and lack of representation of citizen preferences in policymaking led to dissatisfaction with the existing politicians and political system. In their recruitment efforts, the Maoists were able to exploit this disappointment in the Nepalese state by offering an alternative to the current system which promised a more efficient and representative polity. Second, the lack of effective governance in rural areas and the state's withdrawal from these areas as the conflict picked up pace only accentuated the Maoists ability to recruit unhindered and to mobilize the resources of the rural populace to their cause (whether voluntary or by force). The weak state apparatus was thus not only a source of grievance but also a facilitating factor which allowed the Maoists to operate relatively unhindered in large swathes of the country.

Furthermore, the government's law and order response to the insurgency further alienated the populace. The initial response was to crack down with increasingly repressive security measures undertaken by the poorly-trained police force. A government operation in 1998, named Kilo Sierra II was conducted with such blunt force and disregard for human rights that it only strengthened the rebels' recruitment base. After its deployment, the Royal Nepal Army (RNA) also quickly made a name for itself with indiscriminate killings and arbitrary arrests. These repressive measures served to further alienate individuals and drive them into joining the Maoists, motivated by fear of the security forces or a desire for revenge (Schneiderman 2003; Pettigrew 2003; Dixit 2002; Thapa 2001).

These structural factors set the context for insurgency by facilitating or constraining rebel behavior. But given this context, what strategies could the Maoists employ to accelerate recruitment and gain supporters? How did they convince individuals to translate their daily grievances into armed insurgency? How were thousands of disgruntled and aggrieved individuals in Nepal convinced to risk their lives by joining the call to arms? In Nepal, one central recruitment strategy used by the CPN-M was indoctrination and related forms of political education. It is to this specific recruitment strategy that I now turn.

Indoctrination and political education as a recruitment strategy

The latent and widespread grievances experienced by large sectors of the population provided ample potential for recruitment. But to be able to convince individuals to join an armed rebellion – an inherently risky and dangerous proposition – the CPN-M needed to inform individuals about its cause and motivate them to join. Realizing this, the CPN-M began propagating its ideology and training cadres even before taking to arms.

In 1995, the Maoists began a year-long campaign to build support amongst the peasantry in the western districts of Rolpa, Rukum, and Jajarkot. This campaign involved sending political-cultural teams into villages, organizing peasants to challenge local authorities, and mobilizing villagers for infrastructure improvement such as building roads and bridges, etc. (Thapa 2001; Onesto 2005). The primary focus for this campaign, however, was to educate the masses on the goals and tactics of the Maoists. According to a Central Committee member of Rukum district, this was done with various forms of propaganda such as mass meetings, cultural campaigns, postering and walling, pamphlets, newspaper articles, and holding political classes (Onesto 2005: 191). By spreading information about the CPN-M and its goals, the party hoped to educate the masses not only about the Marxist-Leninist-Maoist ideology, but also about the necessity of using violence to change the political system. The importance of this strategy is emphasized by a party District Committee Secretary of Rukum district, "just before the Initiation, the Party leadership gave many political classes to the masses as the basis for the People's War; and so if they were not politically conscious, we could not be successful in carrying out our program" (quoted in Onesto 2005: 190).

With the onset of the People's War in 1996 and the transition of the CPN-M from political party to active rebel group, campaigning amongst the populace increased. The Maoists used a multitude of means to spread information about their movement and educate the peasantry, amongst them mass gatherings; individual motivators who recruited door-to-door; kidnapping of school children; various forms of forced recruitment; and widespread propaganda activities. It was the Schooling Department within the party that was responsible for developing political training programs and for producing propaganda (Mahara 2007).

Means of recruitment

Mass gatherings were generally large-scale affairs that involved not only speeches and information regarding the CPN-M's ideology and activities, but also cultural performances such as dances, music, and skits (see Mottin, this volume, for a detailed description). At the outset of the conflict, such programs were generally held in the evening and in great secrecy, but as the conflict progressed and the Maoists succeeded in largely restricting the police and army to district headquarters, the programs were held increasingly in the open. In fact, as the level of violence in the conflict escalated, so did the frequency of the cultural programs, according to one top Maoist (Pun, T. 2007). Li Onesto (2005) describes a program she witnessed in 1999.[12] After an introduction, there was a minute of silence for Maoist "martyrs", followed by a female Maoist explaining the goals of the People's War and making special appeals to women to join the revolution. Other speeches about the importance of armed struggle for improving villagers' lives were interspersed with songs and poems, all the while emphasizing the need for the villagers to join the People's War. Onesto (2005: 133) provides a brief narration:

> The cultural team has ten members – four women and six men, all very young. They put on an energetic show full of singing, dancing, and skits, accompanied by traditional Nepali drums, guitars, and portable keyboards. Songs of varying rhythm and moods tell tales of guerilla actions and people killed by the police.

Dances combine traditional moves and music with new steps and poses to narrate war stories. The skits move the crowd to laughter as well as tears.

News of battles was recounted, particularly those which resulted in Maoist victories, as were descriptions of Maoist violence against its "revolutionary enemies" such as landowners and petty government officials. Such actions were often viewed approvingly by villagers, particularly in the early years, as landowners and government officials were often seen as the principal agents of economic and social oppression. These depictions demonstrated the ability of the Maoists to take measures against such oppression and inspired hope that the Maoists would indeed be able to affect change. Fujikura (2003: 27) elaborates:

> In Salyan District, Maoists not only used violence, but often after committing a violent act advertised it in newspapers and newsletters as well as during cultural programs, where they skillfully re-enacted the torture and murder of a 'class enemy' . . . The purpose of these 'propaganda activities' . . . was to convince the villagers of the necessity and efficacy of revolutionary violence. What the Maoists aimed to convey was it was only Maoist violence that could eliminate the local 'exploiter' whose power derived in part from his close connection with state power. Through such skillful re-enactments, the Maoists undoubtedly aimed to communicate that they were capable of extreme and hence awe-inspiring violence – calculated use of brutality that they hoped made them appear more formidable and effective than their enemy . . .

Both news of successful battles elsewhere and the elimination of 'class enemies' provided palpable illustrations of Maoists strength and ability to challenge the state that proved popular amongst villagers. Such shows of strength had inspirational effects, encouraging otherwise hesitant villagers to join, "people are not scared if they hear that many police have been killed," stated one villager (quoted in Schneiderman and Turin 2004: 94). Re-enactments also provided a stern warning to potential "class enemies" and introduced an unspoken element of threat to any villager who would oppose the Maoists, for example by becoming government informants. Information about Maoist "martyrs" was also provided, both with a moment of silence and with a skit acknowledging the danger involved in joining the People's War. By acknowledging the risk of death and the difficulties in familial separation inherent in joining, the skit glorified both the courage of the recruit and the sacrifice of the family. The Maoists included amongst their demands that all those who die during the time of the People's Movement should be declared martyrs and their families given compensation, ensuring an individual that his or her death will be glorified in a similar manner as those depicted in the skits. This emphasis on martyrdom may have facilitated recruitment and eased the use of violence, "the Maoist emphasis on martyrdom creates a source of symbolic capital which legitimizes and even encourages violent actions on the part of its participants, just as martyrdom does for suicide-bombers elsewhere in the world" (Schneiderman 2003: 45).

Themes such as those mentioned above – courage, sacrifice, victory – could be found throughout the program in not only the skits and speeches, but also the songs and dances (Onesto 2005). By representing Maoist themes within established cultural practices, the Maoists were able to express complex ideas about ideology and grievances in an easily accessible manner for poorly educated peasants; in the words of one cultural group member, "we conveyed the people's suffering, hardship, and exploitation in the dancing" (author interview 2008). Local cultural practices were co-opted by the Maoists as a means to popularize the ideas behind their movement.[13] Sharma (2004: 46) states:

> Culture is in fact an important aspect of mobilization, where elements of existing cultures are incorporated into mobilization strategies that are themselves varied in different contexts . . . Instead of the songs one hears in the rest of the country, revolutionary songs are much more popular. There has been an unprecedented increase in the local people's capacity for study and analysis.

Although often clandestine and somewhat risky, the mass meetings were generally well-attended by local villagers. The cultural entertainment provided had a reputation for being high quality; even villagers who were not Maoist supports reported attending and enjoying Maoist performances (Pettigrew 2003). Mass meetings therefore served as an efficient means of recruitment; the economies of scale involved in mass meetings meant that many potential rebels and supporters could be reached at little cost.

Another means of recruitment involved individual motivators who worked alone or in pairs going door-to-door (Thapa 2003). These motivators' task was to spread the message of the CPN-M and its armed struggle through individual contacts, sometimes by conducting classes but most often by conversing with individuals. After having met an individual motivator, one villager in Dang district reported, "we now know how to talk to people, why the Maoists are against the government and why it is important to support the Maoists" (quoted in Sharma and Prasain 2004: 159). These motivators would often discuss problems the villagers experienced and frame the Maoist movement in terms of these grievances. They also sought to inform the villagers about their rights and to politicize these individuals by making them aware of how they could affect change by supporting the Maoist cause; Sharma and Prasain (2004: 160) observe that "the villagers . . . say that the Maoists women and men come door to door, provide literacy programs, make them aware of their rights, roles and contribution. The Maoists also talk about how women have been suppressed in the present society, and make them aware that theirs is the only party working for liberation." Motivators were able to move about more easily than cultural groups and were able to interact with villagers without drawing the attention of security forces. Reports of encounters with motivators are fairly common in Maoist-controlled areas, but estimates do not exist on how many motivators were active nor how widespread their activities were.

Schools also provided fertile grounds for recruitment by the Maoists. As the armed conflict progressed and the need for recruits intensified, the CPN-M increasingly took to kidnapping entire classes or schools of children.[14] These children were usually taken to remote areas for several days of indoctrination and then released, though in some cases the Maoists held their political education campaigns at the school itself. These kidnappings filled several functions. First, they allowed the Maoists to assess the relative strengths and weaknesses of the children and determine who to target in future recruitment efforts. Second, it allowed them the opportunity to indoctrinate the children into Maoist ideology and present to them the prospect of joining the rebellion. Despite their schooling, much of the rural youth had few prospects of gaining future employment, and for many the Maoists offered an opportunity to leave their village.[15] The Maoists' romanticized images of martyrdom, victory and courage were also easily sold to impressionable youths. Some observers commented that schools were the *primary* forum for disseminating the Maoist ideology and for recruiting new members (Schneiderman and Turin 2004).[16] In addition to being perhaps more easily convinced than adults, schoolchildren made attractive recruits for other reasons as well. They offered the benefit of having some level of education, which could facilitate training. Moreover, Maoists could again take advantage of economies of scale, by addressing many (young and impressionable) people at once while expending few resources (Macours 2006).

Though most kidnapped schoolchildren were subsequently released, this tactic highlights accusations by human rights organizations that the Maoists coerced individuals into joining their organization and that some recruitment was in fact forced. In particular, this charge is leveled regarding child soldiers, many of whom are argued to have been coerced into membership. Reports suggest that in some areas, the Maoists essentially demanded that every family contribute a family member to the party. It is difficult to determine how widespread coerced recruitment indeed was.[17] It is also unclear whether those who were forcibly recruited attempted to leave the group or were eventually convinced by Maoist rhetoric. The Maoists ability to institute such practices was eased by their control over large swathes of rural territory, where they had effectively driven away local governmental and security officials.[18]

It is clear that many individuals experienced mixed motives, some attended mass meetings or joined the party freely while others did so because of implicit or outright coercion and many did so because of a combination of the two. But indoctrination sessions after joining were designed to convince individuals that they had made the right choice in joining the CPN-M, and even those who were forcibly recruited to the Maoists were subjected to indoctrination in an attempt to win their loyalty. The re-education of captured police officers is a case in point. There were numerous reports about police officers who were kidnapped after armed engagements with the Maoists being subjected to political indoctrination in an attempt to re-educate them and convince them to join the Maoists. The CPN-M's spokesman Krishna Bahadur Mahara has asserted that such re-education was in fact quite successful amongst the lower echelons of the police as this group also suffered from poverty and shared many of the other grievances of the rural populace (Mahara 2007). The distinction between upper and lower echelons of the police and governmental bureaucracy, argues Mahara, mirrors the social hierarchies that have resulted in discrimination. In addition to captured security forces, individuals who were "convicted" in Maoist courts were also taken for re-education. These individuals, usually local businessmen who were accused of exploiting the peasantry, spent their days at the re-education camp working the fields and their evenings learning Marxist-Leninist-Maoist theory. This would help them "learn . . . how to behave in a new society" according to one Maoist cited in *Le Monde* (November 10, 2003). It remains unclear to what extent the indoctrination of such individuals was successful, and the tactic was probably primarily useful in signaling to the masses that the Maoists were resolute in their approach to societal change.

For those who joined the party, receiving continued political education in Maoist ideology was an integral part of the CPN-M's training.[19] The length of this training is unclear, with reports citing a range of one week to months; the confusion may be a result of training practices varying over time owing to the exigencies of war. It is clear that all recruits received a minimum of one week of political training on Maoist ideology and key texts before they were allowed into the party (Mahara 2007). There were numerous roles within the party for an individual, ranging from motivators, cultural performers, spies, members of the armed forces, militia members, and so on.[20] After joining the party, members reportedly worked first as village-level political workers, trying to organize the masses. According to Mahara (2007), it was only after two to three years that these individuals were allowed to apply for military training to join the People's Army.[21] During this time ideological training continued, as it would throughout a rebel's career regardless of what roll s/he held in the party. The experience of working in the political wing ensured commitment and through the subsequent political education that was provided during this time, the rebel was able to attain the confidence necessary to engage in armed combat (Mahara 2007). The Maoist leaders realized that continuous political indoctrination facilitated cohesion amongst the different individuals within the movement so that they all shared a common ideological background, thus deterring factionalization. A steady stream of ideological training also ensured that cadres would be amenable to the changing tactics and strategies of the leadership, because changes were motivated using texts and ideological discourse with which the cadres were familiar. Moreover, it also aided in retention, minimizing attrition rates by continuing to stress and educate the cadres about the importance of the ideology and the armed movement.

Why political education worked

That indoctrination was a successful recruitment strategy for the Maoists can be explained in a number of ways. The different indoctrination campaigns fulfilled perhaps the most basic and essential function of informing the populace about the existence, goals, and methods of the CPN-M. In this sense, mass meetings and individual motivators functioned as a sort of marketing tool that "sold" the public on the Maoist movement. The indoctrination campaigns also provided valuable information about the benefits of joining, in particular, the benefits that would be distributed if the Maoists were to succeed in their aims.[22] The oral nature of cultural programs and individual motivators was particularly important in this context, since many individuals – and particularly those targeted by the Maoists – were illiterate.[23] From a cost-benefit perspective, this information about the potential gains from the redistribution of goods in the event of a Maoist victory may have increased the expected payoff in an individual's calculus (Macours 2006). The CPN-M made it extremely clear that should they come to power, the peasantry would have access to a multitude of political, economic, and social goods currently unavailable to them. Such promises may have outweighed the risks of joining, particularly when so many had so little to lose.

More psychologically-oriented explanations are also central to understanding the success of political education as a recruitment strategy. The Maoist rhetoric at indoctrination sessions often had a powerful effect on the local populace, who were unaccustomed to being addressed with respect by politicians of any sort. Interviews with villagers during the conflict suggest that simply addressing and engaging villagers had a profound effect, "many villagers spoke of their sense of incredulity that such brave and powerful individuals should come to speak with them, ask their opinions on weighty issues, and address them with respect" (quoted in Schneiderman and Turin 2004: 91). By addressing the villagers, discussing their problems, and requesting their assistance, the Maoists encouraged the villagers to be active political agents, a radical departure from villagers' previous experiences of marginalization. Schneiderman and Turin (2004: 88) elaborate, ". . . villagers felt that they were empowered agents shaping and creating their country's destiny, not passive spectators watching from the political sidelines."

For rural individuals who felt marginalized and aggrieved, the Maoist ideology was compelling. The new Nepal that the Maoists proposed would be more inclusive and welcome traditionally excluded groups and individuals. Several analysts have argued that the Maoists sought to redefine identities through political discourse and that these new identities were tied to ideas about the nation. One suggests that "becoming a Maoist may provide a powerful alternative national identity within a 'modern' Nepal for those who have otherwise felt excluded from such national imaginings" (Pettigrew and Schneiderman 2004: 28). Fujikura (2003) provides an example of this alternative national identity, noting that the Maoists adopted national songs traditionally taught and sung in schools and substituted the nationalistic text for Maoist text which exhorts youth to be nation-builders through armed struggle.

This portrayal of the Maoist ideology was especially appealing to rural individuals since it matched well with their own local agendas and grievances.[24] Many of those who joined had previously supported other communist parties, but found these parties to be ineffective and unable to bring about substantive change, which increased the appeal of the Maoists' radical agenda and violent tactics.[25] The Maoist ideology in its purest form, such as in the ideological tracts produced by the Central Committee, differed considerably from the ideology with which villagers were presented; ideological teachings were adapted for those with little experience with politics. The CPN-M employed localized strategies for conveying its complex ideological ideas, using local idiom and references which did not require previous political education or literacy, ". . . it may be useful to differentiate between the theoretical ideology advanced by the Maoist leadership at the national level, and the practical ideology employed at the village level . . . Grassroots redistribution of wealth lent credence to the Maoists' more abstract promises of political power for those who had previously remained excluded" (Schneiderman and Turin 2004: 93). To locals, the CPN-M's complex ideas about class became palpable because they were expressed in a familiar context; for many, Maoism was about bringing justice to "exploiters" (Schneiderman 2003).

According to a former district cultural group leader, the Maoists were able to adjust their rhetoric to the grievances of the differing local communities from which they recruited (author interview 2008). Different rhetorical strategies were employed depending on what the villagers' backgrounds were. In villages dominated by ethnic minorities Maoist demands for ethnic equality were emphasized.[26] Female motivators gave special attention to recruiting other women and educating them on Maoist ideals of gender equality. Sharma and Prasain elaborate, ". . . the full liberation of women and gender equality are to be achieved only in a classless or communist society. Hence there is all the more reason for women to take part in the revolution. Such positions are explained to women, and more generally, through political classes, 'cultural' programs, the party media, and the mass print media" (Sharma and Prasain 2004: 155).[27] This focus on local knowledge and an understanding of local grievances was central to Maoist success in attracting recruits. But at the same time as the Maoists emphasized particular grievances (ethnic, gender, etc.), they were also careful to couch their discussion of these grievances in a Maoist discourse, "the crux of the Maoists ideological work was to construct a narrative that subsumed ethnic counter-narratives as well as other oppositional narratives – including those of women, dalits, the poor, the landless, and small farmers – and to present revolutionary war as the only true remedy for all forms of oppression" (Fujikura 2003: 27). A former district cultural group leader emphasizes this point, asserting that the party's central leadership ensured universality in key themes (author interview 2008). This rhetorical strategy helped to build a common Maoist identity, an essential element for maintaining a cohesive group.

Conclusion

This chapter sought to move from structural factors in explaining rebel recruitment and focus instead on the agency of the rebel group itself by examining particular strategies it can adopt, in particular, indoctrination. It is clear that structural factors are important in the Nepal case: the absence of effective governance and viable channels of influence left the majority of the population with little influence, and the centralization of the state contrasted markedly from the village-up approach that the Maoists adopted. The weakness of the state also facilitated the Maoists ability to expunge the countryside of village-level representation, allowing them a free hand in further recruitment. Inequality, poverty, and social discrimination provided the Maoists with ripe opportunity to recruit from the aggrieved population while government repression drove scores of people into the arms of the Maoists.

This chapter contended that to understand the growth of the Maoists, we must go beyond context and also take into account the Maoists' actual recruitment strategies. Grievances over economic and social inequalities and poor governance are long-standing in Nepal; why was it the CPN-M that was able to take advantage of these grievances? In large part, I have argued, because the CPN-M was the first group to successfully appeal to villagers political interests and encourage their participation through indoctrination practices. Moreover, the CPN-M cleverly linked villagers' grievances about their everyday situation with the larger Maoist ideology, attracting recruits by employing local idiom. At the same time it ensured that all members were educated in Maoist ideology, guaranteeing not only commitment to the cause, but also that the diverse individuals which composed the CPN-M were united by this common ideology. This minimized factionalism and attrition, and ensured that the leadership would be able to exercise control over the cadres. Indoctrination provided villagers with information about the Maoists – their goals, their tactics, their successes – that was essential at the outset of the conflict for promoting the Maoist cause and garnering recruits. Indoctrination also prepared prospective members as to the difficulties they would face as rebels and perhaps lowered their moral threshold for taking to violence (Macours 2006).

One caveat is in order. This chapter focused on the use of indoctrination as an important recruitment strategy used by the Maoists, but it was not the only tactic employed. Coercion and selective benefits were also used to a certain extent.[28] There are also indications in the literature and in the authors' interviews that networks may have been important to recruitment practices;[29] it appears that many individuals were drawn to the organization through personal contacts with friends and family. These other recruitment paths warrant systematic analysis, as does the means by which the Maoists came to dominate the recruitment environment. The extent to which these differing tactics were employed throughout the conflict remains unclear. A prima facie reading of the conflict suggests that the early years of the People's War saw careful recruitment of only highly committed individuals but as the conflict developed, newly recruited cadres were reportedly less ideologically devoted, and the CPN-M was less committed to educating these recruits on its ideology. This indicates that the CPN-M may have shifted its recruitment strategy to a certain extent over the course of the conflict, a suggestion that challenges recent literature which argues that recruitment strategies are static (Weinstein 2007).

Rebel recruitment is central for understanding the duration, intensity, and termination of a conflict. Without recruits, a rebel organization ceases to exist or to be a substantive threat. The Nepal case has highlighted that rebels can adopt strategies which facilitate recruitment. Without the successful recruitment strategy of indoctrination, the CPN-M may never have grown into the large and influential group that it has become today.

Notes

* I wish to thank Manish Thapa and Dhruba Nepal for facilitating my research and generously sharing their contacts, as well as Mahendra Lawoti for many useful comments. I also wish to thank my research team in Kathmandu and Rolpa: Ashik KC, Ojaswi Shah, and Trilochan Malla. Fieldwork was funded by the Theodor Adelswärds Memorial Fund and the Lars Hierta Memorial Foundation.
1 The number of active rebels remains contested. UNMIN's (United Nations Mission in Nepal) verification team concluded in 2007 that of the 31,318 rebels registered after the signing of the CPA, 18,923 were members of the Maoist's People's Liberation Army (PLA). This estimate remains somewhat uncertain since some members of the PLA did not register with UNMIN, and since UNMIN's verification procedures suffered from limitations that potentially allowed for over-counting (interview with UNMIN employee, 2008). It is therefore difficult to know whether there were greater or fewer members of the PLA than the UN estimate indicate.
2 For the purpose of this article, I assume that a rebel group can act as a unitary agent (i.e. the leadership can formulate a policy which is effectively implemented). The analysis of Nepal bears out this assumption, though it may be less applicable in other empirical contexts.
3 This terminology raises a number of problems as the definition of indoctrination varies. The Merriam-Webster dictionary defines it as "to imbue with a usually partisan or sectarian opinion, point of view, or principle" while the Cambridge dictionary defines it as "to repeat an idea or belief frequently to someone in order to persuade them to accept it." The pejorative overtones risk introducing a normative hue to the data presented here. "Political education" does not suffer from the same pejorative connotations, but instead from other weaknesses. Chief amongst them is the question of what political education means, and whose responsibility it is to provide it. Generally speaking, civic education is provided by the state; no other body is mandated to educate the populace politically. Using the term political education provides a veneer of legitimacy to the behavior being described. In short, there is no neutral term available to describe this behavioral phenomenon of the CPN-M. I thus use the two terms interchangeably and any normative overtone implied by the use of either term is not intended.
4 This chapter is focused in the process by which individuals voluntarily joined rebellion, but it should be noted that many individuals were forcibly recruited into the CPN-M; this is an issue to which I will return near the end of the chapter.
5 Popkin also points out the risks of non-participation should the rebels achieve victory, and argues that individuals must weigh the potential consequences of failing to participate in successful movements. Thus, one should expect strong endogeneity of joining in relation to the battlefield outcomes: as a rebel movement grows stronger, it should generate more recruits, not only because they will seek the future gains that seem increasingly likely, but because they will seek to avoid post-victory sanctions by the group for non-participation (Popkin 1979: 258).
6 This point highlights the fact that the collective action approach is vague as to whether it concerns the initial formation of a group, or the mass recruitment which follows, a point noted by Kalyvas and Kocher. I assume that the initial core of the group is composed of first movers driven by what Elster terms unconditional cooperators and altruists. The focus here is thus on efforts to mobilize the masses by the core rebel group.
7 See also Herbst (2000) on how rebel leaders motivate followers to fight, noting that beyond economic incentives, rebel leaders also employ strategies of political indoctrination, ethnic mobilization, and coercion.
8 For an excellent overview of ethnic and regional identities in Nepal, see Sharma (2008).
9 The CPN-M found mixed success in recruiting based on ethnicity. They were able to mobilize many members of some groups, such as Magars, who inhabit the area in mid-western Nepal that made up the Maoist heartland.

10 The bonded labor system (*kamaiya*) in modern times was a system of paying debts with labor. This system was widely abused. The practice, which was widespread in the Terai and mid-western regions of Nepal, was only abolished in 2000, and is still practiced informally.

11 One long-time rebel's comments support this conclusion. Pun, K. (2008) stated that the CPN-M focused its efforts on recruiting from the absolute lowest strata of the population: the very poor and oppressed – people with no clothes, home, or job – were easiest to recruit not only because of their grievances against the state but also because they simply had no other options.

12 It should be noted that Li Onesto was hosted by the Maoists because she is a writer for the *Revolution*, a communist newspaper, and thus has a clear positive bias towards the CPN-M.

13 As an example, a song and dance particular to the Western part of the country was adapted to incorporate Maoist themes and included in the cultural performance (author interview with former district cultural group leader, 2008).

14 To exemplify the extent of these kidnapping, on one day in 2005 over 1,100 primary and secondary schoolchildren and their teachers were abducted in two separate incidents.

15 Youth were a focus for Maoist recruitment efforts, both coerced and voluntary. In part this can be explained by the structure of rural society and economy which offers few opportunities for youths. With little option other than farming, many youths without the resources to move to towns or abroad found the Maoist movement attractive, as it provided them with status and an opportunity for agency that was otherwise not available to them (cf. Pettigrew 2002).

16 Additionally, the Maoists also instituted their own educational programs in many schools in their stronghold areas, revising textbooks to focus on teaching the children a Maoist version of history, politics, sociology, etc. (Pun, K. 2008; Lecomte-Tilouine, this volume).

17 Graham (2007) argues that the fact that the PLA operated in small cells implies that forced recruitment in practice would have been very difficult to sustain as a norm.

18 Arguably, this created a monopoly over the recruitment environment for the Maoists, for both coerced and voluntary mobilization.

19 Joining the party could take many forms. The primary distinction was between part-timer and full-timer. Part-timers remained in their villages and served in various militias that assisted the party. Full-timers, on the other hand, could remain in their village or they could be placed elsewhere. All PLA members were full-timers. There were few distinctions between political and military work in the early years of the conflict (the PLA was only formally announced in 2001), and even in later years the distinction could be blurred as individuals switched between the two (author interviews with PLA cadres).

20 The form of indoctrination seem to have been largely the same irregardless of the audience (PLA member, supporter, general public, etc.) though the extent probably varied. Full-timers had more opportunities to engage in political education, particularly as all PLA units had a political commissar embedded to ensure continuous political indoctrination and control.

21 Another rebel leader states that it took approximately one year of political work before being allowed to move into the People's Army, and that political training was of utmost priority and always preceded military training (Gurung 2007). Author interviews with lower ranking cadres suggest that in fact, many individuals joined the PLA directly or after only limited part-time service to the party. These individuals received political training concurrently with their military training. Again, this discrepancy may explained by when the individual joined.

22 It should be noted that the Maoists were not alone in these practices. What distinguishes the CPN-M's use of such practices is both its elaborate nature, but also its connection to the use of violence: other political parties did not use cultural programs, for instance, to justify selective killings.

23 UNMIN data from the first round of registration (prior to final verification) shows that approximately 1 of 6 (17 percent) was illiterate (Gebremedhin 2007); a survey of Maoist women conducted during the war also shows that 17 percent were either illiterate or had 5 years or less of schooling (Yami 2007).

24 This is in line with theories of frame alignment found in the social mobilization literature (cf. Snow et al. 1986).

25 Yami's (2007) wartime survey of female PLA members found that 78 percent had a Communist family background. Author interviews also support the conclusion that Communist backgrounds were common amongst PLA cadres.

26 See Graham (2007: 242) for a discussion of the "marriage of convenience between Maoism and pre-existing ethno-regional identities."

27 The Maoists had considerable success recruiting women, though exact estimates vary: Yami (2007) asserts that 30–50 percent of the PLA consisted of women, while UNMIN's first round of registration (prior to final verification) found that 19 percent of the PLA were women (Gebremedhin 2007). See Pettigrew (2002) for a discussion of why Maoism was attractive to women.

28 Graham (2007) concludes that selective benefits played only a marginal role in Maoist recruitment.

29 Cf. Snow, Zurcher, and Ekland-Olson (1980) for previous literature on the impact of networks in social movements.

Bibliography

Bhattarai, Baburam. 2003. *The nature of underdevelopment and regional structure of Nepal: A Marxist analysis*. Delhi: Adriot Publishers.

Bohara, Alok K., Neil J. Mitchell, and Mani Nepal. 2006. Opportunity, democracy, and the exchange of political violence. *Journal of Conflict Resolution* 50 (1):108–28.

Collier, Paul. 2000. Doing well out of war. In *Greed and grievance: economic agendas in civil war*, eds. Mats Berdal and David M. Malone, 91–111. Washington, DC: International Peace Academy.

Collier, Paul, and Anke Hoeffler. 2001. *Greed and grievance in civil war*. Washington, DC: World Bank.

CPN-M. 1996/2003. 40-point demands. In *The people's war in Nepal: left perspectives*, eds. Arjun Karki and David Seddon, 183–87. Delhi: Adroit Publishers.

Dixit, Kanak Mani. 2002. Insurgents and innocents. *Himal* 15 (6): 28–38.

Elster, Jon. 2006. Is collective action theory relevant for the study of civil war? Paper presented at the PRIO Workshop on First Movers. Oslo, August 16–17.

Fearon, James D., and David D. Laitin. 2003. Ethnicity, insurgency, and civil war. *American Political Science Review* 97 (1): 75–90.

Fujikura, Tatsuro. 2003. The role of collective imagination in the Maoist conflict in Nepal. *Himalaya* 23 (1): 21–30.

Gates, Scott. 2002. Recruitment and allegiance: the microfoundations of rebellion. *Journal of Conflict Resolution* 46 (1): 111–30.

Gates, Scott, and Mansoob Murshed. 2005. Spatial-horizontal inequality and the Maoist insurgency in Nepal. *Review of Development Economics* 9 (1): 121–34.

Gebremedhin, Amanuel. 2007. Reconstruction, rehabilitation and reconciliation from below. Paper presented at Nepal: Looking Beyond Kathmandu Conference. Brussels, April 20.

Graham, George. 2007. People's war? Self-interest, coercion and ideology in Nepal's Maoist insurgency. *Small Wars and Insurgencies* 18 (2): 231–48.

Gurung, Dev. 2007. Author interview, March 22, Kathmandu.

Hachhethu, Krishna. 2000. Nepali politics: political parties, political crisis and problems of governance. In *Domestic conflict and crisis of governability in Nepal*, ed. Dhruba Kumar, 90–116. Kathmandu: CNAS.

Herbst, Jeffrey. 2000. Economic incentives, natural resources and conflict in Africa. *Journal of African Economies* 9 (3): 270–94

Hutt, Michael. 2004. Monarchy, democracy and Maoism in Nepal. In *Himalayan 'people's war': Nepal's Maoist rebellion*, ed. Michael Hutt, 1–20. London: Hurst & Company.

ICG (International Crisis Group). 2005. Nepal's Maoists: their aims, structure and strategy. Asia Report No. 104.

Kalyvas, Stathis N. and Matthew Adam Kocher. 2007. How 'free' is free riding in civil wars? Violence, insurgency, and the collective action problem. *World Politics* 59 (1): 177–216.

Kumar, Dhruba. 2000. What ails democracy in Nepal? In *Domestic conflict and crisis of governability in Nepal*, ed. Dhruba Kumar, 14–57. Kathmandu: CNAS.

——. 2003. Consequences of the militarized conflict and the cost of violence in Nepal. *Contributions to Nepalese Studies* 30 (2): 167–216.

Lal, C.K. 2001. Nepal's Maobadi. *Himal* 14 (11): 39–47.

Lawoti, Mahendra. 2005. *Towards a democratic Nepal*. London: Sage Publications.

Lichbach, Mark. 1998. *The rebel's dilemma*. Ann Arbor: University of Michigan Press.

Macours, Karen. 2006. Relative deprivation and civil conflict in Nepal. Manuscript, SAIS-Johns Hopkins.

Mahara, Krishna Bahadur. 2007. Author interview, March 19, Kathmandu.

Olson, Mancur. 1965. *The logic of collective action*. Cambridge, MA: Harvard University Press.

Onesto, Li. 2005. *Dispatches from the people's war in Nepal*. London: Pluto Press.

Onta, Pratyoush. 2004. Democracy and duplicity. In *Himalayan 'people's war': Nepal's Maoist rebellion*, ed. Michael Hutt, 136–51. London: Hurst & Company.

Petersen, Roger. 2001. *Resistance and rebellion: lessons from Eastern Europe*. Cambridge: Cambridge University Press.

Pettigrew, Judith. 2002. Guns, kinship, and fear: Maoists among the Tamu-mai (Gurungs). In *Resistance and the state: Nepalese experiences*, ed. David Gellner, 305–25. New Delhi: Social Science Press.

——. 2003. Living between the Maoists and the army in rural Nepal. *Himalaya* 23 (1): 9–20.

Pettigrew, Judith and Sara Schneiderman. 2004. Ideology and agency in Nepal's Maoist movement. *Himal* 17 (1): 19–29.

Popkin, Samuel. 1979. *The rational peasant*. Berkeley: University of California Press.

Prachanda. 1999/2003. The third turbulent year of the people's war. In *The people's war in Nepal: left perspectives*, eds. Arjun Karki and David Seddon, 239–57. Delhi: Adroit Publishers.

——. 2000/2003. Inside the revolution in Nepal. In *The people's war in Nepal: left perspectives*, eds. Arjun Karki and David Seddon, 75–116. Delhi: Adroit Publishers.

Pun, Kirti Bahadur (aka Prakanda Singh). 2008. Author interview, April 29. Unga satellite cantonment, Rolpa.

Pun, Tulsi Ram (aka Himal). 2008. Author interview, April 29, Unga satellite cantonment, Rolpa.

Ramirez, Philippe. 2004. Maoism in Nepal: towards a comparative perspective. In *Himalayan 'people's war': Nepal's Maoist rebellion*, ed. Michael Hutt, 225–42. London: Hurst & Company.

Regan, Patrick M., and Daniel Norton. 2005. Greed, grievance, and mobilization in civil wars. *Journal of Conflict Resolution* 49 (3): 319–36.

Rose, Leo E. 2001. The national political culture and institutions in Nepal. In *The post-colonial states of South Asia: Democracy, identity, development, and security*, eds. Amita Shastri and A. Jeyaratnam Wilson, 114–38. Richmond: Curzon Press.

Schneiderman, Sara. 2003. Violent histories and political consciousness: reflections on Nepal's Maoist movement from Piskar village. *Himalaya* 23 (1): 39–48.

Schneiderman, Sara, and Mark Turin. 2004. The path to jan sakar in Dolakha district: Towards an ethnography of the Maoist movement. In *Himalayan 'people's war': Nepal's Maoist rebellion*, ed. Michael Hutt, 79–111. London: Hurst & Company.

Sharma, Pitamber. 2008. *Unravelling the mosaic: spatial aspects of ethnicity in Nepal.* Kathmandu: Himal Books.

Sharma, Sudheer. 2004. The Maoist movement: An evolutionary perspective. In *Himalayan 'people's war': Nepal's Maoist rebellion*, ed. Michael Hutt, 38–57. London: Hurst & Company.

Sharma, Mandira and Dinesh Prasain. 2004. Gender dimensions of the people's war: Some reflections on the experiences of rural women. In *Himalayan 'people's war': Nepal's Maoist rebellion*, ed. Michael Hutt, 152–65. London: Hurst & Company.

Singh, Sonal, Khagendra Dahal, and Edward Mills. 2005. Nepal's war on human rights: a summit higher than Everest. *International Journal for Equity in Health* 4 (9): 1–7.

Snow, David A., E. Burke Rochford, Jr., Steven K. Worden, and Robert D. Benford. 1986. Frame alignment processes, micromobilization, and movement participation. *American Sociological Review* 51: 464–81.

Snow, David A., Louis A. Zurcher, Jr., and Sheldon Ekland-Olson. 1980. Social networks and social movements: A microstructural approach to differential recruitment. *American Sociological Review* 45: 787–801.

Subba, Chaitanya. 2006. The ethnic dimension of the Maoist conflict. In *Nepal: Facets of Maoist insurgency*, ed. Lok Raj Baral, 31–59. Delhi: Adroit Publishers.

Thapa, Deepak. 2002. Erosion of the Nepali world. *Himal* 15 (4): 26–36.

———. 2001. Days of the Maoist. *Himal* 14 (5): 4–21.

Thapa, Manjushree. 2003. The war in the west. *Himal* 16 (1): 36–42.

UNDP. 2004. *Nepal human development report*. Kathmandu: UNDP Nepal.

Weinstein, Jeremy M. 2007. *Inside rebellion*. Cambridge: Cambridge University Press.

Wood, Elisabeth. 2003. *Insurgent collective action and civil war in El Salvador*. Cambridge: Cambridge University Press.

Yami, Hisila. 2007. *People's war and women's liberation in Nepal*. Kathmandu: Janadhwani Publication.

3 Catchy melodies and clenched fists

Performance as politics in Maoist cultural programs

Monica Mottin*

Introduction

> I want to put forward a short commitment (*pratibaddhata*). This is not only mine. This is the commitment of our whole Samana Battalion cultural movement. I take the commitment to fulfil the dream of the martyrs. [. . .] We, cultural workers, want to give you our commitment. In this coming storm, we will also, at any cost, play our role. This commitment we put in front of you. What we are singing in front of you people, these all are your own songs, including your pains, your tears, your happiness. Through these songs we can stop the hidden royalist system from raising their head and to stop them we will go to Singha Durbar and to the Royal Palace with harmoniums and guitars. Then, if it does not work, we will join the PLA [People's Liberation Army] to enter Narayanhiti [Royal Palace]. This is our oath. You may wonder, 'How can you reach Narayanhiti?' You can see it in our banner, Samana Cultural Battalion, Battalion means warriors, cultural war, cultural army, cultural fighters. We are not only cultural workers. We don't want to be only artists. Political people and intellectuals say that artists should be independent, they should not have any political affiliation, they should not be attached to politics. But we say we are artists and we want to join politics. We want to sing the songs of the people. Politics is a way to free suffocated people. We, artists, want to do the same. This is our commitment as artists.
>
> (Commander, public speech, October 2006[1])

Catchy melodies, colourful dresses, traditional steps broken by classical *mudras* suddenly turning into clenched fists. Since the beginning of the People's War in 1996, Maoist cultural troupes have been travelling the country offering villagers colourful politico-cultural programs. The first 'Cultural Battalion', *Madhya Samana Battalion 6*, was formed in October 2006. It includes the four 'cultural companies' of Central Nepal, Sen Chyang Cultural Company, Anekot Cultural Company, Shiva Sharada Cultural Company and Chunu Shilpa Cultural Company. The battalion is subsumed under the cultural section of the party, *Akhil Nepal Jan Sanskitik Mahasangh* (All Nepal People's Cultural Federation). Maoist cultural groups are active in each of the 75 districts of Nepal. Furthermore, 13 cultural groups are linked to each of the Maoist Federal States, and 11 are connected to their ethnic fronts (Sharma 2004: 41–42). Samana Parivar is the historical cultural group associated to the party's central committee. Cultural groups are also present within the PLA and other workers' organizations although they perform as a leisure activity.

Around 1,500 artists are engaged full time in composing songs, dances and drama which are performed during public political meetings to entertain and educate the audience between the speeches of the party leaders. Cultural programs are also organized for fundraising. About 200 artists[2] lost their lives during the ten-year armed struggle. The cultural troupes' repertoire is regularly created to match the development of the political situation. The task of the party's artists is twofold. During public programs, they aim at getting the people's support for the revolution. During the party's internal meetings, they criticize the leadership whenever they fail, according to them, to follow the people's desires. The Maoist cultural front produces both literary works including magazines, novels, dramas and poetry and performance art such as dance, theatre and songs that circulate through tapes, CDs and videos. Only the latter will be considered in this chapter.

After situating Maoist cultural programs in the context of oppositional performance in Nepal, I will briefly outline the role of art in revolutionary theory. I will then detail how Maoist cultural programs can be conceptualized as both political rituals and popular culture. But first, let us start by unveiling some methodological issues.

Methodology

Following the People's Movement 2006, Maoists were not considered 'terrorists' any longer.[3] Their cultural groups ceased underground activities and started to perform with increasing frequency in public spaces as part of a wider 'strategy' to boost the party's visibility in Kathmandu and to demonstrate their power and popular support. The capital, Nepal's most prestigious 'stage', was turned red through posters pasted thickly on every piece of wall, slogans painted over the façades of buildings alongside roads, red flags at street corners, rallies and the almost weekly national mass meetings of the party's different federations and fronts.

In July 2006, many people in Kathmandu looked at the Maoists with curiosity, suspicion and fear. They were not talked about openly. It was only through word of mouth that I heard a Maoist team was going to rehearse nearby. My friend offered to make introductions discreetly. His attitude suggested a certain degree of sensitivity was required. Opinions about having the Maoists present in one's own environment covered the spectrum from sympathy to overt disagreement. 'They may have killed,' commented one artist[4] with annoyance. 'I don't understand why they should come into our space.'

Ethnographers are required to objectify their 'subjective' position in order to achieve a form of objectivity (Behar 1996: 6; Bourdieu 2003). In such a polarized environment, it is necessary to locate my position before moving into the account of Maoist performances. In the months that followed the first meeting, I was 'given' access to the activities of a Maoist 'cultural company' (*sanskritik company*, otherwise called *sanskritik parivar*, 'cultural family'). I travelled out of the valley with them and attended their programs in Kathmandu. There was both curiosity and apprehension between us. Throughout my previous fieldwork I had always informed a friend about my whereabouts when I travelled outside the capital, and also did so on that occasion. By coincidence, my friend was known to the commander. The commander was surprised to hear that I had told someone that I was going to travel with 'them', but he was also interested in our friend's reaction. Once back in Kathmandu, I discovered that the rumour about my trip had spread throughout the 'artistic community'. My return was greeted with knowing smiles and a pun: *Hindeko?* The verb '*hindnu*' in Nepali means both 'to walk' and 'to follow' and is used by Maoists to talk about joining the party. '*Thuprei hinde* [I walked lot],' I replied, playing with ambiguity of the word.

Expectations and assumptions between the Maoist artists and myself mirrored each other in revealing ways. Although I had met him only a couple of times before, the commander took responsibility for my presence from the beginning of the trip, indicating a certain level of trust. With earphones to answer the incessant phone calls and wearing combat pants which, curiously enough, had just become the latest fashion craze in the city, he looked more like a cool young businessman-in-action than a stereotypical rebel. He asked me if I was afraid. I smiled to conceal my evident tension. I explained that I was quiet not out of fear but because I did not know him and his world. He reassured me, saying I should not worry, and if I felt uncomfortable during the following days, I should tell him.

He soon raised the issue of their armed struggle and questioned what he thought was a common foreign attitude towards weapons. He wished to show me some photos, but said he was not sure if I would like them. 'Many people don't like the use of guns,' he said. 'Maybe you don't either?' I felt unable to convey in a quick answer the complexities raised by his question. He nonetheless then opened a small photo album showing some pictures of him and his comrades patrolling the streets of a hilly area with guns and posing for a night shot. After six years of underground struggle in the jungle as a PLA guerrilla fighter, something inside him had changed, because of the loss of a friend. He then decided to join a cultural group with whom he had travelled for the last two years, from 'Mechi [eastern-most zone] to Mahakali [western-most zone]'. He remembered poor people in the villages, with tattered clothes and not enough food to survive. 'The government is *mathi* [high],' he said. 'They come by helicopter but they don't look *talla* [down]. *Asamanta* [inequality] is the problem, that's what we are trying to change.'

The first journey turned out to be crucial in order to establish a relationship with the group and to gain access to subsequent programs. Travelling together, sleeping on the floor as they did, eating the same food, fighting to be able to help them wash dishes, attending and video-recording programs and rallies probably bridged the artists' 'imagined distance' existing between a 'foreigner' and themselves, and created a feeling of 'inclusion'. Back in Kathmandu the commander commented, 'We got along very well, you are just like us.' This soon turned into, 'You are also a Maoist.'

The ten-year-long conflict had created a situation in which people were associated with either one side or the other. Being an outsider, I was also expected to 'find a location'. Moreover, researching performance inevitably exposes the researcher to a high degree of visibility. My 'contested membership' was later joked about in the group. When some of the artists greeted me with *lal salaam* (red salute) and a raised clinched fist, I waved and said *namaste,* before all of us smiled. I preferred not to use the party's symbols to maintain a certain degree of 'differentiation' while sharing daily moments, activities and interests, even though such behaviour may have seemed strange.

However, since the commander knew I had performed in theatre, I was primarily considered and introduced as an 'artist', like 'them', rather than as an anthropologist. As a result, I was involved whenever it was time to sing and dance, or engaged in technical discussions about the outcome of their performances. My assumed ignorance about party organization and ideology created an open space for 'being taught' and to discuss their ideas and work. One day the commander jokingly suggested I should pick up a gun and go with them should they ever go back to the jungle. I replied I could only write because my 'job' was different. He remarked, 'Then we will explain [Maoism-Prachandapath] and make you a Maoist,' and smiled.

During the time I spent with the group I never felt any sort of pressure. Instead, I perceived a strong feeling of 'involvement', of being part of a community or a family. I felt the paradox of anthropological enquiry framed by the double loyalty of getting the 'natives' point of view' without 'going native' (Behar 1996: 5). Because the artists' choice was 'total', the contradiction between listening to stories of hardship and idealism in cold rooms in Nepal, and then writing about the same events in a warm place in Italy, was deep and uncomfortable. I repeatedly questioned my role. In politically critical moments, when the artists discussed the possibility of returning to the jungle and becoming 'martyrs' before my next trip to Nepal, I indeed felt the differences between 'us': what for them was common talk and a matter of pride, for me was extremely painful. From a professional point of view, their cultural programs were my work; personally, they had become my friends.

What follows can be considered the product of 'collaboration' (Kunnath 2006: 93) between artists and the anthropologist who collects, organizes and phrases the narration of their experiences into academically accepted forms and themes. I have explored the artists' point of view[5] and, in particular, I have conflated various voices into those of the 'commander' and the 'commissar'[6] to protect the identities of my informants. However, to enable the reader to follow the artists' passionate words I have used extensive direct quotations.

Cultural performance as politics

Political opposition and activism have long taken cultural and artistic form in Nepal. Cultural programs (*sanskritik karyakram*) are a well-liked and malleable format including songs, dances and theatre performed by cultural groups. The term 'cultural group' (*sanskritik parivar or sanskritik samuha*) covers heterogeneous groups performing both traditional folk dances and songs, and modern dances based upon pop and Bollywood film music. Cultural groups are innumerable in the capital and a popular form of leisure activity outside Kathmandu. Since the Panchayat years, schools have been encouraged to prepare annual cultural programs for Parents' Day and for Saraswati Puja.[7] Moreover, each ethnic community has its own cultural group performing during local festivals. In Kathmandu and in other tourist places, professional cultural groups perform traditional dances and songs in hotels to entertain tourists.[8] Similarly, cultural programs from different ethnic traditions were cosmetically used by the government and by the Panchayat state to display the fiction of the 'unity in diversity' national culture (cf. Burghart 1993; Des Chenes 1996) during public and official functions, in particular during national celebrations or royal birthdays.

But cultural performances in Nepal also convey deep social and political criticism. This can be seen in the spontaneous women's songs recounting daily life problems sung during the Teej festival (Skinner et al. 1994; Ahearn 1999), or the improvised political satire of the street sketches during Gaj Jatra.[9] Yet, because Nepal's political history has been characterized by repressive regimes, cultural performances have also been a means to enter the banned 'public space'. For example, the activists of the Praja Parishad[10] in early 1940s manipulated religious readings for political purposes (Hoftun et al. 1999: 7). Similarly, Yogamaya, an ascetic and a revolutionary woman, challenged Bhramanic oppressive practices and the Rana ruler himself through her songs called *hazurbani* (Aziz 2001). Yet, it was during the Panchayat rule, when political parties were banned and their leaders were underground, that cultural performances entered the sphere of politics in a more organized way. Political leaders were forced to organize their party work from a 'private' position to avoid arrest. Cultural programs were thus charged with political meanings.[11] Artistic performances carried those messages that could not be openly expressed by politicians and activists. Cultural workers (*sanskritik karmi*), artists and activists associated with the political parties travelled the whole country in teams and made public dangerous political messages. Cultural programs, deeply rooted in the rich oral and folk tradition, were immensely popular, especially in the villages where few other means of entertainment were available. Artists with their songs and dramas were at the front of political campaigning. If they were well received by the people of a particular area, activists would bring in literary magazines first and then political books. When police were nearby cultural workers sang folk or love songs, but once the police left, the repertoire switched to what they called 'progressive' songs (*pragatisil git*) (Rai 2060 BS; Grandin 1994, 2005). While remaining within the musical genre of modern or folk songs broadcasted by Radio Nepal (Grandin 1994: 175), progressive songs introduced innovations both in content and in interaction with villagers. A Maoist commissar explains they were themselves inspired by those artists:

> They travelled from village to village against the Panchayat system to make people aware and get them to stand up. [. . .] Their thinking was that songs should not be about '*saila and maili*', or '*kancha and kanchi*' [that is 'love songs'] but should be about the people.
>
> (Interview, October 2006)

Cultural programs and progressive songs had a lasting and formidable impact on audiences across the country. During the street protests that led to and followed the

People's Movement in April 2006, young and old people alike sang many of those songs.[12] What is more, they created powerful rhetorical images (Grandin 1994; Rai 2060 BS) that constitute the core artistic patterns from which Maoist artistic rhetoric developed.

A cultural army for a cultural revolution

Aesthetics was not a central concern in the writings of Marx and Engels (Moore 2006: 10; Williams 1977; Lang and Williams 1972). Strongly deterministic readings of Marxism included art in the ideological superstructure. As part of the intellectual life, it was deemed to be conditioned by material circumstances, following Marx's dictum that 'social being determines consciousness' (Marx 1859). In contrast, less deterministic views stress the interconnectedness of ideological forms with the economic system, because art has the potential to intervene in the socioeconomic context by spurring the audience to adopt certain attitudes and practices.[13] In this way, 'culture' as artistic performance can affect 'culture' as a system of meanings and practices. Maoist artists' narratives reveal a concept of culture that is indissolubly linked to politics, as a commissar was keen in pointing out the first time I interviewed him:

> Because we are Communist, in our understanding the point of view to see everything is class. Seeing the development of society, every political revolution is a cultural revolution in itself. And in culture the genre that directly affects people is literary art [*sahitya kala*]. Literary art reflects the reality of a society. It also heightens awareness and provides support to society. That's why, in our ten-year experience of people's war, [we have realized that] to fight against the injustice and oppression done upon the people, presenting our ideas in artistic ways, through opera, drama, dance and revolutionary songs, motivates people more than a five-hour speech by a leader. They give the awareness to go forward and rebel. Although other ways can be powerful, art and literature are more powerful. [. . .] When we presented our pains, our sorrows, the reality of war through art, people could easily understand. They could easily follow and appreciate their liberation war.
>
> (Interview, October 2006)

The commissar continues his explanation emphasizing the relation between war-culture, culture-art and thus war-art:

> When we started our People's War, the battle war and the *madal*[14] war went together: pen war and bullet war. The pen supported the war and the war made the pen revolutionary. When these two things went together, the war was not only of bullets and guns but also of thoughts and pens. When Krishna Sen Ichchuk,[15] a magazine editor and Nepal's top literary person, became a martyr in the name of progressive [writing] [*pragatisil*], the soldiers who beat him to death said that a pen was more powerful than thousands of guns because one

bullet from one gun can kill only one army soldier, it kills one enemy, but his pen was killing thousands of soldiers at once.

(Ibid.)

For Maoist artists distinctions are clear-cut and consequential: because there are two classes in society, the oppressor and the oppressed, the bourgeois and the proletariat, there are also two cultures, 'bad culture' and 'good culture'.[16] As a result, while art that simply mirrors the social reality without questioning it can be defined as 'bourgeois art', 'revolutionary art' has to spur people to change society, defining art, as Brecht claims, 'not as a mirror held up to nature but a hammer with which to shape it'. It is the conflation of ideology in culture and art that makes every political revolution simultaneously a cultural revolution.[17] The cultural front is guided by Mao's ideas on art and literature expressed in the Yenan Forum and introduced in Nepal in the 1950s (Onesto 2006: 136). According to Mao, revolutionary art and literature are subordinate to politics because only politics concentrates the needs of the class and the mass, but they are nonetheless important, like 'cogs and wheels' in the revolutionary cause (Mao Tse-Tung 1967: 13).

Moreover, a leader of an ethnic liberation front associated with the CPN-M emphasizes the relation between art and politics, defining art as a vital part of an individual, and thus a privileged and 'natural' means of political expression:

We don't accept the bourgeois view that art and music are the ornaments of the country. We are not ready to accept this. Art and literature are body parts of the country, inseparable organs of the nation. To protect nationality [*rashtriata*] we need art. We need talent. That's why we say that art is not like an ornament to be worn when you feel like, and put into the garage when you don't. This can't happen. That's why today we are taking this music to create a relationship with the government.

(Public speech, September 2006)

In unintended ways, the leader's metaphor echoes Bourdieu's concept of artistic *habitus*. Questioning the Romantic view of the artist as a charismatic individual, independent and disinterested in his work, Bourdieu brings the artist back into the power rules of the cultural field. Therefore, both the ability to be creative and the practice of being creative are seen as effects of the individual artists' *habitus* – the embodied structure developed out of the individual's history, and their social and historical contexts (Webb et al. 2006). I will revisit this issue later in relation to the artist's multiple roles.

Revolutionary cultural programs

Representational practices have the power to reorganize the sense of self, to build alternative perceptions of possible futures and be the engines of social transformation. They can contain dreams and visions. Artistic performances do not simply provide an aesthetic experience. As symbolic performances they 'make it possible for there to be a consensus on the meaning of the social world, a consensus which contributes fundamentally to the reproduction of the social order' (Bourdieu 1991: 166). Extending Bourdieu's view, artistic experience can create a climate of consensus to subvert the social order itself. What Bourdieu suggests is that symbols, in the form of creative presentations, actually construct society by providing people with a specifically social and visible experience of identification that is publicly recognized.

Artistic performances were used in different ways before, during and after the People's War. Maoist artists draw on artistic performances to communicate with the audience, to create a sense of inclusion, to energize the PLA, to popularize Maoist ideology, spread political education and legitimize their political claims. Cultural programs also provide a platform for personal expression of often shared life experiences. These objectives are achieved through the particular character of cultural programs, as I will outline below.

Revolutionary performance as, and in, process

What immediately distinguishes Maoist performances from other artistic performances for social change is their strict connection with the party's political agenda and structure. Cultural groups depend on the party for political organization and thought, while remaining independent in the creative side and practical organization of their work. In this sense, cultural performances cannot be conceptualized as 'products' to be offered to an audience, a commodity, but rather as a process of an interaction through which the link between the party and the audience is created and sustained. The comparison with street performances for social change is intriguing. A commonly perceived flaw in certain street plays (Epskamp 2006; Mottin forthcoming) is the disjuncture between the artists as specialists and the audience, as well the lack of follow-up activities which results in the reduction of the power of theatre to achieve social transformation. The plays thus become more of a show than a form of social intervention. As party members, Maoist artists are backed by a strong institutional structure which embodies the message that they convey. Any person in the audience wishing to follow their message can find an institutional apparatus that sustains their choice.

During political mass meetings, cultural programs usually occupy two or three hours before the arrival of the political leaders and then continue between the leaders' speeches. Artists anchor cultural programs in a performative style. They introduce the songs and provide the audience with links to wider political issues. The audience, the artists and the party are symbolically joined in a single voice by revolutionary rhetoric (cf. de Sales 2003; Lecomte-Tilouine 2006). Artists become the spokespersons of the imagined temporary community that is established through the performance. A crescendo of cross-references plays within introductory speeches like an incantation: plain speaking is enriched with quotations from Maoist poems, which in turn change into revolutionary songs. According to Bourdieu, culture is both 'unifying' (1991: 167) and 'divisive', distinguishing between those who share the same ideals and those who do not.

Cultural productions create symbols of 'us' as communities, as revealed in the following lyrics:

> Look towards the mountains, a new beautiful world is being born
> This is our Nepal, this is lovely Nepal
> This is our Nepal,
> Look towards the mountains, a new beautiful world is being born
> As the snow falls in winter, injustice surrounds us
> In the country of Everest, we practice Malemabaad[18]
> The thought to change the world, born and heightened
> That is Prachandapath, the great Prachandapath, the great Prachandapath
> Look towards the mountains, a new beautiful world is being born
>
> (From *Voices of Faith*)

Therefore, cultural programs can be conceptualized as political rituals that create particular kinds of communities, 'communities of feelings' (Berezin 2001: 93), intense experiential moments of shared identity. As performance, Maoist cultural programs not only make visible the imaginings of people who share the same ideology, but they also emotionally enact their sense of belonging. In other words, cultural programs are both representational and performative. Their strength comes from the immediacy, topicality and emotional response[19] which songs, dances and dramas trigger in the audience. Emotions seem to be at odd with Maoist rhetoric. Although Prachanda (2001) highlights the role of cultural programs in involving the masses both ideologically and emotionally, 'sentimentalism' is often disparaged, as in the opening of the play *After Understanding*:

[Sounds of a crowd, slogans, sounds of bullets, shouts; a girl moans in pain]

A1:   A road? How did I get here? My arm . . . I'm injured. Where [am I]? My friends are not even here. I should not stay here. I should not stay here. I should go somehow [moans] . . . There's nobody here, [moaning], I should go somehow . . .

A2:   Friend . . . are you here? Injured?

A1:   Are you also?

A2:   I'm also injured. Police are coming after us . . .

A1:   Police? And where are the other friends?

A2:   Our friends are moving ahead, they are demonstrating.

A1:   Leave this place quickly. Don't stay here. These human ghosts/beasts won't leave you here. Go quickly.

A2:   How can I go, leaving you here alone . . .

A1:   Listen, in this time cheap sentimentalism (*sasto bhavukta*) will bring you only more loss. Go fast

A2:   This is not cheap sentimentalism, my friend. Police are coming. Let's move from here.

A1:   Look, I've lost lots of blood [lots of my blood has flooded], I will not live . . .

A2:   Friend, what are you saying? You have to live, the country needs you. . . . Stand up, friend, stand up.

This play, a collaborative work between a commissar and his artists, was performed in several districts between August and September 2006 as part of the Maoist Campaign for Republic. Apart from the extended use of Maoist metaphors, both the language and staging were simple and realistic, recalling street theatre. However, more than just acting out roles, artists re-enacted their own lives, many of them having had real-life experience of the performed scenarios. Nepali theatre 'professionals' often regard Maoist acting as amateurish. However, despite being aesthetically simple, the Maoist performance is based on direct personal experience of struggle which make them 'specialized' and 'professional' in their own field. Such a practical competence, a kind of 'feel for the game' (Bourdieu 1990: 66) is what emotionally involves the spectators. Their acting is empowered by their energy, their enthusiasm and the fact that they 'play' themselves as actors and activists.

There may be a feeling that the cultural programs may just be a way of 'preaching to the converted' (Dolan 2005: 65). Yet, as Holly Hughes (in Dolan 2005) suggests, political 'conversion' is unstable. People are never finally converted to anything. Ambiguity and doubt are always present. Cultural programs therefore facilitate the renewal of faith required to sustain political identity.

The content and organization of cultural programs changed during the stages of the People's War, and after April 2006. The evolution of revolutionary performances can be traced through the analysis of the songs, dance and drama over a decade. But that would require a chapter of its own. Placed chronologically, artistic productions offer a meta-commentary of the development of the wider political struggle. This is how the commissar explains how they actively involved and motivated audiences at the beginning of the People's War:

> When we were underground, after 2052 *Falgun* 1st [13 February 1996], we went from village to village at night. We could not walk during the day. We called people and sang for them, playing *madal* with a small voice, sometimes playing bells and glasses:

> Wake up farmer, your right has been ravished
> Your blood and sweat are mixing with the soil
> Without holding a gun on the shoulder good days won't come for the poor
> Without fighting this war, people's culture will never come in this country

> We had to go at night, in the houses, closing the doors, and we used to sing like this. Therefore people's war and cultural war went together.
> (Interview, November 2006)

During the People's War artistic presentations centred on themes of sacrifice, courage and struggle (cf. Lecomte-Tilouine 2006; de Sales 2003):

> Hundreds of new braves have been born in the time of struggle
> The fearful disappear in the floods of the People's War
> The braves have united and fight in the harshness

They are moving ahead, removing obstacles
With their death, the braves keep living era after era
      (Purna Gharti, from 'Songs presented during the great People's War')

In contrast, in autumn 2006 performances dealt with the advent of peace and republic (*ganatantra*). This is how the commander introduced his party's political turnaround in a public meeting:

> The journey of the rebels started in 2052 *Falgun* 1st, the road of blood. Samana Parivar has walked the road of blood for a decade, Samana Parivar, the artists belonging to CPN [Maoist]. Now they are in your cities, in your villages. For a decade they have been singing songs of bombs, weapons, revolution, sacrifice, tears. But now we are singing songs of peace because it's the people's desire. [...] Respecting Nepali people's feelings and desires, our party CPN (Maoist), with deep feelings of responsibility, now comes out to campaign for peace, a journey towards peace. Our Samana Parivar, our people's artists are leaving all the songs of weapons to sing songs of peace and also revolution because the feelings and desires of the 19-day people's movement have not yet been fulfilled.
>
>   (Public speech, October 2006)

The commander's announcement during a public cultural program becomes a form of 'behaviour heightened' (Schechner 1993: 1) that has the power to legitimize political choice while enacting it on stage. In a way, Maoist cultural productions represent the symbolic creative side that contrasts against the destruction generated by the armed struggle. But the post-April 2006 performances also validate the People's War, and serve to guide the audience through the different stages of the subsequent political struggle.

Revolutionary performances as popular culture

Recent debates on popular culture are mostly concerned with mass-media, magazines, TV, cinema or cyber-culture. However, Maoist cultural programs can be conceptualized as a form of popular culture for different reasons. The troupes' organization, described in the introduction, shows clearly that Maoist cultural programs have wide diffusion. Each team performs an average of two to four programs a day during campaigning periods and 10 to 15 shows a month for the rest of the year.

    Like street theatre, Maoist cultural programs are free and therefore reach a wide audience. Moreover, the large number of cassettes, CDs and videos produced and sold contribute to locating revolutionary performance within popular culture. For example, Sen Chyang Cultural Group, a federal team established in 2004 and working in the Kathmandu area, has already produced five cassettes: *21st Century People's War* (2004: 3,000 copies), *We are in war* (in Tamang language, 2005: 3,000 copies), *Voices of Faith* (in Nepali, Bhojpuri and Thami languages, 2006:

10,000 copies), *People going to War* (in Tamang language, 2007: 10,000 copies), *The Sacrifice will never Die* (in Nepali language, 2008, so far[20] 10,000 copies with plans to produce more). Every federal and ethnic troupe has already produced or is in the process of producing cassettes and CDs.

Live performances are the foundation for the popular videos and tapes now available in every bazar. Revolutionary songs, in fact, compete with pop music and can be heard during leisure time, bus trips, weddings and other kinds of celebrations among Maoist sympathizers.

But how do they differ from 'mainstream' Nepali culture? Marxist debate on art often centres on the relationship of revolutionary works with traditional forms (Lang and Williams 1972).[21] As we have seen before, cultural programs are a well-recognized 'old' format that has been adopted and adapted by Maoist troupes. Similarly, revolutionary songs and dances themselves are deeply rooted in the Nepali folk tradition and represent variations and developments from 'old' forms. Since the songs' melodies are usually inspired by folk songs while the lyrics are created anew, audiences find the tunes familiar and thus become instantly involved. While some lyrics are clearly hymns to the party's policies and leaders, praising Prachanda Path and the 'red people' through Maoist jargon, others describe the oppressions and pains faced by villagers and cannot be distinguished from other songs sung by progressive non-party artists.

Songs are often accompanied by dances. At times, 'revolutionary movements' such as raising a clinched fist are mixed with traditional folk or Bollywood-like dance steps. Dancers wear costumes typical of different ethnic groups, as well as Chinese martial art-like suits and military dresses to match movements inspired by martial art or military actions. For example, the song 'Parading' (2006) performed by Sen Chyang is accompanied by a military-style march characterized by regular, emphatic beats and is introduced by spoken military commands. Dancers wear combat dresses and the movements of military drills are transformed into a dance. Yet, as soon as the introduction ends, the sounds of the *madal* and the harmonium start and the song loses its threatening tone. It resembles other sweet folk songs, in stark contrast with the outfit of the dancers and the lyrics about the arrival of the PLA. The 'Nepali' flavour of Maoist art is immediately evident.

Dancers often wear a Maoist red band with a white star on their forehead. A red band across the chest indicates the name of the cultural group. Hammer-and-sickle communist flags and guns were used at times as props. The peace agreements, especially the ban on displaying weapons in public, also affected Maoist dances. In early September 2006 'Parading' was performed indoor with fake weapons. In an outdoor performance the following October, the guns had to be replaced by sticks. In 2007 and 2008 weapons were not used any more. According to the artists, there was no longer any need to display arms.

The rhythms of the songs and dances are usually very energetic and appealing, and it is not unusual to see spectators standing up from the ground to dance. Even during political meetings I heard spectators calling *nach, nach* (dance) in the middle of a complicated speech full of Maoist jargon, making it obvious which of the two forms the audience preferred. Entertainment plays an important role in the success of the cultural programs.

By making reference to different areas, costumes, languages and dancing styles found throughout the ethnic groups of Nepal, cultural programs also create and make visible a 'national'[22] culture, unifying diversity through and into Maoist ideology:

> We are Madhesi [from the plains], we are Pahadi [from the hills],
> We are Himali [from the mountains], we are Nepali
> One caste, one class, all Nepali
> Wake up Nepali, to build a new Nepal
> Unite Nepali, to build a new Nepal
>
> (From *The Flame of Revolution*)

But for the artists, songs performed during cultural programs are also a cathartic expression of the grief caused by the loss of friends and relatives, and are reflections upon personal experiences:

> When the ridge opens across the mountain
> When the rhododendron blooms in the hills
> I wish I were absent-minded while I remember him/her
> While the storm blows and cuts the clouds
> While the heaven of evils falls down
> I wish I could run and call him/her
> When the ridge opens across the mountain
> While the whole world is rising
> While the flame of revolution is dazzling
> I wish I could hum a song for him/her
> When the ridge opens across the mountain
> (Mohanlal Chand, from *Songs presented during the great People's War*)

Therefore, Maoist cultural presentations cannot be confined to the genre of political propaganda. As representations of life experiences, they can be included in the wider field of 'witness art'[23] and for this reason they represent another form of contemporary Nepali popular culture.

Revolutionary artists

What partly characterizes a hegemonic culture is the monopoly of the means of representation. The role of 'symbolic depiction' and/or 'speaking for' is the domain of leaders, experts and artists. The peculiar identity of Maoist artists needs to be considered at this point because of their role in advancing their 'cultural war' against what they conceive as hegemonic bourgeois culture.

The commissar remembers that during the People's War artists could not work inside the cities. People were afraid and did not even attend their programs. So, they used songs to communicate with the villagers, to establish a connection with the audience and persuade them that they were their friends. The commissar explains that they helped villagers and were hosted by them in return:

> We listened to them [villagers] after eating rice. We helped them with their chores, building their houses. We gave medicine to sick people. If we had food we shared it with them as well. We helped farmers plough the fields, and helped with work inside and outside the house. So people came to think that Maoists are good people, and the Maoist party is good [. . .] At that time we did programs. I sang songs. And after listening to my songs, people commented that the songs were 'so nice' [*kati mitho git*], and then I talked, and then again I sang. I had a guitar. Now I can't play the guitar because my fingers have been damaged in a bomb blast . . . People listened and relaxed, and then I talked political and ideological things, about the war, why we had to go into war. We tried to convince them, and they were convinced.
>
> (Interview, September 2007)

The commissar's description gives hints about the organization of the cultural programs as well as the activists' tasks. The role of the cultural workers consisted in singing songs and entertaining people, but also explaining the songs' messages, the reasons of their struggle, listening and engaging in discussions with the audience, as well as living with them. He continues:

> I was also *sena* [PLA soldier], we were artists, we were also in the army, we had to do everything by ourselves [he smiles while raising both hands, to emphasize that there was no other possibility], political leader, cultural member, organizer . . .

Artists therefore had multiple roles and formed a close bond with people in the rural areas. This connection with the audience emerges as crucial in the artists' narratives. Artists coming from a similar background to the villagers give voice and dignity to poor people's life experiences while feeling appreciated by the party:

> This is the main thought: we were born in huts, we are people from remote areas, who suffered from injustice, violence, corruption, oppression, very discriminated communities. Our community is X,[24] we are oppressed by caste, we are also an oppressed class. Only high-class people are active in society and seeing all this we got knowledge that we should fight against this. Then we got involved. Our aim was to be active politically, but what the party said was that if your ability is in music, in writing, in going to war you should follow it. Some people have principally the capacity of explaining, ours is of singing, writing, playing instruments. If you have this ability, you will work in this area. The party gave us this responsibility and in these ten years we worked in this area.
>
> (Interview, October 2006)

Artists often claim that they are amateurs, despite their popularity. In a public meeting the commissar was apologetic about their shortcomings owing to the inexperience of the artists. The distance between artists and audience is thus reduced, as they make no claim to having any special status. On the contrary, what is often emphasized is the fact that the cultural groups are the medium through which the people's voice is amplified and diffused. At the same time, there is a constant appeal to the audience for support for the Maoist campaign. While claiming a shared identification with the audience, artists convey political strategies. However, since the party's entry into mainstream politics, artists in Kathmandu have been taking performance classes, committed to increasing their professionalism.

Bourdieu highlights how class relations are mediated through symbolic struggles. Maoist artists, as 'symbolic producers', legitimize particular definitions and classifications of the social world. They 'hold a specific power, the properly symbolic power of showing things and making people believe in them, of revealing, in an explicit, objectified way the more or less confused, vague, unformulated, even unformulable experiences of the natural world and of the social world, and of thereby bringing them into existence' (Bourdieu in Swartz 1997: 220). Maoist artists therefore embody both the power of intellectuals and the persuasiveness of performers.

Because of the direct contact with the grassroots, artists acquire direct experience and knowledge which then allow them to raise critiques with their political leaders during internal programs. The commissar explains that criticism, while remaining constructive and friendly, works at three different levels: first within the self, then within the organization and thirdly it becomes class struggle. For example, after the Chunwang meeting (2005) the party was on the verge of splitting. Artists produced many songs and dramas that depicted the situation and called for unity:

> Let's walk together, friends
> Let's struggle together, friends
> And preserve the class love inside the heart.
>
> (Hitman Sakya)

A more recent instance in 2007 regards dramas which depicted the urban-centric attitude of the leadership and satirized their living styles: political leaders' big cars and expensive clothes were contrasted against the frugality of lower party cadres. Similarly, artists set the agenda of the politicians' struggle for state power against what they felt as an urgent concern among the people: knowing the whereabouts of the disappeared. Artists therefore also embody a visionary role that allows them to be simultaneously both inside and outside the Party.

Conclusion

In this chapter I have tried to show how the Nepali Maoist revolutionary performance can be viewed as the latest adaptation and evolution of Russian/Chinese

Marxist cultural practice into local folk and political forms. Political songs, dances and drama represent much more than a cultural 'show'. Artists frequently use the word *pratibaddhata* to describe their activities. A *pratibaddhata* is a strong commitment. Not only does it bind the speaker to the words he utters, but it also seeks commitment from the community of listeners who attend the programs. As both representational and performative practices, cultural programs have become political rituals in which messages are spread and where the emotional link between the party and the audience is constantly renewed and strengthened. However, because of the diffusion of both live programs and artistic performances through media, Maoist cultural production is also well on its way to establishing itself as a new form of popular Nepali culture. Maoist cultural programs in fact represent an adaptation and expansion of 'traditional' practices, as well as a new form of artistic 'witnessing' during a critical historical moment.

I chose to present this discussion about cultural programs through the voices of the commander and the commissar because of the artists' unique position inside the party and within the party's political project. The key to the political functioning of the cultural programs is that the performers are simultaneously artists, intellectuals, organizers, activists, guerrillas, leaders and visionaries.

According to Gramsci, intellectuals are the 'agents' of ideological practice. Gramsci conceived ideology[25] as a battlefield, as a practice involving continuous struggle. As ideological transactions (Kershaw 1992), performances become the terrain for the creation of an 'ideological unity' (Mouffe 1979: 184) which, according to Gramsci, is crucial to the establishment of a new hegemony.[26] Maoist cultural programs tackle the moral and intellectual dimension of political struggle that at the same time bears practical consequences. During the People's War, cultural programs were crucial to creating and maintaining the 'ideological unity' and the public sympathy necessary to fight the physical war.

In fact, the Maoist cultural performances that emerged from the ten-year armed struggle can be identified as a 'closed, well-bounded and identifiable' practice, indeed a culture and art form 'of its own'. However, the political scenario has now changed. The CPN-Maoist has emerged from the Constituent Assembly election as the country's leading party. As a result, how Maoist culture and art will open, communicate, blend or perhaps confront and transform mainstream 'Nepali' culture is a fascinating scenario that awaits us.

Notes

* I want to express my deep sense of gratitude to all of my informants whose identities, in keeping with their request, I was unable to disclose during the narration. I mention here the names that have already appeared in the Maoist published materials. I wish to heartily thank the artists belonging to *Sen Chyang Sanskritik Parivar* for their patience in accepting my questions and doubts, and for their support and friendship: Chintang, Rajan Bam, Chiring Lama, Raju Lama, Raman Thami, Parbat B.K, Nirmala Ghising, Kushal Bogati, Rajani Thami, Srijana Lama, Sonu Lama, Umang Lama, Srijana Tamang, Prabha Lama, Asal Tamang, Nirmala Budha, Samip Bohora, Banira Lama, Pratiksha Kathayat, Sanjya Tamang, Sunita Pant, Aroha Nepali, Pratik Tamang, Sunita Hitang, Ritu Prajapati,

Santosh Gurung, Nabin Khadka, Tej Bista, Rajesh Rai, Pusha Pant, Shrijal Lama. My gratefulness also goes to Maila Lama, Rajkumar Karnali, Samana, Bharat Lama, Shushma Shrestha, Surekha Shrestha, *Newa Sankritik Parivar* and *Samana Parivar*. I would also like to thank Mahendra Lawoti, Anup Pahari, Bhaskar Gautam and George Kunnath for their helpful comments on earlier versions of this chapter.

1 All the direct quotations in the paper are translations from Nepali done by the author.
2 Artists often quote two episodes when whole cultural teams were killed by the armed forces: seven artists from Anekot Cultural Group died in Kavre (1999) while 11 died in Palwang, Rolpa (2000). Cultural groups are named after martyrs. For example, Sen Chyang comes from the names of Krishna Sen and Chyangba Lama.
3 At the moment of writing (May 2008) the US government has not yet removed the terrorist tag.
4 I carried out fieldwork for my PhD on theatre for social change from November 2004 to January 2006; I returned to Nepal to follow the development of political performances in July 2006–January 2007, June 2007–September 2007, March–April 2008.
5 The audience point of view has not been considered in this paper.
6 Each Company and Battalion has a double leadership, a 'commander' with mainly organizational tasks and a 'commissar' in charge of political education.
7 Saraswati is the goddess of arts and learning.
8 For example the Tharu's stick dance (*lathi nach*) performed in the lodges of Chitwan or the Gathu dance in the Lakeside of Pokhara's hotels.
9 Gai Jatra is a festival celebrated in the Nepali month of Bhadra (August–September) to worship Yamraj, the god of death.
10 Praja Parishad was an underground anti-Rana and pro-democracy political party established in Kathmandu in 1935.
11 The Jhapa rebellion (Rawal 2047 BS; Khanal 2007) in 1971 was backed by a strong cultural front.
12 'Rise, rise from the village' (*Gaun gaunbata Utha*), sung by Ramesh and Rayan, has become an icon of people's power.
13 Marxism is not a unified and fixed theory. Different positions regarding the relation between art and society coexist (Lang and Williams 1972; Solomon 1979).
14 The *madal* is the Nepali typical hand drum, the backbone of most folk music.
15 Artists remember Krishna Sen as a 'mahan sahid' (great martyr). Krisha Sen Ichchuk was the editor of the pro-Maoist daily *Janadisha* and former editor of the weekly *Janadesh.* Repeatedly arrested and kept in jail through fake charges, Sen was tortured and killed in police custody in 2002 (RSF press releases 2002; Revolutionary Worker # 1160 2002; Li Onesto 2002).
16 Lecomte-Tilouine (2006) interestingly pointed out that although praising dialectics, Prachandapath seems to be based upon binary oppositions between oppressor-oppressed, feudal-proletariat, reactionary-revolutionary and in the military context, unjust-just wars. Binary oppositions work strongly also in art. Revolutionary art is contrasted to bourgeois art, and linked to the other dualistic oppositions resulting from class struggle. Yet, I think it is worth reflecting upon how much such a dualism can be the result of a 'Nepalization' – via the ideology of development – of Marxism, rather than a mere 'reduction' of Marxist dialectics. In fact, dual thinking has been widely documented by Pigg (1992, 1993) who analysed how the ideology of development has created a series of dichotomies along with those of 'developed' and 'underdeveloped'.
17 Parallels between the Chinese Cultural Revolution and the cultural revolution advocated by CPN-M could be intriguing but risk being misleading in such a short space. Suffice it to say that the socio-historical conditions are very different. While in China the Cultural Revolution was implemented at mass-scale by a party in power, in Nepal it is promoted by a revolutionary party. As for daily practices, the cultural revolution in Nepal brings about changes in marriage-related practices (against polygamy, dowry, son preference), gender roles (Onesto 2006), festival celebration, fashion, body display, relationship

attitudes. As for the cultural sector, a leaflet (November 2005) indicated, among other things, the necessity of making government institutions and other media organizations 'progressive', closing 'vulgar third grade cinema halls', dance restaurants and massage centres, creating special days to celebrate the People's War, creating people's literature and art.

18 *Malema* is an abbreviation of Marxism (ma), Leninism (le) and Maoism (ma); *baad* is -ism.

19 In the last three decades emotions had no place in the rationalistic, structural, and organizational models that dominated academic political analysis and were previously associated to irrationality (Goodwin et al. 2001). My research aims to add to the recent trend reincorporating emotions into research on politics and social movements. Audiences, in fact, are not to be regarded as passive receivers of performances. Audiences identify with emotions and representations that touch them.

20 Updated in April 2008.

21 Mao (1967: 5) believed there is no such thing as art above politics or art free from 'politics'. All works of art have a political character and serve one kind of politics or another as they forward a particular view of how society is or should be. Mao also rejected the general assumption that popular forms of art are technically and stylistically inferior to the 'sophisticated' dominant ones. He spurred artists to live among the peasants to understand their problems better (ibid.). For Mao old literary forms should not be rejected but infused with new content (ibid.).

22 Debates over 'national' culture in Nepal are widespread (Des Chenes 1996). The Maoist modality of 'displaying' cultural diversity is similar to the government practices during the Panchayat years and afterwards. The context and process of the performances, as well as the composition of the artistic groups, vary substantially.

23 Behar (1996: 27) suggests that in traumatic situations life stories can play the role of witnessing. She argues that witnessing merges with the genre of *testimonio* literature and cites *I, Rigoberta Menchu* as an example of how personal narratives can help the wider community of readers to come to terms with their shared painful reality. Extending this concept, Maoist cultural/artistic productions may fulfil both an internal therapeutic function (for the party artists) and an external witnessing role (for the wider audience).

24 I omit the name of the ethnic group the commissar belongs to, to avoid identification.

25 Ideology has been defined in different ways as 'false consciousness' or as a 'system of ideas'. Mouffe emphasizes how Gramsci rejected 'epiphenomenalist conceptions which reduce it [ideology] to mere appearances with no efficacy' (1979: 185) while pointing out the material existence of ideology as practice (Gramsci 1975: 1380, 1971: 328).

26 Gramsci defines hegemony not as imposition or domination but as a process of internal coherence.

Bibliography

Ahearn, L. 1999. A Twisted Rope Bind my Waist': Locating Constraints of Meaning in a Tij Songfest. *Journal of Linguistic Anthropology* 8 (1):50–86.

Aziz, Barbara Nimri. 2001. *Heir to a Silent Song. Two Rebel Women of Nepal.* Kathmandu: Centre for Nepal and Asia Studies.

Behar, R. 1996. *The Vulnerable Observer: Anthropology that Breaks your Heart.* Boston: Beacon Press.

Berezin, M. 2001. Emotions and Political Identity: Mobilizing Affection for the Polity. In *Passionate Politics: Emotions and Social Movements*, ed. Jeff Goodwin, James M. Jasper and Francesca Polletta, 83–98. Chicago and London: The University of Chicago Press.

Bourdieu, P. 1990. *The Logics of Practice.* Cambridge: Polity Press.

Brecht, B. 1964. *Brecht on Theatre: The Development of an Aesthetics*. London: Methuen Drama.

Burghart, R. 1993. The Political Culture of Panchayat Democracy. In *Nepal in the Nineties* ed. Michael Hutt, 1–13. New Delhi: Oxford University Press.

Centre for Human Rights and Democratic Studies (CEHURDES). CEHURDES demands launch of independent inquiry into journalist Krishna Sen's death" press release, 12 July 2002 http://www.ifex.org/en/content/view/full/17646 visited on 22 January 2007

Committee to Protect Journalists (CPJ). CPJ asks government to respond to reports of custodial killing, pro-Maoist editor Krishna Sen feared dead, press release, 02 July 2002 http://www.ifex.org/alerts/layout/set/print/content/view/full/16807

Committee to Protect Journalists (CPJ). CPJ protests editor's detention, press release, 07 August 2002, http://www.ifex.org/en/content/view/full/17108

Des Chenes, M. 1996. In the Name of *Bikas*. *Studies in Nepali History and Society* 1 (2):259–70.

Dolan, J. 2005. *Utopia in Performance. Finding Hope at the Theatre*. Ann Arbour: University of Michigan Press.

Epskamp, K. 2006. *Theatre for Development: An Introduction to Context, Applications and Trainings*. London and New York: Zed Books.

Goodwin, J, J. Jasper and F. Polletta. 2001. *Passionate Politics: Emotions and Social Movements*. Chicago and London: The University of Chicago Press.

Gramsci, A. 1971. *Selections from the Prison Notebooks* (edited and translated by Hoare and Geoffrey Nowell Smith). London: Lawrence & Wishart.

Gramsci, A. 1975. *Quaderni dal Carcere (Edited by V. Gerratana)*. Torino: Einaudi.

Grandin, I. 1994. To Change the Face of the Country'. Nepalese Progressive Songs under Panchayat Democracy. *Journal of South Asian Literature* 29 (1):175–89.

Grandin, I. 2005. Music under Development: Children's Songs, Artists, and the (Panchayat) State. *Studies in Nepali History and Society* 10 (2):255–93.

Hoftun, M, Raeper W. and J. Whelpton. 1999. *People, Politics & Ideology: Democracy and Social Change in Nepal*. Kathmandu: Mandala Bookpoint.

Jan Sanskritik Mahasangh (People's Cultural Federation), *Mahan Janyuddha Pratinidhi githaru* (Songs Presented during the Great People's War), unpublished.

Kershaw, B. 1992. *The Politics of Performance: Radical Theatre as Cultural Intervention*. London and New York: Routledge.

Khanal, S. 2007. Committeed Insurgents, a Divided State and the Maoist Insurgency in Nepal. In *Contentious Politics and Democratization in Nepal*, ed. Mahendra Lawoti, 75–94. Kathmandu: Bhrikuti Academic Publications and Sage Publications.

Kiran. 2006. Bhumika (Introduction). In *Sanskriti, Kala ra Saudaryachintan (Culture, Art and Aesthetics)* written by Prachanda. Kathmandu: Akhil Nepal Jan Sanskritik Sangha.

Kunnath, G. J. 2006. Becoming a Naxalite in Rural Bihar: Class Struggle and its Contradictions. *The Journal of Peasant Studies* 33 (1):89–123.

Lang, B. and F. Williams, eds. 1972. *Marxism and Art: Writings in Aesthetics and Criticism*. New York: MacKey.

Lawoti, M., ed. 2007. *Contentious Politics and Democratization in Nepal*. Kathmandu: Bhrikuti Academic Publications and Sage Publications.

Lecomte-Tilouine, M. 2004. Regicide and Maoist Revolutionary Warfare in Nepal: Modern Incarnations of a Warrior Kingdom. *Anthropology Today* 20 (1):13–19.

Lecomte-Tilouine, M. 2006. Kill one. He becomes one hundred': martyrdom as generative sacrifice in the Nepal People's War. *Social Analysis* 50 (1):51–72.

Mao Tse-Tung. 1960. *On Literature and Art*. Peking: Foreign Language Press.

———. Mao Tse-Tung. 1967. Talks at the Yenan Forum on Literature and Art. *Peking Review* 22:5–18.

———. Mao Tse-Tung 1972a. On Literature and Art. In *Marxism and Art: Writings in Aesthetics and Criticism*, ed. B. Lang and F. Williams, 108–19. New York: David McKay.

———. Mao Tse-Tung. 1972b. On The Correct Handling of Contradictions among the People. In *Marxism and Art: Writings in Aesthetics and Criticism*, ed. B. Lang and F. Williams, 120–25. New York: David McKays.

Moore, R. D. 2006. *Music and Revolution. Cultural Change in Socialist Cuba*. Berkerley and Los Angeles: University of California Press.

Mottin, M. (forthcoming). Dramas of Development: Theatre for Development or the Development of Theatre? In Tatsuro Fujukara, *Nepal and Aid. A Reader*. Kathmandu: Martin Chautari Press.

Mouffe, C. 1979. Hegemony and Ideology in Marxism. In *Gramsci and Marxist Theory*, ed. Chantal Mouffe, London: Routledge & Kegan Paul.

Onesto, Li. Killing the News. Censorship and jailing of journalists under the state of emergency. *Revolutionary Worker* 1160, July 28 2002 http://www.lionesto.net/articles/onesto/nepaljournalists.htm

———. Onesto, Li. 2006. *Dispaches from the People's War*. London: Pluto.

———. Onesto, Li. 2007. The Evolution of the Maoist Revolution in Nepal in an Adverse International Environment. In *Contentious Politics and Democratization in Nepal*, ed. M. Lawoti, 120–42. Kathmandu: Bhrikuti Academic Publications and Sage Publications.

Pigg, S. L. 1992. Inventing Social Categories through Place: Social Representations and Development in Nepal. *Comparative Studies in Society and History* 34 (3): 491–513.

———. Pigg, S. L. 1993. Unintended Consequences: The Ideological Impact of Development in Nepal. *South Asia Bulletin* XIII (1&2):45–58.

Prachanda. 2001. Second National Conference CPN (Maoist). http://www.cpnm.com (accessed in February 2007).

Rai, Som. 2060 B.S. Jantaka Git: Nirantara ra Sandarbhikata. *Sramik Khabar*, Cait 5–9.

———. Rai Som. 2060 B.S. Kasari Suru Bhayo Jangiti Gayanko Parampara (How the tradition of People's Songs Started). *Sramik Khabar*, Cait 12–16.

Rawal, B. 2047 B.S. *Nepalma Samyabadi Andolanko:Adbav ra Bikash (Communist Movement in Nepal: Rise and Development)*. Kathmandu: Pairavi Prakashan.

Reporters without Borders (RSF). Pro-Maoist journalist Krishna Sen dies in custody, press release, 26 June 2002. http://www.ifex.org/fr/content/view/full/16761

———. Reporters without Borders (RSF). Report on journalist Krishna Sen's death in detention, press release, 16 October2002 http://www.ifex.org/en/content/view/full/ 17646

———. Reporters without Borders (RSF). Police officer allegedly involved in journalist Krishna Sen's murder receives 'policeman of the year' award, press release, 22 October, 2002 http://www.ifex.org/20fr/layout/set/print/content/view/full/17696

Sales, A. de. 2003. Remarks on Revolutionary Songs and Iconography. *European Bulletin of Himalayan Research* 24, 5–24.

Samana Parivar. 2006. *East Tour*, VCD 1 & 2, unpublished.

Schechner, R. 1993. *The Future of Ritual: Writings on Culture and Performance*. London and New York: Routledge.

Samana Parivar. 2006. *East Tour*, VCD 1 & 2, unpublished.

Sen Chyang Cultural Company. 2006. *Asthaka Swarharu (Voices of Faith)*, MC.

———. Sen Chyang Cultural Company. 2008. *Mardeina Balidan Kahilyai (The Sacrifice Will Never Die)*, MC.

——. Sen Chyang Cultural Company. 2006. *Campaign for Republic*, VCD 1 & 2, unpublished.

Sharma, S. 2004. The Maoist Movement: An Evolutionary Perspective. In *Himalayan 'People's War'. Nepal's Maoist Rebellion*, ed. M. Hutt, 38–57. London: Hurst & Co.

Skinner, D., Holland, D. and G.B. Adhikari. 1994. The Songs of Teej. A Genre of Critical Commentary for Women in Nepal. *Asian Folklore Studies* 53 (2):259–305.

Solomon, M., ed. 1979. *Marxism and Art: Essays Classic and Contemporary*. Detroit: Wayne State University Press.

Swartz, D. 1997. *Culture and Power: The sociology of Pierre Bourdieu*. Chicago and London: University of Chicago Press.

Todd, N. 1974. Ideological Superstructure in Gramsci and Mao Tse-Tung. *Journal of the History of Ideas* 35 (1):148–56.

Webb, J., Schirato, T. and G. Danaher. 2006. *Understanding Bourdieu*. London: Sage Publications.

Williams, R. 1977. *Marxism and Literature*. Oxford: Oxford University Press.

4 The repertoire of scientific organization

Ideology, identity and the Maoist Student Union

Amanda Snellinger*

During my field research[1] with Nepali student organizations, I observed that students who were active in the All Nepal National Independent Student Union – Revolutionary (ANNISU-R), the Communist Party of Nepal-Maoist (CPN-M) affiliated student organization, used the term "scientific organization" in order to convey their sense of what their organization entails. It took me over a year to unravel what they meant by this description and what it encapsulates. The phrase is a referential composite of a complicated number of interrelated factors that they use to define their political organization and frame their political identity. I have come to discover that the aspects that comprise scientific organization weave together the ANNISU-R's organizational structures and day-to-day practices, through which their identity as a political organization is articulated. In this chapter I will deconstruct this description by analyzing the factors it entails in order to understand how the ANNISU-R define themselves as the student organization of the CPN-M and differentiate themselves from the other student organizations and their affiliated political parties. This analysis is meant to reveal what the ANNISU-R's sense of identity is by specifically focusing on how they frame their organization to me in our interactions. I will prioritize organizational forms for the reason that Polletta argues: "Organizational forms . . . are often appealing for their symbolic associations, and especially, their association with particular social groups" (2005: 271). This analysis is meant to make sense of scientific organization as a symbolic association that connects the ANNISU-R to the impoverished, exploited classes of Nepal, their claimed constituents.

It is not my intention to be redundant in my analysis of people's Marxist theoretical orientation that they apply to their everyday lives by using a Marxist theoretical perspective. Rather, I will analyze the aesthetics of political actors' theoretical sensibilities and how it impacts their sense of who they are and their political orientation in the local context of Nepali politics. Put in a different light, I will look at the preferred symbolic associations that influence ANNISU-R's organizational forms – what counts as part of a scientific organization and how they rationalize it through their everyday practices (Lounsbury and Ventresca 2003). It is for this reason that I will focus on ANNISU-R's internal institutional culture. I will analyze how the notion of scientific organization impacts the internal institutional culture of the ANNISU-R, a student organization, and its relationship with its mother organization, the CPN-M.

This analysis is meant to inform what Braungert and Braungert (1986: 219) argue is lacking in the sociological literature when they claim:

> Little is known about the development of shared collective mentalities and how these become activated into a genuine force for political change, nor is there much understating of the interplay between competing political generation units, the maintenance of a political generation's activity, why a political generation comes to an end, and the direct and indirect consequences of a political generation's efforts for change.

Braungert's statement resonates with Tilly's concept of repertoire, which is meant to explain what political activists conceive of as viable options from which to choose their strategy and organization-making ability. Tilly argues that "existing repertoires incorporate collectively learned, shared understandings concerning what forms of claim making are possible . . . as well as what consequences different possible forms of claim making are likely to produce. They greatly constrain the contentious claims political actors make on each other and on agents of the state" (1999: 419). Braungert highlights that repertoires are not stagnant but, at the very least, generational or jointly experiential. ANNISU-R activists are in a particular transitory position, learning the repertoires of their superiors and attempting to imbue them with contemporary values and social change that they consider necessary. This chapter is meant to elucidate the process of changing political values by analyzing the generational repertoires that inform them.

I will also outline how ANNISU-R developed into the organization it has become. My analysis will focus on how its union's history and shared experiences have created common commitments that not only inform its organizational identity but also reinforce its ideological commitment to its political cause. I will specifically focus on the contributions of the ANNISU-R to the Maoist People's War, the second People's Movement of 2006, and its role and agenda on university campuses since the peace talks have brought it and its mother organizations into the political mainstream. I will also consider possible obstacles that its current revolutionary orientation could create as it becomes established in a political mainstream where it must contend as well as compromise with other political forces.

In the last section I will look at internal structures of the organization. Political science engages internal processes and organizational structures as analytics in order to understand how political institutions go about achieving their agenda (Gunther and Diamond 2003; Hachhethu 2002; Katz 1994; Lawson 1994; Monroe 2001; Ostrogorski 1964; Schlesinger 1965; Wright 1971). Yet it must be acknowledged that the basis for all political agendas is political ideology (Panebianco 1988; Prasad 1980; Puri 1980). Ideology informs the end point. Internal processes and organizational structures reveal the means toward that end. But to what degree does the ideology inform the processes of everyday political action? In other words, how closely linked are theory and practice? In this chapter I will unpack the place of political ideology, how it informs the notion of scientific organization, and how the ANNISU-R students orient themselves to it as a political and pragmatic concept within their institution. This analysis will include an overview of their hierarchal structures and the degree to which hierarchy informs the place of cadre and leader not only in ANNISU-R but also in its institutional relationship with its mother party, the CPN-M.

Organization ultimately comes down to the age-old struggle between theory and practice (Djilas 1957; Doolin and Goolas 1964, Lenin 1920). Within the notion of organization there is an insinuation that internal culture and ideology should be recursive (Breines 1989; Downey 1986).[2] It is for this reason that the ANNISU-R students emphasize the necessity of consistency in their organizational practices. They maintain that the main thing that has weakened other Nepali political organizations is the discrepancy between the parties' political ideological aspirations and their internal practices. The ANNISU-R students feel other political parties have lost touch with their "master frames" which are supposed to anchor their agenda and tactics in order to present organizational cohesion (Snow and Benford 1992: 146). I will show how in the transition from revolutionary group to political organization the ANNISU-R students are trying to avoid a party structure that stymies itself and condones an internal culture that serves as a recursive obstacle to their larger political ends. Yet as an underlying caveat, I will consider to what degree a revolutionary orientation is a sustainable long-term structure for a political organization that must rely on mass appeal for survival. In other words, I will explore the degree to which the feedback loops between ideology and internal practice inform ANNISU-R's organizational structure within a revolutionary niche,[3] which may limit its expansion into a larger democratic association (Popielarz and Neal 2007: 77).

Place and role of a revolutionary sister organization

When one considers autonomy within political institutions, it is not only quantified on the level of individual actors but also on the institutional level. This is particularly the case with any of the Nepali student organizations, which are classified as sister organizations to the political parties. As subsidiary organizations, all of the student unions have different relationships with the mother organizations based on their political ideology, history, and particular institutional culture. The degree of autonomy that parent parties allow affiliate student organizations is influenced by the reality that student politics is a rite of passage for aspiring politicians. It is a process of political socialization. In other words, the student organizations are the political training grounds for the parties. Even the terms, mother and sister organization, highlight the sociological dynamics between generations and the hierarchy inherent in cultural forms of ageism (Snellinger 2005, 2006).

Yet in Nepali politics the students play a very particular role that has unfolded through history, which has established them in a very crucial niche. A number of ANNISU-R students, as well as students and party leaders from other organizations, explained to me that the student activists are the Nepali political vanguard. Those in the Nepali political circle commonly consider Nepal to be a feudal society. There has been no labor movement to inspire the exploited classes to rise above ethnic, language, or religious distinctions in order to unite against political, social, or economic injustice the way it has occurred in other industrialized nations. For that reason, student activists are seen to have fulfilled this historic role in Nepal by fighting to push all sectors of society toward social and political progress. They have cultivated this image as the political vanguard because it has been the students who have been at the fore of all the political movements that have contributed to the changing political tides in the last century (Snellinger 2005, 2007).

Despite the tense issue concerning the autonomy of student activists in Nepali politics, the Maoist students and party activists dismiss any tension that polarizes them as mother and sister organizations. They claim this is a false dichotomy that would create splits not only in their overall organization but also in society. Rather, they focus on their unification through their common experience of class struggle. One student asked me:

> Why must there be a disjuncture between a guardian and its offspring? As the offspring will have their own desires, so will the sister organizations. Does that mean that it does not serve the family or party's ultimate end? The sister organization helps in bringing the party line to the public, in which the party educates them in light of the national and international circumstances . . . Our policies and programs are tied up with the way CPN-M is directing its struggle to obtain the political power. With regard to how it is addressed, you have to understand that our main agenda to solve the fundamental problems of the people is what links us all, and it is the basis of our constitution and action plans.
>
> (ANNISU-R central committee member's (CCM) interview, 11/26/06[4])

The ANNISU-R is one wing of the Maoist party. It is the front that represents the students, similar to wings representing other sectors such as workers, ethnic groups, or women. The purpose of these wings is to bring up class issues from each specialized perspective and to implement restructuring policies in each sector that battle inequality in a way that particularly supports the constituents. I have heard this described as the overall division of labor within the Maoist political apparatus.

The tenor of the ANNISU-R students' explanation concerning their relationship with the CPN-M is that it is a symbiotic relationship that is part of a contained system of dialectical materialism. They are both dedicated to the same overall end, yet the students are expected to focus within the realm of education, which is one component of the larger class struggle. The CPN-M gives the ANNISU-R the "ideological nutrition"[5] of Marxism, Leninism, Maoism, and Prachanda Path in order to move ahead in the education sector. The students provide the party with the on-the-ground context in order to frame its political directives. This back and forth impacts both poles and is thought to refine the ever-emerging path of class struggle.

Every student I spoke with made it clear that it is the responsibility of the cadres and students to keep their leaders accountable. When the leaders stray from party ideology towards a revisionist direction, it is the base of the party that must rise up and oppose it. I have been told that it is for this reason that general students and cadres hold more responsibility and ultimately more power within the institution.

They are the ones to whom the leaders are accountable. The organizational dynamic holds implicit the claim that the students represent the masses and must keep their leaders honest and in sync with the overall party ideological agenda.

A very important point that allows the students to forego the struggle for autonomy highlighted by the students is that their education demands and reforms are connected with the overall political agenda. One student metaphorically elaborated it in this way:

> If we are only seeing the branches of a mango tree and expect that it will bear mangoes, our thinking is not holistic since a mango tree with rotten roots can no longer bear the fruit. In the same way, if we say that we are concerned with the educational sector and don't care about other sectors or their bases, which are political, then we will never be able to obtain our objective. In one way or another all issues are connected to politics. Therefore, we contend that the political and the educational movements have to be accordingly linked to one another.
>
> (ANNISU-R CCM's interview, 12/4/07)

This student explained that because other student organizations do not feel politics is any of their business they are not as successful. Rather, they tend to disconnect the educational issues from that of their parties' political agenda. When the party interferes in campus issues, the students feel their autonomy is being violated; the party is encroaching on their sphere. But, he argued, if their role were considered within the larger agenda of their party, one in which they were responsible for one aspect of the overall system that is tended by all, then they would be willing to forego struggles for independence from their mother organization, particularly since, in this student leader's claim, freedom from one's mother party is not productive to the larger political agenda of their organization.

For the Maoists and the ANNISU-R, the restructuring of education and of the state go hand in hand. In order to restructure the state, they must capture it. It is by capturing the state that they can make available to all people the opportunities that have thus far been reserved for the elite, particularly in education, health care, and employment. This agenda is called the New People's State Power (Bhattarai 2003), which, among other things, is meant to ensure the people's education and an education policy suitable to the public interest as defined by the Maoists. One student told me bluntly, "Unless the peoples' sons and daughters have access to the state power, then sons and daughters of the people will not have access to the educational facility. We have linked the issue of equal opportunity education with the capturing of the state power. In the words of Marx, we are clear that everything else except state power is an illusion."[6]

Identity of suffering: beginnings from the underground

In their overall history, the ANNISU-R is not considered an old student organization. Despite the fact that Maoists sympathizers have been active as students in the communist movement since the 1990s, there had not been an official Maoist student wing until the organization of the CPN-M in 1995.[7] Even at the beginning, there was only a loose student following of the Maoist party. They served as a support extension into the campuses during the Maoists' time in parliament. Yet they never participated in Free Student Union elections on campuses nor had they established themselves as an entrenched sister organization (Dangi 2007). Really, their official formation began after the Maoists put out their 40-point demand to parliament. From 1996 to 1998 they served as proselytizers for this political manifesto. As the Maoists went to the jungle to begin their revolution, the students of ANNISU-R stayed on the campuses and informed their fellow students of the progression of the people's war, impressing upon them the need to support the Maoists. It was not until the Maoists were tagged as terrorists during Operation Romeo that the ANNISU-R focused on providing physical support for the war in an official organizational form. ANNISU-R chose to go underground and into the jungle with the Maoists. It was at this time that its responsibilities broadened and encompassed roles not traditional to Nepali student organizations. The ANNISU-R students still worked on the campuses to spread Maoist influence, brokered educational demands, and enforced school closures nationwide, but they also worked as journalists and analysts covering the war, soldiers, local educational overseers, judges in the people's courts, campaigners, and recruiters.[8] They filled the roles that needed to be filled in order make the war a success and address what they saw as the fundamental needs of the people in the parallel government that the Maoists had set up in their stronghold areas.

ANNISU-R students argue that the students' perspective allows them to easily grasp Maoist ideology and they were well positioned to implement that ideology into an action plan during the war. The rationale was that they could recognize the problems but were young and not yet invested in the feudal traditions that reinforced the societal inequalities. In other words, their generational orientation allows them a new repertoire in which to frame political progress and the means for achieving it (Tilly 1995). They recognized that there was opportunity in a changed society and were therefore devoted to societal transformation. Many ANNISU-R students have described the experience of being underground during the war as formative; some even claimed it as their coming of age.

All of the ANNISU-R students I spoke with about their experiences underground look back on it nostalgically. Even those who lost their partners, relatives, or friends still count it as one of the most productive experiences of their life. They believe that while they were underground they were able to witness the everyday realities of Nepali suffering. They had to rely on the poorest of the poor for shelter, food, and protection. The students explained that the common people's experience informs and reinforces their political philosophy. As one student phrased it, they came to "see what our political ideology and struggles were based on."[9] They not only were able to observe the reality that inspired their philosophy, but they experienced it as well. They attributed their deep connection to the public to these underground experiences. As one student explained:

I think that had I not gotten involved in this political movement for change, I would have been born and died like any insect in the world. I have been able to win many people's hearts and read many people's minds. I would never have got the chance to know about the people in their real life situations. We obtained knowledge about the diversity of suffering as well as joy within the Nepalese society.

(ANNISU-R CCM's interview, 11/12/07)

The experience of being underground enabled them to transcend their individual traditional identities and social backgrounds. They believe that their relations with all sectors of Nepalese society allowed them to break from those past identities and study Nepal purely from a class perspective. Furthermore, many students claimed that it was when they were underground that they learned about their own capacity to endure suffering and they built their identities around it. They came to know they could sacrifice anything for their political ideals because they had sacrificed everything and saw progress from it.[10] This common experience of hardship unites the Maoists students, which has buttressed the strength of their individual and organizational discipline. Jeffery Alexander describes the constructing of cultural traumas as a way to relate and form common identities; he writes "Insofar as they identify the cause of trauma, and thereby assume such moral responsibility, members of collectivities define their solidary relationships in ways that, in principle, allow them to share the sufferings of others" (Alexander 2004: 1). The ANNISU-R students formed their personal identities, their organizational identity, and their internal culture based upon on their shared sacrifice and connection with the public and each other during the People's War.

Becoming a mainstream organization

In November 2005, the CPN-M forged an alliance with the seven political parties that had been agitating on the street since the 2001 dissolution of the elected parliament and then against the king's two takeovers in 2002 and 2005. It was agreed that in order to regain state power, all the forces, both democratic and revolutionary, must unify against the autocratic force of the king. The other student organizations were at the forefront of the street agitation that had been ongoing since 2002. During this time there were a number of rhetorical claims concerning the students' political role. They used the position in the political movement to gain more autonomy for their groups as effective political institutions, separate from their mother parties. The movement was also used as a basis from which people launched into national politics. They positioned themselves as today's student leaders overseeing the street agitation, who could become tomorrow's national leaders in parliament (Snellinger 2005, 2007).

ANNISU-R joined the eight student organization alliance in directing the street movement in April 2006 to keep consistent with the new political coalition forged between these organizations' mother parties. During the April 2006 movement the ANNISU-R leaders coordinated Maoist cadres from all sectors of the Maoist political apparatus to participate in the street agitation in the urban areas.[11] The Maoist students consider their organization very different from other student organizations because of their history and their revolutionary orientation. Despite this, their joint efforts with other student organizations in the 2006 April Uprising and their willingness to maintain that alliance after the comprehensive peace agreement has caused them to be collapsed into the category of traditional sister organizations in the minds of the public. They have found themselves within the same political space that they critique as an entrenched, bourgeoisie political role that other student organizations have willingly embraced (Snellinger 2005, 2006).

Since the peace talks, two elements have come to shape the role and responsibilities of the ANNISU-R. The first is the birth of the Youth Communist League (YCL). The second is the role the ANNISU-R plays in campus politics as a part of the Free Student Union while the CPN-M transforms itself into a mainstream party.

The CPN-M organized the YCL in fall 2006 soon after the peace talks were completed. This was a curious organizational move on the part of the CPN-M because it took what is traditionally considered the duties of a Nepali student organization and split it into two sectors, one for the ANNISU-R to oversee and the other for the YCL. Nepali student organizations have traditionally been responsible for both the party's ideological work (indoctrination of students and lobbying for educational issues) and logistical work (organizing of political party events, campaigning, and street agitation), as well as serving as the strong men of the party when their mother organizations needed to rely on force as opposed to diplomacy (Snellinger 2005). When the Maoists instituted the YCL, it was meant to fulfill the duties of maintaining safety and order at political party events, campaigning, political agitation and being the party strong arm. The YCL was particularly active in places where the CPN-M had established strongholds and had created systems of parallel justice to the state. After the peace accord these institutions were supposed to be dismantled but the Maoists did not want to lose their influence in the countryside, so they deployed the YCL to make sure that people complied with the Maoists' sense of how the state and society should be restructured into "New Nepal."[12]

One CNP-M central committee member explained to me that the YCL is very different from the ANNISU-R or other sister organizations because it does not fall within the category of sister organization. Rather, it is a secondary organization. It does not have its own constitution. It does not have a sector of society it represents or oversees. It has no institutional basis from which it can lay claim to autonomy from the CPN-M. It takes orders directly from them. This party member explained:

Before, there were two main wings of our organization, the political wing (CPN-M) and the tactical wing, the People's Liberation Army (PLA). That is what was necessary for the war. Now we are in a new phase and it is not appropriate for the PLA to be organizing the logistical aspects so the CPN-M has organized the YCL to serve this role as we bring our revolution to the next step, from the jungle to the streets and into parliament.

(CPN-M CCM's interview, 1/18/07)

The ANNISU-R works closely with the YCL in campaiging programs and during street protest, or as one student told me "when it is appropriate, we work closely together."[13] Yet the YCL's existence has further defined the ANNISU-R as a unique organization that serves a particular role in the Maoists' overall class struggle.[14] The ANNISU-R takes care of the intellectual and ideological side of traditional student organizational roles and the YCL oversees the physical ones. The members closely cooperate, often living together in communes. The ANNISU-R students teach the YCL cadres the necessary political doctrine but they understand that they have separate responsibilities and play different roles in the overall party structure.

The formation of the YCL is part of the CPN-M current *modus operandi* of restructuring. The CPN-M has chosen to come into the political mainstream in order to show they can solve social injustices by restructuring the governing apparatus. They have chosen to work within the system rather than bring it down. The ANNISU-R's approach on the campuses mirrors this attitude. They not only want to restructure the system of education so it "redeems the proletariat class"[15] but also restructure the Free Student Union (FSU). A Maoist student explained in this way: "We are doing in the education sector what the CPN-M is doing at the government level. We are doing to the FSU what they are doing to parliament. This is our contribution to the overall reform of society."[16]

Thus far the ANNISU-R has not been able to be an active participant in the FSU because as an institution it refused to participate in the last elections before the April uprising of 2006. Nonetheless, the ANNISU-R students feel it is their right to speak out against the injustices, corruption, and lack of transparency as well as the bullying and use of excessive force they see occuring in the FSU structure. I have seen them address this in their speeches and in conversation since they publicly re-entered the campuses. I was told this approach was meant as a multi-pronged strategy to appeal to the general students, to lay out the platform for their larger agenda of educational reform, to establish themselves as a viable political force on campuses, and to set the groundwork for campaigning in the coming FSU elections. Yet this has caused tension and violent clashes on various campuses between the ANNISU-R and the other student organizations.

This tension was supposed to be resolved in March 2008 but the political parties jointly called off the FSU elections because the party leaders felt it would be an obstacle to the constituent assembly elections. The ANNISU-R students did not oppose this decision; they argued that the CPN-M's decision was made with the best interest of the whole organization in mind and that the constituent assembly took higher priority. Yet students of other organizations opposed their mother organization's decision. They were shamed because again the descriptor "Free" was proven a misnomer. This time, however, it seems that the ANNISU-R is as much at the mercy of its mother organization's decisions as are the other student organizations, particularly since the decision was made at the parliamentary level. Furthermore, this decision reveals the degree to which the tensions within the student political organization mirror the latent tensions among the political parties on the national level. If the student organizations could have carried out non-violent, free and fair elections in the FSU, then it would have been the perfect launching point for the national constituent assembly elections. It would have been an appropriate venue in which to mobilize the largest and most energetic demographic to make the constituent assembly elections a success. But like the parliament itself, the FSU is a contested territory. No one wants to let go of their strongholds and there is fear among the other parties and student organizations that if the CPN-M and ANNISU-R members are allowed into the democratic system, then they will capture it and render the entire process undemocratic. Therefore, despite the fact that the ANNISU-R wants to reform the system, it must first and foremost become a part of the system in order to effect change. This process has pushed it into the category of sister organization despite its revolutionary claims, just as participating in parliament has pushed its mother organization to become a parliamentary political party. With this shift come other compromises, such as maintaining a loose alliance with the other student organizations, participating in the democratic institution of the FSU, and bowing to policy directives that its party makes at the parliamentary level. Little by little this will erode ANNISU-R's image as a revolutionary organization that can hold its leaders accountable.

The pragmatics of organization

In order to better understand ANNISU-R's position in the larger Maoist movement, including its relationship with its mother organization, its political agenda on campuses and the degree of autonomy it has to carry out that agenda, it is important to understand the organizational setup and hierarchal system within the union. The ANNISU-R students prize their internal practices as a foundational aspect of their organizational success. They understand that proper organization gives them a political advantage in a landscape of disorganized political groups. Yet what constitutes proper organization? For the ANNISU-R the main concern is having a system of organization that is straightforward and one that appeals to the masses. The students focus on political and revolutionary dedication as the main tenet on which to frame the basis of their organization. The ANNISU-R organizational sensibilities indicate that the students must put their political ideals into practice. This is the definition of being organized and politically active, it allows them to proceed in a well-defined manner and to feel ownership over the political process. In this way, the common cadres pride themselves on knowing that their political ideals are what inform the institutional culture. One ANNISU-R leader explained, "We make the student cadres understand scientific organization and then they support our directives."[17] A number of Maoist students have said that it is this disconnect that makes the students of other student organizations cynical or lost. They feel other student activists see no room for personal expression of political ideals. Rather, these other students seek outlets to exercise autonomy in disruptive ways because they are not encouraged to have dedication to a particular ideology and carry it into practice. The ANNISU-R students claim that political ideology in other organizations comes in the form of sound bites from speeches or rhetoric in the shouting of slogans, but ends there. It does not comfort students that their actions serve a political end that they support.

The concept of hierarchy is very connected with how ANNISU-R students balance autonomy and obedience. The ANNISU-R secretary best expressed this when he asked me if I saw the knives at the NSU conventions. He said, "This is the NSU culture. You would never see this in our culture because we understand the balance between freedom and control. ANNISU-R simultaneously practices the policy of 'freedom and control.' There must be some limitations on freedom in the organization, otherwise the organization will turn into a chaotic mass."[18] He repeated this sentiment when I asked him if he would allow me to interview him. He did not refuse but rather indicated there were proper channels by which to gain access to the information I was seeking. In this case, it was obvious that the freedom to expose the organization was curtailed.

Leadership is achieved through the proper channels. Hence everyone in the ANNISU-R knows how to pursue promotion and everyone respects leadership because there is a protocol for ascension through the ranks. There is no doubt that the leaders are capable of achieving the overall agenda in the positions they fill. I had this progression described to me as a pyramid system. The central committee is at the top, below them are the regional committees, then the district committee and finally the area or unit committees. When I asked a student leader if people are able to bypass a level or was it more like in Cuba where they are required to move up the ranks, he responded:

> The reason behind this is that there is always a system for everything. For example, some sorts of incompetence surface when a person who had worked in the organization in 2052 BS [1996] jumps into the organization again in 2058 [2002] at a higher level. It happens so because he would not know what happened in the course of the student movement in the consecutive years that followed his departure. If he lacked this experience, he would find it really difficult to motivate the people in the movement in the latter stages. Therefore, only those who have passed through all the levels accumulating the knowledge obtained in the course of the successive student movements can be effective student leaders. With this calculation in mind, our friends rise passing through the pyramid structure of the organization.
>
> (ANNISU-R CCM's interview, 1/8/07)

There is a lot tangled up in this student's response. Not only is it expected that one rises systematically through the ranks in order to acquire proper knowledge, but also that one must do so to prove one's dedication in political struggle to superiors and inferiors in order to gain their confidence. Furthermore, one's own experience is considered within the larger realm of historical materialism. When I pushed this student leader on this point he said:

> That is what we mean by scientific revolution. It is not only about looking at the past as lessons in which to base our current policy in order to achieve our goals for the future, but it means being an active participant in the process. One's personal experience must be within the context of the unfolding

revolution. It is only then that they can claim to have a substantial basis in which to know how to go forward. You must realize the personal and the public are one and the same; you must take personal responsibility and personally orient yourself to the revolution at every level, most importantly, making the public your first personal priority.

(ANNISU-R CCM's interview, 1/8/07)

Gaining experience in the process not only places people's personal experience within the revolution but allows them the ability to appropriately explain the party line to their juniors in order to direct them on how they should proceed. Only when one thoroughly understands the basis of party ideology is one able to make decisions to further the party toward its proper political end.

Not every single person that has been promoted has progressed in the orthodox way of the pyramid structure, but when they have not, it is set in a context of what is needed for the progression of the overall revolution. In other words, people can justify the swift appointment of individuals if the leaders deem it necessary because they have faith that the leaders know what is needed and know people's capabilities. Furthermore, the development of the ANNISU-R as an organization happened during a civil war. During war, one does not question one's superiors. The ANNISU-R students pride themselves on what they describe as "militant commitment"[19] to their ideology and their party. War is just one part of revolutionary class struggle. For that reason, even after the war is over they can justify irregularities as being necessary to further the revolution.

One student leader explained to me, "My organization believes that unity is possible through struggle. Unity achieved through struggle is durable. I am willing to compromise the superficial but won't compromise my devotion to class struggle. This is what is real to us."[20] This student went on to explain to me the Maoist understanding of power. He said power is such that it will always enforce a dictatorship on others who are not in power. He claimed people are deluded if they deny that every form of state power enforces a dictatorship on the other classes. Therefore power must be just. The whole point of their class struggle is to negate the capitalists and establish a dictatorship of the proletariat. If people believe that all power takes a dictatorial form, then they are willing to suspend their own personal freedom for the form of power they would like to see installed. Therefore organizational structure for the ANNISU-R is not about compromise or appeasing all participants through any democratic contention, but rather it is about properly indoctrinating cadres with the right sense of discipline and dedication so they follow the orders of their superiors, leaders whom they see as the most capable of furthering the ultimate agenda of their shared struggle.

This is not to say that there is only one political line that people must accept. When discussing this issue, a number of ANNISU-R students highlighted the discursive space within their organization. One student told me that space is given to various opinions and they are encouraged to debate and compete with one another in this capacity. He cited Mao's saying, "Let many flowers bloom," as the basis for which opinion is disseminated. But he was quick to make a distinction between revolutionary and opportunist opinion. He explained, "if the opinion has emerged from an opportunist line, we have to negate it. But if it has come from the revolutionary line, we have to accept it and institutionalize it in a new way."[21] The limitations within the discursive space are not about the opinions themselves, but about the orientation of those opinions. If the students are coming from a revolutionary line, then they are encouraged to express their views in an unlimited way. In other words, they have freedom only within discipline. Where the students lack freedom is outside these revolutionary parameters. If they cannot agree with the basis of the Maoist doctrine, then there is no place for them. Other student organizations make more room for flexibility in this way so they are perceived to be more autonomous. Yet for the ANNISU-R students, this sort of freedom of opinion runs completely counter to what they believe an organization stands for. For them the organization is a shared basis through which they will realize their ultimate political end.

When I have spoken to the Maoist students and leaders about authority within their structure, what they try to highlight is that although there may be power inherent within the hierarchal structure of the organization, they try to limit the power by making sure that everyone is equal in most contexts. They tell me division of labor is necessary in order to progress in a scientific manner. Therefore they must all be pragmatic in accepting how their hierarchal structure works. Everyone fulfills a role but they also understand how their role fits into the overall system of their action plan. They claim that there is no added privilege for a higher role because this would create schisms that would lead people to disassociate from the larger agenda.[22] In order to avoid political alienation, there is an emphasis that all cadres must feel ownership over the larger process in their everyday activities. They do this through a cultural emphasis on equality and uniformity of lifestyle; this is just one example of how they live their politics.

Every student I asked said the lifestyle of leaders and the cadres is not much different beyond their political and military duties. They live together in communes, eat the same food, dress the same and rotate duties to maintain the domestic sphere. One student leader told me that he would be criticized if he took a taxi when his comrades took the bus, or if he ate more expensive food or wore more expensive clothes than others. "I have to refine my thoughts and deeds in order to be a good person; a feeling of collective living should prevail in me rather than an individual one,"[23] he reported. He claimed that this is what has caused splits and weaknesses in other parties. Nobody struggles for anything but power and once they have it, they use it to amass wealth and personal prestige. This has led to resentment and cynicism. He said this political culture is based on a very different lifestyle, a bourgeoisie lifestyle that was premised on one's individual, private orientation. He pointed out that other student leaders are able to leave their offices to go to the private comfort of their home and family. The discrepancy between their lifestyle and that of their cadres does not bother them. Furthermore, in the eyes of ANNISU-R members, other student activists have competing loyalties. Their families usually come first, and their politics is a means to ensure wealth and security and to further their filial influence. Whereas the Maoists work and live together communally, the party is what comes first. The party, which claims to represent the proletariat, is the reason for the students' involvement; it is what they "struggle and live for."[24]

The way this student describes the collapsing of prescribed bourgeoisie boundaries or categories of the personal and professional, or family and party, is similar to the way Rene ten Bos summarizes Agamben's theory of organization as threshold (2005: 20). Agamben describes organization as a zone of indifference between work and non-work or culture and nature that is set up in order to skew categories. In this sense, the categories are skewed in order to imbue every aspect of life with the import of the revolutionary cause.

Conclusion: the sustainability of revolutionary politics

Why, as admitted across political lines, do the Maoist students have more ability to meld their theory (or political ideals) with their practice than other politically active students? One reason, I would argue, is that the Maoists' mission is a complete restructuring of society, politics, culture, family, and individual lives. On the other hand, the other student organizations' political agendas are more narrowly defined as a struggle for democracy, republic, or a socialist economy, but their struggle, especially in latent periods, does not encompass every facet of their life (Snellinger 2006). They can disconnect their family or private life from their political life, which they relegate to the street or their mother organizations' actions in parliament. Yet the success of a party relies on its ability to suspend its agenda so that it is continually progressing at the front and center in the arena of politics, as Warren argues when he writes "associations that are likely to keep the public sphere vital are those that have something to gain by going public, and . . . they must have the capacity to project their voice over time and space" (2001: 164).

Yet it is worth asking how long priority for a mission can be sustained. In Nepali politics, there is a lot of rhetoric focused on the incompleteness of political struggle (Snellinger 2006). The other political organizations have maintained a façade of consistency in articulating their political agendas during active struggle and then putting them aside in their attempt to achieve progress as they move from the streets to parliament and back again. For democratic political activists it is an aesthetic arc that connects the unfolding history within the Nepali political imaginary. Yet the Maoists' sacrifice for class struggle encompasses every single aspect of their lives and every juncture is defined as struggle; it never relents. Now they are faced with the reality that as they compete for power and resources within the political sphere, they will need to adapt in order to survive and maintain their competitiveness (Baum and Singh 1994; McPherson and Rotolo 1996; Ruef 2000). As I have demonstrated, this inevitably invites inconsistencies as they transition from a revolutionary to a mainstream political force.

This reality leads to the conundrum that if you are training your cadres to be uncompromising in your orientation to class struggle, then how can you expect them to accept your flexibility to compromise in the environment of democratic politics? The leaders justify inconsistencies of the CPN-M on the mainstream level as the appropriate means for the current time; they describe it as progressive immediacy toward their ultimate end. This reasoning echoes a prominent justification throughout leftist history for policy and political decisions that might otherwise seem revisionist (Djilas 1957; Doolin and Goolas 1964). Ultimately, the CPN-M and the ANNISU-R will lose cadres or base support to accusations of revisionism just as the CPN (UML) did during the 1990s era of democracy.[25] Furthermore, their party line will be less convincing to those on the outside, who may not be supporters or have any investment in the political organization's success at the government level. This could jeopardize their future ability to amass a larger constituency. Another possibility is that as they go mainstream they will gain voters but lose their radical base, which will push them to redefine their organization and political identity.

What I have tried to demonstrate in this chapter is that the ANNISU-R sensibility of scientific organization may have allowed them the strength to be effective as a revolutionary party and within their transition into mainstream politics it may serve them well, since their discipline, consistency and effectiveness are in contrast to the disintegration of all these qualities in other student organizations. But this revolutionary orientation leaves them inflexible in the complexities of mass-based democratic politics in a way that could undermine their organizational abilities. Ultimately, moving to mainstream politics will inevitably bring the Maoists down to a level of imperfect politics with which the rest of the parties have had to contend. The issue they will grapple with is to what degree is flexibility within the mainstream system going to serve as a revisionist impediment to their ultimate end of resolving class struggle. Yet as Polletta argues, the ANNISU-R can in fact help their mother organization transition into the mainstream political process by establishing hybrid organizational forms that can be transposed onto their mother organization and in a sense mask the hiccups in the transition from revolutionary group to political party. Polletta argues that in the context of the dynamic nature of repertoires, "people can transpose modes of interaction from one setting to another, indeed from one institutional sphere to another, modifying those interactional modes in the process" (2005: 274). In fact their position as a sister organization made up of tomorrow's generation of leaders may be the very thing that provides them a new horizon during a time when people are transitioning from the politics of revolutionary activism to the politics of parliament.

Notes

* I would like to thank Mahendra Lawoti for his invaluable suggestions on how to frame this chapter and Anup Pahari for his substantial content and editorial contributions.

1 This research was conducted during my doctoral field research, which was sponsored by a Fulbright Hays Doctoral Dissertation Research grant from 2006–7 and the Wenner Gren Foundation Dissertation Field Research Grant from 2007–8.

2 In the Nepali context, the more left a party is, the more their practices, agendas, and internal procedures will be informed by a theoretical political ideology (Baral 1995; Borre et al. 1994; Hachhethu 2002; Hoftun et al. 1999; Rana 1995; Shrestha 1996).

3 Niche within the context of organizations can be described as the factors that shape and maintain boundaries between organizational forms; this is a dynamic process of

segregating and blending until an organizational identity is ultimately formed (Hannan and Freeman 1996).

4   All interviews are translated from Nepali.

5   ANNISU-R CCM's interview, 12/4/07.

6   ANNISU-R CCM's interview, 1/8/07.

7   The communist parties of Nepal have one of the most complicated histories of splits and mergers that I have seen in all of my studies of political parties. For a comprehensive visual of this see Thapa and Sijapati 2003.

8   During their time underground the ANNISU-R was most prevalently known for the closures of schools, particularly private schools, and forcing them to pay a tax that would go toward "people's education" in order to create an equitable education system for all. This tax was used to fund indoctrination and the furthering of the Maoists propaganda campaign.

9   ANNISU-R CCM's interview, 10/12/07

10 In "Commitment as an Analytic: Reflections on Nepali Student Activists Protracted Struggle" I analyze the rhetorical use of continual struggle in order to understand how student activists affiliated to the democratic parties make meaning from their political activity.

11 As the April Uprising of 2006 was unfolding, I remember students from other political affiliations telling me that the ANNISU-R was extremely organized in mobilizing its cadres and the common people as well as maintaining control of the agitators on the street. At the time some had indicated fear that after they ousted the king, the Maoists had the strength, numbers, and organizational capacity to oust the democratic parties. Despite the fact that these students were thankful to have the ANNISU-R students and their capabilities on their side of Kathmandu's ring road, they also worried that they had given the Maoists a free pass into the Kathmandu Valley, from which they would take over the country.

12 Many consider the YCL to be a loophole so that the CPN-M could avoid putting all their army members in the United Nations' cantonments after the comprehensive peace treaty was signed. Some of the PLA soldiers were not eligible to stay in the cantonments since they were under 18. Furthermore, the YCL served as a guise for the Maoists to continue recruiting young people, training them and maintaining their influence in the countryside even after their PLA was supposed to give up all activity in accordance to the peace treaty.

13 Notes from an interaction with ANNISU-R student, 11/30/07.

14 Since the YCL has been called upon physically to resolve disputes between the ANNISU-R and other student organizations on the campuses, I had to make a strategic choice not to work with the YCL unless their activities overlapped with ANNISU-R. There was too much tension between them and the other student organizations, often to the point of violent clashes. I could not justify working closely with them because they were not a student organization and that would jeopardize my image as a neutral researcher working across party lines.

15 ANNISU-R CCM's interview, 1/8/07.

16 Notes from an interaction with ANNISU-R student, 7/9/07.

17 ANNISU-R CCM's interview, 12/4/07.

18 Interaction with ANNISU-R activists at their main office, 7/14/07.

19 This term was used by an ANNISU-R central committee member in an interview, 12/4/07.

20 ANNISU-R CCM's interview, 12/4/07.

21 ANNISU-R CCM's interview, 11/12/07.

22 It must be stated that Maoist cadres have criticized their leadership for embracing lifestyles that resemble other mainstream political leaders. At a campaign rally, entitled "Let us study and survive" – an ANNISU-R sponsored campaign that demanded compensation for orphaned children of PLA soldiers equal to that received by orphaned

children of soldiers of the Nepal Army and national security forces – one orphaned cadre gave a speech with CPN-M Chairman Prachanda sitting in the front row, in which she railed against the "mobile and motor culture" that the Maoist leadership was taking on. She went on to say that her parents did not fight and die for their leadership to be indistinguishable from other political party leaders (6/13/07).

23 ANNISU-R CCM's interview, 12/4/07.

24 Notes from an interaction with ANNISU-R student, 7/9/07.

25 The Communist Party of Nepal-United Marxist Leninist (CPN-UML) was the only communist party to have gained the prime ministership during the years of multi-party democracy. It is considered right of the CPN-M, supporting multi-party democracy with a socialist structure without the use of violence against the state. During the late 1990s, the Maoists gained a lot of support from people who were previously loyal to the CPN-UML. These citizens had become disillusioned with the CPN-UML after their government rule because they failed to impact a state structure along radical ideological lines. The Maoists offered a more radical line for these people that the CPN-UML had seemed to abandon in order to engage in party politics (Hachhethu 2000).

Bibliography

Alexander, Jeffery. 2004. Toward a Theory of Cultural Trauma. In *Cultural Trauma and Collective Identity*, ed. Jeffrey Alexander et al., pp. 1–30. Berkeley: University of California Press.

Baral, Lok Raj. 1995. The 1994 Elections: Emerging Trends in Political Parties. *Asian Survey* 35(5): 426–40.

Baum, Joel and Jitendra Singh. 1994. Organization-Environment Coevolution. In *Evolutionary Dynamics of Organizations*, ed. J. Baum and J. Singh, pp. 379–402. New York: Oxford University Press.

Bhattarai, Babu Ram. 2003 The Political Economy of the People's War. In *The People's War in Nepal: Left Perspectives*, ed. Arjun Karki and David Seddon. Delhi: Adroit Publishers.

Borre, Ole; Sushil Raj Panday and Chitra Krishna Tiward. 1994. *Nepalese Political Behavior*. New Delhi: Sterling Press.

Braungart Richard G. and Margaret M. Braungart. 1986. "Life-Course and Generational Politics" *Annual Review of Sociology* 12: 205–31.

Dangi, Shiva Kumar. 2007. *Sangharshaka Sathi Barsha: Neplai Bidhyarthi Andolan ko Gaurabshali Itihas*. Kathmandu: Haidal Press.

Djilas, Milovan. 1957. *The New Class: An Analysis of the Communist System*. New York: Praeger.

Doolin, Dennis and Peter Goolas. 1964. On Contradiction in the Light of Mao Tse-Tung's Essay, 'On Dialectical Materialism.' *China Quarterly* 19: 38–46.

Gunther, Richard and Larry Diamond. 2003. Species of Political Parties: A New Typology. *Party Politics* 9(2): 167–99.

Hachhethu, Krishna. 2002. *Party Building in Nepal: Organization, Leadership and People*. Kathmandu: Mandala Book Point.

——. 2000. Nepali Politics: Political Parties, Political Crisis and Problems of Governance. In *Domestic Conflict and Crisis of Governability*, ed. Dhruba Kumar Nepal. Kathmandu: CNAS/TU.

Hannan MT and John Freeman. 1986. Where do Organizations Come From? *Sociological Forum* 1: 50–72.

Hufton, Martin, William Raeper and John Whelpton. 1999. *People, Politics and Ideology: Democracy and Social Change in Nepal*. Kathmandu: Mandala Book Point.

Katz, Richard and Peter Mair, eds. 1994. *How Parties Organize: Change and Adaptation in Party Organization in Western Democracies*. London: Sage Publications.

Lawson, Kay. 1994. *How Political Parties Work: Perspectives from Within*. London: Praeger.

Lenin, Vladimir Il'ich. 1920. Left-Wing Communism, an Infantile Disorder. In *V.I. Lenin Selected Works Volume 1*. New York: International Press, 1971.

Lounsbury, Micheal and Marc Ventresca. 2003. The New Structuralism in Organizational Theory. *Organization* (10): 457–80.

McPherson, J. Miller and Thomas Rotolo. Testing a Dynamic Model of Social Composition: Diversity and Change in Volunatry Groups. *American Sociological Review* 61: 179–202.

Monroe, J.P. 2001. *The Political Party Matrix: the Persistence of Organization*. Albany : State University of New York Press.

Neupane, Leknath. 2005. *Akhil Gyan*. Kathmandu: Bhijan Prakashan.

Ostrogorski, Moisel. 1964. *Democracy and the Organization of Political Parties*. New York: Anchor.

Panebianco, Angelo. 1988. *Political Parties: Organization and Power*. Cambridge: Cambridge University Press.

Polletta, Fracessca. 2005. How Participatory Democracy Became White: Culture and Organizational Choice. *Mobilization: An International Journal* 10(2): 271–88.

Popielarz, Pamela and Zachary Neal. 2007. The Niche as a Theoretical Tool. *Annual Review of Sociology* 33: 65–84.

Prasad, Naeshwar. 1980. *Ideology and Organization in India Politics: A Study of Political Parties at Grass Roots*. New Delhi: Allied Publishers.

Puri, Geeta. 1980. *Bharatiya Jana Sangh: Organization and Ideology*. New Delhi: Sterling Publishers.

Putnam, Robert. 1976. *The Comparative Study of Political Elites*. New Jersey: Prentice Hall Inc.

Rana, Gobardhan. 1995. *Prajatankrik Andolanma Nepali Bidhyarthi Sang* (Nepal Student Union in the Democratic Movement). Kathmandu: Prakashak Press.

Ruef, Martin. 2000. The Emergence of Organizational Forms: A Community Ecology Approach. *American Journal of Sociology* 106: 658–714.

Schlesinger, Joseph. Political Party Organization. In *Handbook of Organizations*, ed. J.G. March. Chicago: Rand McNally.

Snellinger, Amanda 2007. Student Movements in Nepal: Their Parameters and their Idealized Forms. In *Contentious Politics and Democratization in Nepal,* ed. Mahendra Lawoti, pp. 273–98. Delhi: Sage Publications.

———. 2006. Commitment as an Analytic: Reflections on Nepali Student Activists Protracted Struggle. *PoLAR (Political and Legal Anthropology Review)* 29(2): 351–64.

———. 2005. A Crisis in Nepali Student Politics?: Analyzing the Gap between Politically Active and Non-Active Students. *Peace and Democracy in South Asia Journal* 1(2): 18–43.

Shrestha, Pushpa Lal. 1996. *A Short History of the Communist Movement in Nepal*. Kathmandu: Pushpa Lal Memorial Academy.

Snow, David and Robert Benford. 1992. Master Frames and Cycles of Protest. In *Frontiers in Social Movement Theory*, ed. Aldon Morris and Carol McClurg Mueller. New Haven: Yale University Press.

ten Bos, Renè. 2005. Giorgio Agamben and the Community without Identity. In *Contemporary Organization Theory*, ed. Campbell Jones and Rolland Munro. Malden, MA: Blackwell Publishing.

Thapa D. and S. Sijapati. 2005. *A Kingdom Under Siege: Nepal's Maoist Insurgency, 1996 to 2004.* London: Zed Books.

Tilly, Charles. 1995. Contentious Repertoires in Great Britain, 1758–1834. In *Cycles and Repertoires of Collective Action*, ed. Mark Traugott, pp. 15–40. Durham, NC: Duke University Press.

Warren, Mark. 2001. *Democracy and Association.* Princeton: Princeton University Press.

Wright, William E. ed. 1971. *A Comparative Study of Party Organization.* Columbus, OH: Charles E. Merrill Publishing.

5 Between clientelistic dependency and liberal market economy

Rural support for the Maoist insurgency in Nepal

Madhav Joshi[*]

It looks like the onset of Maoist insurgency has finally brought the political parties, civil society, ethnic minorities and the people together for the establishment of a democratic Nepal – a political mission that has been interrupted quite often. Over the last 50 years, Nepal has had two brief periods of parliamentary democracy, both of which ended with royal interventions. The first democratic government formed by the Nepali Congress party with a two-thirds majority in the parliament in 1959 was dismissed by the king in 1960. A popular uprising in 1990 compelled the king to allow a multiparty system to replace the no-party Panchayat system imposed in 1962 (Khadka 1993). The most puzzling aspect about the multiparty democracy introduced in the 1990s was that the democratic government failed to address the grievances of Nepal's rural/village population. In time, it was this population that came to provide the secure support bases necessary for revolutionary insurgency. If, as Goodwin and Skocpol (1989: 495) have argued, "the ballot box . . . has proven to be the coffin of revolutionary movements," then Nepal's transition to democracy in 1990 should have inoculated that nation against the outbreak of revolutionary insurgency. People were optimistic that the democratic change would give them a central role in the political process by bringing them economic opportunities and a social justice. Even after its transition to democracy, the Nepali state remained an extractive patrimonial state that institutionally neglected people living in rural Nepal. The Maoist insurgency challenged the status quo and rendered the Kathmandu-centric government machinery dysfunctional. King Gyanendra seized this opportunity to dismiss the democratic government in October 2002 and to eventually assume executive power himself in February 2005.

The Maoist insurgency in Nepal presents an anomaly for students of democratic transition, liberal market, and civil war. If democracy is supposed to inoculate a nation against the risk of civil war, why would a revolutionary insurgency emerge in Nepal after the nation made a transition to parliamentary democracy? The answer may lie in the failure of the democratic government to tackle the land ownership question in Nepal. But this raises two further questions:

1   Why did Nepal's democratic government fail to undertake agrarian reform that would have potentially benefited the largest bloc of voters?
2   Why did liberal market policies fail to bridge the gap between the center and the periphery?

This study addresses these questions by exploring how the feudal land tenure system persisted in Nepal in favor of, first, a coalition of the king, the Ranas, the military-bureaucratic machinery of the state; and, second, a coalition of parliamentary political parties with substantial support from landed elites. We also explore the effects of market liberalization on well-being of the rural households compared to those of the urban households. With a functioning market economy, people can have different opportunities to earn livelihood. The rural people were alienated from the benefit of the market economy as a liberal market was not fully functional in the rural villages which further fortified patron–client relations between landed elites and rural people. This study presents argument that the Maoist insurgency bourgeoned on the grievances of people in rural Nepal who were oppressed by the landed elites and systemically neglected by the state. Clientelist politics in Nepal have slowed economic development by discouraging the state from providing public goods and increasing greater dependence of rural people on the local elites. Liberal democracy and market economy did not alleviate the grievances of rural people, and left the field wide open for the Maoists to propose armed insurgency as the means to realize people's expectations.

Ruling coalition, source of political power and democratization

Theories of democratization suggest that equal distribution and access to resources would be conducive to the emergence and consolidation of democracy. Nepal has never had the sort of equitable distribution of wealth resources envisioned in that thesis. Instead, Nepal has always had a centralized state presiding over an agrarian economy. State–society relations have been largely extractive, with a coalition at the center composed of royals, Ranas, and their supporters among the military and state bureaucracy presiding over an economically and politically marginalized peasantry at the periphery. This ruling coalition was groomed over more than two hundred years following the unification of Nepal on the basis of a Hindu kinship system that was patrimonial and caste-based. The state was organized as an extension of the ruler's household along with close allies from upper Bahun (priest) and Chhetri (warrior) castes from the hilly region. The functioning of the state was contingent upon the political power of one individual at the center (the king), and the source of his political power was control over the military. The military rank and file had little influence in politics immediately after the unification of Nepal. The king enjoyed predominant land rights, and military officers and regular soldiers were given land (*jagir*) that raised their social and economic status. Priests and Hindu monasteries were also given lands (*guthi*) as a means of enhancing the Hindu ruler's legitimacy.

The military did gain political influence in Nepali politics following the instability of the 1840s that grew out of power struggles within the palace (Whelpton 2005). The 1846 *Kotparba* massacre of military supporters eliminated many of the royals' political allies and marked the beginning of the Rana regime (Whelpton 1991, 2005). Following the *Kotparba*, the army's loyalty was perceived as crucial for the political survival of the Rana regime. To maintain the loyalty of the military, the Rana rulers raised the basic pay for the military and made available opportunities for career advancement up to a certain level within the military rank. Soldiers were recruited from families already serving in the military, which further strengthened the bond between the military and the Ranas. To build a strong national army and hence preempt the formation of an alternative army, the Ranas recruited ethnic minorities (e.g. Magars and Gurungs, Limbus, Thakuries) into the military, though the highest ranks remained the monopoly of the Ranas themselves (see also Nepali and Subba 2005; Whelpton 1991: 208).

The Ranas institutionalized the caste system with the 1854 Civil Code, and continued the practice of granting lands (*birta*) to priests and monasteries (*guthi*) in order to establish the legitimacy of their rule through the support of Hindu religious institutions. The Ranas also forged marital relations with the royals (Whelpton 1991). This strategy of control over the military and society remained largely intact after the fall of the Ranas in 1951, except the military came under the control of the king. Ranas continue to dominate the military because of their relations with the royal family. After democracy was dismantled in 1960, King Mahendra quickly cultivated the loyalty of the military by taking steps to secure the careers of those in the senior ranks and by ensuring that the military was well paid. He established the Military Secretariat to centralize and tighten personal control over the military (Nepali and Subba 2005). It was not until the April uprising of 2006 that the restored parliament dismantled the Military Secretariat and reduced the military prerogatives of the king, including his role as the supreme commander of the army.

Despite the demise of the Rana regime in 1951, landed elites created in the past century continued to control land-based resources as land reforms initiatives of the 1960s failed to address the grievances of peasants (Regmi 1976). Given the dependence of most of the population on land for their economic well-being, control over land constitutes the main source of political power in Nepal. Those who became politically powerful under the restored monarchy did so through the patronage of kings. Major political parties contesting parliamentary seats in 1991 had radical electoral agendas such as ending a dual ownership of the land and land reform. But, substantial legislative initiatives were not taken to fulfill electoral promises in the post-1990 Nepalese politics, which could alter the existing sociopolitical structure. The politically influential individuals across all political parties are those who derived their power from their land ownership (Khadka 1998: 160), and bequeathed from ancestors who received either *birta* lands as grants from the state or revenue collection rights during the Rana regime (Whelpton 2005: 51). Those with revenue collection rights also received lands that had the additional benefit of being exempt from taxation. Ranas also retained extensive landholdings for themselves, which were also exempt from taxation before 1951. Under the Ranas, these land grants had not established a permanent landed aristocracy because none of these tenure forms involved permanent ownership rights. *Raikar* land granted for service to the state reverted to the state when the recipient's service ended. Similarly, with any change in the alignment of elite factions in the capital, *birta* land could be reassigned to supporters of a newly ascendant faction. In practice, however, only some prominent *bitra* holders were targeted, leaving average *birta* holders alone as long as they were loyal to the political alliance at the center. Nevertheless, a de facto private land ownership was in practice in Nepal as early as 1930s (Regmi 1976).

The tax collected from peasants for the use of land was the main source of state revenue. Tax collection rights were given to the village head (*jimwals* or *mukhiya*) in the hill region and *jamindar* (a person empowered by the state to manage lands for tax collection) in the Tarai (plain) region. The village head and *jamindar* were at the bottom of the pyramid in the power structure of Nepali politics. They had to report tax collections to their regional governor, a high-ranking military official who was either a member of the Rana family or loyal to the king.[1] The political implications of the revenue collection system were that it tied the interests of local "big men" closely to those of the central government. And with the aegis of the central government, local big men emerged as the landlords with formal power to collect taxes from peasants and informal powers as credit providers, arbitrators and mediators between peasants and the state. The result was a closed political and economic coalition between the central state and landed elites as its local agents.

This economic and political coalition survived even after the downfall of the Rana regime in 1951. The interim constitution adopted in 1951 included a provision that guaranteed property rights. This suddenly made the then-current holders of *birta* and *jagir* land into permanent landowners (Regmi 1976). The hierarchy between landed elites and peasants became institutionalized in the permanency of the unequal distribution of land ownership, creating permanent landed elite of government officials, including high-ranking military officers, Brahmins, and members of Rana and royal families. As such, state autonomy from the landed elite was thereafter constrained: the network of landed elites came to serve as the agents of the state at the local level, and the state was dependent upon their support and loyalty to maintain order in the countryside and to collect the taxes necessary to finance the operations of the national government.

Peasant unrest over these developments compelled the government to enact the Tenancy Rights Acquisition Act in 1951. The Act was intended to provide the land title to the tenants who paid tax or rent on the land they cultivated. However, because landlords routinely reported the taxes they collected in their own name, the Tenancy Rights Act had the opposite effect to its intent: it enabled landlords to claim a permanent legal title to the land they had managed in trust for the state (Regmi 1976). In subsequent years, the government made other modest attempts to redistribute land more equitably through the Royal Land Reform Commission in 1952, the Land Act of 1957, the Birta Abolition act of 1959, and the Land Reorganization Act of 1962 (Regmi 1976). None of these measures had much remedial effect on the inequality in landholdings.

The persistence of the feudal land tenure system in Nepal has implications for the democratic transition and survival in Nepal. Contemporary theories of democratization have spelled out a number of conditions under which democracy is more or less likely to emerge and survive. Several recent works have focused on the nature and the distribution of wealth resources as a determinant of a nation's prospects for democratization. Wealth resources are a source of political power, and as the distribution of such resources becomes more equal throughout the society, the diffusion of wealth provides individuals with the means to demand political rights from the government (Vanhanen 1997). For agrarian economies such as Nepal where more than 80 percent of the workforce is employed in the agricultural sector and the vast majority of them are landless peasants, smallholders, or tenants (HMG Nepal Agriculture Census 2001), land constitutes the major source of wealth and income. As such, control over land also constitutes a major source of political power. Equitable redistribution of resources such as land is likely to facilitate democratic transition because it gives people resources to pressure the state for the expansion of political rights, and the state has less reason to resist those pressures. Where land is not equitably redistributed and land ownership is concentrated among few landed elites in the society, democratization is less likely to occur. This is particularly because fewer people in the society have the means to make effective demand for democratic rights, and landed elites are more able to gain the state's support in resisting reforms that are likely to empower the landless and eventually threaten their control over wealth and political power (Midlarsky and Midlarsky 1997; see also Stanley 1996).

In agrarian economies, landed elites have incentives to resist democratization because a democratically elected government is obliged to carry out demands for redistribution, and therefore it would pose a threat to their economic dominance (Boix 2003; Acemoglu and Robinson 2006). Democracy empowers the poor, at least in the sense that it gives them the right to vote. Since peasants outnumber the landed elite in an agrarian economy, the latter are confronted with the possibility of an elected government enacting redistributive policies – whether in the form of taxes or land reform – that would threaten their control over landed wealth and the political power that flows from that control. Because the source of their wealth is a fixed asset – land – they cannot avoid taxation by moving their assets out of the country, as an industrial or financial capitalist could. Therefore, in land-based economies, democracy is less likely to emerge in the first place and, where it does, more likely to fail through some form of extra-constitutional reversion to authoritarian rule (Boix 2003). Moreover, conflict between landed elites and peasant masses is more likely to escalate into civil war than in an economy where industrial or financial assets are the primary source of wealth (Boix 2003; Acemoglu and Robinson 2006). This explains the relapse of democratic government into authoritarianism in Nepal and its failure to adopt radical redistributive policies such as land reform that directly uplift the welfare of rural people at the expense of landed elites.

Liberal market economy and redistribution

Despite the fact that the rural economy is mostly agrarian, Nepal was gradually adopting a liberal market economy. After practicing an import substitution and protectionist trade regime for almost three decades (1956–1985), Nepal adopted a policy of market reform in the mid 1980s (Sharma et al. 2000; Athukorala and Sharma 2004). The market reform policy of 1985 resulted in substantial economic policy reforms on issues related to domestic industries, foreign investment and trade.

After enactment of this policy, the level of protection given to domestic industries declined from 80 percent to 40 percent. This also led to the change in the composition of the industrial sectors. The output share of import substitution industries declined from 78 percent to 72 percent, whereas the output share for export-oriented industries increased from 13 percent to 28 percent (Sharma 2001). The democratic government in 1991 continued with a liberal market economic policy and supported Foreign Direct Investment (FDI) in the export-oriented sector with five years of free tax holidays, which were later extended to ten years (Athukorala and Sharma 2004). During the period 1988–2001, according to Athukorala and Sharma (2004), 721 FDI projects were approved with a total capital commitment of $1153.6 million. It was estimated that these investments would create more than eighty thousand jobs. But only about 37 percent of the approved projects were operational with 18.7 percent of FDI share (about 100 million US dollars). The inflow of foreign capital is contingent upon the terms of return as well as on comparative advantage. Because Nepal is a mountainous and landlocked country and human capital development is low compared to other South Asian countries, Nepal could not attract significant foreign capital investment. Nonetheless, the inflow of FDI rose until the outbreak of violent political conflict in 1996. The economy grew by almost one-third from 3584.38 GDP (Million USD 2000 Constant) in 1991 to 4573.20 in 1996 (World Bank WDI Report 2005).

Shrestha and Chowdhury (2007) find that the economic liberalization in Nepal generated employment in both the urban and the rural areas, but they find a negative relationship between liberalization and bank credits to the poor. They also find that the increased level of liberalization worsened the incidence of poverty in Nepal. This finding is quite surprising but supports the arguments that the economic prosperity did not diffuse evenly, with the rural poor peasants being left behind. In line with privatization priorities, the subsidies given to farmers in seeds and fertilizers were cut off (Deraniyagala 2005: 59). This in turn encourages the factors invested in agriculture to relocate to export-oriented sectors impacting the real earning of laborers working in the agriculture sectors (Cockburn 2002). Therefore, the distributive effect of subsidy cut is disastrous for the rural households compared to urban households because of urban households' lesser dependency on income from land and unskilled labor (Cockburn 2002). The spatial distribution of FDI operation also indicates that the benefits of the liberal market economy are concentrated in urban areas, particularly in the capital city Kathmandu. Of the 270 operating FDI projects, according to Athukorala and Sharma (2004), 57 percent or 153 projects were concentrated in capital city.

The impact of the liberal market economy in Nepal highlights the fact that the fruits of liberalization have been shared very unevenly by people living in urban and rural areas. Perhaps the liberalization process created economic constraints for the government and forced it to cut off welfare programs in response to the structural reforms imposed by the World Bank and the International Monetary Fund. But the burden of structural reforms was disproportionately shared by peasants in rural villages. Between the mid 1980s and the mid 1990s, average levels of urban real income doubled the levels of rural real income, which suggests a rise in rural poverty and a fall in urban poverty rates (Deraniyagala 2005: 58). Had democracy empowered the rural peasants, they would have been able to influence the distributive policy and close the gap in welfare distribution between the urban and the rural people. What explains the urban-centric redistributive policies that the democratic government carried out? Even after the democratic change, rural people were left behind and caught in-between clientelist ties with the landed elites and institutionalized exclusions by the state. To explain this puzzle, we explore the hypothesis that governments in electoral democracies are less likely to carry out redistributive policies when electoral support can be mustered through clientelist ties.

Clientelistic politics, political mobilization and redistribution

One of the mechanisms that forces elected leaders in democracy to come up with a broad redistributive policy is pre-election policy promises that candidates make to voters (Keefer 2007). But the credibility of candidates on whether they will carry out a promise depends on the capacity of political parties and on the candidate herself to influence the political mobilization through the use of formal networks such as party organization or unions, as well as informal networks such as patron–client relations. Where economic activity is mostly concentrated in subsistence cultivation, peasants remain in networks of patron–client dependency that limit the autonomy of their political behavior (Joshi and Mason 2007). With the vast majority of the labor force dependent on agriculture and a substantial portion of their activities concentrated in subsistence cultivations, land ownership is critical for peasant households. The persistence of inequality in land ownership and the very nature of subsistence farming compel peasant households to seek the patronage of local landed elite. These landed elite provide peasants with access to land and other services such as protection from roaming banditry, goods, services, and emergency assistance that amount to a "subsistence floor" (Scott 1976: 29–32).

The relationship between landed patron and peasant client is multifaceted, diffuse, face-to-face and based on personal ties, not written contracts. Landlords provide peasants some insurance against the prospect of a subsistence crisis that would put their very lives in jeopardy. The bond between peasants and patrons is perpetual because the loss of patron's support would cast peasants into the pool of landless laborers, devoid of any subsistence securities and exposed to the market uncertainties for land, labor and food. In exchange for these services and use of a plot of land, peasant cultivators are expected to provide the landed patron with some mix of rent, crop shares, free labor and other services. They are also expected to support the patron politically by complying with his instructions even on political matters such as whom to vote for in elections. Joshi and Mason (2007) explain that the emergence of Maoist insurgency in Nepal after the democratic transition in 1991 is partly due to this form of clientelistic dependency in which the local patrons acted as buffers between peasants and candidates running for elective offices (and their party organizations). Peasants' interaction with all outside authorities (including candidates for elective office) is mediated by the patron, and the patron uses his ability to "deliver" the support of his peasant clients as a bargaining chip in his

Table 5.1 Distribution of household (HH) and area owned by size of land holding (in %)

Size of holding	1961 HH	1961 Area	1971 HH	1971 Area	1981 HH	1981 Area	1991 HH	1991 Area	2001 HH	2001 Area
Holdings with no land	1.43	0.00	0.80	0.00	0.37	0.00	1.17	0.00	0.85	0.00
Less than 1.0 ha	73.89	24.03	76.77	27.2	66.32	17.33	68.63	30.5	74.15	38.88
1–4 ha	19.56	35.68	18.39	39.29	28.05	46.13	27.68	50.8	23.7	50.45
More than 4 ha	5.13	41.42	4.03	33.74	5.35	36.54	2.51	18.7	1.3	10.67
Total	100	100	100	100	100	100	100	100	100	100

Source: Central Bureau of Statistics, Agricultural Census of Nepal (1961, 1971, 1981, 1991 and 2001).

dealings with political parties and candidates running for office. The clientelistic dependency of peasants on the rural elite has several implications for democratic political process and for the onset of Maoist insurgency in Nepal.

Table 5.1 summarizes patterns and distributions of land ownership over time. The data suggest that the proportion of households with larger holdings has declined over the years and the proportion of smallholders who own less than one hectare of land has increased substantially. Part of the reasons related to decrease in large-scale landlordism in Nepal is related to land fragmentation, which has a cultural explanation. Most of the fragmentation occurred because of the tradition of inheriting family property among male siblings. As such, land is still held by different member of the same family, not outside family. Therefore, land fragmentation did not bring change in the relationship between patron and client because many of those who inherited land from ancestors still have surplus lands. Smallholders do not own enough land to support their subsistence needs and most of them need favor in kind from local patrons or access to lands to meet subsistence security. Since supply of land is more limited than supply of agriculture labor forces (joined by landless peasants and smallholders), landed elite gain a predominant bargaining position that influences the nature of relationship between peasant household and the landlord. Table 5.2 gives descriptive statistics from the National Agriculture Census 2001 on different patterns of tenancy arrangement. This suggests the nature of the relationship between the patron and the clients and the strength of that relationship.

The implication of patron–client relationship is that the peasant households would not be able to elect the candidates they prefer in elections. Among political parties fielding candidates in elections, the radical left parties, such as the predecessor of Maoist party, had the most radical demand for agrarian reform and sought redistribution of resources through welfare policies. As the agrarian reform is directly related to the welfare of peasant households, peasant cultivators have incentives to vote for those left-leaning parties. But peasant voters would jeopardize their access to land and other subsistence guarantees if they vote against the directive of their patron (Joshi and Mason 2007). Joshi and Mason (2008) find that the voter turnout was greater where land tenure patterns gave landed elite greater influence over peasant political behavior. The three parliamentary elections and two local elections in the 1990s produced governments dominated by Nepal's local

Table 5.2 Households cultivating lands in different tenancy arrangements

	Obs.	Mean	St. Dev.	Min.	Max.
Landless households (1,000s)	75	11.854	22.962	0.171	181.763
% Smallholders households	75	18.184	12.976	0.162	63.641
% Share cropping households	75	6.602	5.418	0	24.527
% Renting for service households	75	0.319	0.607	0	3.741
% Rent for fixed cash households	75	0.833	0.972	0	5.43
% Rent for fixed product households	75	1.704	3.406	0	23.843

Source: Central Bureau of Statistics, Agricultural Census of Nepal, 2001.

elites whose source of power comes from their control over land-based resources (Khadka 1998, 1993: 52). Khadka (1993: 52) argues that the local elites controlled about 90 percent of the seats in the first parliament. According to Mannan (2002: 84) the elected representatives in the national parliament in Nepal possessed an average of over 16.8 hectares of land in the hill areas and nearly 10 hectares in the plains. By contrast, 50 percent of farming households (who elected them) possessed 0.15 hectares per household.[2] As such, landed elites did not only work as a buffer between peasants and candidates running for elected offices, but also influenced policies of the post-1990 democratic government. This perhaps is correlated to the failure of the democratically elected government to enact land reform policies even if major political parties had recognized the importance of land reform to peasant households.

The network of landed elites, therefore, substantially reduced the cost of political mobilization for political parties, at least in those districts where land ownership was concentrated in the hands of a relatively small landed elite, and where a large section of the peasantry worked as sharecroppers and smallholder tenants. As a result, those political parties who advocated reform and promised to bring about change in the distribution of resources could not persuade enough peasants to vote for their cause (Joshi and Mason 2008). Under conditions of rural clientelism, dominant political parties have an incentive to look out for the welfare of the landed elite rather than the interests of the peasant cultivator. As a matter of fact, successful clientelistic mobilization of the rural voters allows the government to divert resources to urban districts where voters are not necessarily bound by patron–client networks. In urban areas where social control mechanisms are diffuse and people are not under the influence of landed elites, and where economic activity is not centered around subsistence cultivation, political parties must credibly commit to a redistributive agenda and to providing public goods and must carry out those commitments. Welfare of urban people is important to avoid possible urban unrest (Bates 1984). As long as the governing parties make sure that the urban constituents are taken care of, it enables them to gain electoral support from urban voters and avoid any unrest that could possibly challenge the political legitimacy of the regime. This argument is best summarized in figure 5.1.

As suggested in figure 5.1 (lower right cell), costs of political mobilization and social control mechanism are concentrated in rural areas. The effective social control mechanism is patron–client relations between landed elites and peasants. In this regard, political parties could maximize their gains by mobilizing the already existing social control mechanism (landed elites) and taking care of their welfare (no land reform and no access to resources for peasants) rather than actually carrying out redistributive polices that could possibly uplift the welfare of peasant households. This control mechanism is not readily available in urban settings (upper left cell). People are educated and affiliated with different organizations and unions. Social control mechanism is diffused, making the cost of political mobilization higher in those districts. Under such circumstance, candidates contesting for elected offices and political parties fielding candidates for election have incentives to make credible policy commitment and actually carry out that policy to

		Cost of mobilization	
		Diffused	Concentrated
Social control mechanism	Diffused	Untargeted (urban)	Mixed
	Concentrated	Mixed	Targeted (rural)

Figure 5.1 Social control mechanism and provision of public goods/redistribution in democracy

retain urban support. Upper right and lower left cells in figure 5.1 represent mixed scenarios.

The theory developed above allows us to make a claim that a ruling coalition in Nepal has incentives to provide economic opportunities and carry out pre-electoral redistributive commitments for urban voters rather than peasant voters in rural villages. We can test this hypothesis by making a distinction between urban and rural districts in Nepal and looking at the difference in the Human Development Index (HDI) available from the United Nations Development Project (UNDP 1998 and 2004) between urban districts and rural districts. One of the indicators that we can use for this purpose is road density. Murshed and Gates (2005) have also used a road density index to highlight the horizontal inequality between the urban and the rural districts. It measures the paved road in each district, an indicator of urbanization. This variable is available from District Level Development Indicator from Government of Nepal (2003). The mean of this variable is 0.19, with the highest road density in Kathmandu district with value of 2.0578, and about nine districts have no paved road (zero value in road density index). For the purpose of comparison, we categorize urban districts as having a road density index above the mean and rural districts as when the road density is below the mean. As such, among 75 districts, we have identified 24 and 51 districts as urban and rural districts, respectively.

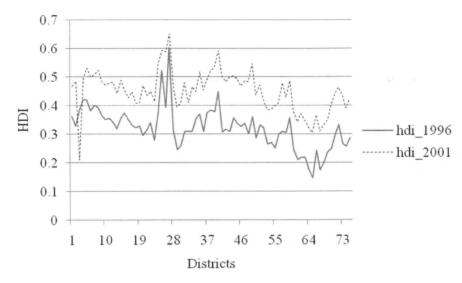

Figure 5.2 Average human development index, years 1996 and 2001

HDI reports from UNDP-Nepal suggests that there have been some positive changes in the status of most of the districts, from 1996 to 2001 (see figure 5.2), but a great disparity exists in human development between rural and urban districts (also see Murshed and Gates 2005; Deraniyagala 2005). The mean difference between the urban and the rural districts is 0.084 in the HDI index in 1996 (see figure 5.3). With 95 percent confidence interval, this difference is between 0.052 and 0.194. It suggests that after two rounds of parliamentary elections, government

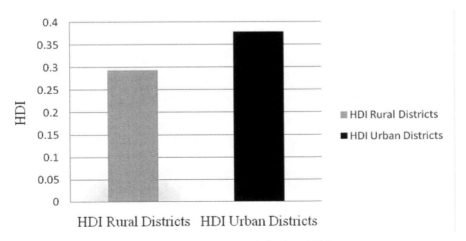

Figure 5.3 HDI difference between urban and rural districts, 1996

policies and programs were not targeted in uplifting the socio-economic status of peasant households. This difference becomes even more glaring when comparing life expectancy at birth between the urban districts and the rural districts. On average, people in urban districts are likely to live 6.1 years longer than people in the rural districts.

This, however, does not hinder the welfare of the landed elites in rural districts. This is particularly because landed elites were provided with targeted goods, particularly access to institutional credit offered at lower interest rates from government-owned financial institutions. In Nepal, the government provides low interest rate loans from the Agriculture Development Bank, which has extensive branches across all districts in Nepal. Because it is available at a lower interest rate and the loan can be paid back after the harvest, it is very attractive for peasant households. Interestingly, access to such credit is not easily available to all peasant households as it requires collateral (title of land in most cases). Many peasant households (especially smallholders, sharecroppers and landless peasants) do not have access to institutional credit. Even if they get credit, they are more likely to default on loans. In other words, institutional credit is mostly targeted to landed elites, which further fortifies their stronghold, because peasants are compelled to borrow from them. The Maoist party in its original 40-point demands to the government in 1996 demanded that:

> Poor farmers should be completely freed from debt. Loans from the Agricultural Development Bank to poor farmers should be completely written off. Small industries should be given loans.[3]

Baburam Bhattarai (1998) succinctly portrays the politico-economic implication of lack of access to institutional credit as:

> Peasants are usually in need of loans for production and consumption purposes. Taking undue advantage of this situation the feudal-usurers provide credits to the peasants at high interest rates and with oppressive conditions and by entrapping them in a vicious circle of indebtedness they enforce semi-feudal exploitation through interest and labour-service payments.

Using data from UNDP (2004), we performed a mean comparison test on difference in households' access to institutional credit between urban and rural districts. In the test performed, we find that the mean difference in the percentage of households' access to credit in the urban and the rural districts is statistically insignificant. The difference is from negative 4.53 to positive 11.57 percent. From this test, we cannot make the inference that access to institutional credit is different between urban households and the rural households. Nevertheless, the findings support that the landed elites in the rural villages and urban districts have equal access to the institutional credit. Since landed elites have greater access to institutional credit, it further confirms urban-centered redistributive policies adopted by the government, provision of targeted goods to landed elites, and grievances among peasants against the central government and its agent "landed elites" in the villages.

Mobilization for armed insurgency

The Maoist insurgency in Nepal is the outburst of grievances among rural people. After the people's movement in 1990, peasants were optimistic that the democratic government would carry out land reform and social welfare programs as most of the political parties prioritize these issues in their election manifestos. But rural people could not successfully change the attitudes of political elites through the democratic process. The persistence of clientelist dependency inhibited peasants to vote for pro-reform candidates.[4] Patrons' capacity to mobilize peasants for electoral purposes made it politically costly for elected government to carry out land reform and other redistributive policies and thus address the grievances of rural people. Under such circumstances, the Maoist party convinced peasants that they could bring about change and meet the needs and aspirations of rural people. When Maoist insurgents launched an insurgency in a rural Nepal, they targeted landlords among others in rural districts. By targeting landlords and local elite, the Maoist insurgents, on the one hand, challenged the feudal state (see Deraniyagala 2005; Ganguly and Shoup 2005), and, on the other hand they reduced the costs for peasants to join the insurgency. After all, when local power bases are destroyed, peasants are free from the clientelistic obligation that had bound them. Driving out the local elite from rural villages created a power vacuum, which was quickly filled up by the Maoist insurgents who promised to relieve landless and poor peasants from all kinds of debts and labor-services and other charges levied on them.

A Common Minimum Policy and Program (CMPP) of the United Revolutionary People's Council (URPC), which was the Maoist party-commissioned parallel government (also called *Jana Sarkar*), stated that:

> The main policy of agrarian revolution shall be to abolish the feudal, semi-feudal and bureaucratic capitalist production relations in the land and develop national capitalist relations, of which "land to the tiller" shall be the main policy tenet. In other words, the land owned by feudal, bureaucratic capitalists and various guthis (a type of feudal ownership by social and religious institutions) in the places where the old reactionary power structures have been smashed, shall be seized without any compensation and distributed to landless and poor peasants, and the tillers shall be made the owners of the land.
>
> (URPC 2001)

The land redistribution policy that the Maoists espoused during the insurgency was very popular among landless peasants and smallholders as the Maoists convinced them to join and support the insurgency. The CMPP of the URPC further elaborates the policy of land and property redistribution as:

> Land and property shall be distributed to the office-bearers of the People's Army, People's Governments and mass-organizations and their families who come from the villages like other common peasants.
>
> (CMPP of URPC 2001)

With the arrival of Maoists in villages, previous local elites lost their power base substantially, especially with threat of elimination and other actions. They redistributed lands that belonged to local elites among the supporters of insurgency, destroyed bondage papers, cancelled debts, and constituted the "people's government" and "people's court" in the villages.[5] They targeted branches of the Agriculture Development Bank in various districts and destroyed legal documents. In a sense, the arrival of insurgency in the rural districts brought social justice, by establishing the rights of peasants to the land they farmed and by emancipating them from debt servitude.

There is ethnic element in the land tenure issue as the share of ethnic minority households that are landless, small and marginal cultivators is greater than their proportion of the national population (Joshi and Mason 2007: 410; UNDP 1998). Adoption of majoritarian democratic institution in 1990 and major political parties' insensitiveness to the grievances of ethnic minorities further marginalized ethnic minorities from access to state resources and power (Lawoti 2005). As such, grievances among ethnic minorities increased a pool of rebel recruitment for the Maoist party. In order to gain support from ethnic minorities, Maoists demanded cultural rights, ethnic federalism and elimination of gender and caste-based inequalities. Using cultural programs, they energized and appealed to wider audiences in rural villages (Mottin, Chapter 3) which helped to recruit and mobilize peasants and ethnic minorities against local elites (Eck, Chapter 2).

Within a brief period, the Nepal Communist Party (CPN-M) -initiated revolutionary insurgency established a support base in certain parts of the country sufficient to afford it a degree of local control that rendered the Kathmandu-centric administrative machinery of the state dysfunctional. In some regions, rebel control progressed to the point that CPN-M commissioned "people's governments" and "people's court" that serve as the *de facto* political authority and dispense justice in those communities (Seddon 2005: 33). Over the course of the next ten years, Maoist insurgents captured about 80 percent of the countryside, disrupting the traditional local social structures and practices (Seddon 2005). Perhaps the support that the Maoist insurgency received from the rural villages might be generated from coercion and intimidation. But for peasant households a change in the socio-economic structure that would relieve them from debt servitude and give them an access to land is enough for them to support the Maoist insurgency.[6] The failure of the democratic government to resolve the Maoist rebellion and bring peace and security led King Gyanendra to dismiss the government in October 2002 and eventually to suspend democracy altogether in February of 2005. He assumed autocratic power and this led the parliamentary parties to join the CPN-M in a series of mass demonstration, which forced King Gyanendra to restore parliament in April 2006.

The conflict was so intense in the rural districts that more than 10,000 people were killed compared to about 2,700 killed in urban districts (INSEC 2005). Nevertheless, the Maoist insurgency changed the rural political economy and challenged the feudal establishment sufficiently to change the perceptions of political elites at the center. The Maoist rebels and the government agreed to a ceasefire and a series of power-sharing deals. All agreements signed between the Maoist party and the Seven Party Alliance, as well as the common minimum program of government unveiled on April 10, 2007, includes provisions for extensive land reform and investments in rural development projects. Hopefully, people in rural Nepal will see more equitable distribution of resources and greater opportunities after the restoration of peace and stability.

Conclusion

In this chapter, we tried to present the argument that the Maoist insurgency in Nepal is mostly related to the grievances of people living in rural villages. Because of the clientelistic bond they had with the peasants, landed elites influenced their political behavior. The restoration of parliamentary democracy in 1990 did not alter the concentration of economic resources in the hands of a small elite coalition. The political parties contesting parliamentary elections gave peasants hope for agrarian reform and for improvement of their living conditions but turned to landed elites for support in parliamentary elections. It constrained the capacity of the new democratic state to enact meaningful reforms. As a matter of fact, the democratic state did not seek to faithfully implement land reform policy and efficiently redistribute resources. Successful mobilization of peasants through landed elites created political incentives for governing elites to enact urban-centric redistributive policies.

The Maoist insurgency gained support for their promise to enact radical land reforms, redress grievances and establish equitable society where people in rural villages have more equitable access to state and economic opportunities irrespective of caste and ethnicity. In order to successfully enact redistributive policies to promote welfare of people in the villages, the post-conflict Nepal should aggressively pursue land reform and investment in rural development projects.

Notes

* I would like to thank T. David Mason, Mahendra Lawoti and Anup Pahari for comments and suggestions in developing this chapter.
1 During the Rana regime, the tax collection authority was given to those loyal to the Rana prime minister.
2 One of the reasons related to the performance of radical parties is perhaps related to the electoral institutions that have failed also to integrate ethnic minorities in the political process. For more discussion on inclusive political institutions and democracy in Nepal, see also Lawoti (2005, 2007).
3 For more discussion of the 40-point demands made by the Maoist see Pathak (2005).
4 CPN-UML, a reformist if not a radical leftist party, received considerable votes and seats in parliamentary elections held in 1991, 1994 and 1999. It formed a minority government as the largest political party in the parliament after the 1994 election and introduced some rural-oriented populist programs such as a block grant to village development committees (VDCs) and allowances for senior citizens.
5 Even if they distributed lands to their supporters and peasant cultivators, titles to the lands still belong to the landlords ousted from villages. In a comprehensive peace agreement signed on November 21, 2006, the Maoist party agreed to return seized property to the owners. There is no credible information on the implementation of this agreement.
6 The results of April 10, 2008, constituent assembly election show that the Maoist party

consistently performed well in rural districts and received better than expected seats from urban districts. If fear and intimidation were used to generate support during the insurgency and that fear and intimidation still existed at the time of elections, they would have not received electoral support in the urban districts. Rural people voted for the Maoist party because they believed that the Maoists would bring change by redistributing resources while urban residents voted for the Maoists because of fear that the Maoists would return to armed conflict if they did not receive enough seats.

Bibliography

Acemoglu, Daron and James A. Robinson. 2006. *Economic Origins of Dictatorship and Democracy*. New York: Cambridge University Press.

Athukorala, Prema-Chandra and Kishor Sharma. 2004. "Foreign Investment in a Least Developed Countries: The Nepalese Experience." Paper presented in 10 Years of Australia South Asia Research Center Conference, Canberra, April.

Bates, Robert H. 1984. *Markets and States in Tropical Africa: The Political Basis of Agricultural Policies*. New edition. Berkeley: University of California Press.

Bhattarai, Baburam. 1998. "Politico-economic Rationale of People's War in Nepal" http://www.cpnm.org/worker/issue4/article_dr.baburam.htm, accssed on September 18, 2006.

Boix, Charles. 2003. *Democracy and Redistribution.* New York: Cambridge University Press.

Central Bureau of Statistics. 2001. *Agriculture Census 2001: HMG Nepal.* http://www.cbs.gov.np/Agriculture/Agriculture%20Census2001/District%20Summary/content.htm, accessed on August 3, 2005.

——. 2003. *District Level of Indicators of Nepal for Monitoring Overall Development.* HMG-Nepal.

Cockburn, John. 2002. "Trade Liberalization and Poverty in Nepal: A Computable General Equilibrium Micro Simulation Analysis" CSAE WPS/2002–11.

Common Minimum Policy and Programme of United Revolutionary People's Council, 2001. http://www.cpnm.org/worker/issue8/urpc.htm, accessed on January 9, 2007.

Deraniyagala, Sonali. 2005. "The Political Economy of Civil Conflict in Nepal." *Oxford Development Studies* 33(1): 47–62.

Ganguly, Sumit and Brian Shoup. 2005. "Nepal: Between Dictatorship and Anarchy." *Journal of Democracy* (16)4: 129–43.

Goodwin, Jeff and Theda Skocpol. 1989. "Explaining Revolutions in the Contemporary World." *Politics and Society* 17(4): 489–509.

Informal Sector Service Center (INSEC) Human Rights Violation Data 2005: Kathmandu, Nepal. http://www.inseconline.org/download/Killings_Data.pdf, accessed on November 11, 2005.

Joshi, Madhav and T. David Mason. 2007. "Land Tenure, Democracy, and Insurgency in Nepal: Peasant Support for Insurgency versus Democracy in Nepal." *Asian Survey* 47(3): 393–414.

——. 2008. "Between Democracy and Revolution: Peasant Support for Insurgency versus Democracy in Nepal." *Journal of Peace Research* 45(6): 765–82.

Keefer, Philip. 2007. "Clientelism, Credibility, and the Policy Choices of Young Democracies." *American Journal of Politicsl Science* 51(4): 804–21.

Khadka, Narayan. 1993. "Democracy and Development in Nepal: Problems and Prospects." *Pacific Affairs* 66(1): 44–71.

——. 1998. "Challenges to Developing the Economy of Nepal." *Contemporary South Asia* 7(2): 147–65.

Lawoti, Mahendra, 2005. *Towards a Democratic Nepal: Inclusive Political Institutions for a Multicultural Society*. New Delhi: Sage Publications.

——. Lawoti, Mahendra. 2007. "Political Exclusion and the Lack of Democratization: Cross-national Evaluation of Nepali Institutions using Majoritarian-Consensus Framework," *Commonwealth and Comparative Politics* 45(1): 57–77.

Mannan, Manzurul. 2002. "South Asia's Experience in Land Reform: NGOs, the State and Donors," in *Whose Land? Civil Society Perspectives on Land Reform and Rural Poverty Reduction: Regional Experiences from Africa, Asia and Latin America*, ed. K. B. Ghimire and Bruce H. Moore. Rome: The International Fund for Agricultural Development (IFAD).

Midlarsky, Manus I. and Elizabeth Midlarsky. 1997. "Environmental Influences on Democracy: Aridity, Warfare, and Land Inequality," in *Inequality, Democracy and Economic Development*, ed. Manus I. Midlarsky. New York: Cambridge University Press.

Murshed, S. Mansoob and Scott Gates. 2005. "Spatial-Horizontal Inequality and the Maoist Insurgency in Nepal." *Review of Developmental Economies* 9(1): 121–34.

Nepali, Prakash and Phanindra Subba. 2005. "Civil-Military Relations and the Maoist Insurgency in Nepal," *Small Wars and Insurgencies* 16(1): 83–110.

Pathak, Bishnu. 2005. *Politics of People's War and Human Rights in Nepal*. Kathmandu: BIMIPA Publication.

Regmi, Mahesh C. 1976. *Land Ownership in Nepal*. Berkeley: University of California Press.

Schneiderman, Sara and Mark Turin. 2004. "The Path to *Jan Sarkar* in the Dolakha District: Towards an Ethnography of the Maoist Movement," in *Himalayan People's War: Nepal's Maoist Rebellion*, ed. Michael Hutt, 79–111. Bloomington: Indiana University Press.

Scott, James C. 1976. *The Moral Economy of the Peasant: Rebellion and Subsistence in Southeast Asia*. New Haven: Yale University Press.

Seddon, David. 2005. "*Armed Violence and Poverty in Nepal: A Case Study for the Armed Violence and Poverty Initative*." http://www.smallarmssurvey.org/files/portal/ spotlight/country/asia_pdf/asia-nepal-2005.pdf, accessed January 9, 2007.

Sharma, Kishor. 2001. "Liberalization, Growth and Structural Change: Evidence from Nepalese Manufacturing." *Applied Economies* 33(10): 1253–61.

Sharma, Kishor, Sisira Jayasurya and Edward Oczkowski. 2000. "Liberalization and Productivity Growth: the Case of Manufacturing Industry in Nepal." *Oxford Development Studies* 28(2): 205–22.

Sharma, Kishor. 2001. "Liberalization, Growth and Structural Change: Evidence from Nepalese Manufacturing." *Applied Economies* 33(10): 1253–61.

Shrestha, Min B. and Khorshed Chowdhury. 2007. Impact of Financial Liberalization on Welfare: Evidence from Nepal. *Applied Econometrics and International Development* 7(1) http://www.usc.es/~economet/journals1/aeid/aeid7115.pdf.

Stanley, William. 1996. *The Protection Racket State: Elite Politics, Military Extortion, and Civil War in El Salvador*. Philadelphia: Temple University Press.

UNDP.1998. *Nepal Human Development Report*, Kathmandu, Nepal.

——. 2004. *Nepal Human Development Report 2004: Empowerment and Poverty Reduction*. Kathmandu, Nepal.

Vanhanen, Tatu. 1997. *Prospect of Democracy: A Study of 172 Countries*. London: Routledge.

Whelpton, John. 1991. *Kings, Soldiers and Priest: Nepalese Politics and the Rise of Jang Bahadur Rana, 1830–1857*. New Delhi: Manohar.

———. 2005. *A History of Nepal*. Cambridge: Cambridge University Press.

World Bank (2005). *World Development Indicators*. http://publication.worldbank.org/DWI/.

Appendix 5.1: Proof for mean difference test

a. Institutional credits difference between urban and rural districts.

Combined variance for rural and urban districts

$$s^2 = \frac{\Sigma[(Y_1)] - \overline{Y_1})^2 + \Sigma[(Y_2)] - \overline{Y_2})^2}{(n_{1-1}) + (n_{2-1})} \tag{5.1}$$

$$= \frac{14954.73 + 3672.69}{50 + 23} \tag{5.2}$$

$$= 225.17 \text{ (combined variance)} \tag{5.3}$$

Standard deviation $s = \sqrt{225.17}$ $\qquad$ (5.4)

$$= 15.97 \tag{5.5}$$

Mean difference in institutional credit

$$= \mu_1 - \mu_2 = \overline{y}_1 - \overline{y}_2 \mp t_{0.025} \, s_p \sqrt{\frac{1}{n_1} + \frac{1}{n_2}} \tag{5.6}$$

$$= 24.59 - 21.07 \mp 2 * 15.97 \sqrt{\frac{1}{23} + \frac{1}{50}} \tag{5.7}$$

$$= 3.52 \mp 2 * 15.97 * .252 \tag{5.8}$$

$$= 3.52 \mp 2 * 4.03 \tag{5.9}$$

$$= 3.52 \mp 8.06 \tag{5.10}$$

$$= -4.53 \text{ to } 11.57 \text{ (the difference is between } -4.53 \text{ to } 11.57)$$

b. Human Development Index difference between urban and rural districts.

Combined variance for rural and urban districts

$$s^2 = \frac{\sum [(Y_1)] - \overline{Y}_1)^2 + \sum [(Y_2)] - \overline{Y}_2)^2}{(n_{1-1}) + (n_{2-1})} \tag{5.11}$$

$$= \frac{0.605 + 0.557}{50 + 23} \tag{5.12}$$

$$= 0.016 \text{ (Combined variance)} \tag{5.13}$$

Standard deviation $s = \sqrt{0.016}$ (5.14)

$$= 0.126 \text{ (Combined standard deviation)} \tag{5.15}$$

Mean difference in HDI $= \mu_1 - \mu_2 = \overline{y}_1 - \overline{y}_2 \mp t_{0.025} \ s_p \sqrt{\frac{1}{n_1} + \frac{1}{n_2}}$ (5.16)

$$= 0.422 - 0.292 \mp 2 * 0.126 \sqrt{\frac{1}{23} + \frac{1}{50}} \tag{5.17}$$

$$= 0.130 \mp 2 * 0.126 * .252 \tag{5.18}$$

$$= 0.130 \mp 2 * 0.032 \tag{5.19}$$

$$= 0.130 \mp 0.064 \tag{5.20}$$

$= 0.066$ to 0.194 (the difference is between 0.066 to 0.194)

Part III
Revolutionary governance

6 Political change and cultural revolution in a Maoist Model Village, mid-western Nepal

Marie Lecomte-Tilouine

Despite the number of publications on the Maoist movement in Nepal, little is yet known about its impact on the lives of peasants in rural areas where the Party ruled the villages. However, the documentation published by journalists and members of the Maoist Party allows drawing a general picture of the changes introduced by the Cultural Revolution in western Nepal.[1] These pages offer an outline of the latter in the year 2005, taken from the Maoist weekly *Janadesh*. This picture serves as a framework to situate my observations at the time on the changes introduced in Deurali, a locality in the hills of mid-western Nepal, which was selected by the Communist Party of Nepal-Maoist (CPN-M)) to be a Model Village.

Deurali is located 250 kilometers to the west of the capital. I lived there for two years between 1986 and 1989 and visited it each year afterwards until July 1996. The People's War intensified during the following years but until my trip in September 2005, I had no idea what the situation was there, as little information had been published on this district, which is faraway and not considered to be the cradle of the revolution. Yet, in the Maoist description of the country, the district where Deurali is located was included in the base region and in the Magarant autonomous region created by the CPN-M.

Cultural revolution in the base region

The Magarant autonomous region was roughly speaking superimposed on the base region. The latter was designed as a model, where the Party undertook activities of creation, not just of destruction as in the rest of the country. The CPN-M's program was to form an autonomous region based on ethnic identity, under the Party's supervision. The first election of the Magarant autonomous region took place in September 2002.[2] Although Deurali was inhabited by Magars, three years after the creation of this region (in autumn 2005), few villagers were aware of the fact that Deurali was included in the Magarant, or Magar country.[3] On the other hand, for the urban Magars of Tansen who did not live under Maoist rule, the idea of Magarant was very important and they flew the Magarant flag in the middle of their city.

The base region was the pride of the revolutionaries. Maoist journalists recounted their wonderful feeling when traveling to these villages full of war heroes and of peasants thought to be fully lacking in any selfishness. This is also where foreign journalists were led, accompanied by Maoist activists, on a guided tour to witness the great achievements of the People's War.

Yet, the local population was far from enthusiastic. The Maoist writer Anpe Kancha (2005) acknowledges this when he compares the Cultural Revolution in the base region to a newborn baby that appears "disgusting to his father and close relations" (up until the age of five months) because he was born bloody; yet is loved by his mother, because she made sacrifices for him. The bloody baby stained his cradle as the whole base region has been transformed into a sanguinary universe by its renaming. Cultural groups bearing names such as "the blood seeds cultural family" wandered from village to village that were themselves renamed according to the new fashion: Martyr village, Respect-for-the-Martyrs village, and so on. Maoist comrades bearing revolutionary surnames such as Revenge, Struggle or Terrible would go shopping at the Self-Sacrifice Fancy Store, take the Road of the Martyrs, and work at the Immortals' Commune.

Cultural programs were the most important form of propaganda used by the CPN-M. They included songs and dances, as well as a vast body of literature – poetry, novels – which circulated in the remotest places (see Mottin, this volume, for a detailed analysis). The Nepali Cultural Revolution was based on the idea, expressed by Kumar Malla (2006), that "as long as class society lasts, all writers, artists, singers and musicians are divided into two sides: the oppressor class and the oppressed class . . . Art cannot be for all."

Therefore, the Maoist program not only included the creation of a new culture, but also the destruction of the "indecent"[4] or "declining" culture. Included in this category were "the official media, television, radio and newspapers, the indecent journals, publishing houses, film production houses, exhibitions, as well as massage centers and Miss Nepal contests."[5] In 2005, G. Bhandari (2005) assesses that "the horrible bad practices" have been destroyed in the base region, while the "flood of art and literature emerging from these areas bring[s] an essential energy to the cultural revolution." The bad practices officially included consumption and sale of alcohol, early marriage, polygamy, and social discrimination (particularly against Dalit and women). On the other hand, no texts banning religious practices were published, probably because this was far from being popular locally (and internationally).[6] While this ban remained unofficial, opposition to religious practices was not only an important dimension of the Cultural Revolution, in Deurali as elsewhere, but also something which the local Maoist activists did not conceal. Thus, when asking a local Maoist in Western Nepal, "Why don't you let people worship the gods?" he replied: "The worship of gods and goddesses is a conservative tradition [*rudhivadi parampara*]. It is not good to worship stones, trees, cows or statues because this does not change the society. This thing should be finished."

Contrary to revolutionary movements like the Mozambican Renamo, the Nepali Maoist Party was much concerned with social reform and created various structures like People's tribunals and correction houses to sanction deviant behavior.

On people's tribunal, working camps and self-criticism

In January 2004, Comrade Dayamand, a judge in Kalikot, explained that he applied the "natural law," with no legal code, which was appreciated because it was rapid and public. Most of the cases he settled were related to landed properties and monetary loans. Those found guilty were not sent to jail but to a "correction house." There, they attended four days of schooling per week, but were allowed to go back home one day per month and for festive occasions.[7]

Based on this natural law, a Maoist Code of Law was drafted in 2003, and used for instance in 2005 to sentence two "Royal Army informants" to five and six years of forced labor.[8] The People's tribunals could even sentence to death, as happened for instance in April 2004, in Jumla district, where Candra Bahadur Shahi and Amrit Shahi were condemned to capital punishment and executed.[9]

A case at a People's tribunal in Rukum in summer 2005 reveals that the inhabitants of the base region were not free to move. It reads, "Ram Bahadur Pun, headmaster of the Lukum school, used to give letters of recommendation to his students to go to Banphikot through the village headman, and provided them with the means of going to Khalanga . . . in exchange for 1,000 rupees." Ram Bahadur is presented as an "exploiter of the people," and was sentenced to three years of forced labor. But the fact that his students were ready to pay such an amount in the hope of reaching the district headquarters shows that they could not otherwise escape their village and that they were determined to do so.[10]

In addition to correction houses, purification of the Party and of each of its members was encouraged. Maoist journalists made high-ranking members of the CPN-M confess their main weaknesses to readers. Comrade Visva (2005b), central member of the Party, is thus asked his opinion about his brother who has deserted the Party, and then what, according to him, were his main weaknesses, to which he answered: sentimentality (*bhavukata*) and perversion of the mind (*manogat*). A week earlier in the same journal Comrade Visva (2005a) had signed an article on "The question of discipline in the Communist organization," which he stated should be "an iron discipline," otherwise it would be "an anarchic crowd of locusts." He added: "Criticism and self-criticism is the method which helps purify oneself and purify the Party. The more we can make our weakness public, the more we can be good representatives of human society. To present our excuses for our weaknesses and to transform our habits in this way is for us, revolutionaries, a matter of pride, whereas it is more difficult than death for the feudal." Some places, such as the martyr parks, were described as places of purification, without it being clear if it was symbolic or literal. In a less ambiguous manner, open sessions of criticism by the people are reported. Thus a meeting for the Party's purification took place in spring 2005 in the locality of Respect-for-the-Martyrs and was attended by the head of the district, the district secretary and other leaders. Comrade Sagar addressed the people with these words: "The one who does not say something now, remember, wants to see the party deteriorate and is an enemy of the revolution. That is why you, the people, shall speak." The youth and the women noted that the Party showed half a dozen weaknesses.[11] Another sector of revolutionary reform was education.

On education and training centers

For Purna Bahadur Simha (2005) all problems stem from education as "old teaching limits teachers and students to the university compound. In their minds, a mass of sterile knowledge is forcibly introduced, in order to develop dependence, slavery and mental perversion." To address this problem, the Party supervised the schools, making sure that teachers carried out their duties, and did not teach conservative topics or make the pupils sing the national anthem. The party also provided training in various sectors, such as medicine[12] and engineering.[13] However, the training and schooling centers were very much military oriented. Military training for schoolchildren, though reported by villagers in Deurali, is not mentioned in Maoist journals. But military training of political activists is quite openly publicized.[14] For instance, the Party provided "historical teaching" in its Central Schooling Department in Rolpa, which Kamala Roka (2005) describes as a "powerful front aimed at destroying the bad things which are in people's spirits and at developing new thought and conscience." Roka adds that, by forming their spirits, the schooling "allows hundreds of thousands of warriors to sacrifice themselves on the military front."[15] The subjects studied included dialectic, historical materialism, and Prachandapath, negation of the self and frugality in order to show that pro-people practices are linked to military priorities and that these priorities require self-sacrifice and renouncement. Self-sacrifice of political activists happened indeed, as the journalist S. Majhi (2005) who covered the VK operation in March 2005, attested. There he met a friend, Samjog, whom he describes as "a writer but who is now going to handle the weapons as a necessity of war." Samjog died on the expedition after they met.

The year 2005 also saw the development of the militia in the base region. That year they received a specific uniform in the Magarant. Comrade Cancal, a militia, explained: "our main task is to serve and protect the population. We warn them if the enemy comes, we observe informers. In case of problems . . . we do ambush and mining." As for Hikmat Budha, he walked from village to village "to attract young boys and girls to the People's Liberation Army." Comrade Hitman, who had 50 persons under his command in north-east Rolpa, even claimed that it was necessary to provide military training to the whole population (Kunwar 2005).

Collectivization, communes and cooperatives

Within the Cultural Revolution it was a question of "developing an economy of war, without profit" (Bhandari 2005). In the base region the project was to form collective production units or communes. It was also a question of modernizing farming by destroying the "parcelized form of production" and regrouping the lands, and to use scientific methods of farming. For instance, Comrade Natural (*Prakritik*) wandered and distributed improved vegetable seed in the villages.[16]

The communes were apparently limited in size and number but were viewed as the avant-garde, playing the role of model. Many of them were in fact created on land seized by the Maoists from the government or from "exploiters." Thus the commune of Obang, Rolpa, was located in the "old government's center of agriculture." Production was said to be higher on collective land and the peasants were said to be envious.

The oldest commune was created in March 1999 in Jajarkot, and included 105 members, all Magars except for one Dalit family.[17] A description of the Self-Sacrifice People's Commune (*balidan jana komyun*), Pvang, Rukum, asserts that it was created in August 2004 "to develop collective work, shared living and to end private property and the nuclear family."[18] But the circumstances of its creation bring out another picture. In February 1996, on denunciation by the Congress leader Bhim Bahadur Pun, the police killed Dil Bahadur Pun and Jog Bahadur Pun, and brought their severed heads to the district headquarters. The commune was dedicated to them and housed on the property of Bhim Bahadur Pun's, who was responsible for the murder of these two activists, but whose own fate the Maoists have not revealed. The commune was made up of ten families among whom 18 members worked full-time for the Party: seven in the People's Liberation Army (PLA) and 11 in the political organization. Another 30 persons, including 15 children, worked and lived in the commune.[19] Comrade Sisir, who was in charge of it, complained about a shortage of manpower since the young and able persons "must go to the front." Like the common house, the commune's cattle were probably also the property of the same person, as it included only four buffaloes, four cows, and twelve sheep and goats. The yield from the landed property covered the commune's needs for six or seven months.[20] In addition, it owned some forests and vegetable gardens as well as a shop (the Self-Sacrifice Fancy Store where only 15 percent profit on goods is taken), an inn (the Self-Sacrifice Hotel, with a total revenue of 5,000 rupees per month) and a tailor's shop.

The Ajambari commune of Thabang, Rolpa, grouped together 34 individuals (among whom 22 were youngsters) from seven Magar families, linked to martyred CPN-M members. In 2003, the "enemy" burnt down three houses and destroyed a fourth one in the commune, and in March 2004, when the journalist visited them, all the residents lived in stables. They did not have enough clothing or blankets and possessed only ten plates to eat out of, which they did in turn. They told him that they were poor in everything, owning only 12 cows. They reported planting fruit trees which had all died because they could not look after them. The old women of the commune made nettle thread. They had land, but it was far from their settlement. The commune was in need of manpower, and Mitra Bahadur summarized: "Our commune is in a problematic situation," but they hoped that the Party would provide them with facilities in the future. The report by M. Dhital (2004)[21] on this commune contrasts sharply with other articles on the subject that praise results of this type of organization.

Besides these structures, in several places the term "commune" referred to collective land only. Thus, in some areas of Rolpa, peasants worked one day a week on the "lands of the commune," the other days on their own land (Shila Sharma 2005). Though it is not actually stated, this common land probably belonged to villagers who fled or were killed, as was the case in places which I visited. There, the product was given to the People's Village Government.

Cooperatives were also sometimes distinct from a commune. Thus, in Ghartigaun, Rolpa, a cooperative "hotel" (i.e. eating place) opened in July 2005. The Family of the Martyrs, the Family of the Full-Time Activists and the Family of the PLA borrowed some money from the cooperative bank and joined ranks to form this "hotel." It served a meal for 22 rupees instead of the 30 rupees charged elsewhere, so the place was popular.[22]

For the journalist K. B. Bhandari (2006), the establishment of communes in Nepal should be considered a historical act, as in the case of China they were only set up nine years after the revolution in August 1958, whereas in Nepal, "even if the communes are small and weak in infrastructure, they were created during the revolution." The simultaneity of revolution and Cultural Revolution is a matter of pride.

Deurali, a Maoist Model Village

In 2005, Deurali was declared a Maoist Model Village and the local Maoist leaders were active in trying to introduce various forms of collectivization. At the time, the villagers endured a state of terror, notably because of the ceaseless abduction of children by the Maoists.[23] I went back again to Deurali in September 2006, after the Seven-Party Alliance was formed. The locality was still headed by a People's government, but all Maoist activists who were not originally from the village had left the place and the rules had become less authoritative. At the same time, however, the Maoist design to create small collective units of production took concrete shape in the village.

In 2005, no element of the landscape in Deurali itself hinted at the Maoist presence. While the village hall was in ruins following its destruction, the new seat of political power was not yet visible. A visit one year later, in 2006, showed that this absence of territorial markers had changed, with one third of the houses in Deurali now flying the Maoist flag on their roofs. A house in the village had been transformed into the People's Government office with a red banner. The entrance to major administrative units, such as the district and the district headquarters, were now marked by huge "martyr gates," and Maoist gates had also been erected at both entrances into the settlement of Deurali. These gates emphasized a notion of boundary that had not materialized in any manner in the past. Though they were usually dedicated to martyrs, they evoked victory gates in that they signified both a spatial closure and a withdrawal of the conquered territory from the rest of the country. They reinforced the reality of the Maoist seizure of power, expressed by the term "*kabja*" (capture) to designate the process of establishing a People's Government in a given locality and the accompanying destruction of the symbolic presence of the "old power," the administrative buildings.

The inhabitants of Deurali say that during the first years of the People's War, their village was just situated on a "Maoist path." Strangers started to be seen on this path leading nowhere but to the top of their remote valley: it became, in effect, a red corridor leading to the Maoist base region. At times strangers would come in large groups and organize meetings in Deurali, and the entire population was expected to attend. Since the 1990 movement for democracy, the Deurali School had become the seat of Marxist political activism. In 2003, a few villagers, grouped around a Magar schoolteacher, helped with the nomination of the first People's Government. This was headed by the schoolteacher, a native from the village who had been posted to Baglung for several years in the 1980s and 1990s. The teacher left the village soon after his nomination as the head of the People's Government to become what the villagers call a "walking Maoist." This expression referred to those who have joined the CPN-M, and underlined their mobility. As a matter of fact, mobility formed an essential feature of the Maoist organization. First, it helped the party to operate over a much larger area than would have been possible if its activists and soldiers were posted in one place; and second, it helped it to expand and to maintain control. Let us take an example from Deurali. A majority of the population clearly suffered from the Maoist rule in 2005 and wished to be rid of it. I asked them why in this case they did not revolt collectively against it. The answer I got was that doing so would cause the red army to come in and "cut out all our tongues." This type of incident never actually happened anywhere. But the fact that no one knew where this army was added to its strength, as it could be anywhere. Indeed, though the structure of the Maoist Party and army was territorialized, their mode of operation was not: a western battalion, for instance, could attack in the center or the east of the country.

Many of those who had been appointed to the People's Government in Deurali repeated "it was not our wish," and explained that once appointed, to refuse would make them likely to be considered a class enemy and punished. It should be recalled that conditions in Deurali were not like those typically reported by the media, that is to say villagers suffering the double violence of both government security forces and Maoist rebels. The district headquarters was far away, and the army had rarely ventured into this area. Therefore, the fear of refusing a Maoist position was much greater than that of being the target of the security forces for accepting it. Still, villagers' conceptions, as well as the experience they acquired outside the village, were marked by this dual oppression, as all villagers from a so-called Maoist territory were credited with the Maoist label. Appointments were not limited to political or administrative positions only, but also applied to membership in committees and the militia.

There was thus a double impetus to the implantation of a People's Government: a small core of local sympathizers and the existence of a powerful and intimidating organization, which did not have to be present to be effective. In some cases a core of local supporters may even be absent, as in the case of the locality next to Deurali, where "Maoists from Deurali" came with weapons, assembled the population and appointed some to the People's Government in 2005.

With the implantation of a People's Government, Deurali became a kind of refuge for young Maoist activists who wandered from house to house, eating freely here and there. The local people did not know the exact occupation of these Maoist youth. In addition, there was a small Cultural Group stationed in the village during my visit in 2005.[24]

The People's Government in Deurali

Caught within the gigantic and mobile Maoist superstructure, the village of Deurali was ruled by a local People's Government, which was no different from the previous forms of local government regarding administrative spatial divisions. The locality had kept the same boundaries and had simply been renamed *Gajasa* or Village People's Government instead of *Gabisa*, Village Development Committee (1990–2001) and *Gaun Panchayat* (1962–90). It was still divided into the same nine wards, called *ikai* by some instead of wards, with representatives from each ward. The Village People's Government was headed by a *pramukh*, or chief, and an *upa-pramukh*, or vice-chief, as well as a secretary, as in the past. Like the spatial divisions, the structure of Deurali's political administration thus did not change, but the names used to designate the different positions did, as they did in the past after each political reform. Thus, the traditional *mukhiya* (Main Person) was replaced by the *pradhan* (Head Person) in 1962, by the *adhyaksha* (President) in 1990, and then by the *pramukh* (Chief) with the Maoist rule in 2003. The representatives of each ward were also called *pramukh* (*wardko pramukh*). In addition, two men from each ward were appointed as militia, and this was new, since there had been no policing in the village in the past. They were equipped with battered local weapons and their task was to keep a lookout day and night for any possible approach by the army, which was posted six hours' walk away to the south, in a very inaccessible old royal fortress. But, according to the villagers, except for one helicopter attack against a group of PLA fighters in 2003, during which bombs fell on Deurali, the army had never entered their area.

The Chief of the People's Government: a weak position

A closer investigation shows that the Maoists introduced deeper changes in the political sphere than what appears at first sight. Indeed in 2005, the appointed chief of the Village People's Government or *pramukh* was a Brahman from a small remote hamlet, while in 2006, a Magar from an even more remote hamlet was nominated. These two *pramukh* had in common their extreme isolation in terms of their location, while all the former heads of the locality lived in the two major hamlets of Deurali. In fact, the spatial isolation of these two *pramukh* reflected their isolation in terms of kinship as well. Indeed, the Magar *pramukh* is the only representative of his lineage in the locality, while the Brahman is from a lineage of two households only. In both cases, the *pramukh* was thus not backed by any relative, whereas until 1990 all the village headmen had been members of a large Magar lineage. With the multiparty system in 1991, the village representative was elected from a large Chetri lineage.

Comparative data are needed to support the overall validity of this observation (i.e. the selection of isolated individuals as village headmen), which indicates a will to break the traditional forms of power based on the clan's numerical dominance and network of relations. It is impossible to say whether the choice of an "isolated" chief was deliberate or not, but it is striking that it happened twice in Deurali, and that Deurali is not the only locality where it happened. Indeed, the same phenomenon could be found, for instance, in the locality of Dullu, which attracted media attention after the person appointed against his will as head of the main ward in the local People's Government was killed by the security forces, leading to popular uprising. It happens that the person in question, a Newar, was also recruited from among one of the smallest groups of Dullu, since there were only two Newar households there when I conducted some research in this locality in 2000 and 2003.

Interestingly in Deurali, the rupture of tradition signified in the selection of an isolated chief paralleled the reduction of powers vested in the chief, while the official functions remained unchanged since the 1960s. This obviously happened in an indirect manner, as a consequence of the increased independence and decision-making powers provided by the Maoist political organization to two administrative spatial levels framing the *gajasa* locality: the area (which includes five *gajasa*) and the wards (i.e. the nine sub-divisions of *gajasa*). Their empowerment weakened the role of the *gajasa*. What remains unclear is whether this weakening was induced by the nomination of powerless people at the head of the *gajasa* or whether it was just made manifest by this choice.

Let us now examine the two spatial units that have gained importance: the area and, to a lesser degree, the wards.

The Chief of the area: a potentate

In the Maoist organization, the *gajasa* localities (or Village People's Governments) were grouped into areas, or *ilaka*. In the case studied here, the *ilaka* encompassed five localities including Deurali. This was not an innovation, since in the past the localities were also gathered in different *kshetra*. Though of a comparable size, the *ilaka* where Deurali was located did not correspond to the former *kshetra*: it covered the territories included on both slopes of the same valley, while the *kshetra* included a locality which depended on Deurali for its water supply. The person in charge of the area (*ilaka*) was omnipotent in his or her region and was sometimes called *komandar* (i.e. commander) but more commonly *incharj* (i.e. area In-charge). This position conferred membership to the Maoist District Committee. On the other hand, the In-charge (*incharj*) was not chosen from among the various *pramukh* placed at the head of the *gajasa* localities included in the area but was directly nominated by the Party and could be from a region other than the area he or she administered. In 2005, the In-charge of the *area* studied was a Magar woman from Rolpa. She was based in Deurali but was extremely mobile over the whole area she administered. Somehow, she was the de facto ruler of its whole population numbering approximately 15,000 persons. It should be stressed that political changes in the past had never placed the locality under the direct control of a stranger, and that the In-charge's externality probably helped to destroy local institutions and to impose new rules. Indeed, according to the villagers, the new rules were all dictated by her and the Village People's Government had almost no deciding role.

A number of rules concerned religious practices, which were severely restricted. Rituals including animal sacrifice were forbidden, and given the fact that the great majority of rituals included such sacrifice, collective religious life almost totally stopped. The temples remained closed for the most important ritual of the year, Dasain. But some people celebrated it at home anyway, and an old man went to sacrifice his goat in front of the closed temple. No rituals or dances were allowed on the fifth day of Tij, because it celebrates ancient polygamous sages: the Rishis. The *shraddha* or rituals addressed to ancestors were forbidden on the charge that they were superstitious. Even death mourning rituals were limited to three days instead of the 13 normally required.

The attitude of the local Maoists towards shamanic practices was more complex. According to the lady In-charge of the area whom I questioned on the subject, shamans were not allowed to perform, because, she said, their practices were "not scientific." However, a villager who described to me the cessation of all religious activities in the village, made this point: "as for the shamans, they still 'sit' [i.e. perform], because *they* too fall sick" (the pronoun "*they*" refers to the Maoists, who were rarely referred to directly). This local situation may be due to the fact that the first chief of the People's Government in the village was a famous shaman before he became a famous "walking Maoist."

All the purity rules restricting inter-caste relations were forbidden and several inter-caste weddings were organized by the Party. Three weddings between Damai and Magar, which used to be strictly forbidden by local custom in the past, were organized in the very hamlet where I resided. Parents were forced to accept the new in-laws, but as soon as the Maoist rules became less binding they went back to the old customs. For example, already by 2006, the Dalit daughter-in-law of my Magar neighbor was no longer allowed inside her husband's house.

In theory it was strictly forbidden to refuse cooked food from anyone, or entry into the house. In such a case, a notice to the lady in charge of the area was enough to transform the guilty ones' behavior, for people were frightened of being considered a class enemy and tried at a People's tribunal. My observations, however, show that Dalit continued to stay outside their so-called "pure caste" neighbors' houses, while professing that they were free to enter!

In 2005, most of the Dalit and Magar families declared that they now ate cow meat, and pretended that the high castes did the same. Locally, no one was forced to do this publicly, as had happened elsewhere. People explained that given their present situation, nothing was of any importance anyhow. They were forced to transgress so many things that the holiness of the cow had become, according to them, a somewhat negligible detail. However, this change also did not last, as a year later in 2006, a pure caste householder who had shown me their "cow cooking pot" in 2005 served me and other unmarried members of the family buffalo meat outside, as was customary in the 1980s. However, in 2006 as in 2005 during "the terror," villagers of all castes accepted tea from Dalits, which would have been unthinkable in the 1980s.

The abduction of children was not attributed to the In-charge, but to the Headmaster, who was said to be involved in identifying teenagers suitable for the Maoist PLA. Regardless of who facilitated the abductions, this practice had major consequences in the locality in 2005. Once married, girls were no longer at risk of abduction. This led frightened parents to marry off their daughters early. As for boys, around the age of 16 they were sent off as far as possible, to the Tarai or to India. The presence of a large population of young females and the absence of young men led to an increase in polygamy, though it was officially condemned by the Maoists. I thus saw cases of men married to three women, something unheard of in the 1980s. In addition, the age difference between husband and wife became greater than in the past – as much as 40 years in one case.

At school teachers were forbidden to speak about religion, morals and the monarchy, but they did not have any Marxist books and asked me to send them some. Apparently, the standard of education had improved but in spite of this, I was told that the parents of the neighboring villages sent their children to other high schools, fearing that their children would be abducted if they studied in Deurali.

Money was a serious concern for villagers in Deurali. All the families who had some sort of income were highly taxed by the Maoists. The fact that they no longer had to pay their land taxes to the government did not compensate for the loss, as land taxes had been minimal over the last few years. Most of the local revenue in Deurali used to come from the army or the police, in the form of pensions and salaries. But in September 2006, not a single individual working in the police or the army (not even those serving in India) had come back to the village since 2001. Still, their families were asked to pay enormous amounts of money, or to let the Maoists have their child.[25] People simply did not have 50,000 rupees to pay to the Maoists, and some had already left because of fears arising from this inability to pay the fine. They were forced to abandon their houses and fields, which no one could or would buy. Neighbors or relatives cultivated the abandoned land, but the vacated houses started to crack from neglect. While the absence of men between the ages of 16 and 40 was particularly striking, there were only a few cases in Deurali where an entire household abandoned the village. This was in contrast with places such as Taka, in Rukum, which was affected by the revolution earlier and where, in addition, a large proportion of people owned land in the Tarai as well as in their native village. According to villagers from Taka who migrated to Dang and with whom I discussed in 2005, 75 percent of the village population had left their homes.

In Deurali, the pauperization of Magar families, in particular, was striking and attributable to the fact that in addition to reducing or terminating their income from the army and police, the Maoists had forbidden the sale of home-made beer and alcohol, which was the main source of local income for Magar women. I was told that the Maoists did not spend any of the money collected locally for local consumption. Rather, they were said to use locally collected funds to buy weapons and food for the members of the Party.

More than the militia, who tended to be older men appointed against their will, it was the In-charge who went from house to house making inquiries about infringement of the new rules. A few words were sufficient, so people said, since they were frightened of being taken to a People's tribunal and even more so of being sent to a forced labor camp outside their territory. Thus, the most severely punished case was that of a Damai boy, who was caught singing with a married woman and who was sentenced to six months' forced labor. However, the villagers of Deurali insisted collectively that he carry stones in the village instead of being sent to a labor camp as initially ruled.

Collectivization

Given the way in which the In-charge presented the situation, her area (or Deurali and the neighboring localities) was headed for the Cultural Revolution, which had been thoroughly achieved in Rolpa, her region of origin. In 2005, the In-charge declared Deurali a Model Village (*namuna gajasa*), which was then supposed to be an example in the vicinity. I attended the inaugural meeting in September 2005 and people expressed a mixture of pride and fear in view of its implications for the future, notably regarding collectivization.

The new Maoist code in Deurali was revealed by girls, who told me, while touching my hair, "The In-charge says that we should cut our hair, and that we should not wear jewelry." Others repeated, "We shall not say mine, *mero*, everything should be ours, *hamro*," or "The In-charge says that one person should cut grass all day long, everyday, and another person bring water and another bring wood. Each person should have one task."

However, though collectivization was discussed daily at meetings, it had not yet really taken place in Deurali, except for taxes, which were fixed as a quantity of grain to be paid by the entire village. Collective taxation of the village represented 80 *muri* of cereal (or 6,400 kilos), and this apparent innovation may just have been transplanted into central Nepal from similar systems prevalent in regions to the west.

In principle, collectivization did not come as a blow to anyone, since work was already organized collectively in the past[26] before collective land disappeared in the 1980s with land registration. The gradual disappearance of collective land and work was a subject of regret, notably for women, while men claimed that work was not properly done collectively, with workers wasting their time playing and flirting. Arable land had always been individualized, but forest and pastures were collective. With time, villagers restricted free access to the uncultivated "sides" of their fields and exploited them intensively for grass and wood, planting trees and Graminae in these spaces. They also privatized the *khar bari*, or grass fields, which used to be exploited collectively in the past.

Like the headmen of the past, the In-charge organized collective work for common infrastructures: reservoirs, paths, and suchlike. But this took on a new dimension with the Maoist rule, as one person from each house was asked to work 30 full days to construct the road leading to Deurali. The Maoist ruler insisted that the village "big men" go and work in person instead of sending some other member of their family. This was quite popular, and villagers rejoiced at the sight of them piercing the rock. In addition, the organization of collective work by the In-charge sometimes applied to individual plots as well, where she would ask people to go and help one household in particular when it needed extra manpower. This type of help had been informally recruited in the past. Mina told me:

- Six persons came to plant my millet, because my daughters are too young to help me.
- Did you like it?
- Yes.
- And what about them?
- They may also need help some day.

These two ways of requisitioning manpower did not meet any resistance, as it was perceived as beneficial. In particular, the construction of the road was quoted as the main improvement over the last few years, although a year later in September 2006 it was already badly damaged; in all, only one tractor had reached Deurali just after completion of the road in 2005.

On the other hand, villagers had a good idea of the limits of collectivization within their own territory, and strongly reacted to the idea of creating a collective cattle herd, although they had had one in the past, when the population was smaller and the agricultural system completely different. In 2005, men protested: "How can we round up all the animals or even 30 cows? We don't have much pasture land here." Since very few entire families had left the village and the few that had left had relatives living there still, no collective arable land could be used by the Maoists to create a commune (*komyun*). In another village in the district I visited, the Maoists had seized the land of a "landlord" whose house they had bombed after he had already moved to settle in the south. The villagers cultivated the land and gave the products to the Village People's Government.

Forest management was another bone of contention. Village authorities had always governed forest land according to a rotation system between the high and low areas, to allow vegetation to grow back. In 2005, this system was completely abandoned at the In-charge's decision to "close the forest." This introduced a major imbalance, since the local agro-pastoral system relied on the seasonal displacement of animals grazing at different heights of the slope, which also was useful in directly fertilizing the fields. Most villagers had fields at three different levels of the slope in the 1980s. In 2005, many had ceased to take their cattle to their fields at altitude because animals were no longer allowed to graze in the forests. Instead they carried dung on their backs and the fields were not manured as well, or they simply sold the fields located far from their houses.[27]

The project of collectivization went hand in hand with a project of industrialization. One day I was discussing "class struggle" with the In-charge, and I raised the point that the concept was meaningless as there were only peasants in Deurali. She countered that her project for the village was aimed at "creating a class of workers, *majdur*." This process consisted of gathering artisans (blacksmith and tailors) under the same roof, to create a "factory." But the local artisans resisted, fearing that they would lose the ownership of their tools and machines. Some Damai women announced the news to me, their eyes filled with joy. But the old man of the family stopped them and reacted against this rule and the Maoist factory project: "We are worried . . . it is my machine, I brought it back from India on my back. I like to go to different places; they offer me tea and food, beer, cigarettes. It won't be like that in the factory." In 2005, the Damai tailors were already forbidden to go to their patrons' houses as was the custom in the past and, instead, the patrons had to come to them. Forbidding tailors to go to their patrons and asking them to work at home loosened the traditional bond between the patrons and tailors. Customarily, the latter sewed for all the members of the formers' families in exchange for a certain quantity of grain. In 2005, girls brought fabrics to tailors who could sew the latest fashion models and paid them directly in money per item.

With regard to infrastructures, the In-charge announced at a meeting during my stay that the "health post" should be moved from the main hamlet of Deurali, where there was already a high school, and be set up in the distant hamlet of Bukicaur, which did not have any equipment. Again nobody took kindly to this idea, with villagers pointing out that it was nonsense to try to make the wards equal to each other. The children, 700 in total, were at school all day long, and "if something happens to them, the health post will be too far away to take them there."

Empowering the wards

The In-charge was replaced in 2006 by the Magar schoolteacher who had initially set up the People's Government in Deurali. Villagers commonly attributed the relaxation of the rules to this change. Since the former teacher was a member of the locally dominant Magar lineage, the villagers seemed to believe that a more traditional form of power had been restored. Interestingly though, he belonged to a junior branch (*khalak*) of this lineage, which maintained a conflicting relationship with the elder branch that had always monopolized local political power. Indeed, prior to the Panchayat reform in 1962, the Deurali slope was divided into two halves each ruled by a different Mukhiya headman. The teacher belonged to the family of the Mukhiya "of the heights," who lost his position when the Panchayat was created unifying the territories of various Mukhiyas. Within one year, the new In-charge authorized ritual activities again, as well as the free consumption and sale of alcohol, arguing that these customs were traditional. However, he also introduced a form of collectivization based on the ward units, which was welcomed by the population, while contributing to a weakening of the Village People's Government. This also provided the In-charge with a more stable form of authority over his area and he became a kind of governor over the whole valley, visiting its different settlements accompanied by a court made up of Village chiefs.

As they were created in 1962, the local Panchayats were made up of nine *wards*. During the Panchayat era, two persons were elected in each ward, and would attend the Panchayat councils. In Deurali, these had practically no decisional role and would simply listen to the Pradhan Panch and agree. Within the People's Government, a small council of five persons, headed by a *pramukh*, was appointed to manage each ward. The militia was also created on the basis of the ward. The first In-charge demonstrated her will to make these ward units the basis of village equality by attributing an infrastructure to each of them, which went against the centralization process initiated in the 1980s with the creation of a school, then of some shops and administrative offices. With the second local In-charge, the wards gained greater independence when the locality's collective lands, such as the forest and the pastures, were divided into nine parts and attributed to each ward. Each ward council managed his own resources according to its own rules and used the money collected from it for its own infrastructures. They raised money from the trees, firewood and fodder collected in their zone of forest, as did the Panchayat in the past for the whole forest. In addition, the various wards built fences around the pastureland which was allotted to each of them, left the grass to grow, and made their ward's inhabitants pay to cut it. Three remote wards built a primary school with money raised this way.

Conclusion

It is too early to say if the type of organization of the territory introduced by the Maoists in Deurali will last or not. This reflects the growing importance of the ward, which has progressively become not only a significant administrative unit, but also a major territorial pattern used to identify belongingness, and even, in many cases, a distinct ritual unit. We may formulate the hypothesis that the growing importance of the ward is due to its political neutrality on the one hand, and to its "human dimension" on the other. Indeed in Deurali, well-known Congress supporters were nominated as the head of wards during the People's War, notwithstanding their political affiliation, because of their management skills. The wards were small enough in spatial and human terms[28] to create a strong sense of solidarity among their residents. They clearly expressed that paying their ward council for cutting grass was a way of improving their own daily life in that it financed the construction of new community infrastructures. Proximity with council members led to people trusting them: they had a good idea of their ward's management by mastering its source of finance as well as its use since money was not invested in large-scale or external projects.

The future importance of the areas (*ilaka*) is less ascertained, as this relied mainly on the fearsome organization represented by its head, and from which the In-charge received clear support through visits from Maoist leaders, as well as by the coming and going of numerous activist strangers. The exact occupation of these was not known to villagers, who had thereby less knowledge and control of the global administrative network of which they were made a part. In these circumstances, they placed their trust in the ward council's politics of proximity.

Faced with the new set of Maoist rules, the villagers of Deurali offered no arguments to protect their traditional cultural and religious practices against charges that they were superstitious. They just complied until traditions were authorized back. By contrast, they did react immediately to the decisions concerning their natural and economic resources, as they viewed themselves as more competent in this matter than the stranger in charge of their area, who, they said, did not "know the village." They were probably right, in that she was trying to apply a form of collectivization that was perhaps suitable to her region of origin, Rolpa, where villages are dense and where pastureland abounds as the population density is low, without taking into consideration the specificities of a place like Deurali, where houses are extremely scattered and most land is cultivated.

In Deurali, the Maoist organization finally succeeded in introducing some collective structures but only to exploit common land at the smallest scale – that of the wards, and only when people had the feeling that they were the masters of their own destiny and to be relieved from what some called "a long nightmare."

Notes

1 Restricting to the facts reported in Maoist writings is a way of avoiding what could be "reactionary" misinformation.

2 In *Janaawaj* 1 (39–40), December 2002, "the Magarant autonomous region" is said to have been established by the CPN-M, but the government of the Magarant comprises members of the CPN-M, as well as of the Magarant National Liberation Front. The latter is clearly affiliated with the former but there is still a slight difference in their approach, as one ethnic leader says: "we are fighting for ethnic liberation and the CPN-M is fighting for class liberation." The Magarant's government includes: a chief, a vice-chief, a secretary, a head of the PLA, a head of the militia, and an assembly of elected representatives. *Janadesh* 14 (30), 5 July 2005, announced that elections were organized in June 2005 in all the localities of the ten "special districts," whereas the old government did not have the means to do so. This information is not true about the district where Deurali is located, even on Maoist fringe.

3 The Magarant is a vast region, including districts of Rapti zone (Rolpa, Pyuthan, Salyan, Rukum), Dhaulagiri zone (Mustang, Baglung), Lumbini zone (Gulmi, Arghakhanci, Palpa) and the mountainous part of Nawalparasi, as well as some parts of Syangja and Tanahun districts, or "the mountainous region located between the Kaligandaki and the Bheri rivers," *Janadesh* 13 (47), 9 November 2004.

4 Risiraj Baral, secretary to the People's Great Cultural Association, quoted in *Janadesh* 14 (39), 6 September 2005. Ganesh Bhandari (2005) states: "the non-scientific and declining culture must be torn out by the roots and a new, fresh and improved scientific culture shall be implemented." The latter includes: "Marxism-Leninism-Maoism and the Prachandapath, the history of communist parties and of the revolts."

5 *Janadesh* 14 (34), 2 August 2005, also published a long text criticizing pop music by Bhim Kumakhi. Some actions along these lines have been carried out, such as the destruction of NTV archives in Palpa, *Janadesh* 14 (24), 24 May 2005.

6 In *Janadesh* 15 (3), 6 December 2005, M. Dhital reports on the transformation of an altar into a martyr memorial in Sinja. At this spot the victory of Pilli (Kalikot) was celebrated for five days. "During this celebration, no *dhami* [medium] danced, no one manipulated sacred rice in a superstitious manner. No one spent money on the banners" and the journalist concludes: "it's a great change to see people ready to move the altars, in the Karnali."

7 Referring first to a "correction house," he then uses the term "forced labor camps," suggesting that besides their schooling "culprits" probably also had to work (Dayamand 2004).

8 *Janadesh* 14 (42), 27 September 2005: they were sentenced "according to sub-section 4 of section 4 of part 4 of 'the collection of laws of democratic Nepal 2060'," indicating that the code of law had been used in certain regions since its drafting. Journalists and human rights activists were present at the tribunal, and a lawyer defended the culprits.

9 "Janatadvara mrtyudanda phaisala," *Janadesh*, 13 (21), 20 April 2004.

10 A report published in *Janadesh* 14 (34), 2 August 2005.

11 "Shahid park ra suddhikaran" (Martyr park and purification), *Janadesh* 14 (28), 21 June 2005.

12 Thus, the People's Medical College of Butwal trained groups of 75 persons over 45 days at basic level, and two higher levels were also provided. As in all other fields, the Party's structures were presented as the best: "Patients who were not cured in great hospitals were cured in Maoist hospitals: this increases the people's confidence," *Janadesh* 14 (34), 2 August 2005.

13 See Om Sharma's article in *Janadesh* 15 (7), 3 January 2006: "Comrade Janak, who went to school only two days in his life, was trained in the Engineering department. His team makes thousands of grenades and hundreds of weapons. Comrade Avir, a member of this team, declares: 'My hands are all burnt, my eyes became weak. I have blisters. But while handing the hammer . . . we recall the martyrs and we internalize the Prachandapath.'"

14 Thus, Bhakta Bahadur Pun in *Janadesh* 14 (42), 27 September 2005, reports that a group of 47 political activists were taught ambush techniques and how to make grenades.

15 She followed a two-week session in spring 2005, with the following teachers: Divakar on political science, Ravindra on political economy and military science, Sudarsan on ideology, Sunil on scientific socialism, Pasang on military science, Namuna on women's movement.

16 *Janadesh* 15 (8), 1 January 2006.

17 The commune owns ten goats, eight buffaloes and 40 cows, as well as a lot of land, but one member says that their production is low. They also exploit a stone mine.

18 See K. B. Bhandari 2006.

19 This commune, we are told, is different from the others because it includes Dalits, Ksetris, Magars and one Chaudhari (or Tharu), suggesting that in other cases, communes are not multi-ethnic/caste.

20 It amounts to 1,000 kilograms of rice, 2,400 kilograms of maize and 1,200 kilograms of wheat, or altogether four quintal and a half of cereals.

21 It also describes the Juni commune of Kalikot in similar terms.

22 H.P. Sharma (2005). Another article, published in *Janadesh* 14 (34), 2 August 2005, refers to two other cooperatives in Rolpa, producing respectively bananas and stones. In Jajarkot, a wool cooperative where 15 workers make sweaters, shawls and gloves started in 2001. Two other examples of small cooperatives described by Upendra Sharma in Kalikot show that they were formed in each case by four or five families of the same clan. *Janadesh* 13 (22), 27 April 2004.

23 On this subject, see Lecomte-Tilouine, forthcoming.

24 It was formed by three musicians and one dance teacher who taught revolutionary songs and dances to three schoolchildren from the neighborhood who had been abducted for training by the party. No one spoke to these children, nor tried to know from where and when they were abducted. During my stay in 2005, three other teenagers, studying at the school in Deurali, were taken away for such training elsewhere and seven abducted two months before had still not come back.

25 On the day of my departure in 2005, six householders from the hamlet where I was residing were summoned by the People's Government to pay 10,000 rupees each for having a son in the army or the police. In 2006, a villager whose son was in the police told me that he had given a total of 38,000 rupees to the Village People's Government during the preceding years.

26 On the history of agriculture, see Lecomte-Tilouine and Michaud 2000.

27 Most of the villagers used to send the cattle with an elder or a teenager for two months at the lower part of the slope and two months at its summit. In addition to the closure of the forest, the creation of a high school in 1987 gradually reduced the practice and political violence after 1990 made villagers fearful to send someone alone to a shed.

28 Both the size and population varies from one ward to another: densely populated ones are smaller and include between 200 and 500 people.

Bibliography

All the *Janadesh* issues quoted below are available at cpnm.org

Anonymous. 2004. "Janatadvara mrtyudanda phaisala" (Sentenced to death by the people), *Janadesh*, 13 (21), April 20, 2004.

Anpe Kancha. 2005. "Adhar kshetrako raksha ra vikas sambandhana" (About the development and the protection of the base region), *Janadesh* 14 (28), 21 June.

Bhandari, Ganesh. 2005. "Samanti pratigaman, loktantra ra samskritik andolan" (Opposition to feudalism, democracy and Cultural Revolution), *Janadesh*, 14 (42), 27 September.

Bhandari, Khil bahadur. 2005. "Adharkshetra bhitra adhunik kheti pranalisangai samuhikatako samskriti" (With scientific method of farming, the culture of collectivity in the base region), *Janadesh* 14 (34), 2 August.

Bhandari, Khil bahadur –. 2006. "Nivargiyatako samaj banirahecha: Balidan janakamyun" (Creation of a society without class: the Self-Sacrifice People's Commune), *Janadesh* 15 (9), 17 January.

Dayamand. 2004. [interview by Upendra Sharma], "Jana adalat bhaneko jantako khula adalat ho" (The People's tribunal are tribunals open to the people), *Janadesh* 13 (8), 20 January.

Dhital, Manarishi. 2004. "Jajarkotko Juni Kamyun ra Rolpako Ajambari kamyun" (The Juni Commune of Jajarkot and the Ajambari Commune of Rolpa), *Janadesh* 13 (15), 9 March.

Kunvar, Cetan. 2005. "Janamilisyaharu ke gardeichan?" (what are the people's militia doing?), *Janadesh* 14 (45), 15 November.

Lecomte-Tilouine, Marie. Forthcoming. "Terror in a Maoist Model Village, mid-western Nepal, in J. Pettigrew and A. Shah eds.

Lecomte-Tilouine, Marie and Catherine Michaud. 2000. "From the mine to the fields" in P. Ramirez ed. *Resunga, the Mountain of the Horned Sage*, Kathmandu, Himal Publications.

Majhi, Surya. 2005. "Aitihasik abhiyankai bicma kalamka sahayatri gumaepachi" (After the loss of a fellow-writer in an historic expedition", *Janadesh* 14 (42), 27 September.

Malla, Kumar. 2006. "Abhyasta sipahi, srasta ra rato tara" (Trained soldiers, creation and red stars), *Janadesh* 15 (10), 24 January.

Roka, Kamala. 2005. "Kendriya skulingle aitihasik shikshaharu" (Historic teachings at the Central Schooling), *Janadesh* 14 (40), 13 September.

Sharma, H. P. 2005. "Rolpama badhdaichan sahakari hotelharu"(Cooperative hotels are increasing in Rolpa), *Janadesh* 14 (35), 9 August.

Sharma, Shila. 2005. "Rolpama yuddhasangai vikas" (In Rolpa, development with war), *Janadesh* 15 (2), 29 November.

Simha, Purna Bahadur. 2005. "Adhar ilakama saisksik krantibare choto carca" (A brief description of the teaching revolution in the base region), *Janadesh* 14 (42), 27 September.

Visva. 2005a. "Kamyunist sangathanma anushasanko prasna" (The question of discipline in the Communist organization), *Janadesh* 14 (41), 20 September.

Visva. 2005b. [interview by Govinda Acarya], "Janayuddha kunai yatra hoina, yo ta nirantar utsaha ra utsavako yatra ho" (The People's War is not just any journey, it is a journey of endless energy and rejoicing), *Janadesh* 14 (42), 27 September 2005.

Part IV
Ethnic dimension

7 Ethnic dimensions of the Maoist insurgencies

Indigenous groups' participation and insurgency trajectories in Nepal, Peru, and India

Mahendra Lawoti[1]

Despite the discrediting of communism after the end of the Cold War, Maoist insurgencies have grown in some parts of the world.[2] An important dimension of these communist rebellions was the significant participation of indigenous groups. Why do indigenous groups participate in such avowedly class-based insurgencies? What are the consequences of participation on the trajectory of the insurgencies? I look at the insurgencies in Nepal, Peru, and India, the more successful and enduring Maoist insurgencies in the past several decades, to examine these questions more closely. Apart from the similarity of initial high ethnic participation, the three insurgencies developed varied relationships with the indigenous groups. Furthermore, the insurgencies' trajectories also varied – from termination to eventually joining a government as an influential partner and eventually winning the post-conflict election. This chapter investigates the attitudes and policies of both the state and insurgencies towards indigenous groups in order to explain their varied participation in and resulting varied trajectories of the insurgencies. An investigation of the ethnic dimension of violent class-based rebellions is important for understanding the growth of Maoist insurgencies even in the changed circumstances of a post-Cold War world.

Class-based insurgencies and violent ethnic conflicts

The world has primarily seen two types of insurgencies: class-based insurgencies guided by Marxist ideology and led by communist organizations and violent ethnic conflicts spurred by ethnic and nationalist aspirations. Extensive mobilization is necessary for insurgencies to become viable and have a wide impact. Both communist and ethnic leaders attempt to mobilize as many people as possible but they are only able to mobilize certain sections of the population with particular sets of grievances and aspirations.

Gurr (1968) argued that relative deprivation defined as the gap between expectation and achievement or the perceived deprivation could frustrate people and lead them to violent conflict. Muller and Seligson (1987), on the other hand, argue that income inequality is the cause of violent conflicts. On similar line, others have argued that inequality in land distribution is the cause of violent conflict (Russett 1964). Economic inequalities, either real or perceived, could fuel class-based violent conflicts. Scholars have pointed out, on the other hand, that political and cultural discrimination, exclusionary national ideologies, loss of autonomy and ethnic geography, group history, repression and other related factors contribute toward mobilizing ethnic groups (Gurr 1993, 2000; Brown 2001). Ethnic insurgencies are known to mobilize both rich and poor members of the communities.

Communists have traditionally focused on class inequalities and not attached much importance to ethnic grievances. Many reject nationalist aspirations outright. Communist movements, however, often encounter nationalist groups while mobilizing larger masses. The "national question" bogged down the Marxists from early on, and they interpreted it as "the social consequences of capitalism, or more generally from economic motivations and economic change" (Smith 1998: 47). Even when the "national question" was reluctantly recognized, the Marxists have often subordinated it to the issue of class. Some, like Hechter (1999), attempted to explain the nationalist movements as arising from regional and economic inequalities while others have argued that nationalism reflects "imagined communities" (Anderson 1991).

Despite claims of being classed-based, mobilizations by communist organizations nevertheless have been influenced by ethnic dynamics. Scholars have noted that, more often than not, communist parties are dominated by particular ethnic groups, and are naturally influenced by the interests of that group. Horowitz (1985: 9–10) recorded the domination of communist parties by different ethnic groups in various countries: by Ansaris in the Sudan, by Sinhalese in Sri Lanka, by Javanese in Indonesia, by Greeks in Cyprus, by Chinese in Malaysia, and by different groups in different states in India. Despite their abhorrence of ethnic/nationalist movements, the communists could not rise above their own ethnic boundaries, and failed to universally mobilize different ethnic groups.

The end of Cold War witnessed the decline of class-based and communist-led violent mass mobilizations. Some successful Maoist insurgencies, however, have emerged in this period. How did they overcome adverse historical conditions? Did mobilization of ethnic groups allow such communist movements to grow and remain relevant? I attempt to answer these questions by looking at reasonably successful Maoist movements with varied ethnic participation.

Despite the seeming contradiction, mobilization of ethnic groups by communist insurgencies should not be a very difficult adjustment, provided the communists conduct an ideological shift to recognize ethnic identities and nationalist movements. Often, class oppression and ethnic exclusion share a sizeable overlap. If the two types of grievances are mobilized within a single rebellion, the resulting movements could become powerful.

Some have argued that an exclusionary polity fuels rebellions (Goodwin and Skocpol 1989). This framework could be used to analyze ethnic exclusion and its contribution to class-based insurgencies. The recognition of ethnic grievances and ethnic mobilization, however, is a new phenomenon in communist movements and hence there is a dearth of studies on the subject. Studies of communist insurgencies and movements to date lack a systematic analysis of ethnic group participation and its impact on the trajectory of the insurgencies. Where they exist, such works have analyzed the pre-1990 communist parties and movements (for example, Scalapino 1969). Scholarship on country-specific Maoist insurgencies has looked at participation of indigenous groups, but systematic comparative analyses are lacking.

This study aims to fill a number of gaps. First, it conducts a comparative analysis of the Maoist movement. Second, the study looks at the effect of ethnic participation in violent communist rebellions. Comparative studies have generally analyzed either class-based insurgencies or violent ethnic conflicts but not mobilization of both class and ethnic grievances together. This study aims to analyze them jointly through a systematic comparison of participation of indigenous groups in Maoist insurgencies in India, Nepal, and Peru.[3] I look at the attitudes of the Maoists and the state, the principal opposing parties in insurgencies, towards indigenous groups, and seek to uncover linkages, if any, between the attitudes and trajectories of the insurgencies. Third, this study analyzes a particular subset within ethnic groups – the indigenous peoples. It seeks to understand why indigenous groups participate in the violent insurgencies, and with what consequences.

Insurgencies and indigenous people in Nepal, Peru, and India

The oldest Maoist insurgency, among the countries compared here, began in India in 1967. The Naxalbari (the movement is known as Naxalite) uprising occurred in

Table 7.1 Evolution of the Maoist rebellions in the 1990s and early twenty-first century in Nepal, Peru, and India

	Nepal	*Peru*	*India*
1990	—	War	Minor
1991	—	War	Minor
1992	—	War	Minor
1993	—	War	Minor
1994	—	Intermediate	Minor
1995	—	Intermediate	Minor
1996	Minor	Intermediate	Minor
1997	Minor	Intermediate	Minor
1998	Minor	Intermediate	Minor
1999	Minor	Intermediate	Minor
2000	Minor	— (Terminated)	Minor
2001	Intermediate	—	Minor
2002	War	—	Intermediate
2003	War	—	Intermediate
2004	War	—	Intermediate
2005	War	—	Intermediate
2006	Minor	—	Minor

Source: UCD, accessed on September 16, 2007.

Note: UCD ranked 2006 as *Minor* for India, probably owing to there being fewer than 25 deaths in the year, but its detailed report says the insurgency was growing.

the state of West Bengal. The tribal group, Santals, participated significantly in the uprising. Even though the uprising was suppressed by the state, many other indigenous tribal groups have participated in other Maoist uprisings since then: the Kols, Mundas, and Orans of east India, Bhils and Meos of the north, and Koyas and Girijans in the south (Banerjee 1984: 9–10; Duyker 1987: 175). The Naxalbari movement went on to establish the revolutionary Communist Party of India-Marxist-Leninist, which was formed on April 22, 1969.[4] For a considerable time the movements did not grow significantly. According to University of Uppsala's Uppsala Conflict Database (UCD) (Uppsala Conflict Data Program 2007), the conflict reached an *Intermediate* level in 2002, after being categorized as minor till 2001 (see table 7.1).[5] By 2004, the Naxalite or the Indian Maoists affected 125 districts in 12 of 28 Indian states (such as Andhra Pradesh, Bihar, Jharkhand, Madhya Pradesh, Orissa, Chhatisgarh, and Maharastra) and the government suspected another 24 districts were being "targeted."[6] The rebellions were largely confined to forested tribal regions. The MCC and PWG merged in 2004, becoming the Communist Party of India-Maoists (CPI-M), heralding perhaps a more concerted rebellion in a hitherto fragmented movement.

The Shining Path or the Maoist rebellion in Peru began from the Quechua-speaking indigenous regions of Ayacucho, Apurimac, and Huancavelica of southern Andes in 1980 with considerable support from the indigenous groups (Isbell 1994; Palmer 1994; Starn 1995).[7] A philosophy professor and his followers, including student recruits, formed a base at a newly reopened university at Ayacucho and launched the insurgency. It has been estimated that 30,000 persons died from the hostilities during the 1980–95 period (Ron 2001). The UCD categorized the Shining Path insurgency as *War* from 1989 to 1993 and *Intermediate* from 1994 to 1999. The UCD considered the insurgency terminated in 2000.[8] Even though the Shining Path lost much influence since the mid-1990s, it affected large parts of rural Peru as well as its capital, Lima, during its peak years.

The Maoist insurgency in Nepal began in February 1996 and rapidly broadened its influence to most regions of the country. It began with significant participation of the Kham Magars, an indigenous group inhabiting the mid-western hill districts of Nepal (Lawoti 2003; de Sales 2003). The UCD categorized the Nepali insurgency as *Minor* from 1996 to 2000, *Intermediate* in 2001, and *War* since 2002. More than 13,000 persons were killed. The Maoists reached a settlement with the government and signed a comprehensive peace treaty in November 2006. The Maoists joined the Parliament in 2007 after keeping its combatants and arms in cantonments under UNMIN (United Nations Mission in Nepal) supervision and joined the government in early April 2007. They emerged as the largest party in the Constituent Assembly election held in April 2008 and are leading a coalition government since August 2008. Based on the influence across the country during the insurgency and post-conflict electoral success, the Nepali insurgency is the most successful among the three insurgencies.

Nepal, Peru, and India: similarities and differences

In addition to indigenous groups' participation, all the three Maoist insurgencies have a number of other similarities to make them comparable. All the three countries were open and democratic when the insurgencies were launched. The rebels had the option to use the electoral path to pursue their political objectives. India had the longer democratic experience of two decades when the Naxalite rebellion began. Nepal had six years of democratic practice. The Shining Path rebellion began in Peru the same year democratic elections were held after the end of a military regime.

Table 7.2 The Maoist insurgencies in Nepal, Peru, and India

	Nepal	*Peru*	*India*
Rank based on influence at movement's height	1	2	3
Highest level reached in UCD ranking	War, 2002–5	War, till 1993	Intermediate, 2002–5
People killed	13,000 (1996–2006)	30,000 (1980–1999)	6000 (up to 2007)
Status, 2008	Settlement in 2006, heading government since 2008	Declared terminated in 2000 by UCD	Ongoing, growing
Indigenous people's participation	Yes	Yes initially, resistance later	Yes, occasional resistance
Size of indigenous groups in the countries in percent	36	45	7.5
Diversity	Ethnic, linguistic, caste, religious	Ethnic, linguistic, religious	Ethnic, linguistic, caste, religious
Governance effectiveness, 1999 (higher index = more effective)	–0.95	0.11	0.91
Military expenditure percentage of GDP, 2004 (actual)	1.5 (99.2 millions)	1.5 (829.3 millions)	2.5 (16.98 billions)
Population, 2005	27,676,547	27,925,628	1,080,264,388
Area in km^2	147,181	1,285,220	3,287,590
Rugged terrain, forests	Yes	Yes	Yes
Literacy %, 2003	45.2	90.9	59.5
GDP per capita in PPP in US$, 2004	1,500	5,600	3,100
GNP per capita in US$ in years close or start of the insurgencies	141 (1995)	730 (1979)	150 (1976)

Source: UCD (2007), World Bank (2007), and CIA (2007)

All three are developing countries, suggesting that all of them faced the challenge of poverty (see table 7.2). The World Bank categorizes India and Nepal as low-income countries and Peru as a middle-income country. Nepal had the lowest GDP (gross domestic product) per capita in purchasing power parity in 2004 at $1,500, while Peru and India had $5,600 and $3,100 respectively. At the time of initiation of respective insurgencies or in years close by, the GNP (gross national product) per capita in US dollars was $150 in 1976 for India, $730 in 1979 for Peru and $141 in 1995 for Nepal (World Bank 2007).

All three countries are very diverse culturally. They have different mixtures of ethnic, linguistic, and religious groups. India and Nepal are more internally diverse with multiple religious, linguistic, ethnic/nationalities, and caste groups while Peru is diverse ethnically and linguistically. All the three countries have rugged terrain and/or forests (see table 7.2).

All three countries had well-established communist parties. In Peru and Nepal, the Maoists were marginal communist factions at the time they began their insurgencies. In India, the Maoists split off from a larger communist party. The existence of communist parties,who have long argued in favor of violent rebellion for transforming society, meant that the discourse of violent rebellions existed in the three countries. Apter (1997) has argued that violent discourses legitimize violence when it occurs.

The similarities make the countries comparable while differences in other aspects allow for teasing out factors that were active in producing varied trajectories of the insurgencies. In India, the Maoist insurgency was repressed in West Bengal, the place of origin, but spread in other regions. The growth, however, has been slow. In Peru, the Shining Path grew rapidly initially but began to falter by the mid-1980s and lost much influence by early 1990s; the UCD labeled it terminated in 2000. In Nepal, the Maoists spread all over the country, though their influence in the urban areas was less during the insurgency years. The Nepali Maoists are leading a coalition government since August 2008. It is the most successful Maoist insurgency in the past few decades.

India is a federal country while both Peru and Nepal were unitary states. Among the three, Nepal was the most centralized state while India was the most decentralized.[9] India and Peru have more effective states compared to Nepal. The State Failure Task Force labeled India as being more effective in governance in 1990 (0.13) and 1999 (0.91) than Peru and Nepal (higher score mean higher effectiveness). Peru obtained middle positions in both years, 1990 (–1.00) and 1999 (0.11). Nepal had negative score in both years, 1990 (–1.06) and 1999 (–0.95) (State Failure Task Force 2000).

India has the largest and the strongest military. Its wars with China and Pakistan led the country to strengthen defensive capabilities. Its military expenditure in 2004 was 2.5 percent of GDP while Nepal's and Peru's expenditures were 1.5 percent. Peru's military is also experienced. It has fought wars with it neighbors and it was beefed up by the military regimes. On the other hand, the Nepali military is weak and has been called ceremonial (Mehta 2005). It has not fought any war for nearly two centuries. Its size and capabilities were, however, increased after 2002.

Attitudes and behaviors of the state and Maoists

Attitudes of the state towards indigenous groups

Among the three countries, the Indian state has been more positive toward the indigenous groups in terms of recognition and specific public policies. It has provided quotas to indigenous groups in political offices, administration, and educational institutions. The Indian state is secular and more multicultural than the others and contributed in fostering tolerance towards minorities. The government recognized many nationalist movements' demands and created new states or gave more autonomy in, for example, the Northeast and Tamil Nadu, Andhra Pradhesh and Punjab (Kohli 1997). The Tribal Advisory Councils were instituted to involve indigenous groups in governance that affect them. India has formally protected land rights of the indigenous groups. The problem, however, lies in implementation. For instance, alienation of tribal lands continues, often under the guise of industrialization and development (Sarma 2006).

Some regional governments' policies have positively affected the indigenous population. West Bengal's moderate communist government initiated large-scale land reforms that benefited the tribal population as well. On the negative side, the state has killed innocent indigenous groups in its actions against the Naxalites but since India is a better-functioning democracy with active civil society and since India has primarily relied upon the police in its counter-insurgency activities, it may have engaged in less brutality and fewer killings than Nepal and Peru.

The Peruvian state is moderately positive toward the indigenous groups. Peru has conducted major structural reforms; the military regime initiated the second largest land reforms in Latin America after Cuba in the 1970s that benefited the indigenous groups as well. The termination of haciendas gave the indigenous groups access to landed resources (Yashar 2005). However, the hill indigenous groups did not benefit as much as the coastal people owing to fewer large landholdings in the mountains (McClintock 1984). Peru also initiated legal reforms that have recognized the "informal" enterprises of the poor migrants in urban areas. De Soto (2002) argues that it facilitated providing poor entrepreneurs with opportunities, depriving the Maoists of their support base. Corporatist policies also provided the indigenous groups with some autonomy. Formal linguistic rights of the groups were protected even though in practice they have not yielded much positive result. In 2002, the state required political parties to nominate 15 percent of electoral candidates from the indigenous groups of the Amazon, whom the state recognizes as native communities (Htun 2004). The quota, however, is not applicable to the less mobilized but more numerous indigenous groups from the Andes. The representation of the indigenous groups in the influential decision-making institutions is still weak. The Peruvian state initiated some policies that addressed certain indigenous concerns. With regard to coercive methods, the Peruvian state's role appears to be mixed. Initially it engaged in killing villagers suspected to be Maoists, but later on provided arms, training and support when the indigenous groups asked for them to resist the Shining Path (Degregori 1998; Starn 1995).

The Nepali state's attitude, on the other hand, was negative. It was the least accommodative among the three countries. Even though the 1990 Constitution recognized the multicultural nature of the society and was better than the Panchayat Constitution, cultural discrimination continued through various articles of the Constitution (Lawoti 2005). The state was declared Hindu, and the Khas-Nepali language was provided with special privileges over other native languages. Most of the public holidays and state-declared national heroes were "high caste" hill Hindus. The royal government announced reservations in educational institutions and administration in 2003 but political reservation was not awarded. Land rights of the indigenous groups were not recognized. In fact, indigenous land rights were taken away by the land reforms in the 1960s through the abolition of *Kipat,* communal landownership (Caplan 2000; Forbes 1999). The Tharus and other Tarai indigenous nationalities were displaced by Madhesi encroachment but primarily by hill migrants after the government-instituted resettlement policy that encouraged migration to the Tarai in the 1950s after malaria was eradicated (Guneratne 2002; Gaige 1975). Unlike in India, the Constitution banned ethnic parties, constraining political mobilization of the indigenous and other disadvantaged groups.[10] During the insurgency, the state, controlled by the dominant groups, suspected indigenous groups of being sympathetic towards the insurgency and disproportionately "disappeared" and killed them in counter-insurgency activities (OHCHR 2008).

Attitudes of the Maoists towards indigenous groups

Class-based rebellions might frame issues to attract and mobilize marginalized indigenous groups. They might extend solidarity, raise indigenous demands, and promise to fulfill the groups' demands after the revolution. The Nepali Maoists raised many issues of the indigenous groups such as language equality, secularity of the state, and self-determination rights. The Maoists also formed various ethnic fronts and declared autonomous ethnic regions. They launched campaigns against the caste system and ethnic prejudice and resisted imposition of compulsory Sanskrit in schools, a language alien to most indigenous groups. Among the mainstream political forces, the Maoists were the most positive towards issues important to the indigenous peoples (Thapa and Sijapati 2003; Lawoti 2007; Tamang 2006; Shneiderman and Turin 2003; de Sales 2003).

The violent activities of the Maoists affected the indigenous groups but as the Nepali Maoists engaged in selective violence, they did not generate widespread resistance (Weinstein 2007). The Maoists killed fewer indigenous people than the state. From 1996 to 2005, of the killed who were identified along ethnic/caste lines, 28 percent of Maoist victims were indigenous while it was 40 percent in the case of the state (INSEC 2008).

The Indian Maoists have also incorporated the issues of indigenous groups in their policies and programs. They have raised the grievances of tribal living in the forested areas of Central India, including rights on forest and land-based resources. They have accepted the self-determination of tribal people, including self-determination rights to secede (Dasgupta 2005). Indian Maoists supported the

Table 7.3 State and Maoist attitudes toward indigenous groups (IG) and their consequences on conflict in India, Peru, and Nepal

Country	Attitude of the state toward IG	Attitudes of the Maoists toward IG	Consequences	
			IG participation in rebellion	Conflict status
India	Highly positive – land rights protected; secular state; quotas to IG; linguistic and ethnic/national federal division; weakness in implementation of laws protecting IG rights	Positive – fighting to end inequalities toward IG; support to nationalist movements; recognition of right to secede	Considerable in some regions; occasional resistance; erosion of support in few areas	Conflict continues after three decades; evolved to intermediate level in 2002 in UCD ranking; growing
Peru	Fairly positive – Amazon IG recognized (not Andean); language rights formally protected; quotas in political parties for Amazon IG; massive land reforms	Somewhat positive initially but rejection of IG culture and values at later stage	Initial participation, widespread resistance at later stage	Shining Path influence declined after achieving considerable growth; UCD termed conflict terminated by 2000
Nepal	Negative during insurgency – Hindu State; no reservation; ethnic parties banned; formal discrimination; land alienation	Highly positive – recognition of self-determination rights; declaration of autonomous ethnic regions; support to ending Hindu state and Hindu caste chauvinism	High participation	Insurgency grew rapidly; Maoists signed a comprehensive peace agreement in November 2006; joined interim government in April 2007 and lead a coalition government since August 2008

nationalities struggles in Chhatisgarh, Jharkhand, Tamil Nadu and elsewhere during the 1980s (Mohanty 2005). Among the 38 points in the party program of the Communist Party of India (Marxist-Leninist) adopted in 1970, one was clearly worded to support the rights of indigenous peoples:

> In the name of "national integration" these enemies of the people have been suppressing the genuine rights of all the nationalities and national and religious minorities. The right to self-determination is being denied to the Kashmiris, Nagas and Mizos. Equal status to all the national languages is being denied and Hindi is sought to be imposed on the people by them.
>
> (Duyker 1987: 175)

The Indian Maoists also resorted to popular actions such as moving against the rich money lenders and engaging in development activities in tribal areas. Mohanty (2006: 3164–65) argues that overall the Indian Maoists' ideological formulation on the issue of class, caste, tribe (indigenous), gender and religion, however, was less adequately developed than that of their Nepali counterparts.

Human rights organizations report that the indigenous groups in India suffered occasionally from Maoist violence. ACHR (2006) reported that 70 indigenous people were killed by the Maoists in 1992–93 to repress the indigenous rebellion against them. The participation of some indigenous group members in self-defense groups in Chhattisgarh state suggests that some indigenous people could have been pushed towards it by Maoist violence.

In Peru, initially the Shining Path's class-oriented activities such as punishing cattle thieves and drunkards and killing rich farmers rhymed well with the indigenous groups' class-based grievances (Isbell 1994). However, the party's position became antagonistic to local culture and traditions soon after. The party replaced communal authorities with its commissars and ignored the communal decision-making processes (Degregori 1998; Isbell 1994). Writings of Guzman, the supreme leader of the Shining Path, and party policies rejected local values, practices, and traditions. Guzman attempted to impose "scientific" aspects of Marxism and denigrated the cultural traditions and values of the indigenous groups.[11] Orin Starn labels it as the "refusal of history":

> ... the writings of the Shining Path founder stand out for the total lack of interest, or even mention, of the distinctive textures of Andean life. A dependence on the Maoist typology of poor, middle and rich peasants substitutes for an engagement in the politics of language for Quechua and Aymara-speaking villagers ...
>
> (Starn 1995: 414)

The Shining Path increasingly employed coercive methods against the indigenous communities, beyond killing the village elite. People were killed for demonstration affect, to discourage opposition (Marks 1996). According to Degregori (1998: 147), while the military demolished communities up to 1988, the Shining Path was engaged in rampages in later years. It was involved in at least 16 massacres of 12 or more persons between December 1987 and February 1992.

Consequences of differential attitudes and policies

Indigenous groups' participation

The indigenous groups are economically and culturally marginalized and perceive their identity and survival to be under threat (Gurr 2000, 1993). Extremes of marginalization and neglect by the state may increase their alienation and attract them towards the radical promises of rebels. Davidhieser (1992) argues that vulnerable groups may join revolutions because breakdown of stability makes them fluid and open to new worldviews and values. The discrimination, marginalization, and vulnerability occurred at different levels in the three countries and they pushed the indigenous groups toward the Maoists at different rates in the three countries.

Horowitz's (1985) notion of ranked and unranked ethnic group system suggests that indigenous groups may participate in rebellions at a higher rate. In a ranked system, groups are situated in a hierarchical ordering. Some groups are subordinate while others dominate and social class is based on ethnicity. All or most members of a group are either below or above most members of other groups. On the other hand, in an unranked system groups are not subordinate or super-ordinate – they are more or less parallel. All groups have an elite as well as a lower class in an unranked system. Horowitz argues that violent ethnic conflicts may be more frequent in unranked systems because members of different groups compete with each other for resources, status and domination. The ranked system may often be stable, on the other hand, because members of a group do not compete with members of others groups as the hierarchy divides them. However, when the ranked system encounters changes, it often witnesses social revolutions because the dominated group seeks to thoroughly overhaul the political and social structure. The indigenous-dominant group relationships in the three countries are closer to ranked systems as the indigenous groups are subordinated socio-culturally and economically. This subordinate position may have attracted the indigenous groups to the rebellions that espoused total transformation of the society.

The indigenous group in the three countries participated in insurgencies at varying levels in varying phases, depending upon the attitudes and behaviors of the state and the Maoists. In Peru, the indigenous group was initially attracted toward the insurgency owing to the norms of economic justice. The Shining Path punished "public enemies" such as cattle thieves, new rich peasants, and drunkards. The poor indigenous peasants sympathized with these acts and the less-educated youth participated in the rebellion (Isbell 1994; Berg 1994). However, even at the initial stages the indigenous participation in the leadership level was weak. Starn (1995) writes that the cadres were filled with dark-skinned indigenous Indians while the leadership was composed of lighter-skinned Peruvians.

The initial support soon turned sour, however. The Shining Path did not recognize community authority, demanded regular supplies of food, and closed down markets and fairs (Isbell 1994). The rejection of local culture, tradition, and values, and attempts to impose non-local values and violence against community members alienated the indigenous groups. It pushed the indigenous community to form civil defense groups to resist the Shining Path. Mallon (1998) writes that the outside leftist workers in Peru succeeded in mobilizing the indigenous communities during the land invasion movements in the 1970s in areas where they adapted to communities' tradition and failed where the outsiders did not respect local ways. Similar dynamics may have occurred between the indigenous group and the Shining Path. The army trained and supported the civil resistance groups but the indigenous groups were clearly taking initiatives to defend their communities (Degregori 1998; Starn 1995).

State attitudes and behaviors also affect participation of people in rebellions, either by creating conditions for joining insurgencies, remaining neutral, or resisting them. The attitudes and policies of the Peruvian state, for instance, contributed in turning the indigenous groups against the Shining Path. The Peruvian state was reasonably responsive to the indigenous groups. The massive land reforms the state conducted initially did not prevent the indigenous groups from supporting the insurgency, partly because it had not affected the highland indigenous groups significantly owing to the availability of less land for redistribution in the Andean hills (McClintock 1984), but when the attraction toward the Shining Path wore off, the indigenous groups found the state relatively more bearable and responsive. Further, the state initiated massive economic development projects in the insurgency-affected regions that reduced poverty considerably (McClintock 1984). Even in the formation of civil defense groups, the state's role was significant. It provided training as well as arms. These activities put the state in a favorable light, and among the two competing entities the indigenous groups chose the group they perceived as beneficial to them. The Peruvian case more clearly illustrates the agency of the indigenous groups. Initially they supported the Shining Path, hoping it would address their marginalization, but once they lost hope from the Shining Path, which began to impose its Marxist values on them, often employing violent means, the indigenous groups turned to the state that had initiated reforms in the past and was willing to do so again.

The indigenous participation in the Maoist insurgency in Nepal was very high.[12] The participation is significant because indigenous participation in other mainstream political parties is much lower. The Maoists have included the indigenous people in higher numbers at the middle and higher middle level leadership than the mainstream parliamentary political parties (Lawoti 2003). The people's government of the Maoists at the village, district, and regional levels had many indigenous members. Even though the Caste Hill Hindu Elite (CHHE) still dominate top leadership, a few indigenous peoples were in the politburo of the party. Among the three countries, the available information shows that the Nepali Maoists had a higher proportion of indigenous people in the leadership.[13] The presence of significant indigenous people at the leadership probably influenced the Maoist policies and made them more pro-indigenous group oriented, further reinforcing the support among the group.

The negative attitude of the state pushed many indigenous people to the Maoist fold in Nepal. The mainstream parties largely excluded indigenous members from influential leadership positions. The few ethnic parties were not successful and hence did not attract a significant indigenous following. The state announced few reforms but they were mostly tokenistic in nature. The absence of substantive reform in Nepal meant that the support base for the Maoists was not eroded by government policies. The negative attitudes of the state pushed the indigenous people away from it while the positive attitude of the Maoists attracted the indigenous groups. Many indigenous group members who were seeking recognition and an end to ethnic inequality participated in the insurgency.

Violent activities of the Maoist and dictates against traditional practices produced occasional reactions against them. The most prominent collective resistance

Table 7.4 Indigenous groups' participation and resistance in the Maoist insurgencies

Countries	Participation		Resistance	Net participation ranking
	Cadres	Leadership		
India	Moderately high	Some presence at the central level	Occasional resistance, participation in anti-Maoist self-defense committees in one state	2
Nepal	High	Significant presence at the central level (though not proportionate)	No collective resistance	1
Peru	Moderately high initially	None or at insignificant level	Widespread collective resistance at later phase of the insurgency	3

occurred in a district in western region (Shah 2008) and the government and the army attempted to form civil defense committees and distributed arms to such groups in later phase of the insurgency; but the indigenous groups were not involved in such episodes of collective resistance.

In India, the Maoists have been active in the tribal (indigenous) regions and they have received considerable support from the indigenous groups. Many of the Naxalite cadres married into the tribal groups. Despite the Indian state's formal positive measures and policies, the tribal groups still are marginalized and oppressed. The ineffective implementation of the positive policies and failure to protect the rights of indigenous groups, on the other hand, meant that the positive formal laws and policies had less affect on the tribal groups. Further, the larger society and informal norms and practices denigrate the tribal. In such a context, the insurgents fought against discrimination and exploitation, protected tribal interests, and worked to empower the tribal groups. This provided the insurgents with the support of tribal populations.

However, the accommodative policies of the state have reduced the alienation to some degree. The Indian polity formulated policies targeted at the tribal groups and co-opted the tribal leaders. India adopted accommodative policies toward regional/ nationalist groups within the federal dispensation. The mainstream political parties in India nominated tribal leaders to public offices because they had to come up with winning candidates in seats reserved for the indigenous groups. The tribal groups also can field their own candidates in reserved seats where only the tribal candidates can compete. The major dominating party in India's history was also accommodative, providing seats to influential regional leaders. The Indian National Congress facilitated the election of minority leaders, including tribal leaders, in the constituent assembly which introduced significant pro-minority articles (Chiriyankandath 1999). These provisions and processes engaged many tribal leaders in the polity.

The Naxalite movement had tribal members in different levels of leadership positions. For instance, in the early revolutionary phase during the late 1960s and 1970s, the Santals dominated the organization in the Maoist Communist Center (MCC), which operated in the Kanksa-Budbud regions on the Burdwan-Birbhum border (Dyuker 1987).[14] Even though the current leadership of the Indian Maoists is not publicly known, as the base area of the Indian Maoist continues to be the tribal areas, it is likely that the leadership may contain some indigenous members. Occasional news of senior tribal Maoist leaders being captured indicates the presence of tribal leadership at the central level (Bhaumik 2006). The martyrs' lists of the CPI-ML and MCC, however, show low percentages of tribal martyrs (Louis 2002).[15] Likewise, ACHR (2006) found that even though most cadres were tribals, the leadership in Chhattisgrah in 2006 was not. The top Maoist leader in Chattisgarh hailed from Andhra Pradesh. Such evidence suggests that the indigenous groups may have only limited presence in the leadership ranks.

Maoists' use of violence within the indigenous groups, however, has led to dissatisfaction among some indigenous communities. It has led to occasional retaliation against the Maoists and to indigenous participation in anti-maoist defense groups in one state (ACHR 2006; Sundar 2006). Since 2005, Indian authorities have mobilized indigenous tribes to form a civil defense group called Salwa Judum (Peace Mission) in the state of Chhattisgrah. Some indigenous groups participated in Salwa Judum voluntarily due to Maoist excesses, whereas others have been recruited forcefully or with the promise of jobs in the security forces by the government side (ACHR 2006).

The Maoists actively recruited indigenous groups in Nepal and India by co-opting indigenous nationalists' demands, adapting the rebellions' objectives accordingly, and fighting for indigenous rights. The positive attitude of the Maoists toward indigenous groups in Nepal and India and its absence in Peru explains the long-term involvement of indigenous groups in the former countries but not in the latter. On the other hand, relatively more violent atrocities by the Maoists in India, including elimination of rival Maoists, led to occasional reaction by sections of indigenous groups and may have lessened their participation in India.

Explaining differential insurgency trajectories

The three insurgencies reached different level of success and growth. The Nepali insurgency was the most successful. They grew rapidly and forced the state to reach a settlement that strongly favored the insurgents. In the subsequent election, the CPN-M emerged as the largest party. The Shining Path also grew considerably and at one stage some commentators thought that the Peruvian state was in the danger of takeover. However, with the capture of its leaders in early 1990s, the rebellion's influence eroded rapidly and only small bands of rebels exist today. The Indian Maoists, on the other hand, did not grow rapidly but have persisted over four decades despite losing ground in their place of origin. In recent years, the movement is expanding slowly.

Several factors such as capabilities and policies of states played a role in the growth or decline of the insurgencies but the discussion below shows that the level of participation of indigenous groups in the three insurgencies, or the lack of it, explain the varied trajectories of the three insurgencies. The initial involvement but resistance by the indigenous groups at later phase explains the Shining Path's rise and fall. The decline of the Shining Path is often attributed to the capture of Guzman and other top leaders in popular discourse. Even though the capture of top leaders brought down the Shining Path rapidly, scholars have pointed out that the base of the Shining Path had eroded prior to the captures.

The Shining Path insurgency grew from the Andean mountains, mobilizing the indigenous groups. But as it began to impose its ideology-based policies, and as it became more violent toward the indigenous communities, indigenous support waned (Isbell 1994). In the late 1980s and early 1990s, numerous civil defense organizations sprang up in the Andean highlands that pushed the Shining Path away from their traditional strongholds (Starn 1995; Berg 1994). Scholars believe that the large-scale formation of self-defense committees by the indigenous groups was instrumental in pushing back the Shining Path and undermining the insurgency (Degregori 1998; Starn 1995). The weakened social bases may have contributed to the captures of the Shining Path leaders by limiting shelters and defensive networks, and strengthening government intelligence.

The Indian case is interesting because the indigenous groups have participated both in the Naxalite rebellion and in state counter-insurgency. The pro-indigenous attitude of both the Maoists and the state in India has divided the support of the indigenous groups. The participation of indigenous leaders and their supporters in the polity and specific pro-indigenous state policies has denied the Maoists an extensive fertile support base of alienated people. The persistence of the insurgency in India, however, is due to its support base in the tribal regions, which are backward and whose inhabitants are exploited by corrupt government functionaries, exploitative traders and money lenders.

Violent activities of both the state and rebels, on the other hand, repelled sections of the indigenous groups from both sides. The mixed participation not only helps to explain the inability of the Naxalites to reach the stage of civil war, unlike the Nepali and Peruvian Maoists, but also can explain the inability of the strong and effective Indian state to wipe out the insurgents. The indigenous support for the Maoists has contributed to the persistence of the insurgency despite the formidable power of the Indian state and its accommodative attitude. The Indian experience also shows that the overall share of the tribal population in India (7.5 percent) may have limited the growth of the rebellions. The limitation of the rebellion to tribal areas, on the other hand, suggests that indigenous groups may be more prone to rebellion than other disenfranchised groups like the Dalit.

The experience of West Bengal, the birthplace of the Maoist movement, is instructive with regard to state policies. The Maoist influence weakened in West Bengal despite its expansion elsewhere. This is partly due to the massive land reforms initiated by the West Bengal government headed by the moderate communists. The insurgency continues to thrive in other tribal areas of India where significant reforms have not been initiated. This shows that policies that address the underlying factors can help to erode the support base of insurgencies. The West

Bengal experience also shows that federalism facilitated reforms by giving power to states to initiate large-scale land reform policies.

Despite the Indian state's positive policies and formidable coercive power, it has not been able to repress the growth of the Maoists. The Indian state repressed the insurgents in West Bengal and captured the top leaders, including the founder and general secretary Charu Mazumdar, after a few years of the insurgency. But this failed to arrest the expansion of the movement in other regions. This shows that coercive capabilities of the state can repress the conflicts for some time but not permanently (Gurr 1968) and that the state's reformist policies, rather than repression, can contribute to undermining insurgencies.

The coercive and violent methods of the Naxalites, such as expelling or killing local leaders, undermining tribal institutions, and killing those suspected of being government or other party supporters, however, alienated segments of the tribal population. The tribals have occasionally resisted the Maoists and some have even joined self-defense groups as in the state of Chhattisgarh. The division among tribals and the opposition of some tribals meant that the rebellion faced challenges within its support base that constrained its unhindered growth.

The contribution of higher participation of indigenous groups to insurgency trajectory is perhaps more clear in Nepal. The insurgency began from the land of the Kham Magars, an indigenous group, in the mid-western hills. The group and the region provided the initial fighting cadre and a base area, and still provide the CPN-M with cadres and leaders to run and head Maoist organizations in other parts of the country. The participation of the indigenous groups, which constitute 37 percent of the population, made a difference in the insurgency owing to the size as well as the quality of indigenous participation. The cadres were ready to die for a cause. This was important especially at the initial stages of the insurgency when the common people did not think the Maoists would become a major political force that could dominate a large part of the country. The western hills, because of their relative inaccessibility, also provided shelter to leaders and the Maoist army. Often the Maoist cadres fell back to the region when the security forces pursued them after raids on towns and government installations. On the other hand, the state contributed indirectly to the growth of the insurgency by repressing poor villagers on the suspicion of being Maoists or Maoist sympathizers, especially during the counter-insurgency programs in the mid-western hills at the start of the insurgency. This only pushed local Kham Mager people towards the insurgency.

The ethnic fronts opened by the Maoists came in very handy in the course of the insurgency. When there was a lull in the activities of the PLA (People's Liberation Army) and the party, these fronts stepped up their activities. During the royal regime (2002–5) when the security forces intensified counter-insurgency activities and claimed that they were winning the war, the Tamuwan, Magarat and other ethnic fronts organized blockades of their respective regions and the capital and dealt psychological blows to counter-insurgency efforts. This boosted the morale of the Maoists who were demoralized after the capture of leaders and cadres, and the lull in the offensive activities of the party and PLA against government forces. It also demoralized the resurgent state and helped to change the public mood by showing the inadequacy of a military solution in suppressing the multi-pronged Maoist rebellion.

The argument is not that all members of the indigenous groups participated and supported the insurgency. Many members of the marginalized groups were in the security forces as well as other state agencies. However, the nature and extent of participation made a significant difference. First, the indigenous groups who participated in the insurgency were more committed. The readiness to die for a cause is a potent force in itself. Second, the higher participation of the indigenous groups than in other mainstream political parties meant that the establishment side was weaker owing to non-participation of the indigenous groups, and the significant difference in participation meant that this indigenous participation was much more important for the insurgency than the numbers indicate.

Conclusions

The chapter has made clear that, in addition to other factors, varied ethnic participation has strongly impacted the trajectories of the insurgencies in Peru, India, and Nepal. This study has also shown that insurgents groups like the Maoists can innovate and adapt to counter the ideological challenges they face in the twenty-first century. They can mobilize alienated and vulnerable groups like the indigenous groups by raising cultural and other grievances, going beyond the sole focus on class inequality. Violent communist rebellions may, thus, not yet be past history despite the fall of communism in many parts of the world.

The policy recommendation of this chapter is that governments should not alienate and exclude specific ethnic groups, particularly indigenous groups, and that they should formulate policies that address particular problems and grievances. The Peruvian and Indian cases show that government's inclusive reform policies can blunt the growth of the insurgencies. If states remain unresponsive and insensitive to indigenous issues and grievances, as in Nepal, ethnic groups may support class-based insurgencies if the rebels pursue a policy of mobilizing them. The support of ethnic groups for class-based insurgency could transform the nature of the insurgency itself, making it more formidable than a purely class/ideology-based insurgency.

Notes

1 Earlier drafts were presented at the Annual International Studies Association Meeting (March 1–5, 2005), Annual South Asia Conference (October 7–9, 2005), Symposium on Divided States and Contested Territories in South Asia, Michigan State University (March 8, 2006), and Annual Mid-west Political Science Conference (April 12–15, 2007). I would like to thank Anup K. Pahari for comments on an earlier draft.

2 See Thomas A. Marks (1996) for Maoist insurgencies in Thailand, the Philippines, Sri Lanka, and Peru.

3 Indigenous people are labeled as tribal (formally Scheduled Tribes) in India, indigenous nationalities in Nepal, and Amerindians in Peru.

4 A faction splintered later in the same year to form the Maoist Communist Center (MCC). Another faction split from CPI-ML in 1980 to form the Communist Party of India (ML)

People's War Group (PWG). The MCC and PWG were the two most prominent Maoist groups engaged in violent rebellion in India at the turn of the century.

5 The UCD data covers India from 1990 onwards only. The conflict level was *Minor* for most years, if not all, prior to 1990. The intensity level is coded as *Minor* (at least 25 battle-related deaths per year and fewer than 1,000 deaths during the course of the conflict), *Intermediate* (at least 25 battle-related deaths per year and an accumulated total of at least 1,000 deaths but fewer than 1,000 in any given year), and *War* (at least 1,000 battle-related deaths per year).

6 According to Dasgupta (2005), the Indian home minister conceded this in a meeting of chief ministers of the Maoist-affected states on September 21, 2004.

7 According to the UCD, the first battle-related death occurred on August 15, 1981, and conflict-related deaths reached 25 on August 22, 1982.

8 Media have reported a resurgence of the Shining Path. They have attacked and killed police and military personnel in 2007 and 2008 (Forero and Neary 2008; Sanchez 2007).

9 India was considered centralized till the 1980s. The regional governments obtained more power in the 1990s because the judiciary intervened to stop the center's power to dismiss regional governments; more regional parties emerged and gained more influence, and coalition politics at the center increased the role of regional parties (Dasgupta 2002; Manor 1998).

10 Many reforms, such as the declaration of the state as secular, public holidays on various groups' festivals, and quotas in the Constituent Assembly, have been introduced since the 2006 political transformation.

11 The founder of the communist party in Peru in the early twentieth century, Jose Carlos Mariategui, had called for incorporating indigenous values, but Guzman, though praising Mariategui in other respects, negated the indigenous issues (Starn 1995: 417). Likewise, the founder of the Nepali communist movement, Pushpa Lal Pradhan, had elaborated extensively on ethnic autonomy, but the issue was relegated in the interregnum by the mainstream communists until the Maoists picked up the issue (Tamang 2006).

12 Gurung (2007) has shown that there were fewer deaths in many districts with a higher indigenous population, and Tiwari (this volume) also finds that population concentration of indigenous groups does not explain district death levels during the insurgency. Such aggregate analyses do not capture the nuanced differences among different groups within districts toward indigenous issues and the Maoists. For instance, Newar from Kathmandu Valley demand ethnic autonomy but Newar settled outside the valley are not enthusiastic about it because they are not indigenous outside the valley.

13 Formal organizations of the indigenous nationalities, such as the Nepal Federation of Indigenous Nationalities (NEFIN), did not formally support the insurgency but many activists associated with it were sympathetic to the Maoists' ethnic agenda.

14 A tribal leader (Jangal Santhal) and one dalit leader (Santosh Rana) are listed among 16 top leaders during the initial phase of the insurgency. Both were central committee members (Roy 1975). Duyker (1987) also mentions other influential tribal Naxalite leaders such as Gunadhar Murmu, Leba Chand Tudu, and Rabi Manjhi.

15 Some 2.3 per cent of known martyrs in the CPI (ML) Party Unity during 1982–98 and 8.9 per cent in the MCC for 1973–99 were tribal. In both parties the scheduled caste had the highest number of martyrs (Louis 2002: 186, 194).

Bibliography

ACHR. 2009. *The Adivasis of Chhattisgarh: Victims of Naxalite Movement and Salwa Judum Campaign*. Asian Centre for Human Rights 2006 [cited January 28 2009]. Available from http://www.achrweb.org/Review/2006/117–06.htm.

Anderson, Benedict. 1991. *Imagined Communities: Reflections on the Origins of and Spread of Nationalism*. 2 nd ed. London: Verso.

Apter, David, ed. 1997. *The Legitimization of Violence*. New York: New York University Press.

Banerjee, Sumanta. 1984. *India's Simmering Revolution: The Naxalite Uprising*: Zed Books.

Berg, Ronald H. 1994. Peasant Responses to Shining Path in Andahuaylas. In *Shining Path of Peru*, edited by D. S. Palmer. New York: St. Martin's Press.

Bhaumik, Subir. 2006. India police identify 'top rebel'. Review of Reviewed Item. *BBC News*, http://news.bbc.co.uk.

Brown, Michael E, ed. 2001. *Nationalism and Ethnic Conflict*. Revised ed. Cambridge: MIT Press.

Caplan, Lionel. 2000. *Land and Social Change in East Nepal*. 2nd ed. Lalitpur: Himal Books.

Chiriyankandath, James. 1999. Constitutional predilections. *Seminar*: http://www.india-seminar.com/1999/484/484%20chiriyankandath.htm.

Dasgupta, Jyotirindra. 2002. India's Federal Design and Multicultural National Construction. In *The Success of India's Democracy*, edited by A. Kohli. Cambridge: Cambridge University Press.

Dasgupta, Tilak. 2005. Whither the Naxal Comrades? *Himal South Asian*, September–October.

Davidheiser, Evenly B. 1992. Strong States, Weak States: The Role of the State in Revolution. *Comparative Politics* 24 (4):463–75.

de Sales, Anne. 2003. The Kham Magar Country: Between Ethnic Claims and Maoism. In *Resistance and the Nepalese State*, edited by D. N. Gellner. New Delhi: Social Science Press.

De Soto, Hernando. 2002. *The Other Path: The Economic Answer to Terrorism*. Reprint ed. New York: Perseus Books.

Degregori, Carlos Ivan. 1998. Harvesting Storms: Peasant *Rondas* and the Defeat of Sendero Luminoso in Ayacuho. In *Shining and Other Paths: War and Society in Peru, 1980–1995*, edited by S. J. Stern. Durham and London: Duke University Press.

Duyker, Edward. 1987. *Tribal Guerrillas: The Santals of West Bengal and the Naxalite Movement*. Delhi: Oxford University Press.

Forbes, Ann Amcrmbrecht. 1999. Mapping Power: Disputing Claims to Kipat Lands in Northeastern Nepal. *American Ethnologist* 26 (1):114–38.

Forero, Juan, and Lynn Neary. 2008. Shining Path's Return Raises Violence. *NPR*, November 15.

Gaige, Frederick H. 1975. *Regionalism and National Unity in Nepal*. Delhi: Vikas.

Goodwin, Jeff, and Theda Skocpol. 1989. Explaining Revolutions in the Contemporary Third World. *Politics & Society* 17 (4):489–509.

Guneratne, Arjun. 2002. *Many Tongues, One People: The Making of Tharu Identity in Nepal*. Ithaca and London: Cornell University Press.

Gurr, Ted Robert. 1968. A Causal Model of Civil Strife: A Comparative Analysis Using New Indices. *The American Political Science Review* 62 (4):1104–24.

——. 1993. *Minorities at Risk? A Global View of Ethnopolitical Conflicts*. Washington, D.C.: United States Institute of Peace Press.

——. 2000. *Peoples Versus States: Minorities at Risk in the New Century*. Washington, D.C.: United Institute of Peace Press.

Gurung, Harka. 2007. Social Exclusion and Maoist Insurgency. In *The Inclusive State: Reflections on Reinventing Nepal*, edited by A. Aditya. Kathmandu: SAP Nepal.

Hechter, Michael. 1999. *Internal Colonialism: The Celtic Fringe in British National Development*. Revised ed. New York and London: Transaction Publishers.

Horowitz, Donald. 1985. *Ethnic Groups in Conflict*. Berkeley: University of California Press.

Htun, Mala. 2004. Is Gender like Ethnicity? The Political Representation of Identity Groups. *Perspective on Politics* 2 (3):439–58.

INSEC. 2008. *Documentation and Dissemination Department, INSEC*. INSEC 2008 [cited October 2008].

Isbell, Billie Jean. 1994. Shining Path and Peasant Responses in Rural Ayacucho. In *The Shining Path of Peru*, edited by D. S. Palmet. New York: St. Martin's Press.

Kohli, Atul. 1997. Can Democracies Accommodate Ethnic Nationalism? Rise and Decline of Self-Determination Movements in India. *Journal of Asian Studies* 56 (2):325–44.

Lawoti, Mahendra. 2003. Maoists and Minorities: Overlap of Interests or the case of Exploitation? *Studies in Nepali History and Society* 8 (1):67–97.

——. 2005. *Towards a Democratic Nepal: Inclusive Political Institutions for a Multicultural Society*. New Delhi, London, and Thousand Oaks: Sage Publications.

——, ed. 2007. *Contentious Politics and Democratization in Nepal*. Los Angeles, London, New Delhi and Singapore: Sage Publications.

Louis, Prakash. 2002. *People Power: The Naxalite Movement in Central Bihar*. Delhi: Wordsmiths.

Mallon, Florencia E. 1998. Chronicle of a Path Foretold? Velasco's Revolution, Vanguardia, Revolucionaria, and "Shining Omens" in the Indigenous Comunities of Andahuaylas. In *Shinging and Other Paths: War and Society in Peru, 1980–1995*, edited by S. J. Stern. Durham and London: Duke University Press.

Manor, James. 1998. Making Federalism Work. *Journal of Democracy* 9 (3):21–35.

Marks, Thomas A. 1996. *Maoist Insurgency since Vietnam*. London and Portland: Frank Cass.

McClintock, Cynthia. 1984. Why Peasants Rebel: The Case of Peru's Sendero Luminoso. *World Politics* 37 (1):48–84.

Mehta, Ashok K. 2005. *The Royal Nepal Army: Meeting the Maoist Challenge*. New Delhi: Rupa and Co.

Mohanty, Manoranjan. 2006. Challenges of Revolutionary Violence: The Naxalite Movement in Perspective. *Economic and Political Weekly*, 3163–68.

Muller, Edward N., and Mitchell A. Seligson. 1987. Inequality and Insurgency. *The American Political Science Review* 81 (2):425–51.

OHCHR. 2008. Conflict-related Dissappearances in Bardiya District. Kathmandu: United Nations Office of the High Commissioner for Human Rights.

Palmer, David Scott. 1994. *The Shining Path of Peru*. Second ed. New York: St. Martin's Press.

Ron, James. 2001. Ideology in Context: Explaining Sendero Luminoso's Tactical Escalation. *Journal of Peace Research* 38 (5):569–92.

Russett, Bruce M. 1964. Inequality and instability: The relation of land tenure to politics. *World Politics* 16 (3):442–54.

Sanchez, W. Alejandro. 2009. *Shining Path's Resurgence in Peru*. Power and Interest News Report 2007 [cited January 30 2009]. Available from http://www.pinr.com/report.php?ac = view_report&report_id = 723.

Sarma, E A S. 2006. The Adivasis, the State and the Naxalit: Case of Andhra Pradesh. *Economic and Political Weekly* 41 (15):1434–37.

Scalapino, Robert A., ed. 1969. *The Communist Revolution in Asia: Tactics, Goals, and Achievements*. 2nd ed. Englewood Cliffs, NJ: Prentice-Hall, Inc.

Shah, Saubhagya. 2008. Revolution and reaction in the Himalayas: Cultural resistance and the Maoist "new regime" in western Nepal. *American Ethnologist* 35 (3):481–99.

Shneiderman, Sara, and Mark Turin. 2003. The Path to Jan Sarkar in Dolakha District: towards an ethnography of the Maoist movement. In *Himalayan People's War: Nepal's Maoist Rebellion*, edited by M. Hutt. London: Hurst & Co.

Smith, Anthony D. 1998. *Nationalism and Modernism: A Critical Survey of Recent Theories of Nations and Nationalism*. London; New York: Routledge.

Starn, Orin. 1995. Maoism in the Andes: The Communist Party of Peru-Shining Path and the Refusal of History. *Journal of Latin American Studies* 27 (2):399–421.

———. 1995. To Revolt against the Revolution: War and Resistance in Peru's Andes. *Cultural Anthropology* 10 (4):547–80.

Sundar, Nandini. 2006. Bastar, Maoism, and Salwa Judum. *Economic and Political Weekly*, 3187–92.

Tamang, Mukta S. 2006. Culture, Caste and Ethnicity in the Maoist Movement. *Studies in Nepali History and Society* 11 (2):271–301.

Thapa, Deepak, and Bandita Sijapati. 2003. *A Kingdom Under Siege: Nepal's Maoist Insurgency, 1996 to 2003*. Kathmandu: The Printhouse.

The CIA. *The World Factbook*. The CIA 2007 [cited. Available from https://www.cia.gov/cia/publications/factbook/.

The State Failure Task Force. 2000. The State Failure Task Force Report: Phase III Findings. Washington, D.C.: Political Instability Task Force.

The World Bank. *World Development Reports*. The World Bank 2007 [cited. Available from http://web.worldbank.org.

Uppsala Conflict Data Program. *Uppsala Conflict Database*. Uppsala University 2007 [cited. Available from htt://www.pcr.uu.se/database.

Weinstein, Jeremy. 2007. *Inside Rebellion: The Politics of Insurgent Violence*. New York: Cambridge University Press.

8   Maoist–Madhesi dynamics and Nepal's peace process

*Pramod K. Kantha**

> After the Maoists attain their political goals and seek to demobilize, the ethnic genie, raised on ambitions of secession and separate statehood, may not wish to go back into the bottle so quietly: ethnic chauvinism has a tendency to take on a life of its own. Unlike Mao and Stalin, the Nepali Maoists would not have the wherewithal to contain the ethnic firestorm they had ignited.
>
> (Shah 2004)

> Despite resentment against the Nepalese government's economic policies in the rural areas of the tarai and resentment against the government's efforts at Nepalization in the urban centers, the tarai is not a sea of discontent, ready to drown the government in a high tide of revolution. The government is able to suppress quickly overt opposition, but it appears unable to provide the leadership at local levels that can compete with the opposition parties for support among many segments of the tarai population.
>
> (Gaige 1975)

The year 2007 began for Nepal amidst hope as well as despair. The Comprehensive Peace Agreement (CPA) signed in November 2006 between the Maoists and the government signaled the end of the decade-long Maoist insurgency. On 15 January 2007, the Seven Party Alliance and the Maoists (SPA-M) announced an Interim Constitution to facilitate Constituent Assembly elections. The very next day, SPA-M leaders were confronted with a largely unexpected Madhesi protest against the Interim Constitution. Spearheaded by a little-known group calling itself the Madhesi People's Rights Forum (MPRF), the campaign against the Interim Constitution turned immediately into a standoff with the Madhesis engulfing most parts of Nepal's southern plains in an escalating cycle of protests, violence, terror and anarchy. The more the Maoists and the government sought to suppress the Madhesi movement, the larger it grew. By churning "a sea of discontent," and rendering the government unable to suppress "overt opposition," the Madhesi agitation of 2007–8 did the unexpected. It drastically altered the political landscape in the Tarai in what proved to be a radical departure from Gaige's summation of oppositional Tarai politics made three decades earlier.

The Madhesi protests soon took on an anti-SPA as well as anti-Maoist character. While the constituents of the SPA struggled with both intra- and inter-party differences over the best way to approach the Madhesi protest, the Maoists took an openly confrontational route, thereby making the Maoist–Madhesi contest a salient feature of the peace process. What made the Maoists the main foe of the Madhesis? Why could not the Maoists show solidarity with the Madhesi movement, whose demands were largely a mirror image of the Maoists' own positions on regional autonomy and non-discrimination? How does one explain the strength and intensity of the massive Madhesi protests? Answers to these questions are critical to understanding Nepal's still unfolding peace and democratization process. This chapter seeks to answer these questions by focusing on the dynamics of Maoist–Madhesi interaction in the context of Nepal's peace process. The first part sets the context of this interaction; the second part focuses on the dynamics of interaction between the Maoists and Madhesi groups and the government. Finally, the third part examines the impact of the Constituent Assembly elections on the dynamics of the Maoist–Madhesi relations in the context of the formation of a new coalition government that includes the MPRF. This case study of the interface between Nepali Maoists and the Madhesi movement will be useful in understanding the complex interactions between a weak and embattled transitional regime fraught with internal contradictions and alienated ethnic, regional forces seeking to optimize their bargaining power by leveraging favorable internal and external factors.

Madhesh/Madhesis and discrimination

For the sake of simplicity, I have used Gaige's definition of Madhesh or Tarai:

> [T]he plain region [is] adjacent to the foothills within Nepal's national boundaries. This foothill range is called the Siwaliks or sometimes the Churia range … the Nepal tarai is approximately 500 miles long, from its western boundary, the Mahakali River, to its eastern boundary, the Mechi River. At its widest point the tarai has a span of 33 miles and at its narrowest 2–3 miles. The estimated average width of the tarai along its entire east–west axis being 20 miles.
>
> (Gaige 1975)

The term Madhesi refers to people living in the Tarai whose mother tongues are of what Gaige calls "the plains language category." This category includes Hindi, Urdu, Maithili, Bhojpuri, Bengali, and dialects of these such as the Awadhi and Morang Pradesh dialects, and some languages spoken by relatively few people – languages such as Jhangar, Marwari, and Raji (Gaige 1975). According to the 2001 census, the Madhesis are 33 percent of the total population. Tarai currently consists of 20 districts. All the Tarai districts have varying proportion of Siwalik and mid-mountain areas, the highest being 77.5 percent in Nawalparasi district, 51.5 percent in Chitwan district, 50.8 percent in Banke district and 41 percent in Kailali district, down to the lowest 7 and 8.9 percent in Jhapa and Sunsari districts respectively; the average being 32.4 percent for the 20 districts (Shah 2006).

Awareness of the internal heterogeneity of the Madhesi population is important to understanding the acrimony that surrounds both articulation and representation of Madhesi interests. In Nepal's political parlance, the Madhesi population is divided into four groups: indigenous nationalities groups living in Madhesh for generations, such as Tharus; people belonging to traditional Hindu caste hierarchy; businessmen of Indian origin (Marwaris, Sikhs, and others); and Muslims (Shah 2006). Madhesi leaders tend to underplay these internal cleavages to emphasize a broader unity among the Madhesis. Pahadi leaders, on the other hand, not only religiously invoke these to undermine the Madhesi leaders' demands and claims but also encourage various groups to emphasize their differences and raise particular demands based on their particular geographic and historical attributes. For example, the Tharu community has drawn considerable attention from both the Madhesi leaders and the Pahadi leaders, who claim that the Tharus do not want to be lumped in with the Madhesis. The MPRF leader Upendra Yadav has accused the other political parties of trying to undermine the Madhesi movement by raising the Tharu issue (Nepalnews.com July 2, 2008).

The use of Hindi has remained a hot political issue since Nepal's entry into the modern world in 1951. Though used widely as a lingua franca in the plains region, any suggestion of using of Hindi as one of Nepal's official languages arouses frantic reactions from many native speakers of Nepali who see in this demand a further extension of Indian hegemony in Nepal. In July 2008, the newly elected Vice-President of Nepal, Parmanand Jha, polarized the nation by taking his verbal oath of office in Hindi rather than in Nepali. Earlier, the newly elected Constituent Assembly members of the Tarai-based parties had drawn strong objections from other parties over their use of Hindi to take the oath of office and to participate in the Constituent Assembly.

Closely related to the language issue is the migration and government-sponsored resettlement of hill people into the Tarai plains. Madhesis harbor deep-seated resentment against what is known as "Nepalization" program launched by King Mahendra following his December 1960 coup against Nepal's first elected government. Under this campaign, the state sponsored the resettlement of hundreds of thousands of hill farmers into the Tarai as homesteaders. This program has produced considerable demographic and cultural changes in the region and in local people's lives. Govind Shah's 2006 analysis points to these changes:

> The linguistic characteristics of the population in Madhesh districts changed significantly between 1961 and 1981 due to the influx of the hill population in Madhesh as well as inclusion of some parts of Siwaliks and mid mountains to Madhesh districts. This marginalized the population speaking plains languages. This resulted in the dominance of hill culture, tradition, practices and languages in Madhesh region particularly in Jhapa, Chitwan, Dang and Kanchanpur districts where about 67 percent to 85 percent of the districts' total population consist of hill linguistic groups. The current trend of changing cultural equation indicates that in three to four decades' time, the plains culture, tradition and practices will gradually disappear from most of Chitwan, Jhapa, Kanchanpur, Dang, Nawalparasi, Kailali, and Morang districts, while half and more of Sunsari, Rupendehi, Banke and Bardia districts, and the

northern third of Sarlahi, Bara, Parsa and Rauthat districts will be dominated by hill culture.

(Shah 2006)

The Madhesis have encountered discrimination in many other aspects of life. It is beyond the scope of this chapter to provide a detailed account and analysis of discrimination against the Madhesis in different sectors. Suffice to say that the Madhesis remain grossly underrepresented in government bureaucracy, police, military, and diplomatic services. It is a common Madhesi perception that not only are the Madhesi people treated as "second-class citizens" but their "Nepali identity" is often questioned because of their cultural and geographical proximity to India.

The dawn of the democratic era in Nepal in the wake of Nepal's 1990 first democratic movement did widen the room for political participation as well as for the articulation of the demands of the Madhesi people. Lawoti notes that after 1990 the identity movement of various underrepresented groups gained momentum and greater visibility (Lawoti, 2007). This opening, however, did not result in effective representation of Madhesi grievances. At a rhetorical level, the 1990 constitution did embrace multiculturalism and grant recognition to several other languages, including Tarai languages. However, various studies have indicated that these changes were more cosmetic than real. Once again, as Lawoti has pointed out, the representation of many underrepresented groups, including Madhesis, really declined during the democratic era of 1990–2002 (Lawoti 2008). Moreover, the political instability resulting from coalition politics and frequent change of governments during 1994–99 and the impact of the Maoist insurgency after 1996 left the state besieged for survival and security.

A Madhesi party, Nepal Sadhvawana Party or Nepal Goodwill Party (NGP), did take up the Madheshi issue but with very limited success. Established as a political party in 1990 by the late Gajendra Narayana Singh, a long-time Nepali Congress activist, the Sadbhavana party raised many of the Madhesi grievances such as amendment of the citizenship laws to allow citizenship to more Madhesis, official recognition of Hindi, reorganization of the state into a federal system, and a greater representation of Madhesis in the civil service and security forces (ICG 2007). However, NGP's popular appeal and electoral clout remained too narrow to draw the attention of the mainstream parties. In the 1991 elections, the party won only six seats and 4 percent of the popular vote. Its performance in the 1999 elections was worse as it won only five seats and its share of popular vote fell to 3 percent.

Maoist insurgency and the Madhesi resistance

The role of Maoists has been instrumental in ethnic mobilization in Nepal as well as in the Tarai. As Gellner observes, "current unrest and ethnic conflict in the Nepalese Tarai would perhaps have been inevitable at some stage or other, but the role of the Maoists in giving ethnic militancy a voice there has certainly been considerable" (Gellner 2007). However, the Madhesi issue did not figure prominently on the Maoists' agenda in the initial stages of the insurgency. The Maoists did build their support base by rallying the marginalized groups' grievances against the state and included in their demand an end to regional discrimination between hills and Tarai (Hutt 2004). Their demand for regional autonomy for backward areas also had implications for the Tarai. But the Tarai figured in the Maoist agenda in a peripheral way, at best, because the insurgency in its first four years drew its numbers and strength largely from a few ethnic groups – mainly the Kham-Magars from the Midwestern Nepali hill districts of Rolpa and Rukum.

In the year 2000, the Maoists established a Madhesi Rashtriya Mukti Morcha (Madhesi National Liberation Front, MNLF) in Siliguri, India, under the leadership of Jai Krishna Goit. This was part of their strategy to use identity politics to win the support of excluded communities. MNLF's demands were quite comprehensive and included proportional Madhesi representation in state institutions; full distribution of citizenship certificates; use of Maithili, Bhojpuri, and Awadhi as local official languages, protection of other cultural rights, and reinvestment of Madhesh revenues in the region; revolutionary land reform; and an end to dowry, women's exploitation, untouchability, and social discrimination

A major weakness in Maoist efforts to reach out to the Madhesis was the lack of practice rather than of advocacy. As the International Crisis Group reported, the MNLF's role was "largely subordinate: supporting the CPN-M by providing a regional front, developing locally popular policies, recruiting and organizing." The ICG report also points to important differences of perspectives between Pahadi and Madhesi Maoist leaders. For example, the Pahadi Maoist leaders saw Tarai problems as resulting from both "pahdai ruling-class policies and Madhesis' own exploitative feudal and caste structure." The Maoist's division of the Tarai into Tharuwan (region of indigenous Tharu) in the west and Madhesh in the east also infuriated the Madhesi Maoists (2007).

The Tarai was never a bastion of communist ideology; instead, it had remained a stronghold of the democratic movement during both the anti-Rana protests and anti-King protests following the royal coup of December 1960. During the period 1951–60, as Gaige has observed, the Tarai saw considerable activism over the status of Hindi. The systematic attempt by the royal regime to impose Nepali as the only official language was resented in the Tarai as an "effort to force the hill culture upon the plains people" (Gaige 1975). Even though the Tarai Congress made the status of Hindi and regional autonomy for the Tarai its main agenda, the Hindi movement had significant support among other national parties. The Tarai leaders, therefore, saw the success of democracy in Nepal as critical to the realization of their regional aspirations (Gaige 1975). Hence, the idea of a centralized communist government had little appeal in the Tarai.

During the national referendum campaign for multiparty system (1979–80), I travelled through many villages campaigning in support of a multiparty system. To the astonishment of multiparty campaigners, many rural people equated a multiparty system with communism and expressed multiple fears and suspicions about a communist takeover. They thought the communists would not allow people to pray; that they would take away their land, would kill the landlords, and would

impose a one party dictatorship like that in China. At the time, most Madhesis identified with the King or with the Nepali Congress Party. The Maoist emphasis on the
land reform program reinforces the landowner's fears about losing their land and
property; they also see land reform as a further attempt to transfer land from
Madhesis to the Pahadi population.

Ellie Loveman's analysis of Nepal's Maoist movement lists some key regional
differences. Explaining the success of the Maoists in Western Nepal she writes:

> First, the government loosely controls the western areas and communications
> are poor. Likewise, Hindu influences are weak and thus less of a threat to the
> revolutionary actions and thoughts of the Maoists. Finally, in the West, people
> belong primarily to Mongolian ethnic groups, which are free from upper-caste
> chauvinism. Mongolians are also more receptive to Marxist ideas and make
> very good fighters. In order to prevent a moral "putting-all-your-eggs-in-one-
> basket" situation, the Maoists launched struggles in other parts of the country
> as a means of spreading and weakening police forces.
>
> (Loveman 2008)

The expansion of Maoist activities in Nepal's Tarai region followed the breakdown
of negotiations with the government and the declaration of emergency in
November 2001. As the Maoists came under pressure from security forces in their
base areas, they sought support and resources in the Tarai region, often through terror and intimidation. As Thomas Marks observes, "Outside the cores areas, they
held sway only through terror, through their ability to call upon guerilla formations
to act as enforcers." People in those areas had a difficult choice between surrender
and confrontation, with most people yielding to the Maoist demands (Marks 2003).
The mobilization of the army against the Maoists also brought the Tarai population
under double pressure, from the Maoists as well as from the security forces.
Moreover, the terrain in the Tarai is much easier than the hills for conducting
security operations.

Another factor limiting the Maoist influence in the Tarai is their anti-Indian
stance. The Maoists have used anti-Indian rhetoric as a mobilization tool to consolidate their support by exploiting what Hutt labels "the ordinary Nepali's ambivalent attitude to and inherent distrust of the southern neighbor." The first nine of the
40 points submitted by the Maoists to the government before they embarked upon
their insurgency were related mostly to their plan to restructure relations with India.
The first two points called for ending the 1950 Nepal–India Treaty, Mahakali treaty
and Tanakpur Treaty. Their demands also called for greater regulation of the open
border, termination of Gurkha recruitment, and work permits for foreign workers
etc. (Hutt 2004).

The Maoist's anti-Indian rhetoric, typical of Nepal's left groups, has little reso-
nance among the Madhesis. While Nepalis without ethnic and cultural roots in the
Tarai have always harbored a sense of vague threat from India's dominant status and
from Nepal's heavy dependence on India, the Madhesis feel a natural affinity with
India. Common linguistic, cultural and caste backgrounds are constantly reinforced

by widespread matrimonial ties across the open border. Many people along the border depend on India for their life needs. Instead of being a threat, many Madhesis expect India to use its power and influence to support the Madhesi demands for greater equality in Nepal; many also express dismay at hitherto Indian indifference to the Madhesi cause. These deep-seated differences in perceptions and perspectives regarding India between Madhesi and non-Madhesi Nepalis remain among the most formidable challenges for achieving national integration within Nepal.

The Maoists' influence in the Tarai has thus remained largely limited to areas with a dominant hill population and to a certain extent among the Tarai indigenous nationalities, mainly the Tharus. According to 2003 reports on areas of Maoist operation, only one Tarai district of Dang was classified as Sensitive Class B, and none as sensitive class A (South Asian Terrorism Portal).[1] As the Maoists moved into the Tarai and into the physical and social space of the Madhesis, they imported their standard operating procedures perfected in the hills – usurping private land, extortion, killing, and kangaroo courts. As a result, the Madhesis' long-standing reservations and antipathy towards the Maoists became all the more real as the Maoists' presence in the Tarai grew.

The defections of high-profile Madhesi Maoists from the party further exposed the hollowness of the Maoist claim to represent Madhesi interests. Both Jaya Krishna Goit and Jwala Singh deserted the Maoists, alleging discrimination in the party against Madhesi members. Goit was the co-coordinator of the Madhesi National Liberation Front of the CPN-M. Goit formed Janatantrik Tarai Mukti Morcha (Republican Tarai Liberation Front, RTLF) in July 2004. In August 2006, Jwala Singh broke away from Goit's group and formed his own RTLF-J. Both Goit and Jwala Singh demand an independent state of Tarai. The RTLF factions have also demanded an end to Maoist atrocities including extortion and the return of land and property captured by the Maoists (ICG 2007). The MPRF has remained at the forefront of the Madhesh movement since 2007. Launched in 1997 by Madheshi academics and students as an NGO, the MPRF focused its activities on Madhesi issues through research, publications, and holding public debates and discussions. Before leading the forum, the MPRF leader Upendra Yadav had contested elections in 1991 as a CPN-UML candidate; he is also known to have briefly joined the Maoists. According to an International Crisis Group report, Mr. Yadav had attended the Maoist-affiliated MNLF and was detained by the Indian authorities along with two other Maoist leaders. The MPRF, unlike the two factions of the RTLF, have demanded a federal republic with autonomy to the Tarai region and greater representation of Madhesis in the Nepali government and bureaucracy. The organization showed a meteoric rise in popularity and staying power during the Madhesi movement. The MPRF registered itself as a political party in April 2007 to contest the Constituent Assembly elections.

Maoists and the Madhesi movement

As pointed our earlier, on January 16, 2007, the Forum appeared prominently on the national scene in opposition to the SPA-led peace process and the promulgation of the Interim Constitution. The forum members burnt the Interim Constitution on the streets of Kathmandu, protesting the failure of SPA and the Maoists to include any reference to the federal system and proportional representation in the Constitution. In a commentary, the London-based *Economist* succinctly summarized the grievances of the Madhesis in the following words:

> The ethnic group known as Madhesis, who dominate the Tarai, fear they will be cheated. Nepal's censuses have always underestimated Madhesi numbers. Ethnically and culturally, they are indistinguishable from the Indians across the border. They probably make up more than 40 percent of the population but are barely represented in the bureaucracy, army or police and their "Nepaliness" is constantly questioned. Ahead of the elections there is a drive to give millions of Madhesis the citizenship they lack, allowing them to vote.
>
> (*Economist*, January 25, 2007)

The Forum leaders early on recognized the extent and the depth of frustration and alienation among the Madhesi population arising from their long-accumulated grievances fuelled further by the singular focus of the post-April 2006 regime on mainstreaming the Maoists. The Forum became the first political party to succeed in capturing and channeling this widespread sentiment among the Madhesi population of being excluded in the context of the evolving peace process. Under the Interim constitution, the Maoists were to nominate 73 of the 330 members of parliament, whereas 48 others were to be nominated by the SPA parties. The SPA parties were also seen as shutting the door behind them in order to keep other parties from competing for power. For example, a provision regarding party registration required 10,000 signatures of voters to register new political parties. These stipulations were seen by the Madhesis and others as an attempt to create a monopoly of the SPA-M parties over the political process.

The absence of any role for the Madhesi leaders in the wake of the April 2006 movement in critical deliberations on issues like mainstreaming the Maoists and the Interim Constitution was clearly a major factor in igniting the protests. As a journalist wrote: "Their [Madhesis'] demand was for participation not only representation" (Pathak 2008). Following the burning of the Interim Constitution, the forum leader Upendra Yadav and 28 other forum supporters were arrested. The fuel to the ongoing fire of Madhesi movement was provided again by the Maoists. On January 19, 2007, a Maoist cadre heading for Chitwan from eastern Nepal shot dead an MPRF supporter participating in an MPRF strike (*bandh*) in Lahan, a town in Eastern Tarai. The victim was a 16-year-old student, Ramesh Kumar Mahato. The killing sparked violent protests. The Madhesi protesters destroyed dozens of government buildings, party offices of the ruling parties and the Maoists, media houses, and houses of the SPA leaders (*Kantipuronline*, January 30, 2007). The forum called for an indefinite *bandh* and protests. The MPRF, along with other Madhesi organizations, launched major rallies and shutdowns across the Tarai to protest the killing. The protestors also demanded the resignation of the Prime Minister and the Home Minister; the latter's continuation in office became a lingering issue between the government and the Forum for several months, stalling any progress toward a negotiated settlement.

The huge participation and intensity of the protests baffled everyone including the Madhesi leaders. In July 2007, the MPRF leader Upendra Yadav described to me the avalanche of protests in the Madhesh as a "spontaneous outburst of deep-seated Madhesi resentment against the discriminatory policies and practices of the state as well as against the atrocities committed by the Maoists in towns and villages of the Tarai."

Here it is important to mention that the protest against the Interim constitution had occurred in the immediate aftermath of a massive riot in Nepalganj, a town in Western Nepal, on December 25–26, 2006. A report prepared by a civil committee appointed by the government found that the violence in Nepalganj damaged or destroyed a total of 211 houses and shops with a loss totaling over 78 million Nepali rupees. A more telling report was by the People's-Level Civil Investigation Committee consisting of human rights defenders. This Committee found that only 14 percent of the property destroyed belonged to the Pahadis; the rest belonged to the Madhesis. It appears, thus, that the Nepalganj riots were the first explicit Pahadi–Madhesi riots in Nepal. While calling on the government to punish the culprits, the report also blamed the Tarai-based Sadbhavana Party (Anandi Devi), still a part of the government, for causing the eruption of violence by calling for a Tarai *bandh* (*Nepalnews*, January 30, 2007).

Beginning with the Nepalganj riot, the Madhesi–Maoist antagonism became the defining feature of the Madhesi movement and it has remained the most critical energizing factor since. On February 23, 150 activists of MNLF, the Maoist outfit, were reported to have intervened in a MPRF mass meeting in the western town of Bhairahawa to be addressed by the MPRF leader Upendra Yadav. The Maoists had also taken a large number of MPRF supporters and their vehicles into custody. The intervention of the Office of the High Commissioner for Human Rights (OHCHR) secured the release of MPRF supporters (*Kantipuronline*, February 24, 2007). Another intervention in an MPRF mass meeting was reported on February 25 from Nepalganj. The MPRF leader Upendra Yadav called the Maoist intervention in the forum's program the height of "terrorism and militant philosophy." Mr. Yadav also alleged that the Maoists had tried to attack him personally in the Nepalganj incident (Pandey 2007). In my July conversation with Mr. Yadav, he mentioned that he could not operate freely owing to continuing Maoist threats to his life. The fact that Mr. Yadav is now the Foreign Minister in the Maoist-led coalition is a clear testimony to the power of shifting political alignment in Nepal.

For the Maoists the MPRF and its Madhesi agitation came as a rude awakening of a level of resistance to its atrocities and activism that the party had not at all anticipated. At a time when the SPA government was widely seen as caving in to Maoist pressure on many fronts, the Madhesi challenge to the Maoists in the plain region drew both national and international attention and also support for the Madhesi grievances. Suddenly, the Maoists were faced with an enemy whose hostility to the Maoists conveniently coincided with the desire of many others to stall the Maoists' advance to power. The Madhesi movement was labeled as a "reverse wave against the reds." Two factions of the RTLF started destroying the Maoists' and CPN-UML's offices in Tarai. As one of the commentators pointed out, "Maoist leaders themselves are provoking the people of Tarai by terming them as a bunch of criminals and supporters of regressive forces" (*Nepalnews*, February 2, 2007).

The worst confrontation between the supporters of MPRF and the Maoists took place in the border town of Gaur in south-central Nepal in March 2007, resulting in the deaths of at least 27 Maoist supporters, including four women and a 17-year-old girl. The violence erupted after the Maoists attempted to hold their public meeting at the same venue where the MPRF had already announced their program. Gaur became what Lal called "the battleground for collisions between the Madhesi Janadhikar Forum and the CPN-M" (Lal 2007a). The aftermath of the Gaur carnage presented the Maoists with perhaps the greatest and most direct challenge since they joined the peace process. While the Maoists vowed revenge, they displayed political maturity by not retaliating against the MPRF and its supporters. An investigation by the OHCHR-Nepal pinned most blame on the inaction of law enforcement agencies. The report maligned the Nepal Police and Armed Police Force for their failure to either prevent violence or to protect its victims (*Nepalnews*, April 20, 2007).

A report by Nepal's National Human Rights Commission (NHRC) also reached a similar conclusion. A member of NHRC told me in an interview in December 2007 that the local administration in Gaur was under instruction from superiors in Kathmandu to refrain from acting pro-actively to prevent the looming confrontation. The inaction on the part of the administration raised fears in the Madhesi community of collusion between the government, especially the Home Minister Krishna Sitaula, and the Maoists to suppress the Madhesi protests. The Maoists had repeatedly asserted that they could successfully confront the Tarai agitators.

Explaining the Maoist–Madhesi confrontation

The Maoists' stated position on marginalized people and regions was clearly at odds with their utter dismissal of the Madhesi movement. Each confrontation between the Maoists and the Madhesis elevated resentment and antipathy among the Madhesi population toward the Maoists. As Lal remarks:

> But the indifference of the Maoists to the plight of Madhesis defies logic. The mainstream parties took years to degenerate into their unresponsive state. The Maoists seem to have acquired that trait within days of entering the interim legislature.
>
> (Lal 2007b)

By consistently denouncing any agreement reached between the Madhesi leaders and the government, the Maoists kept reinforcing their opposition to Madhesi demands. The government response ranged from repression to rhetoric without any serious commitment to negotiations. Yet, opposition to the Maoists, to their atrocities, and to their ideology became the principal defining themes of Madhesi agitation. Each time the government and the MPRF reached some agreement, the Maoists routinely expressed their rejection and blamed foreign influence (Indian/American) for the agreement or concessions.

Singular focus on the Maoists and the Madhesis will not adequately explain the dynamic of their relationship. Instead, one must try to understand the nature of this relationship in the broader national and international context of Nepal's political and security landscape. Despite their engagement in the peace process, the Maoists failed to inspire confidence about their commitment to it. Nepal's mainstream SPA parties were as alarmed by the Maoists' non-conformity with the provisions of agreements as were the international stakeholders. The Maoists' outlook exuded an overconfidence combined with a tendency to see their role as central to Nepal's political transformation. As the Maoists had managed to repeatedly get their way in dealings with the SPA parties, their scornful attitude towards the Madhesis was not difficult to understand. As brought home by the following quote, the Maoists had made no space for sharing power with the Madhesis:

> The dependable friends of the Maoists are all their old foes: Madhav Kumar Nepal, Kirti Nidhi Bishta and Sher Bahadur Deuba. Perhaps Marich Man Singh and Nava Raj Subedi will also get a visit from Maoist interlocutors one of these days. But Mahanta Thakur, Surendra Chaudhary and Chitra Lekha Yadav must wait. Madhesis haven't figured in the itinerary of the revolution-aries yet. The Maoists' negotiating team does have a Matrika Yadav, but what does Comrade Yadav have for his fellow Madhesis?
>
> (Lal 2003)

The Maoists also saw the Madhesi movement as an attempt by various elements in India opposed to the mainstreaming of the Maoists to exert their influence on Nepali politics. New Delhi's support for the peace process in Nepal involving power sharing with the Maoists had been controversial and contested. Many in India's security establishment as well as national political parties feared that the Maoists would eventually take over the Nepali state and control its military, which was and would remain the only effective force to challenge and resist the Maoist forces in Nepal. For example, India's main opposition party, the Bhartiya Janata Party, had openly expressed its objection to the inclusions of the Maoists in the government. The complexity of Maoist–Madhesi relations grew further as the Maoists entered government in early 2007 and became a part of what Bermeo calls "semi-opposition parties," that is to say groups that are part of the government but still oppose the government on certain issues/policies (Bermeo 1987). The Maoist's Youth Communist League (YCL) was also used to intimidate/subdue the Madhesi population. While the ethnic overtones and the potential political chal-lenge posed by the Forum were detested, the SPA parties found some psychologi-cal comfort in the anti-Maoist posture of the Madhesi movement.

The Maoists' and government's efforts to undermine the Madhesi movement were stifled by the Forum supporters' ability to choke off the route of essential supplies to Kathmandu and other parts of the country. All the transit points for land-locked Nepal pass through Tarai's major industrial cities such as Biratnagar, Janakpur, Birganj, and Nepalganj. The disruption of economic activities in these cities proved detrimental to Nepal's economy. During my trip in December 2007, several business leaders in Birganj expressed deep dismay over the business climate that was causing massive disruption and capital flight. However, the rise of the Madhesi movement had emboldened the business leaders to resist Maoist attempts at extortion.

The Maoists and negotiations with the Madhesi forces

Unlike the Maoists, the SPA parties called for negotiations with the Madhesi parties; but a common desire to undermine the Madhesi leaders and their movement kept them united. Interestingly, all the SPA parties as well as the Maoists admitted that the demands raised by the Madhesis regarding under-representation and discrimination were legitimate; the Maoists projected the Madhesi demands of a federal state, proportional representation and delimitation of electoral districts on the basis of population, and self-determination as their own (Acharya 2007). While remaining vague over the demands raised by the MPRF, the Maoists flatly denounced the militant Tarai groups, including both factions of the RTLF, as criminal outfits and dismissed any possibility of negotiations with them.

The government launched a well-orchestrated multi-pronged campaign to undermine the Madhesi movement. The first element of this approach was to categorize some of the Madhesi demands as "genuine"; both the government and the Maoists showed their openness to negotiations on these demands. The second element was counter-mobilization of other groups to undermine the Madhesi movement. One such group concocted by the SPA constituents is the Chure-Bhawar Unity Society. The society claims to represent the interests of the hill migrants in the plain region. The society has staked claim for a separate state in northern areas of Madhesh with a predominantly Pahadi population. The third element was to discredit the Madhesi leaders. The SPA leaders as well as the Maoists routinely alleged that the "reactionary forces," that is to say forces supportive of the beleaguered king and opposed to the holding of the Constituent Assembly elections, had infiltrated the Madhesi movement. These charges were repeated despite categorical statements by Mr. Yadav that his movement was in favor of a republican Nepal.

The government also sought Indian help to deal with the Madhesi movement. Prime Minister Koirala suggested repeatedly that India was the key to resolving the Tarai problem. Soon after the protests started, leading politicians from all major constituents of the SPA-M reached Delhi to urge India's cooperation in tackling Nepal's Tarai problem (Khanal 2007). To their dismay the SPA-M leadership failed to obtain Indian support against the Madhesi movement; instead, India kept calling on the government to meet the reasonable demands of the Madhesis.

In February, the Maoists and the SPA reached an agreement to address some of the demands raised by the MPRF. The Prime Minister's address to the nation on February 9 contained a guarantee of a federal system after the CA election, a mixed-proportional electoral system, and reconstitution of election constituencies in Tarai based on population. In a further government move to end the Tarai protests, amendments were made into the Interim Constitution on March 9 to incorporate the latest concessions. The MPRF responded by calling off its general strike; however, a stalemate between the government and the MPRF continued over Home Minister K. P. Sitaula's continuation in office, ignoring the MPRF's demand for his resignation. Mr. Sitaula had strong support from the Maoists.

A 22-point agreement with the government on August 30, 2007, was the most important breakthrough in negotiations. The agreement included provisions for compensation to those killed during the Tarai movement, guarantee of inclusion of Madhesis and other marginalized groups in the constituent assembly, autonomy to the states in the future federal system, and so on. The government also recognized the deceased of the Madhesi movement as martyrs (*Nepalnews*, August 30, 2007). The Maoists described the agreement as "utterly objectionable and scandalous in terms of both the procedure and the essence, and full of conspiracy." They specifically objected to the 15th clause in the agreement that referred to the CPN-Maoists for "seizure of property" and called for its "return." Prachanda called the agreement a "direct violation of the basic procedure and norms of running a coalition government" (Nepalnews.com, August 31, 2007). The Maoists also claimed that the agreement was made at "the behest of Indian forces" (*Kantipuronline*, September 2, 2007).

Soon after the agreement with the MPRF, the Maoists pulled out of the government in September to press for a fresh set of demands including the declaration of republic through parliament and the adoption of a proportional electoral system for all seats. As a result, the entire peace process faced the most severe challenge. The Maoists returned to the government in December following a compromise with the SPA parties over their demands.

Maoist–Madhesi dynamics ahead of the constituent assembly elections

Another 23-point agreement between the SPA and the Maoists on December 27, 2007 raised fresh hopes for the Constituent Assembly elections. The Maoist decision to rejoin the government followed an agreement for the adoption of the declaration of republic by the parliament with the implementation of this declaration suspended until the first meeting of the Constituent Assembly. Setting April 10 as the new date for the Constituent Assembly elections, the SPA and the Maoists formed a joint coordination committee to launch a joint front to hold major assemblies around the country to rally support for the elections.

The new situation also produced realignment of forces among the Madhesis. The Madhesh movement got an extra impetus with the defection from the Nepali Congress of its senior leader, Mahantha Thakur. Blaming the SPA parties for lack of seriousness towards the Madhesi demands, Mr. Thakur formed a new political party, the Tarai-Madhesh Democratic Party (TMDP), on December 28, just the day after the Maoist SPA reached agreement with the Maoists. The TMDP also committed itself to the demand for an autonomous Tarai with the right to self-determination.

On February 9, the MPRF, NGP led by Rajendra Mahato, and the TMDP joined to form a United Madhesi Democratic Front (UMDF). The Madhesi leaders accused the government of ignoring the implementation of the 22-point agreement reached in August and threatened to launch fresh Tarai agitation if their demands were not met by January 19. The UMDF announced a protest movement in Tarai beginning on January 23 and threatened to boycott the Constituent Assembly elections. In the meantime, Nepali media carried reports of a 23-point agreement between Upendra Yadav and other groups, including the armed groups such as Jwala Singh's RTLF, the Tarai Liberation Front and the Madhesi Liberation Tigers. The Madhesi groups also opposed the deployment of a special police force in the Tarai as a non-political and unconstitutional move (*Nepalnews*, January 26, 2008).

The Maoists, in turn, threatened to mobilize their YCL members to insure that Constituent Assembly polls took place as scheduled. The government also mobilized a paramilitary force, a special security task force, in the Tarai region. The Madhesi leaders objected to the deployment of this force as an attempt to intimidate the Madhesis into submission. This latest Tarai agitation caused a severe shortage of fuel in the capital and disrupted normal life all over the country. The government had to impose a curfew in the Tarai towns in order to insure the passage of fuel tankers.

On February 28, the MPRF and government signed an eight-point agreement, bringing an end to the nation-crippling indefinite strike in the Tarai. The latest agreement pointed to the inability of the SPA-M and Madhesi leaders to hammer out a deal independently. The last rounds of negotiations were held in the Indian Embassy in Kathmandu, mediated by the outgoing Indian ambassador Shyam K. Mukherjee. The main sticking point was the UDMF's demand for single autonomous Madhesh province with the right to self-determination. The Maoists did not directly participate in the negotiations. Strong reservations were raised in the Nepali media and political circles about the Indian role in the negotiations. Observers also saw a direct Indian role in the formation of TMLP as well as increasing evidence of New Delhi's reliance on the Madhesi groups to bolster its leverage vis-à-vis the rising influence of the Maoists and apparent inability of the SPA parties to resist the Maoist pressure (Thapa 2008).

Maoist–Madhesi dynamics in the post-election scenario

The results of Constituent Assembly elections catapulted the Maoists as the largest party with 220 seats. The Maoists recorded wins throughout the country, including various districts of the Tarai region. The results were devastating for the two leading parties of the SPA, the Nepali Congress and the CPN-UML. The MPRF, TMDP, and other Tarai parties made an impressive showing in the elections although their win was not overwhelming. Unlike the Maoist sweep of the hilly regions, the Tarai-based parties presented an effective challenge to the Maoists as well as other parties in the Tarai region.

The MPRF and the TMDP emerged as the fourth and fifth largest parties in the Constituent Assembly. The electoral contests in the majority of Tarai districts showed stiff competition between various parties. The Maoists' sweeping victory in both the far-eastern and far-western districts of the Tarai will remain a challenge to the Madhesi parties' claim to represent the entire Tarai region and will undermine their demand for turning the region into a single autonomous Madhesh Pradesh. The MPRF and TMLP had their best showing in Eastern and Western Tarai districts. The demographic features outlined earlier showed their direct impact, with the Maoists and other parties having overwhelming support in districts with dominant hill populations and Madhesi parties overwhelming success in districts with dominant Madhesi populations.

The trajectory of the Maoist–Madhesi relationship is far from certain. The formation of an unlikely alignment between the Maoists, the CPN-UML and the MPRF for forming the Maoist-led ruling coalition on August 18, 2008, could prove little more than an alliance of convenience. The MPRF has used its new political strength to secure key positions of power in the emergent politics of Nepal. After negotiations between the Maoists and other political parties failed, the MPRF entered into an alliance with the Nepali Congress and the CPN-UML to secure the Vice-President's position for the MPRF in return for supporting the Nepali Congress candidate, another Madhesi, for President. Then, the MPRF abandoned the Nepali Congress and joined the CPN-UML to support the Maoist leader Prachanda to lead the Nepali government. The MPRF, under the agreement, heads four cabinet portfolios; for the first time, a Madhesi leader is heading the country's foreign ministry.

Political compulsions of both the Maoists and the MPRF could jeopardize their uneasy partnership. The Madhesh movement slogan of a "Single Madhes State" will complicate political choices; electorally less successful Tarai political groups may try to undercut the MPRF's popular support if the latter shows willingness to compromise. Internal rivalry within the Madhesi leadership over power and policies could also undermine the Madhesi leverage and make compromise more divisive and difficult. The Maoists, along with the Nepali Congress and the CPN-UML, will face a similar dilemma. There is strong resistance among these parties to the idea of a "Single Madhesh State." Many of their supporters also resent the sudden prominence of the Madhesis in national leadership positions. In the aftermath of the Constituent Assembly elections, the leaders of these parties have even called for rescinding the eight-point agreement reached with the Madhesi parties.

On the other hand, the fractured mandate in the Constituent Assembly makes pragmatism and compromise indispensable. The Maoists must have drawn some critical lessons in pragmatism from both the delay in their ascendance to power after the Constituent Assembly elections, and from the defeat of their Presidential candidate. Even the Madhesi parties may not find prolonged stalemate and confrontation a sustainable posture; there are reports of "a yearning among Madhesis for an agenda that goes beyond just identity" (Jha 2008). Hence, the current ruling partnership could herald closer cooperation on constitutional issues, especially the federal structure and the inclusion of Madhesis in Nepal's bureaucracy and military. As the mainstream political parties remain hamstrung between their urge for immediate power, and the need to expand their electoral appeal, a shifting realignment of political forces will continue. One can only hope that this process will favor cooperation over conflict.

Notes

* I would like to express my deep appreciation to Mahendra Lawoti and Anup K. Pahari for their valuable comments on the earlier drafts of this chapter; Dr. Lawoti's support and encouragement was critical. I would also like to thank Research Council, Wright State University for their support for field study in Nepal in November–December 2007.

1 The guerrillas operated to varying degrees in 68 of the 75 districts of Nepal; their influence varied between moderate to extreme in these districts. The districts of Rolpa, Rukum, Jajarkot, Salyan, Pyuthan, and Kalikot in mid-western Nepal were classified as "sensitive Class A" – the highest penetration areas with the government presence confined to district headquarters. Nine other districts, namely Dolakha, Ramechhap, Sindhuli, Kavrepalanchowk, Sindhupalchowk, Gorkha, Dang, Surkhet, and Achham, were classified as "Sensitive Class B." Seventeen other districts, Khotang, Okhaldhunga, Udaypur, Makwanpur, Lalitpur, Nuwakot, Dhading, Tanahu, Lamjung, Parbat, Baglung, Gulmi, Arghakhachi, Bardiya, Dailekh, Jumla, and Dolpa, were put into the lowest category, "Sensitive Class C."

Bibliography

Acharya, Yuvraj. 2004. "PM, Prachanda Differ on Talks Offer to Tarai Groups," Kantipuronline January 24. http://www.kantipuronline.com/kolnews.php?&nid = 98517

Bermeo, Nancy. 1987. Redemocratization and Transition Elections: Comparison of Spain and Portugal. *Comparative Politics* 19 (2): 213–31.

Economist (London).2007. "Ethnic Violence Threatens Nepal's New-found Peace," January 25. http://www.economist.com/world/asia/displaystory.cfm?story_id = 8597143

Gaige, Frederick H. 1975. *Regionalism and National Unity in Nepal.* Berkeley: University of California Press.

Gellner, David N. 2007. Nepal: Towards a Democratic Republic. *Economic and Political Weekly,* May 19: 1823–28.

Hutt, Michael (ed.). 2004. *Himalayan's People's War, Nepal's Maoist Rebellion.* Bloomington: Indiana University Press.

International Crisis Group. 2007. *Nepal's Troubled Tarai Region, Asia Report N0136–9* Kathmandu/Brussels available at http://www.crisisgroup.org/home/index. cfm?id = 4941&l = 1 (accessed August 7, 2008)

Jha, Prashant. 2008. "Madhesi Groups Will Now Have to Move to the Next Stage." *Nepali Times Weekly* May 16–23, http://www.nepalitimes.com. np/issue/400/TaraiEye/14793

Kantipuronline. 2007. "Rautahat Tense; Madhav Nepal's Ancestral House Vandalized," January 25. http://www.nepalnews.com/archive/2007/jan/jan26/news13.php

——. 2007. "Task Force Asks Eight Party Leaders to Reach Consensus on Madhesi Demands," January 30. http://www.kantipuronline.com/kolnews.php?&nid = 99094

——. 2007. "Maoists Release 94 MPRF Cadres from Custody,"

February 24. http://www.kantipuronline.com/kolnews.php?nid = 101738

Kantipuronline. 2007. "India behind MPRF-Govt Agreement: Dev Gurung," September 2. http://kantipuronline.com/kolnews.php?&nid = 121275

Khanal, Gopal. 2007. "Indian Help Sought to Resolve Tarai Impasse," Nepalnews.com, January 29. http://www.kantipuronline.com/kolnews.php?nid = 99044

Lal, CK. 2007. "Mainstream Parties and Civil Society Must Challenge the Extremists," Nepal Times, March 23–29, Issue 341. http://www.nepalitimes.com/browse/Stateofthe State?p=2

Lal, CK.2007. "Lament for Lahan," *Nepali Times*, January/February, 333 http://www.nepalitimes.com.np/issue/333/StateoftheState/13147 accessed August 6, 2008.

Lal, CK. 2003. "The Tarai Cauldron," *Nepali Times*, February/March, 134 http://www.nepalitimes.com.np/issue/2003/02/28/StateOfTheState/4189

Lawoti, Mahendra. 2007. *Contentious Politics and Democratization in Nepal.* New Delhi: Sage Publications.

———. 2008. Exclusionary Democratization in Nepal 1990–2002. *Democratization*, 15 (2): 363–85.

Loveman, Ellie *MAIC,* "Non-State Actors in Nepal," http://maic.jmu.edu/journal/8.2/feature/loveman.htm, accessed September 4, 2008

Marks, Thomas A. 2003. *Insurgency in Nepal.* A Strategic Studies Institute (SSI) Monograph. http://www.carlisle.army.mil/ssi/

Nepalnews.com February 2, 2007. http://www.nepalnews.com.np/contents/2007/english-weekly/spotlight/feb/feb02/ coverstory.php

Nepalnews.com, Apr 20, 2007 http://www.nepalnews.com.np/archive/2007/apr/apr20/news08.php

Nepalnews.com, "Govt-MJF reach 22-pt agreement; MJF withdraws protests," Aug 30, 2007, http://www.nepalnews.com/archive/2007/aug/aug30/news11.php

Nepalnews.com. "Prachanda Sees Conspiracy behind Govt-MJF Agreement," Aug 31, 2007, http://www.nepalnews.com/archive/2007/aug/aug31/news13.php

Nepalnews.com, "Armed and Unarmed Tarai Outfits Reach their Own Pact of Cooperation," January 26, 2008 http://www.nepalnews.com/archive/2008/jan/jan26/news03.php

Pandey, J. 2007. "Maoist Activities Example of Terrorism and Militant Philosophy: Yadav," Kantipuronline.com February 25. http://www.kantipuronline.com/kolnews.php?&nid=101851

Shah, Shree Govind, 2006. "Social Inclusion of Madheshi Community in Nation Building," a paper presented at the Civil Society Forum Workshop for Research Program on Social Inclusion and Nation Building in Nepal, Organized by SNV–Netherlands Development Organization on 13 February 2006, Kathmandu, Nepal), p. 2 <http://madhesi.files.wordpress.com/2006/07/social-inclusion-of-madheshi-community-in-nation-building.pdf>, accessed June 7, 2007.

Shah, Saubhagya. 2004. "A Himalayan Red Herring? Maoist Revolution in the Shadow of the Legacy Raj," in *Himalayan People's War, Nepal's Maoist Rebellion,* edited by Michael Hutt, 192–224. Bloomington: Indiana University Press.

Thapa, Manjushree.2008. "The Impact of the Maoist Victory in Nepal," May 7. www.opendemocracy.net http://alternatives-international.net/article2065.html

Part V
Military and state dimension

9   Military dimensions of the "People's War"

Insurgency and counter-insurgency in Nepal

Ashok K. Mehta and Mahendra Lawoti[1]

Introduction

As important as military capability, strategy and performance are in civil wars, the role of the People's Liberation Army (PLA) and Royal Nepal Army (RNA) during Nepal's Maoist insurgency have rarely been thoroughly analyzed.[2] This is to a certain extent due to the sensitivity of the sector and as a result reliable information is not publicly available. By definition, the sector's many aspects are kept secret. A major source of information about the PLA and RNA and their activities are their public statements, and the documents they have made available and interviews with personnel, but such information may contain positive bias about their respective organizations, omission of certain facts and sometimes deliberate misinformation about the other side. Newspaper reports are another source of information, but except for a few investigative reports "the reliability of news reports is always in doubt as some sensationalize the issue and others become protagonists of conflict, and some even play an advocacy role" in Nepal (Dhruba Kumar 2006: 103), while reports filed based on short trips in dangerous zones may contain information that may not have been verified with multiple sources. However, in the absence of other reliable sources of information, there is not much choice except to use this available information to describe and analyze the two armies' performances. Our recognition of potential biases in the available information, we believe, has allowed us to weed out positive biases and misinformation. Further, collaboration between two authors, one with extensive experience in another country's army, including counter-insurgency activities, and the other in academia, has allowed us to interrogate the available information with experiential and academic bases of knowledge. Hence, even though this study should not be taken as definitive in all aspects, we believe that until more in-depth analyses come forth, the chapter will provide urgently needed analysis of an important topic.

This chapter looks at Nepal's state and rebel armies to analyze their contribution to their respective objectives. The question we ask is why a large, better-trained and equipped state army was not able to contain an insurgency with a poorly trained and ill-equipped army. First, we will briefly discuss the context of the military dimension in insurgency and counter-insurgency. In the second section we will describe the two armies; the third section will analyze the contribution of the two armies in achieving their respective objectives. Finally, we will argue that differential characteristics of the two armies and the political contexts in which they operated contributed to their differential performances.

Military dimension of insurgency and counter-insurgency

Violent rebellions, by definition, aim to capture the state through the use of force. The rebels establish an army for fighting and eventually defeating the state forces. They have to ensure a regular stream of recruits, provide them with training and equipment, and obtain a regular supply of ammunition and other essential items such as food and shelter. These require superior recruitment abilities and huge resources. Establishing and maintaining a regular army requires almost state-like capabilities. Often, the army has to be started from scratch, and the recruits have to not only forego safety but also be ready to die.

Because the rebels challenge the state's legal monopoly over violence, the state will attempt to eliminate or contain rebellions, employing its coercive apparatus. Inevitably, the rebel and state army confront each other with the aim of defeating the other side. The question is who will win. History shows that rebels or the state have succeeded in their goals at different times and places. In China, Cuba and Nicaragua, among others, the rebels defeated the establishment side. In Malaya, Bolivia, Venezuela, Peru and many other countries, the state was successful.[3] In many countries, on the other hand, civil wars have been ended with settlements, often after a period of stalemate between the rebel and state forces (Kumar 1998; Jarstad and Sisk 2008; Weitz 1986).

The success of either side will depend upon the strategies of the respective armies, key among them being the ability to secure local support, in addition to the larger socio-political environment and strategies and the role of external actors. It will also depend upon the activities of the enemy. One side's mistakes are benefits to the other side.

Contribution of the militaries in the civil war outcome

Both the state and the rebel army did not achieve their ultimate goals – repression of the rebels by the RNA and capture of state power through war by the PLA. However, if one were to compare the two armies, the evolution, growth, and performance of the PLA is remarkable because it literally started from scratch and without significant external support. The PLA contributed to the political victory of the Maoists by helping produce a stalemate that facilitated a settlement, which was favorable to the rebels. The PLA's own offensives, as well as resistance to the RNA offensive, helped to generate the strategic stalemate.

The PLA raided police posts, security bases, and district and zonal headquarters, and looted arms, ammunition and cash from banks. The PLA, however, was never able to control any district headquarters. Thus, despite its remarkable growth, the PLA had not grown into a force that could defeat the RNA in direct confrontation. The Maoists had the heart but did not possess the wherewithal to overwhelm Kathmandu. Despite the limitations, the PLA's raids and attacks, however, furthered the rebellion significantly.

Table 9.1 Major skirmishes between security forces (SF) and PLA, 2001–06 (incomplete list)

Date	Place	Attacker	Remarks
11–23–01	Ghorahi Military Barrack, Dang	Maoists	Major casualty
11–23–01	District Headquarters, Syangja	Maoists	Major casualty
11–25–01	Salleri, DHQ, Solukhambu	Maoists	Major casualty
12–08–01	Ratmate Telecom Tower, Rolpa	Maoists	Foiled
12–09–01	Kapurkot Telecom Tower, Salyan	Maoists	Foiled
02–16–02	Mangalsen, DHQ, Sanfebagar Airport, Accham	Maoists	Major casualty
03–16–02	Maoist Training Centre, Rolpa	SF	Major casualty
04–11–02	APF Camp in Satbaria; APF Training Centre in Bhaluwang; Lamahi Police Station, Dang	Maoists	Major casualty
04–11–02	Tulsipur and Ghorahi Army Barrack	Maoists	Foiled
04–14–02	Mukutti, Dang	SF	Moderate casualty
05–02–02	Lishne, Rolpa; Khida jungle, Doti	SF	Moderate casualty
05–07–02	SF Base Camp, Gam, Rolpa	Maoists	Major casualty
05–07–02	SF Base Camp, Khara, Rukum	Maoists	Foiled
09–08–02	Sandhikharka, DHQ, Argakhanchi	Maoists	Major casualty
10–27–02	Rumjatar Airport, Okhaldhunga	Maoists	Foiled
11–14–02	Khalanga, Regional Headquarter, Jumla	Maoists	Major casualty

Second Ceasefire: January 29 to August 27, 2003

03–03–04	Bhojpur Bazzar, DHQ, Bhojpur	Maoists	Major casualty
03–20–04	Beni Bazzar, DHQ, Myagdi	Maoists	Major casualty
01–05–05	Maoist base in Bankhet, Kailali	SF	Major casualty
03–04–05	Sandhikharka, DHQ, Argakhanchi	Maoist	Major casualty
04–07–05	SF Base Camp, Khara, Rukum	Maoist	Foiled
04–09–05	Charikot, DHQ, Dolakha	Maoist	Moderate casualty
05–09–05	Bandipur Company, Ransingh Battalion, Area Police Office in Mirchiya, Siraha	Maoist	Moderate casualty
06–19–05	Diktel, DHQ, Khotang	Maoist	Major casualty
08–07–05	Army Road building Camp Pilli, Kalikot	Maoist	Major casualty
01–11–06	Dhangadi, DHQ, Kailali	Maoist	Moderate casualty
01–31–06	Tansen, DHQ, Palpa	Maoist	Major casualty
02–07–06	Dhankuta, Regional Headquarter, Dhankuta	Maoist	Moderate casualty
03–05–06	Illam, DHQ, Illam	Maoist	Moderate casualty
04–23–06	Chautara, DHQ, Sindhupalchowk	Maoist	Moderate casualty

Sources: Dhruba Kumar and Sharma (2005), SATP (2008), Mehta (2005) and various issues of *Kantipur*, *The Kathmandu Post*, and *The Himalayan Times*.

Note:
Major casualty = major casualty on opponent; moderate casualty = raid on opponent and some casualty on the opponent; foiled = attack repelled.

A major contribution of the PLA in the Maoist rebellion was dismantling the state presence in rural Nepal. After successful raids and attacks on security posts in rural areas, the government often relocated security posts and state and private agencies such as banks and agricultural extension service centers. This helped the Maoists to consolidate their hold in rural regions (Pasang 2064 v.s./2007; Lawoti 2007a).

The PLA also contributed to the rebellion by generating wide publicity through its raids and the capture of government officials and security personnel. The news caught national and international attention and probably influenced opinion about Maoist strength significantly among both Maoist supporters and opponents. The government's propaganda, which often claimed the participation of thousands of rebels in the raids, may have been counter-productive as it conveyed a sense of the massive mobilization capacity of the Maoists.

Finally, the PLA contributed to the eventual success by helping to create a stalemate even after the RNA was expanded and trained and supported by the Indians and Americans. The RNA may have inflicted casualties on the PLA after 2002 but the PLA continued to regroup and conduct raids in district headquarters and other places. The attacks in Bhojpur district headquarter (DHQ) on March 3, 2004, Beni, Myagdi DHQ on March 20, 2004, Sandhikaharka, Arghakanchi DHQ in April 2005, in Pilli, Kalikot on August 2005, Tansen, Palpa DHQ on January 2006, and so on, dampened the confidence of the RNA and its supporters and helped to create an environment of stalemate.

As for the RNA, its inability to repress the PLA was more than obvious. This was despite considerable military support by the Indians and Americans after the turn of century.[4] The RNA, especially under the cover of the state of emergencies, did inflict serious losses on the PLA. The Maoist themselves acknowledge such losses in places like Ratamata and Kapurkot (Pasang 2064 v.s./2007). The Maoists were also unable to overcome military installations in some instances even when they overran district headquarters. The subsequent rise in casualties after the deployment of the RNA increased the cost of joining the PLA and the decline in recruitment disadvantaged the PLA.

The RNA began to claim that it was winning the war. In May 2005, the Royal Government claimed it had broken the back of the Maoists and killed 600 of them since February, captured 350 guns and 13,700 bullets. On September 16, 2005, the RNA claimed that 4,546 Maoists had been killed and 2,889 had surrendered since the end of ceasefire in August 2003. Security force losses for the same period were put at 562. To some extent, further military advance by the Maoists was checked for a time. After the breakdown of the ceasefire in August 2003, except for the attacks in Beni, Myagdi DHQ and Bhojpur DHQ in early March 2004 the Maoists were engaged only in hit and run raids for around 18 months. The RNA may have succeeded in demonstrating to the Maoist leadership that it was very difficult to defeat them in direct confrontation, which was amply revealed in the April 2005 battle of Khara, where the Maoists suffered a big defeat. This may have forced the Maoists to abandon the military option and to seek a peace settlement. The Maoists resumed major attacks only after March 2005 (see table 9.1), when the RNA became engaged in enforcing King Gyanendra's February coup, providing security and logistical support to the King's felicitation tours, and directing the suppression of movement against the coup.

People's Liberation Army[5]

The Maoist started with a few dozen people and a few simple weapons but within a decade they had established an army with three divisions and nine brigades and had acquired modern weapons such as sub-machine guns, rocket launchers, and mortars.[6] The estimate of PLA size has varied. In early 2005 the Maoists claimed to have 10,000 cadres and the RNA estimate also supported this claim (ICG 2005). After the peace agreement the UNMIN (United Nations Mission in Nepal) verified the PLA as having around 20,000 cadres. More than 10,000 were disqualified for either being under age or having joined the PLA after the peace agreement.

The PLA was not well equipped, however. Various photographs and videos taken during training and attacks clearly show that many cadres were armed with sticks and socket bombs only (Cowan 2008; Mehta 2005; Douglas 2005). Experts estimated that around 85 percent of the weapons were looted from the Nepal Police or the RNA while others were collected in villages, manufactured by the Maoist themselves in makeshift factories around the country, or purchased in the international arms market. Some of the weapons could have been acquired from the Maoist Communist Center (MCC), People's War Group (PWG) and the United Liberation Front of Assam (ULFA) of India and the Liberation Tigers of Tamil Ealam (LTTE) in Sri Lanka. The RNA estimated that the PLA had around 3,000 weapons in 2004 (Shah 2004),[7] consisting of locally made guns, various types of rifles, various types of machine guns and a few rocket launchers and mortars.

The early Maoist combatants were called "fighting units" (*ladaku dal*), "security units" (*suraksha dal*) and "volunteer units" (*swayamsevak dal*), and had little equipment. The development of the People's Army took place only after the government's operation Kilo Sera Two (May 1998–April 1999) (ICG 2005: 9). Some Maoist leaders were initially trained outside the country, possibly by the Indian Maoists. On their return, they conducted extensive training for other commanders and cadres for a year in 2053–54 v.s. (1997). The Maoists also received training from some Indian ex-servicemen. Approximately ten Indian Army ex-servicemen were actively involved with the Maoists and most were part of previous ethnic movements which were subsumed into the Maoists. Some Indian Army deserters and discharged personnel were involved as well. Serving soldiers from the Indian Army on leave in Nepal in some instances ran three-to-four-day training capsules for Maoist recruits in lieu of the donation demanded by the Maoists (Mehta 2005).

In August 1998, the fourth expanded central committee meeting (plenum) decided to build up military strength and "base areas" and began to expand the military. They utilized the first ceasefire with the government declared in July 2001 to strengthen military capacity. Finally, in September 2001, the Maoists announced the establishment of the People's Liberation Army at a gathering of guerillas from around the country in Kureli in Rolpa district (ICG 2005: 9).

In June 2002 the central committee plenary formed brigades while in August 2004 the brigades were incorporated into three divisions of three brigades each. Twenty-nine battalions, companies, platoons and squads were under the brigades.[8] People's militias, armed with a few small arms and local weapons, were established in villages to support the PLA in its activities as well as to help govern and expand party activities (see figure 9.1).

The Maoists recruited people into the party and military voluntarily as well as forcefully. Indiscriminate police repression of villagers during the initial counterinsurgency operations may have pushed some into the fold of the PLA while others

GENERAL HEADQUARTERS

Supreme Commander – Puspa Kamal Dahal ("Prachanda")

WESTERN DIVISION

Commissar – Dev Gurung
Commander – Janardan Sharma
Vice Commander – Unknown

BRIGADES

1. Ghorahi–Satbariya Second Brigade
2. Lisne–Gam Third Brigade
3. Bahubir-Yoddha Eight Brigade

MID DIVISION

Commissar – Post Bahadur Bogati
Commander – Nanda Kishor Pun
Vice Commander – "Barun"

BRIGADES

1. Mangalsen First Brigade
2. Basu Memorial Fourth Brigade
3. Parivartan Memorial Nith Brigade

BATTALIONS (29)

COMPANIES

PLATOONS

SQUADS

EASTERN DIVISION

Commissar – Ram Bahadur Thapa
Commander – Barsa Man Pun
Vice Commander – "Rajesh"

BRIGADES

1. Bethan Memorial Fifth Brigade
2. Solu-Salleri Sixth Brigade
3. Mechi-Koshi Seventh Brigade

PEOPLE'S MILITIAS (organized locally, and separate from military units)

Figure 9.1 Structure of the People's Liberation Army, 2005 (ICG 2005)

joined after recruitment drives by the Maoists (see Eck, this volume). The Maoist also forcibly recruited through programs such as "one house, one guerilla" (Shah 2008; ICG 2005).

The Maoist did not receive significant external material assistance. However, the open international border with India helped the Maoists. The initial training and supply of some arms and probably regular supply of ammunition and explosives via Indian Maoists, their network, or other channels were crucial in their growth. Prachanda has said that he lived eight out of ten years underground during the insurgency in India. The presence of 12 million Nepalis in India (many of whom are part of AINUS–All India Nepali Unity Society) helped the rebels in networking with Indian sympathizers, getting shelter, and collecting funds.[9]

Maoist military strategy

The Maoist military strategies were greatly influenced by Mao's writing on the protracted People's War in China. The notion was to encircle the center by first winning the rural regions.[10] It was a useful strategy for the Maoists because it allowed them to grow in rural areas away from the reach of the central state. The classic three-stage Maoist guerilla warfare philosophy was discernible in their military strategy: strategic defensive, strategic stalemate and strategic offensive. The first phase lasted from 1996 to 2001. It relied entirely on guerilla tactics and focused on attacking the police and scrupulously avoiding the RNA. The hit and run tactics raided police posts, destroyed communication centers, looted banks and destroyed government offices (Dhruba Kumar 2006; ICG 2005).

After a review of five years of People's War, the Maoist fused the Maoist and Leninist modes by adopting Prachandapath, whereby both rural and urban mobilization was emphasized. This change in strategy came after the realization that Mao's Chinese strategy alone would not work in a highly centralized Nepal where the ruling elite was not much bothered about the goings on in the hinterland. A range of urban insurrection tactics such as "to use fraternal organizations to carry out strikes and street demonstrations, to foment revolt within the RNA and to seek to polarize sympathetic and opposed political forces" were applied, especially by its student front during the 2001 ceasefire (ICG 2005: 23–24).

The second stage saw a dramatic shift to direct confrontation with the RNA which commenced with the breakdown of the peace talks and simultaneous attacks on RNA posts and government buildings in Dang on November 23, 2001. This led to the imposition of the state of emergency, deployment of the RNA, and the formation of composite posts (RNA, civil police and armed police). The Maoists incurred losses in the confrontations with the RNA. Before the state of emergency was declared on November 25, 2001, the Maoists and the state had killed 811 and 992 persons respectively in nearly six years, but in the next nine months during the emergency the state killed nearly three times more Maoists and Maoist suspects than the Maoists – state and Maoists killed 2,580 and 948 persons respectively (INSEC 2008). As a result of the increasing losses (Hill 2004), the Maoist called for peace talks and dialogue at least six times during the second half of 2002 while the government appeared confident in repressing the Maoists and rejected their offers. However, the Maoists continued to regroup and conducted major raids at Sandhikharka (September 8, 2002) and Khalanga (November 14, 2002), Argakhanchi DHQ and the zonal headquarters of Karnali respectively. The Maoist also began to resort to high-value targets to exhibit that they were a potent force to reckon with: the Armed Police Force (APF) chief and his wife were assassinated in Kathmandu. The raids and high value targets within Kathmandu Valley probably forced the government to sit for the second round of talks, which began in January 2003.

After the end of second ceasefire, the Maoists announced the beginning of the third stage, the strategic offence, in August 2004 after the central committee plenary. It followed the selective targeting of the RNA, political leaders and government officials. However, major raids hardly occurred until March 2005, partly because the RNA camps were fortified. The Maoists, in fact, suffered a major reverse during the ill-advised attack on Khara military camp in April 2005. However, the Pilli raid on August 2005 on the RNA road construction team provided a psychological boost to the PLA.[11] The Maoists conducted around a half-dozen major raids after March 2005 when the RNA got tied up in enforcing the King's takeover. The raids on Tansen (January 31, 2006), DHQ of Palpa, led to major casualties while raids at Dhangadi (January 11, 2006), Dhankuta (February 7, 2006) and Illam (March 5, 2006) headquarters of Kailali, Eastern Region, Illam, were only partially successful (they destroyed some government buildings but could not completely overrun the security bases). Despite Maoist claims, a strategic stalemate prevailed for most of 2004 and thereafter. The Maoists did not capture and control urban areas and DHQs, which the government was determined to defend. The long-announced strategic military offensive actually never took off.

The Royal Nepal Army

The RNA traces its origin to 1748, when the Shri Nath Gan was raised under the order of King Prithvinarayan Shah as a preparation for the conquest of Nepal. Over the next 20 years the total strength of the army was raised to ten Gans (infantry battalions) and a number of independent companies called "gulmas" were raised to administer captured territory. Nepali security thinking was influenced by the expansionist ways of the British East India Company. At the time of Indian independence RNA had 16 to 18 infantry battalions and approximately 25 independent companies. The organized soldiery had increased slowly in nearly 200 years.

The RNA was very loyal to the monarchy. The structural and historical loyalty of the RNA to King and Palace was a legacy of the past when its forebears were used by the Rana and Shah rulers to prop up their feudal interests. The culture made state security synonymous with the security of the institution of monarchy (and national unity) and the security policy was fashioned by the Palace-monarchy-RNA trio.

Organization and deployment of the RNA

At the time of the Maoist attack on the RNA camp at Dang on November 23, 2001, the 53,000-strong RNA had one division deployed in the West at Nepalganj, one brigade in the central region at Pokhara and a brigade in the East at Dhankuta. By early 2003, the two brigades had been upgraded to divisions. In November 2004, two more division headquarters were raised at Hetauda and Dipayal making the RNA an army of five operational divisions in addition to the Kathmandu Valley Division. The army deployment in early 2005 was:[12]

- Valley Division – Kathmandu
  One brigade, Royal Guards brigade and ten Special Forces brigades
- Mid-West Division – Surkhet
  One brigade each at Surkhet, Dang and Jumla
- Far West Division – Dipayal
  One brigade each at Dhangarhi and Dadeldhura
- Eastern Division – Dhankuta
  One brigade each at Hille, Ilam and Udayapur
- Central Division – Suparitar, Makwanpur
  One brigade each at Barreni, Chitwan and Sindhuli
- Western Division – Pokhara
  One brigade each at Pokhara, Butwal and Baglung

The other brigades are Special Forces, Air Assault, Artillery, Engineers, Signals, and Logistics. The brigades are numbered from 1 to 25. The seven fighting brigades were expanded to 15 operational brigades, including one in Kathmandu (excluding the Royal Palace Guards Brigades). In early 2005 the RNA could support one or two battalion groups for combat for four days. By the end of 2005, the RNA had expanded to around 90,000.[13]

Indian support to the RNA

While the PLA did not receive external material support, the RNA benefitted from American, British, and especially Indian military assistance. India provided arms and ammunition, training and other military support as part of a 500 crore rupees Military Modernization Package agreed in 1991 (there was a break for some time in the implementation of the agreement).[14] India's concern had grown with the rise of the Maoists and their occasional shrill anti-India rhetoric, security of thousands of ex-servicemen and family members of 50,000 Gorkha soldiers serving the Indian Army and paramilitary forces,[15] and the possibility of opening an insurgency corridor, the Compact Revolutionary Zone (CZR), stretching from the coastal areas of Andhra Pradesh to Bihar's long and porous border with Nepal.

After the Maoist insurgency flared up, the training and military advice for the RNA was revived. A bilateral India-Nepal Bilateral Consultative Group on Security Issues (INBCGSI) was set up in 2003 with the aim of meeting twice a year (it did not function during the royal takeover). India's military assistance and training programs increased the RNA's fighting capabilities considerably.

Factors responsible for the RNA and PLA's performance

Ceremonial RNA and motivated PLA

The RNA's largely ceremonial character hindered it from containing the Maoists despite its disproportionate size, better equipment and training and external support. The RNA had not engaged in combat for a long time. The last time it was involved in extensive combat operations was against Tibet in 1892, and before that against the British in 1814–16. More recently one battalion was involved in evicting Tibetan Khampa rebels from Nepali soil in Mustang and Mugu in the far northwest region in 1974. The army was also used briefly to put down the Nepali Congress revolt in Okhaldunga during the Panchayat regime.

The RNA had never envisaged an internal threat such as the Maoist rebellion. Even in the 1923 and 1950 security treaties with India, an internal threat was never considered (Muni 1992). Likewise it has never been clear whether the RNA seriously factored into its planning any external threat, either from north or south. The RNA's deployment mainly in the Tarai in the 1970s suggested that it envisaged a primary threat from the south – India – though logistics was mentioned as a prime consideration for RNA "looking south." The RNA has been a defensive army maintaining neutrality in foreign policy. The operational concept was to fight delaying battles in the plains and mountains with independent companies, battalions and brigades.

The RNA's deployment pattern – heavy concentration in Kathmandu and, unlike other armies, units in many DHQs instead of near command headquarters – and the recruitment pattern of the top brass – Rana, Shah, and Chhetris with close connection with the palace – reveals RNA's prime concern: royal regime security. The military doctrine was to protect a Hindu King, who was considered a reincarnation of the god Vishnu. The objective was strengthened through various means, such as loyalty ensured through recruitment of the top brass largely from the ruling community, naming RNA's units with names of Hindu gods and goddesses, socializing military officials into a culture of divine worship, and heavy reliance on the propitiation of Hindu gods and religious ceremonies. An organization developed to protect the interests of a royal dynasty and the ruling community's interests through loyalty inculcated from selective recruitment and rituals does not stand on a solid foundation to meet the threats that emerge from large-scale political-military mobilization.

The RNA was fashioned into a ceremonial force, with a flair for United Nations peacekeeping operations, which can entail danger in some missions but are not a preparation for a country's security. All armies have significant elements of ceremony, but rituals and ceremonies are used to reinforce larger objectives and are not an end in themselves. The RNA continued to focus on peacekeeping even during the insurgency. As many as 3,000 soldiers on average were on such missions at any one time during early 2000s. Nepal even offered to send a battalion to Afghanistan as part of the ongoing operations but the offer was declined by the US. The attraction of a peacekeeping force is largely due to monetary reasons – soldiers earn many times more in a United Nations mission than their meager salaries and hence the United Nations mission is an attraction for joining the army. Such an incentive need not necessarily become problematic but it can if it overshadows the main objectives of an army.

Even after the state of emergency, the RNA was governed by traditional Kathmandu culture: a panoply of ceremonial activities, no let-up in United Nations peacekeeping missions and a heavy concentration of troops in Kathmandu. The Shree Kali Bahadur Battalion and Shree Gorakh Nath Battalion were permanently earmarked as Palace Guard battalions. One of the two was always deployed in the Palace while the second battalion for the Palace was chosen by the King from remaining infantry battalions. In addition, a light battery and anti-aircraft guns were deployed in the Palace. Another two battalions were employed in protecting wildlife parks. Ministers had aides-de camp and retired and serving generals had squads of soldiers as batmen. Army orderlies were used to build the houses of senior officers and provide other personal services. It was estimated in June 2002 that at least four battalions could have been raised from troops located in the Kathmandu valley for counter-insurgency operations.

One reason for the RNA's weakness was its Palace orientation. The RNA motto decreed that the safety, honor and welfare of King and Country came first. Promotion and posting of top officials depended upon networking with and loyalty to the Palace. All the army chiefs came from families with an aristocratic/military background and traditional links to the monarchy (Nepali and Subba 2005: 89). The ethnic and caste network affected promotion and posting of officers down the ladder. The Rana, Shah, and Chhetri content was much higher among RNA officers.[16] These practices resulted in loyalty and an appropriate network trumping professionalism in the army. When a big challenge emerged, the top brass did not have the operational capabilities to handle it.

The absence of sound professionalism led to wrong priorities, missed opportunities, and underutilization of resources. An army busy in ceremonial functions and practices did not devote time and energy to developing a sound intelligence system, which undermined its understanding of society and hindered its operations.[17] The RNA was able to defend its bases and reduce its casualties through fortification but it "robbed the RNA of the initiative and left them with a limited capacity of mount offensive operations" (Hill 2004). Likewise the army's insistence on the declaration of a state of emergency for its deployment proved shortsighted. A culture of impunity led to indiscriminate killings and human rights violations (see Conclusion) and reduced its support in society. Without popular support it is hard to isolate insurgents, and counter-insurgency in such conditions rarely succeeds (Weitz 1986). The 2005 royal coup, which the RNA supported (if not instigated), put the parliamentary political parties, media, human rights groups, intelligentsia, and international actors squarely against the state and military. Even a capable and professional army would rarely have succeeded in counter-insurgency programs in such an adverse situation. Likewise, unlike the Maoists, the RNA made very little effort to mobilize British and Indian army ex-servicemen, many of whom were experts in counter-insurgency.

While the RNA was bogged down in ceremonialism, the Maoists demonstrated a high degree of motivation and commitment, and developed sound strategies and tactics, making the best use of available resources and opportunities. The Maoists adeptly avoided the army until they perceived that they were ready to confront it. Even though they had circled an army group pursuing them in Holleri in July 2001, Pasang writes that they let the army retreat (2064 v.s./2007). This strategy worked partly because of the gullibility of the state and the RNA, which did not consider the Maoists as a serious threat.

The Maoists compensated for insufficient weapons and numbers by preparing an extremely physically fit army, which contributed to the success of the raids. The PLA would often travel for several days before attacks and conduct the raids in the night and retreat, often with the RNA in hot pursuit on the ground and in the air, for several days to reach their safe shelters. The rugged terrain also helped the guerillas.

The PLA often mobilized local supporters in their base areas to help in the attacks by creating distractions or as volunteer support units. For instance, during the raid in Dhartigaon on February 19, the Maoists acknowledge that 2,000 local people took out torch rallies, beat drums and shouted slogans to distract and terrorize the government security forces (Pasang 2064.v.s.).

The PLA also envisioned and prepared for counter-insurgency actions of the RNA by studying various counter-insurgency tactics of the American, British and Indian armies. Pasang said that they developed a strategy of "search and clean" to counter RNA's "search and destroy" counter-insurgency offensive.[18] The aim was to eliminate active government supporters and sympathizers in villages. After the success of raids the PLA claim that they released police and army personnel but deliberately killed local government sympathizers who aided the security forces (Pasang 2064 v.s./2007). This selective violence conveyed a message to commoners that it was fatally risky to help the government with information and in other ways while they would be unharmed if they did not actively support the government security agencies. The strategy, which contrasted with indiscriminate abuses by the security forces, allowed the Maoists to gain operating support in many villages.

The success of armies also depends upon their spirits. Leo Tolstoy, in *War and Peace* (1869), argued that the reason the poorly equipped and outnumbered Russian troops defeated the Germans in the 1812 war was, in addition to the Russian winter that created problems for the Germans, because the Russians were engaged in a spirited defense of their country.

The difference between the RNA and PLA in terms of spirit and motivation is clear. The PLA was fighting for a cause. Part of the spirit came from motivated recruits whereas others joined PLA to take revenge for the RNA and state repression. The CPN-M also regularly indoctrinated (see Eck, this volume) and conducted post-death commemoration to develop a cult of sacrifice that attracted soldiers seeking martyrdom (Lecomte-Tilouine 2006). The indoctrination and socialization made the PLA cadres ready to sacrifice their lives. The PLA's spirits were bolstered before attacks through days of motivational lectures, which included not only specific responsibilities during attacks but also political objectives for particular attacks, by commanders and commissars (Pasang 2064 v.s./2007).

The motivational spirit of the PLA is clear from the description of the attacks and raids. Pasang (2064 v.s./2007) describes the deaths of several cadres in the snow during the trek along the rugged and unknown terrain on the way to the Dunai raid. The PLA attacked various police posts, district headquarters and other government agencies even during difficult situations such as rain and snow. To prevent detection, the PLA often travelled to the raid sites for several days in order to just arrive ahead of the actual attack. This meant that they often were sleepless and tired during the raids. The PLA sometime had inadequate supplies of food, not only during retreats but on their way to raids. All the fighters were also not fully equipped and many carried only home-made equipment. Nevertheless they launched many successful raids and attacks.

On the other hand, the motivation among the RNA to fight the Maoists was not exceptional. In fact, desertions from police and army ranged from 5 to 10 percent and increased after the Maoists began targeting families of RNA soldiers, especially in the west (Mehta 2005). According to a retired army officer, the problem had become serious enough to prepare an internal report on the phenomenon.[19]

The low motivation among the RNA was partly to be expected because they were not fighting for a cause as the PLA were. Many officers joined the RNA for social mobility whereas lower-level cadres joined for job and economic security. This is, however, true for most armies. The difference between the RNA and other armies is the inadequate regimental system and spirit of camaraderie. Regular army cadres are indoctrinated into the regimental spirit and on the battlefield they risk their lives to protect their brothers in the regiment. In Nepal, as the regimental system was not strong, the regimental spirit was weak and as such the cadre corps lacked an immediate cause to put their lives in the line of fire. Further, a distance existed between officers and soldiers, and the roughshod treatment of soldiers did not make for strong bonding. Higher and junior officers were reluctant to confront the Maoists initially. Sustained combat against Maoists improved the quality and cohesion of the RNA, but as the next section shows, the success of an army depends upon larger political contexts as well.

Political division versus coordinated movement

Political decisions and environment affect an army's performance in civil wars. Division and mistrust among the establishment actors had a perverse effect on the performance of the RNA even as the Maoists, when necessary, managed to effectively coordinate the activities of different organizations and fronts that, otherwise, often operated in a decentralized manner. Beyond the stated principle of "high centralization" under which they claimed to operate, mobile phones and signal communications as a command network enabled the Maoists to coordinate important activities such as raids.

One major political decision – or lack of decision – that affected the RNA's effectiveness against the Maoist was its delayed deployment. While the Maoists began nibbling from western Nepal, Kathmandu chose to ignore the threat and let it grow. The uprising was conveniently but mistakenly diagnosed as a local law and order problem. Despite the graffiti on the wall, Nepal failed to mobilize and prepare the RNA to contain the Maoists. Successive governments failed to create a national consensus on how to deal with the Maoist threat, and civilian governments could not get the royal assent to deploy the RNA. The Nepali state first deployed the ill-trained and poorly equipped police force to contain the Maoists. The Maoists were not only able to overcome the police actions but in fact looted weapons and ammunitions from the police. When the RNA was finally deployed in late 2001, six years into the insurgency, the Maoist armed rebellion had grown considerably. The failure to mobilize the sword arm enabled the Maoists to develop capability and clout.[20] The PLA grew in size, gained battle experience, and developed support areas. Its successes against the police force increased the confidence of its fighters and sympathizers and increased its attraction for rural youth, hence facilitating recruitment. In Peru, as in Nepal, the initial deployment of the police had allowed the Shining Path insurgency to grow and expand (Obando 1998).

An earlier deployment of the RNA does not necessarily mean that RNA would have been successful in crushing the PLA; but the possibility of crushing the Maoists, if it ever existed, would have been higher when the PLA was still in its formative years. Scholars have argued that military options are more effective in the initial years of insurgency before the insurgents have the opportunity to consolidate influence in any region (Weitz 1986: 409).

A major reason for the delay in RNA deployment against the PLA was mistrust among the establishment side: between the politicians and the King and between the politicians and the army top brass. The civilian political leadership suspected that the King and army could stage coups against them, as in 1960. The attitudes of the civilian leadership, on the other hand, made the RNA mistrustful of the politicians. The new political class in Nepal was unfamiliar in relating to the RNA. Owing to historic mistrust, the Nepali Congress did not attempt to cultivate the army after it came to power in 1990. In fact it attempted to promote, expand, and use the police. In the late 1990s the budget of the police was increased drastically while the RNA got a smaller increase. In the course of the insurgency, an armed police force was established and the army perceived its establishment as an attempt to counter or dilute its power.[21]

The mistrust largely grew from the perceived as well as real loyalty of the RNA to the monarch. During the 14 years of fractious democracy, RNA allegiance to the Palace was never in doubt. Senior army officers were fiercely loyal to the King. The RNA had historical contempt for the political establishment and was reluctant to accept civilian political control. Any challenge to monarchy was regarded as a threat to the RNA.

The army was loyal to the King for historic as well as contemporary reasons. The army did not only perceived itself as a force that helped the ancestors of the monarch to "unite" the country, but felt that kings had treated the army well. The Royal title was given to the RNA by King Mahendra in 1965 after it helped him quash democracy.

The RNA was also loyal to the monarchy because the King controlled it through promotions and postings. Article 119 (1) of the 1990 Constitution conferred the King as Supreme Commander, and the appointment of the Commander-in-Chief of the RNA was to be made by the King on the recommendation of the Prime Minister according to Article 119 (2). However, it was the King who made the selection, and the monarchy controlled the promotion of top army officers through its influence over the Commander-in-Chief. For the officer corps, the King was *sarkar* (government).

The control of the army by the King was partly due to the weakness of the civilian politicians in exercising power awarded to them by the 1990 Constitution. The politicians had fought hard to put the army under the National Defense Council (NDC) during the constitution making process in 1990 (Lawoti 2007b; Hachhethu 1994). The 1990 Constitution clearly stipulated that the RNA would be guided by the NDC headed by the Prime Minister. Article 118 (2) stated: "His Majesty shall operate and use the RNA on the recommendation of the NDC." However, according to former Chief of Army Staff (CoAS) General Dharam Pal Thapa, no government forced its prerogative under either Article 118 (2) or Article 119 (2). The NDC consisted of the Prime Minister, the Defense Minister and the CoAS. During the whole decade of the 1990s, a separate Defense Minister was never appointed. Since the Prime Minister was also his own Defense Minister, a tie existed between the Prime Minister and the CoAS. As the Prime Minister was too occupied, the CoAS effectively controlled the army. Nomination of a separate Defense Minister would have easily turned the balance of power toward the civilians and changed the loyalty dynamics, but a Defense Minister was appointed only in 2000. Rational and career-oriented officers would have understood where the real power lay.

The government's mistrust of the army made it reluctant initially to deploy state troops against the rebels. Likewise, the civilian governments did not support the RNA's initiatives against the insurgency. After the insurgency began, the army had submitted a plan to the government for deploying the army with a development package of 6.3/6.5 million rupees, but the government rejected the proposal and continued to use the police. Further, Prime Minister Koirala preferred to give the Integrated Internal Security and Development Program (IISDP) funds to the police instead of to the RNA. The civilian government did not want to strengthen the RNA, whose loyalty it suspected (Nepali and Subba 2005; Gordon 2005).

As the police failed to control the Maoists and the insurgents' influence grew, the government sought to deploy the army but the King was ambivalent about it. The King felt it ought not to be used against its own people, while the parties feared the consequences of using it. In July 2000, PM Koirala had to resign because the RNA did not respond effectively to rescue the police following abductions of nearly six dozen policemen from the Holleri Police Post. The army did not show direct insubordination but sought to evade implementing the civilian government's order (Nepali and Subba 2005).

The army has consistently denied the charge that it was unwilling or untrained to deal with the Maoists. General Dharampal Thapa has said he was alive to the developing Maoist threat. He claimed he had sent a team to Surkhet under Brigadier Chitra Gurung to monitor the insurgency soon after it started and proposed the IISDP in tandem with the use of force. An operational plan to deploy three brigades in Rukum and Rolpa under Major General Prajwalla Rana (who later became CoAS) was ready in 1997, which had the political approval of Prime Minister Chand and Deputy Prime Minister and Home Minister Bamdev Gautam. However, King Birendra was in two minds.[22]

The frequent changes in government contributed to failure in developing a coherent military strategy against the Maoists. During the period from 1996 till April 2006, 13 governments were formed. Some of the civilian leaders had a better relationship with the military top brass while others did not. Short-lived coalition governments shifted focus from policy debates to coalition formation. Different priorities of different governments, bickering among political parties to form governments, and divisions within the establishment prevented development of a common position against the CPN-M.

The counter-insurgency's effectiveness was further compromised by governance failures. In Peru, Bolivia, and Venezuela previous land reform and other pro-poor policies of the government generated support among the peasants towards counter-insurgency programs (Weitz 1986; McClintock 1992; Starn 1995; Marks and Palmer 2005). The RNA was also disadvantaged by the government policy of pulling back government agencies from rural areas after Maoists raided police posts and security camps. During the insurgency around 65 percent of police posts were withdrawn (Lawoti forthcoming 2009). When the Deuba government discontinued local governments in 2002 primarily because the opposition CPN-UML controlled a large majority of them, the vacuum further increased. The vacuum allowed the Maoists to easily fill the void, establish control in the rural regions, and cut off the RNA and state from local information, and made it increasingly difficulty for the RNA to get a foothold in the regions later on.

While the lack of coherent strategy and tactics on the establishment side hindered its counter-insurgency efforts, the Maoists successfully coordinated the party, PLA, and numerous fraternal fronts for a common objective. The PLA was firmly under the control of the party. Each PLA unit was under a political commissar. The PLA carried out raids the party ordered even in difficult circumstances. For instance, the PLA made dramatic raids in Bhojpur and Beni in March 2004 and on an army base in Pilli in August 2005 to counter the RNA's propaganda of winning the war, which was based on the RNA's claims of killing and capturing Maoist leaders and destroying shelters. The hold of the party and the PLA's obedience can be witnessed in the attack on Khara in April 2005. A former British general says that it was impossible for the raid to succeed but the PLA nevertheless carried out the orders from the party high command (Cowan 2008).

When the PLA and the party were unable to launch raids and activities, the Maoists relied on fraternal organizations like the ethnic and student fronts to blockade district headquarters, the Kathmandu valley, and regions – some times for months – and called strikes (Lawoti 2003). For instance, the party launched the surprisingly effective economic blockade of Kathmandu valley in August–September 2004. It showed that the tactics of intimidation and psychological warfare were sometimes more powerful than the use of firearms and targeted assassinations. Fusion of military and political strategies together with the coordinated actions among the PLA, the party, and fraternal organizations allowed the movement to continuously engage the enemy and garner political achievements even when the PLA and the main party organization encountered setbacks.

Strategic stalemate and political settlement

The PLA and RNA invested heavily in the civil war even though neither achieved their ultimate objectives. Without the PLA, the Maoist movement would not have reached the height it did. On the other hand, the RNA defended the establishment and foiled the Maoist's attempt to take over the state violently. The civil war was eventually settled by political moves and strategies.

The Maoists have emerged triumphant largely owing to political foresight and strategies and not through military victory. The Maoists abandoned the military option because by 2004 they had realized the difficulty of defeating the RNA in direct confrontation. There were reports that the Maoists were debating whether to reach an understanding with the King or with the parliamentary political parties and India.

The RNA, on the other hand, emerged as a loser despite not being defeated militarily. Its loss resulted from its strategic mistake to support the February 2005 Royal coup (Angbuhang 2009). The RNA appeared to be more confident and started to bask in the glory of having become a new power center in 2005, as the King attempted to transform the RNA through proposed salary hikes, promotions, overseas appointments and other perks. However, the coup isolated the King and the RNA. International actors denounced the coup while internally it pushed the parliamentary parties toward the Maoists. The coup eventually contributed to the end of monarchy and marginalization of the Nepal Army. More importantly, however, it facilitated peace settlement by neutralizing the RNA and producing a stalemate.

The Maoists too were surprised by the King's takeover of power and called him a "national betrayer." Some say that Prachanda was angered because King Gyanendra had betrayed him in an understanding the two sides had. Whether this is true or not, the unforeseen consequence of the coup was unity among the King's foes. Prachanda rescinded punishment of Baburam Bhattarai, who had been put in Maoist imprisonment, and reinstated him in the party; he sent him to negotiate with political parties and India, which eventually facilitated an understanding between the parliamentary parties and the Maoists.

After RNA's active support for the King, the mistrust between the RNA and the parliamentary political parties peaked, and the military option was no longer seen as viable by the parliamentary parties. They negotiated with the Maoists from a weakened position without the backing of military force. Four months after the

Royal takeover, the political parties were able to forge an alliance with the Maoist for the restoration of "total democracy." The joint movement of the Maoists, seven parliamentary political party alliance and civil society eventually forced the King to give up power in April 2006. Along with the King, the popular uprising weakened the RNA. With the neutralization of the Nepal Army, the Maoists marched on to political victory, first negotiating favorable terms during the 2006 peace agreement and eventually winning the election to the Constituent Assembly in 2008, when fear and intimidation also played a role.

Notes

1   We would like to thank political leaders, including Maoists, and PLA and Nepal Army officers for sharing their views and experiences, and anonymous Nepal Army officers for commenting on an earlier draft.
2   The RNA's name was changed to the Nepal Army after the April 2006 People's Movement.
3   However, even when states were successful, repression alone was insufficient. Unless the underlying causes of rebellions are addressed, as the Indian experience with Maoist insurgency shows, repression in one period may not eliminate the rebellion altogether.
4   The Nepal army has complained that the Indian aid included INSAS rifles that heated up and did not perform well after repeated firing. Nepal army sources also state that the Cheetah helicopter provided by India had almost completed its service period.
5   This section draws from ICG (2005) and is supplemented by other sources.
6   Pasang (2064 v.s./2007: 19), the commander of PLA, writes that in the first attack on the Holeri Police Post to launch the war, three dozen fighters with one rifle (nicknamed "whole timer"), 15–20 local muskets (*bharuwa banduk*), and home-made *sutali* bombs were used.
7   Shah, a retired RNA general, presented the data in a paper at a seminar in India.
8   Military experts question whether the Maoist formations (such as divisions and brigades) were of regular military size and allege that they were created to project at par size with the RNA.
9   The government of India banned AINUS on July 1, 2002, and deported several active and suspected Maoist leaders to Nepal (SATP 2008).
10   Pasang said that they also developed military strategies and tactics by reading military theorists such as Giap and Caluswitz and learning about American and Indian counter insurgency policies.
11   The Maoists were successful because the RNA had deployed a unit without establishing a good defense mechanism (Cowan 2008).
12   Information obtained from RNA sources in December, 2004 by first author. A battalion has roughly 800 soldiers. A brigade has three battalions and a division, three brigades. The rest of the forces are combat and logistics support forces.
13   The police had the strength of 63,000 while the armed police 18,000 in 2005.
14   India has had long standing security interest in Nepal. In 1919, a British Foreign Office document noted: "Nepal is in a position to exercise powerful influence on India's internal stability and if it were disaffected, the anarchy would spill over . . ." (Mehta 1975). Nepal and British India signed a security treaty in 1923 and its successor treaty of Peace and Friendship in 1950. The Indian military assistance was first sought at the height of anti-Rana revolution in 1950. Two companies of Indian soldiers were on call to be flown to Kathmandu but in the end were not required. At one time, India had established 21 joint border check posts on the Nepal–Tibet border. In 1959, the Indian Army signalers helped Nepal in its first multi-party elections. The Indian Military Mission in Nepal was set up in 1952 in Kathmandu at the request of King Tribhuwan for reorganizing, training

and modernizing the RNA. The task was carried out over the next ten years with the nomenclature of the assistance changing to Military Training and Advisory Group in 1958 and thereafter Military Liaison Group in 1963. From 1963 onwards, RNA started looking to other countries for training and modernization, despite a clause in the 1965 Memorandum of Understanding requiring Nepal to acquire its military needs through India. China, UK, USA and Israel were the countries whose help was sought. However, the bulk of RNA needs were met by the Indian Army. The Indian military aided in the reorganization of the RNA into Army Headquarters and three infantry brigades and setting up of training institutions and logistics installations. The Military Liaison group and border check posts were withdrawn in August 1970 after a request by Nepal.

15 Based on a tripartite agreement, Nepalis serve in the armies of UK and India.
16 There were just a handful of Madhesi soldiers. Although Muslims had been enrolled in the Mule companies, these units were disbanded. In September, 2005, RNA announced the raising of a Tarai and Kiranti (from east) battalions.
17 In Peru, the capture of many top leaders of Shining Path in early 1990s by the intelligence agency gave a severe blow to the rebellion (Obando 1998).
18 Interview, August 2008.
19 Interview, summer 2006.
20 Despite weaknesses, the RNA was still much more professional and coherent than the Nepal Police, which had been racked by partisan politics and corruption in the 1990s.
21 The army, on the other hand, dragged its foot on delivering arms to the armed police force.
22 There are other versions why the RNA was held back. Then general secretary of the National Democratic Party (NDP) Pashupati Shamsher Rana said that King Birendra did sanction the use of RNA but the government changed. Veteran diplomat Bhekh Bahadur Thapa said Koirala was keen to use the army but King Birendra wanted to first build a national consensus.

Bibliography

Angbuhang, Ranadhoj Limbu. 2009. Lessons of War I & II. *The Kathmandu Post*, February 23 & 24.
Cowan, Sam. 2008. The Lost Battles of Khara and Pili. *Hima Southasian*, October.
Dhruba Kumar. 2006. Military Dimension of the Maoist Insurgency. In *Nepal: Facets of Maoist Insurgency*, edited by L. R. Baral. New Delhi: Adroit.
Dhruba Kumar, and Hari Sharma. 2005. *Security Sector Reform in Nepal: Challenges and Opportunities*. Kathmandu: Friends for Peace.
Douglas, Ed. 2005. Inside Nepal's Revolution. *National Geographic*, 46–65.
Gordon, Stuart. 2005. Evaluating Nepal's Integrated "Security" and "Development" Policy. *Asian Survey* XLV (4):581–602.
Hachhethu, Krishna. 1994. Transition to Democracy in Nepal: Negotiations Behind Constitution Making, 1990. *Contributions to Nepalese Studies* 21 (1):91–126.
Hill, John. 2004. Royal Nepalese Army adapts to counterinsurgency role. *Jane's Intelligence Review*, July 1.
ICG. 2005. *Nepal's Maoists: Their Arms, Structure and Strategy*. Kathmandu/Brussels: International Crisis Group.
INSEC. 2008. *Human Rights Year Book 2008*. Kathmandu: INSEC
Jarstad, Anna K., and Timothy D. Sisk, eds. 2008. *From War to Democracy: Dilemmas of Peacebuilding*. Cambridge: Cambridge University Press.
Kumar, Krishna, ed. 1998. *Postconflict Elections, Democratization, and International Assistance*. Boulder: Lynne Rienner Publisher.

Lawoti, Mahendra. 2003. Maoists and Minorities: Overlap of Interests or the case of Exploitation? *Studies in Nepali History and Society* 8 (1):67–97.

——. ed. 2007a. *Contentious Politics and Democratization in Nepal*. Los Angeles, London, New Delhi and Singapore: Sage Publications.

——. 2007b. Democracy, Domination, and Exclusionary Constitutional Engineering in Nepal. In *Contentious Politics and Democratization in Nepal*, edited by M. Lawoti. Los Angeles, London, New Delhi, and Singapore: Sage Publicaitons.

——. Forthcoming (2009). Nepal. In *Encyclopedia of Human Rights*, edited by D. P. Forsythe. New York: Oxford University Press.

Lecomte-Tilouine, Marie. 2006. "Kill One, He Becomes One Hundred": Martydom as Generative Sacrifice in the Nepal People's War. *Social Analysis* 50 (1):51–72.

Marks, Thomas A., and David Scott Palmer. 2005. Radical Maoist Insurgents and Terrorist Tactics: Comparing Peru and Nepal. *Low Intensity Conflict & Law Enforcement* 13 (2):91–116.

McClintock, Cynthia. 1992. Theories of Revolution and the Case of Peru. In *The Shining Path of Peru*, edited by D. S. Palmer. New York: St. Martin's Press.

Mehta, Ashok K. 1975. Excercise Tribhuvan, edited by M. The College of Combat.

——. 2005. *The Royal Nepal Army: Meeting the Maoist Challenge*. New Delhi: Rupa and Co.

Muni, S. D. 1992. *India and Nepal: A Changing Relationship*. New Delhi: Konark Publishers.

Nepali, Prakash, and Phanindra Subba. 2005. Civil-Military Relations and the Maoist Insurgency in Nepal. *Small Wars and Insurgencies* 16 (1):83–110.

Obando, Enrique. 1998. Civil-Military Relations in Peru, 1980–96: How to Control and Coopt the Military (and the consequences of doing so) In *Shining and Other Paths*, edited by S. J. Stern. Durham, NC: Duke University Press.

Pasang, Nandakishore Pun. 2064 v.s./2007. *Itihaaska Raktim Paila: Januddhaaka Mahatwapurna Fauji Karbahiharu (History's Bloody Step: Peoples War's Important Military Operations)*. Kathmandu: Sambad.

SATP. 2008. Akhil Bharatiya Nepali Ekata Samaj (ABNES): South Asia Terrorism Portal.

——. 2008. Fatalities in Major Clashes between Security and Insurgent Forces: South Asia Terrorism Portal.

Shah, Sadip. 2004. Assessment of Strategic Military Balance: RNA and Maoists. In *Restoring Peace and Stability in Nepal*. New Delhi: India International Center.

Shah, Saubhagya. 2008. Revolution and Reaction in the Himalayas: Cultural Resistance and the Maoist "New Regime" in Western Nepal. *American Ethnologist* 35 (3):481–99.

Starn, Orin. 1995. To Revolt against the Revolution: War and Resistance in Peru's Andes. *Cultural Anthropology* 10 (4):547–80.

Tolstoy, Leo. [1869] 2006. *War and Peace*. Harmondsworth, UK: Penguin.

Weitz, Richard. 1986. Insurgency and Counterinsurgency in Latin America, 1960–80. *Political Science Quarterly* 101 (3):397–413.

10 Unequal rebellions

The continuum of "People's War" in Nepal and India

Anup K. Pahari

Introduction

South Asia has seen several major waves of Maoist armed insurgency since the founding of Maoism in China in the 1940s. Three of these unfolded in the subcontinent, while the fourth erupted in Sri Lanka in several episodes starting in the early 1970s. This chapter will be concerned with explaining the differential evolution and outcomes associated with three distinct waves of Maoist "People's War" in India and Nepal over a period of roughly four and a half decades starting in the mid-1960s.

The first of these occurred in India between 1965 and 1975 and is known as the Naxalite movement, named after Naxalbari, the locale in which the Maoist-inspired tribal/peasant revolts first erupted in the State of West Bengal. At its peak, the first wave of Naxalite insurgency engulfed sizeable portions of three states in India's north and indirectly impacted half a dozen others. A number of factors jointly contributed to ending this first wave of South Asian Maoist "People's War" as quickly as it had started. These included: inherent weaknesses of the West Bengal Maoist party; the response and adjustments made by the major political parties to the Maoist challenge; successful counter-mobilization by various layers of the Indian State and state institutions; and finally, historical contingencies like the Bangladesh war of Independence and Indian Prime Minister Indira Gandhi's Emergency Rule.

The second wave of Maoist armed insurgency in South Asia ignited from the dying embers of the original West Bengal Naxalite movement. Naxalite cells in Bihar, Andhra Pradesh and Orissa were active simultaneously with the Bengal Naxalites, albeit on a smaller scale (Banerji 1984; Dash 2006). Many of these splinter Maoist cells had a longstanding nexus with the West Bengal Naxalite movement and its leaders, and with India's first and original Maoist party, the Communist Party of India (Marxist Leninist) – CPI-ML. With their displacement from West Bengal, India's head Maoist party – CPI-ML – shifted its attention to a half-dozen neighboring Indian states and began re-partnering with regional revolutionary leaders to rekindle the "People's War." Thus, even as West Bengal transitioned to post-Naxalite politics dominated by the parliamentary left, dozens of Naxalite cells regrouped in the neighboring states of Bihar, Orissa and Andhra Pradesh and resolved to pursue the "People's War" agenda anew, eager to implement lessons learned from the defeat of the original Naxalite movement (Ramana 2006). Through the 1990s and into the new century, when much of India's attention and energy were focused on riding the wave of globalization, dozens of neo-Naxalite cells were on a quiet but furious mission to reestablish themselves in the largest and most densely populated tribal heartland of India, stretching from the Bihar and West Bengal all the way to the Andhra Pradesh–Maharastha border, including the newly created and heavily tribal states such as Jharkhand and Chattisgarh (Guha 2007a, 2007b; Sengupta 2006). In 2004, two of the largest Maoist parties in India, the Andhra Pradesh-based People's War Group (PWG) and the Bihar-based Maoist Coordination Committee (MCC), merged to form the Communist Party of India (Maoist)–CPI-M. Since then the "People's War" movement in India has expanded steadily, with Maoist physical presence and organizational reach now extending to 170 districts spread over 13 States of India (Chakma 2007; Guha 2007a; Ramana 2006). The scale, tactics, and persistence of this latest neo-Naxalite wave of Maoist "People's War" prompted Prime Minister Manmohan Singh to acknowledge that this wave of Maoist expansion represented the "single biggest internal security challenge facing India" (Guha 2007a).

Appearing some 30-odd years after the original Naxalbari revolt, the third wave of Maoist insurgency in South Asia unfolded in Nepal from 1996 to 2006 under the leadership of the Communist party of Nepal (Maoist) – CPN-M. The CPN-M was formed in 1995 after the coming together of a number of Maoist left parties under the leadership of those active in its largest front organization – United People's Front Nepal. The United People's Front Nepal tried its hand at parliamentary democracy for up to half a decade after the restoration of democracy in Nepal in 1990, and even managed to become the third-largest party in the House, commanding a total of 11 seats in the first parliament.[1] But in 1996, like its Naxalite counterparts in India, the CPN-M set out on a path to replace Nepal's parliamentary system with a "New Democracy" – a concept rooted in Mao's thought. Neither Nepali political actors and stakeholders nor the international community paid much attention when the CPN-M withdrew into the mountains of mid-western Nepal to prepare for a "People's War."

Within five years, the CPN-M's "People's War" had grown strong enough to not only disrupt social, political and economic life in far-flung districts, but also to bring political and economic processes at the national level to a near standstill. As a result of the insurgency and the state's inept counter-insurgency response, serious cracks and rifts appeared in the political and constitutional consensus upholding Nepal's post-1990 political order. Having concluded that it was both advantageous and timely to end the phase of armed and underground politics, the CPN-M used the wide ramp of the 2006 People's Movement to forge a deal with the other political parties to end the "People's War" and re-enter the fray of electoral politics. After winning an impressive victory in the Constituent Assembly elections, the CPN-M has gone on to form and head a coalition government with the support of a number of smaller parties. As the largest party in the Constituent Assembly, they are on their way to playing a formative role in the writing of the new constitution. Some view the Nepali Maoists' entry into competitive politics as indicative of a permanent shift in their ideology, while others have doubts about the Maoists' real strategic goals (Nayak 2007; see Lawoti and Pahari, this volume).[2]

The remainder of this chapter analyzes the principal factors that have influenced the evolution and travel of three distinct waves of South Asian "People's War" along this continuum. The continuum, as discussed, ranges from failure in West Bengal, to limited yet growing success of the current wave of India's neo-Naxalite revolutionary parties, to relatively comprehensive, yet not full strategic success in the case of the Communist Party of Nepal (Maoist). Methodologically, it is instructive to put major focus on the two "extreme types" along the continuum – the failed "People's War" of West Bengal and the relatively highly successful application in Nepal of Mao's doctrine of waging and winning a "People's War." A discussion of the two extreme types may offer a better critical understanding of how and why "People's War" models fail or succeed in the socio-economic and political milieu of South Asia. The intermediate case of ongoing neo-Naxalite armed insurgencies in India will be discussed briefly at the end of each section to illustrate why such armed struggles are caught in the middle between success and failure, and what factors might push them over time towards one or the other pole along the continuum.

Fundamentally, insurgents and state actors compete at the level of mobilizing and counter-mobilizing people, resources, ideas, and issues; and, more often than not, the fate of insurgency and counter-insurgency is decided by the degree of success in proactive mobilizing along some core and particular conflict-specific axes. I shall look at two broad classes of factors that have shaped and continue to govern the evolution and prospects of "People's War" in the subcontinent: (i) levels of rebel mobilization; and (ii) state and institutional counter-mobilization. Three distinct dimensions of rebel mobilization against the state are analyzed: military, ethnic/tribal and political mobilization.

Rebel mobilization

While all armed rebel movements intend to reach their strategic goals, in reality only a very few do, and those, too, only partially. Taking on and neutralizing a modern state, with all its institutional and organizational capacity and complexity, are not easy propositions even for the best motivated and equipped rebel groups.[3] In this task, the principal means available to the subcontinent's partisans of "People's War" has been multi-level mobilization aimed at eroding the state's powers, presence, and viability itself. In the following section I examine the form and extent of anti-state mobilizations, from the Bengali Naxalite movement to the most recent Nepali Maoist "People's War."

Military mobilization

West Bengal Naxalites

Charu Mazumdar and fellow original Naxal leaders like Kanu Sanyal and Jangal Santal quit the larger and older Communist Party of India (Marxist) – CPM –

largely on account of the latter's reluctance to follow Mao's "Peoples' War" model in India. In many of his famous writings, chief Naxal ideologue Charu Mazumdar emphasized Mao's successful armed campaign in China as the model that Indian Maoists and revolutionaries ought to adopt (Dasgupta 1974: 132–33). Naxal leaders believed that the Bengal countryside was ripe for mobilizing a revolutionary armed group from within the rural landless and exploited peasantry (Banerji 1980).

However, the Naxalite theoretical commitment to "Peoples' War" never translated into practical actions towards forming a fighting army. Instead, Mazumdar believed that a "Peoples' War" would follow naturally and logically from peasant-led annihilation campaigns (Dasgupta 1974: 174; Pandey 1985: 76). Naxalite leaders advocated reliance on native weapons at the disposal of poor peasants – bows and arrows, spears, machetes, and other farm implements (Chakrabarti 1990: 74–76; Dasgupta 1974: 45–46; Duyker 1987; Samanta 1984: 233). But compared with their complacency about mobilizing a standing army, Mazumdar and the Naxalite cadre were quite taken up with spreading terror in urban areas. Chakrabarti writes:

> The tactics of individual killings did not necessitate any military training for them. Once in a while, they did talk of building a PLA, based on the Chinese model but actually made no attempt towards it.
>
> (Chakrabarti 1990: 76)

As much as the Naxals idealized Mao's "Peoples' War," they failed comprehensively in achieving the basic prerequisites for starting (much less successfully waging) a protracted "Peoples' War." The CPI-ML seriously misgauged the strength of the various layers of the Indian State, and its own military/armed capacity to withstand the state's security response. As a result, the rural component of the Naxalite movement in West Bengal collapsed within a few months after the state mounted a series of sustained police actions across a broad sweep of area in which the Naxalites operated (Dasgupta 1984; Jawaid 1979).

Nepal's Maoists

The Nepali Maoists' handling of the military and armed component of the "Peoples' War" could not have been more different. While the Naxals remained conflicted and complacent with regard to the need and modality for raising a guerilla army, the Nepali Maoists never wavered from Mao's famous dictum – "without a people's army, the people have nothing." In September 1995, six months after its formation, the CPN-M adopted Mao's "protracted People's War" as the official policy of the party, and the top leaders went underground. Thereafter, the party wasted little time in raising armed militia units in its strongholds. It used these trained and mobile armed fighting units to gradually dislodge the state and rival political actors and institutions from across much of rural Nepal. Between 1996 and 2000 the CPN-M deployed its armed militias to accomplish four major tactical objectives: first, to project the romance of being a "freedom fighter" in communities that historically idolized military service, and thereby to attract a regular supply of rural youth to join the Maoist party and take up arms;[4] second, to accumulate arms and weaponry by raiding poorly staffed and ill-equipped state security and police posts; third, to try to instill fear in the ranks of opponents, including the supporters and functionaries of rival political parties; and fourth, to roll back the presence and function of state institutions so as to create a trail of political vacuum across the country.

By 1999 the CPN-M militias had driven out the police from the interiors of the party's base areas, and from many other rural areas where police presence was propped up by no more than weak and overextended logistical and organizational networks. By 2004, the majority of village-level police posts were shut down, and the dislodged police personnel moved into the relative safety of district headquarters (see Lawoti and Metha, this volume). In brief, the success of the Maoists to implement classic Mao-style protracted guerilla warfare was instrumental in enabling them to keep the conflict tilted to their advantage, and to keep the state from mounting an effective counterinsurgency.

By 2002, the CPN-M possessed a full-blown PLA. The Maoists claimed to have a force of 62,250, although the more accurate figures were lower than half that, going by the number of Maoist combatants that registered with the UN after the peace settlement in 2006 (Kumar 2006: 102).[5] The PLA was divided into two Divisions, seven Brigades, and 19 Battalions, making them easily capable of attacking army patrols and barracks in all but the most fortified conditions. In addition to the enlisted PLA fighters, the Maoists had access to a militia of at least 50,000 and up to a 100,000 rural youngsters (Kumar 2006: 102). Starting with their audacious raid on the army's regional headquarters and arsenal in Dang in November 2001, the PLA launched opportunistic attacks on the RNA whenever the latter's guard was down.[6] The government and the RNA looked to wage and win conventional battles, but discovered quickly that the PLA never intended to fight a conventional or frontal war against the much larger and better-equipped national army (Philipson 2002). Instead, the PLA adapted and applied Mao's guerilla warfare doctrine to hit at RNA vulnerabilities at every opportunity.

To summarize, early successes in mobilizing a rural militia, and eventually raising a full-fledged guerilla army allowed the CPN-M to achieve four vital goals. First, it bought the civilian wing of the party the time and space to develop into an entrenched political power across the entire country. Second, by helping achieve a stalemate against the state security forces, the PLA gained the Maoists the upper hand in the domestic political conflict, and put rival parties on the defensive. Third, the armed movement was instrumental in extending the conflict for a whole decade, which forced domestic and international stakeholders to re-examine and ultimately redefine the conflict as more of a civil war than simply a law and order (terrorism) crisis as initially portrayed by the state and accepted by regional and international players.[7] Fourth, the CPN-M's successful military strategy forced domestic political rivals to ultimately enter into a peace settlement premised on accepting the key political demands of the rebels.

India's Neo-Naxalites

In the wake of the West Bengal debacle, neo-Naxalite "People's War" campaigns in India quickly jettisoned Charu Mazmdar's romantic fascination with peasant weaponry, and aggressively pursued a goal that had always eluded the early Naxalites – namely, raising fighting units armed with modern weapons. Starting in the 1980s, neo-Naxalite groups in Bihar, Orissa and Andhra Pradesh amassed a considerable cache of modern arms including bolt-action rifles, AK47s, semi-automatic guns, and handguns (Banerjee 2008; Dash 2006). Regular and successful raids on government infrastructure, police personnel, and other representatives and symbols of the state were carried out precisely on the strength of such modern weaponry. Today, the CPI-Maoist, the largest and most formidable Indian Maoist outfit, is estimated to possess 6,500 conventional weapons, including rocket launchers (Ramana 2006). In addition, they are said to have become skilled at laying landmines (Ramana 2006). Reminiscent of quintessential Nepali Maoist tactics, Indian Maoist groups have resorted to attacking their targets with a large human shield of hundreds of "people's militia" and civilian sympathizers in tow (Bakshi 2008). This is indicative of a growing "base force" and the ability to wage mobile guerilla warfare (Ramana 2006, 438–39). Estimates put the armed strength of the CPI-Maoist fighters at close to 20,000, which may be small for a huge country like India, but it is a substantial force if one considers that the majority operate within the borders of three or four contiguous states including Bihar, Jharkhand, Andhra Pradesh, and Chattisgarh (Sengupta 2006).

Still, while the numbers and quality of fighters and weapons may have increased, the neo-Naxalite "People's War" campaigns in India have not yet achieved the success of the Nepali Maoists in putting together a formal, well-structured and trained PLA. Like the Nepali Maoists, the current wave of Indian "People's War" relies on guerilla warfare. But such guerilla units have not approximated the wide range of operation achieved by the Nepali PLA units. Even within the context of highly affected individual states like Andhra Pradesh and Chattisgarh, the movement and combat range of guerilla units is proscribed by the state security's superior numbers and retaliatory fire power. The Nepali Maoists, by contrast, had taken on sections of the national army within five years of declaring the "People's War." And yet, the military strength, organization, and planning capacity of the CPI-Maoist seem to have reached the critical levels where continued state inaction or misstep can turn the momentum dramatically in favor of the rebels, a course of events amply demonstrated by the case of Nepal (Bakshi 2008; Nayak 2007; Ramana 2006).

Political and organizational mobilization

West Bengal Naxalites

Among communists in West Bengal in the 1960s, the Naxals possessed neither the most organized party nor the most politically well-trained cadre. That distinction belonged to the Communist Party of India, the parent left party from which the Maoist faction led by Charu Mazumdar and Kanu Sanyal had officially separated in 1969 to form the Communist Party of India (Marxist-Leninist) – CPI-ML. After the split, CPI-ML leaders were keen to establish themselves as a more radical and militant party than the parent outfit. In the process, the CPI-ML leadership neglected party building and organization. In the following passage written more than 30 years ago, Dasgupta thus articulates the Naxalite distaste for systematic party building and organization:

> Other forms of activity like political propaganda, building mass organizations, and participating in the struggles for raising economic demands, amount to revisionism and should be avoided.
>
> (Dasgupta 1974: 174)

Charu Mazumdar strongly pushed for annihilation campaigns over systematic party building and propaganda as the preferred tactic to achieve revolution. Dasgupta writes:

> In the tactic of individual annihilation they thought they had found an alternative to mass organization and mass ideological propaganda. . . . Whenever a annihilation took place in a new area, the event was equated with the spread of revolution to that area.
>
> (Dasgupta 1974: 173)

In fact, Mazumdar believed that political work among the masses could easily amount to "aimless political propaganda," detracting from the more important task of eliminating class enemies, which to him was the real basis for entrenching the party in the rural areas and endearing it to the masses (Dasgupta 1974). The focus on targeted assassinations made the party reliant on secret networks commanded by a select "conscious" segment of the peasantry, rather than based on cultivated political support based on a "mass line."

The upshot of this deliberate neglect of political mobilization among the masses was brought home as soon as the state decided to respond to Naxal violence with overwhelming force. With neither width nor depth in their political organization, the Naxalites could not count on becoming the proverbial "fish" in the ocean of the people.

Charu Mazumdar himself was captured in Calcutta on July 16, 1972, and he died in custody on July 28. In the aftermath, the CPI-ML suffered a setback from which it never fully recovered. The relative ease with which the leaders and their immediate followers were captured was indicative of the organizational disarray that typified the CPI-ML from its earliest days. Chakrabarti aptly summarizes the state of party organization in the main Naxal movement:

> Even after the CPI-ML was formed it lacked many features of a proper organization. As a united group it did not even survive its third birthday and broke

into several factions, each opposed to the other with no signs yet of any proper reunification.

(Chakrabarti 1990: 81)

Compared to the CPI-ML and the Naxal leadership, the Nepali CPN-M put inordinate emphasis on building a strong and disciplined party and in propagating its politics among rural and urban audiences. Initially, the Naxalites and Nepali Maoists were faced with similar a political landscape and range of choices. West Bengal and Nepal both had established mainstream/moderate left parties that operated within a constitutionally defined electoral multi-party, democratic set up. Both parties were looking to displace and dislodge the established parties from power, and to completely restructure the existing constitutional political order. In pursuit of those goals, the CPI-ML adopted tactics focused almost entirely on sponsoring disparate violent actions against perceived oppressors and individual "class enemies."

Nepali Maoists

The Nepali Maoists, on the other hand, set out to actually implement Mao's three-stage tactics for winning a "People's War" – strategic defense, strategic stalemate, and strategic offence (Ogura 2008a; see Lawoti and Metha, this volume). But this focus on waging a "People's War" was not simply a matter of making raids against individual enemies, or even about forming a roving peasant militia. Rather, it was about building a full-capacity military within the overall control of an expanding and disciplined and political party. When the Maoists launched their "People's War" the party had fewer than 100 full-time workers, including the top leadership (Ogura 2008a: 13). Within ten years the party had managed to raise an army of 20,000, and had built a significant political and armed presence in the majority of the 75 districts of the country. Thorough, systematic and sustained political work among the rural population featuring a mixture of indoctrination, propaganda, threat, rewards and punishment were the basis for the dramatic expansion and organizational success of the CPN-M (Ogura 2008b). Even as the armed attacks on state security, institutions and installations multiplied, the CPN-M managed to put the political leadership of the party in firm control over the PLA by mandating that all military actions be approved through a political chain of command (Ogura 2008b).

The Nepali Maoist's strategy was to use the PLA to first create a multi-level vacuum in the countryside, and then to fill this with CPN-M designated "people's governments" (jan sarkar) (Ogura 2008b; Sharma 2004). At their peak, the Naxals may have operated in a wide area, but they controlled very little of it. The Nepali Maoists, on the other hand, started by operating in limited areas, but figured out ways to convert these into "base" areas and then use them to make calculated and largely irreversible forays into the surrounding region. By 2005 the CPN-M had installed "people's governments" in over 50 of the 75 districts of the country, albeit some operated only in name. Additionally, the Maoists ran FM radio stations, "people's courts," an efficient nationwide tax/donation collecting network, cultural program troupes, and multiple front organizations – in short, a series of parallel governments (Ogura 2008b). Remarkably, through this journey, the CPN-M was able to check and manage the fatal internal fissures that typically plague communist parties that embark on the taxing and high-risk path of armed struggle. The type of "People's War" pursued by the West Bengal CPI-ML ultimately enabled the state to paint the party into the impossible corner of having to retreat from the country-side and resort to urban terrorism against a vastly superior state security machinery. By contrast the Nepali Maoist's "People's War" managed to paint the state, the Monarchy and all non-Maoist political parties into a corner by systematically attacking and eroding their social and political bases. Separated by 40 years, these radically different political and strategic outcomes in West Bengal and Nepal were fundamentally influenced by the two parties' differential approaches and achievements in terms of political mobilization and party organization.

India's Neo-Naxalites

Internal splits and fractionalization plagued the original Bengali Naxalite party – the CPI-ML. But neo-Naxalite parties in India have witnessed an opposite trend since the late 1990s, with "expansion, consolidation, and merger" being the rule (Ramana 2006: 439–40). Unlike the original Naxalites (and more akin to their Nepali counterparts), the neo-Naxalite Maoist outfits in India have forged extensive ideological and practical links with other radical left parties in South Asia and abroad (Ramana 2006). Further evidence of the growing political presence and organizational clout of contemporary South Asian Maoism can be seen in the formation of the Co-ordinating Committee of Maoist Parties and Organizations (CCOMPOSA) in July 2001 to, "unify and coordinate" South Asia-wide Maoist activities in order to "hasten and spread" protracted People's War (Ramana 2006: 441). Compared with the Bengal Naxalites, the CPI-Maoist has a defined party hierarchy, like the Nepali Maoists, and has been able to put the military under command of a political hierarchy. The party coordinates state-wide military and political actions from the party's base areas located deep inside the tribal belt. The latest waves of Naxalites in India operate in 170 districts covering a range of 13 states from Bihar to the borders of Tamil Nadu, Andhra Pradesh and Maharastra (Guha 2007a, 2007b; Ramana 2006). Marginalized tribes, dalits, and the rural poor continue to be the main base of India's current wave of Naxalite political mobilization (Banerjee 2008). A few "People's War" groups have made some headway in capturing the imagination of wider urban audience based on the party's advocacy of popular anti-globalization slogans. The CPI-Maoist has been successful in forming alliances with multiple front organizations that incorporates artists, writers, journalists, left intellectuals and human rights groups. In many ways, the neo-Naxalite groups in India seem poised to make dramatic advances in membership and organizational reach as soon as the state falters or commits a major misstep in its counter insurgency campaigns. All this explains the intermediate position of the neo-Naxalite movement in India between the failed Bengal Naxalites and the highly successful Nepali Maoists.

Ethnic identity mobilization

West Bengal Naxalites

One early and important tactic followed by the Maoist party in West Bengal as well as in Nepal was to reach into tribal regions and recruit pre-existing ethnic discontent in the service of the party's strategic ends. West Bengal contains at least six major ethnic tribes, in addition to the large population of Nepali speakers who form the majority in Darjeeling, the northernmost district in the state. Of these, the Santals form the largest tribal group in the State, with a range that spans Bihar, Jharkhand, and South Eastern Nepal all the way to Bangladesh (Duyker 1987). The CPI-ML developed a closer association with this tribe after the Naxalbari uprisings in which the Santals played a lead role. Jangal Santal, an indigenous educated Santal and a member of the CPM, later became a key link between the CPI-ML and the land-hungry Santal tribe who deeply resented local landlords and state agents that supported them, including the police (Duyker 1987; SinghaRoy 2004: 91). Santal militancy and activism against extreme landlord oppression in the region was so strong and spontaneous that in most instances Naxal leaders, and later the CPI-ML, sought to simply ride the wave of Santal tribal discontent rather than rearticulate and channel the identity-based movement into the wider ideology of liberation represented by Maoism.

Other than vis-à-vis the somewhat pre-mobilized Santal tribe, the CPI-ML pursued only a secondary policy of mobilizing tribal and ethnic enclaves in West Bengal to form a long-term "united front" under the ideological and political banner of the party. In fact, the majority of urban cadre that initially followed the party into the rural districts retreated to the cities in haste.[8] Samanta observes:

> About 65% of the Calcutta students who went to the countryside were overwhelmed by the physical difficulty encountered in the villages and had to come back to the city. This retreat brought about a compulsive ideological change in the CPI-ML.
>
> (Samanta 1984: 231)

Muslims, who made up to 25 percent of the population of West Bengal, were another minority community that the CPI-ML might have brought into its ideological camp. Compared to the dominant Bhadralok ("gentle-people") class/castes of West Bengal, Muslims were considerably behind in terms of political clout and socio-economic status (Franda 1973: 187). But the Naxalite movement had little penetration in the Muslim community, in part perhaps because the Naxal leadership was itself composed of largely Bhadralok intelligentsia. The same was true about the distinct, Nepali-speaking community of the Darjeeling district with whom the Naxalites were not able to form any political or symbiotic ties. Ultimately, even the Santal tribe grew disillusioned with the Naxalite's annihilation campaigns (Jawaid 1979: 39).

Nepali Maoists

The heights reached by the Nepali Maoist movement would have been unthinkable without the successful mobilization of ethnic and tribal support in the heartlands of Nepal. It was no accident that the Nepali Maoists initiated and later expanded their "People's War" based out of the mountainous mid-western districts of Pyuthan, Rukum and Rolpa. Mohan Bikram Singh, a native of Pyuthan district and a senior patron figure among revolutionary communists in Nepal, lived for decades among the Kham Magar communities in Rukum and Rolpa and helped build a radical communist underground movement from the ground-up (de Sales 2000: 61; Thapa and Sijapati 2003). Radical communist activism and mass mobilization in Pyuthan, Rukum, Rolpa and the surrounding districts with large ethnic Magar populations relied heavily on the Magar community's collective perception of marginality and discrimination (de Sales 2000). In seeking to base their movement in the heart of Kham Magar country, the largely non-Magar senior leadership of the CPN-M demonstrated a keen awareness of the value of tapping into Magar tribal identity-based grievances in order to recruit their support and loyalty. The rise of Maoism and resurgent Kham Magar identity politics were closely intertwined. Some of the serious Nepali pro-Maoist leadership (Kiran Baidya, Prachanda, Ram Bahadur "Badal," Dev Gurung) spent long years living and propagating Maoist-communism among the Kham Magar; and in the process the CPN-M identified, trained and allied with scores of Kham Magar activists and organic intellectuals.

Ethnic activists, leaders, and leadership aspirants who felt betrayed and short-changed by the slow and sometimes backwards pace of progress on issues of fairness and inclusion after the transition to multiparty democracy in 1990 were attracted to the radical platform of the Maoists with its promise of language/ethnicity-based new federal entities with full autonomy and right to self-determination (Lawoti 2005; Subba 2006; see also Lawoti, this volume). Between 1996 and 2005, the Maoists expanded quickly and successfully out of their base areas towards the east, west, and south. Much of this unexpectedly rapid spread of the armed insurgency can be attributed to the tactical alliances forged between the CPN-M and regional ethnic liberation fronts, which at peak numbered more than ten.

In particular, the expansion of the Maoists to the east and south of their base areas depended crucially on the ability of the CPN-M to mobilize ethnic communities around cultural and political rights issues and then to successfully sell "People's War" as the appropriate platform to organize and pursue particular ethnic agendas.[9] By 2002 the Maoists had managed to either create or align with ten ethnic liberation fronts which secured them strategic access into areas and populations in which they previously had only sparse or sporadic presence.[10] Without the benefit of such access, it is doubtful if the CPN-M could ever have broken into such regions as the western Tarai (Tharuwan Liberation Front), the central and eastern Tarai (Madhesi National Liberation Front), and the eastern and far-eastern hill districts (Kirat and Limbuwan Liberation Front). There can be no doubt that the Maoist strategy of protracted war and surrounding cities from villages succeeded in good measure on the strength of mobilization of ethnic youth across Nepal.[11]

India's Neo-Naxalites

India's second wave of pro-"People's War" political and military mobilization has been nearly synonymous with tribal mobilization. The CPI-Maoist has laid down deep roots among indigenous tribal populations in Bihar, Jharkhand, Chattisgarh, and Andhra Pradesh (Banerjee 2008; Dash 2006; Guha 2007a, 2007b; Sengupta 2006). Tribal mobilization has been a fundamental part of the revival of Naxalism in India, with the CPI-Maoist reaching into the deep wells of tribal resentment against India's central and state government neglect of tribal welfare, and exploitation of the rich mineral, forest, and other natural resources in tribal lands (Banerjee 2008; Guha 2007a, 2007b). While West Bengal Naxalites mobilized Santal peasants and landless laborers only superficially and sporadically, the connection between the CPI-Maoist and tribal populations in the Indian heartlands is much more organic and extensive, with tribal populations and areas making up the core of the mass support and "base areas" so fundamental in sustaining a protracted "People's War." Like the Nepali Maoists, the CPI-Maoist has adapted many tribal symbols and cultural practices into Maoism, including organizing indigenous cultural performances for tribal audiences in the base areas (Sengupta 2006; see Mottin, this volume). This extensive and almost exclusive dependence on tribal support in conducting the "People's War" may ultimately become the Achilles heel of Indian Maoism, to the extent that it prevents or retards mobilization of a wider circle of support among non-tribal/ethnic populations. The Nepali Maoist movement had significant tribal/ethnic support, but was also able to mobilize sympathy, if not support, from among a wide cross section of Nepalis (Sneiderman and Turin 2004). Further, maintaining the continued interface between class and ethnicity/caste under the rubric of Maoism is a significant challenge, as the Nepali Maoists are discovering in Nepal. Still, given the heavily forested, large, and contiguous nature of tribal territory in the Indian heartlands, heavy mobilization and support for "People's War" in tribal regions will pose a long-term, serious security and political challenge to India's central and regional governments, even if it were possible to confine the "People's War" within the tribal zones. Finally, in the absence of strong and reformist left parties in the states currently facing armed insurgency, political counter-mobilization has become increasingly unfeasible. Thus, in Chattisgarh, for example, the ruling government has had to resort to the dubious strategy of creating right-wing vigilante squads – known as the "Salwa Judum" – to confront the Maoists on the ground, and to try and retake the political and physical space lost to the rebels over the past decade and a half (Guha 2007b). In West Bengal, the CPM more than fulfilled this role, and it did so through natural and lasting political processes (Basu 2002; Kohli 1990).

State and institutional counter-mobilization

The fate of an armed rebel movement or insurgency rests only in part on factors internal to the movement itself. The other side of the equation rests under the control of the state and state actors, and the form and efficacy of counter-mobilization to deal with rebel challenges to their legitimacy.[12]

West Bengal Naxalites

The Congress Party was expected to win the 1967 elections, and the CPM, in fact, planned the Naxalbari agitations to embarrass and cripple the Congress Party after its imminent victory (Franda 1971: 157). Instead, the Congress Party lost the elections, and the CPM won the most seats, paving the way for the first term of a shaky and fractured United Front Government (Kohli 1990: 267–96). Faced with the dilemma of being part of an elected ruling coalition expected to maintain law and order in the state, including cracking down on Naxalite violence, the CPM settled on a solution of least cost to its political future in West Bengal electoral politics. This solution entailed a two-pronged approach; first, to discourage and thwart a strong security reprisal against the armed Naxalbari constituency with which it retained extensive links (Kohli 1990: 274–77); and second, to out-maneuver the Naxalites by embarking on a frenzied campaign to remobilize the rural masses in its favor (Kohli 1990: 274–85). But this strategy was proving to be insufficient to check the rise of Naxalism whose influence (but not necessarily infrastructure) had spread to more than half of the 17 districts in West Bengal (Banerji 1984; Franda 1973).

By June 1967 Naxal rebels had managed to amass some guns, even as continued indecision and complacency by the United Front Government in dealing with the armed Naxalbari rebellion led to spillover into neighboring districts (Franda 1971: 161–68). Finally in July 1967, after much internal debate and lingering dissention, the first United Front Government decided to approve a full security operation against the Naxalbari armed insurgents. The 1500 police who moved into the region quickly arrested hundreds of cadre, activists and leaders, and effectively ended the actual Naxalbari armed movement within three weeks (Franda 1971: 162).

In January 1968, the "distant state" (Delhi) imposed President's Rule in the face of continued inability and unwillingness of the "near state" (Calcutta) to address the armed insurgency (Kohli 1990: 278). Between 1970 and 1971 alone there were 3,500 "incidents" of Naxalite violence in West Bengal, and guerilla violence was heading towards the crowded urban sprawl of Calcutta (Franda 1971: 169). In July 1971 alone there were 646 violent political incidents and 125 political murders in West Bengal, although not all may have been committed by the Naxalites (Franda 1973: 211). Business and industry were in a state of constant paralysis owing to strikes and shutdowns called by various left parties intent on wooing the proletariat.

The immediate and precipitating factors behind the armed Naxalite movement must be sought in the chaos, conflict and complacency that characterized the institutional response of the state under the two United Front Governments during the most formative years of the Naxalite movement between 1967 and 1971. Based on the West Bengal Naxalite experience, Kohli makes this crucial retrospective assessment:

> Disintegration of state power may well be an important precondition for trans-
> formation of latent socioeconomic hostilities into overt conflict.
>
> (Kohli 1990: 279)

Indeed, the Naxal insurgency in West Bengal might have escalated into a full-blown protracted internal civil war in the region. But the decentralized structural character of the Indian State, with constitutionally built-in layers of government and division of powers and prerogatives between the center, state and local governments, ensured that periodic regional turmoil, inevitable in any new democracy, would not escalate to systemic crisis. Responding directly to the mishandling of the Naxalite insurgency by state-level political institutions and actors, the New Delhi Government stepped in on two separate occasions (1968 and 1971) to put West Bengal under President's Rule.[13]

Besides setting the stage for a coherent security-led counter-insurgency, Delhi's direct rule brought about three key turning points in the Bengal Naxalite movement. First, Delhi put all its weight behind the efforts of the Governor of West Bengal, Anthony Lancelot Dias, and urged him to use every tool and tactic in his power to hold the 1972 elections as scheduled (Franda 1973: 211). The elections in turn set the stage for a transition to the majority government of the Congress Party, which immediately received strong support and endorsement from Delhi where the Congress already held sway under Indira Gandhi.

Failure to hold the 1972 state assembly elections would have widened the political vacuum, and led the state farther down the path of anarchy, providing the Naxalite movement with additional fuel and staying power.

The second turning point came in the wake of the 1971 Bangladesh war of independence which India supported with armed troops.[14] With large contingents of Indian Army troops amassed in the West Bengal border with what was then East Pakistan, the Government of Indira Gandhi used the opening provided by President's Rule to divert sections of the army to assist the police in decisive counter-insurgency drives across Naxalite-impacted areas. "Operation Steeplechase," a police and army joint anti-Naxalite undertaking, was launched in July–August 1971. By the end of "Operation Steeplechase" over 20,000 suspected Naxalites were imprisoned including senior leaders and cadre, and hundreds had been killed in police encounters (Sen 2002: 111–14). It was a massive counter-insurgency undertaking by any standards.

The third turning point came with the 1972 victory of Congress and the arrival of the strongly pro-law and order Chief Minister, Siddharth Shankar Ray. The Ray Government came into office in March 1972, and by July 16, 1972, Calcutta police had Charu Mazumdar in custody. He died in police custody several weeks later on July 28, 1972, dealing a moral and political blow to the West Bengal Naxalite movement from which it could never recover. With the declaration of Emergency Rule by the Indira Gandhi Government in 1975, what remained of the Naxalite movement in West Bengal was subjected to one final round of organized and concerted state persecution. Between 1975 and 1977 up to 25,000 persons were arrested, including thousands of non-Naxalite, CPM leaders and cadre (Kohli 1990: 285).

Delhi's direct intervention in quelling the Naxalite violence in West Bengal between 1971 and 1977 also helped to set the stage for the moderate CPM to make a major political comeback in West Bengal politics, enabling it to more than fill the vacuum created by a decade of Naxalite violence (Kohli 1990: 285–95). This had two important consequences for returning peace, democracy and stability to the disquieted state.

First, Delhi's intervention spared the CPM from having to directly conduct the security ("stick") end of the anti-Naxalite counter-mobilization. Given that it shared approximately the same rural support base as the Naxalites, this allowed the moderate CPM to maintain its credibility among the Bengali electorate, and to focus instead on political counter-mobilization. Second, Delhi-backed anti-Naxalite security mobilization helped maintain and expand the political space for the parliamentary, moderate left to counter-mobilize among the rural masses and regain lost ground. Throughout this period, CPM championed popular causes such as land reform, and additionally worked to expand the class support of the party by forming linkages with the rural and urban working and middle classes.[15]

Nepali Maoists

Responses to the Naxalite challenge to state legitimacy came from multiple layers within the Indian state structure. Nepal, on the other hand, was set up as a unitary and centralized state entity under the 1990 Constitution, making it structurally impossible to formulate a counter-mobilization response to the Maoist "People's War" that involved multiple levels of state and political institutions. The 1990 Constitution concentrated all powers in Kathmandu, allowing for no decentralized entity or mechanism to absorb and deflect the regional crises and upheavals that are bound to crop up in the life of any nation state. In short, extreme centralization of political, administrative and governance powers and functions of post-1990 Nepal played a major role in the translation of a regional crisis into a national security crisis, and in the translation of a national security crisis into state implosion within ten years.

When the actions and decisions of various West Bengal-elected state governments in response to Naxalite armed mobilization proved inadequate or ineffective, it invited the decisive and constitutionally prescribed intervention of the central government. The Indian polity faced no risk of deep internal political fissures or constitutional crisis from the central government's deployment of overwhelming force to contain and eliminate the Naxalite challenge to the state's authority and legitimacy. In Nepal, on the other hand, there was no "central government" to look to when successive elected governments faltered in formulating coherent and effective state counter-measures to the armed campaign of the Maoists. At best, there was a constitutional monarchy that was designed to remain above the daily political fray even as it was awarded certain emergency powers in the 1990 Constitution to deal with national contingencies. The national army was placed under the command of the government and a National Security Council as defined in the Constitution. Yet, informally the King continued to wield power and influence over the Army Brass, as the official Head of the State of Nepal. And mistrust between the monarchy and the government/political parties over army deployment began to corrode the political compact behind the 1990 political transition.[16] Thus, instead of inoculating the newly democratized polity against constitutional crises, and helping it manage unforeseen situations, the constitutional monarchy in Nepal itself became a lightning rod for controversy the very first time that the elected Prime Minister Girija Koirala requested the King to mobilize the national army against Maoist rebels.

Whether this decision to withhold the army was by design or default, the result was that it allowed the Maoists five relatively unhindered years to organize, propagandize, mobilize, and recruit support across the heartlands of the country. Towards the end of 2005 the army was beginning to have some impact on slowing down the insurgency. But before the full potential of that success could be realized on the ground, the Maoists forged an anti-monarchy/army alliance with the constitutional parties, and took the army completely out of the picture, along with the constitutional monarchy.

Constitutional kingship in Nepal – particularly during the short yet catastrophic tenure of former King Gyanendra – had become a liability rather than an asset in the state's battles against the armed and tactically astute Maoist party. But the rest of the Nepali state and state actors proved equally incapable of mounting a coherent and effective counter-mobilization in the face of galloping mobilization by the Maoists on multiple fronts. Convulsed by fits of inter- and intra-party rivalry, no post-1990 government served a full five-year term, and no national or local elections were held after 1998. Unlike in India, there was no legitimate, alternative national entity to push through critical elections which might normalize and stabilize a political system racked by intra-party conflict and teetering under the Maoist's armed siege. And if all that were not enough to embolden the Maoists to press on with the "People's War," in two final acts that completed the implosion of post-1990 democratic rule in the country the last elected government of Nepal under Prime Minister Deuba brought about the dissolution of the national Parliament, and refused to extend the tenure of thousands of local elected bodies even when it was clear that they were in no position to hold elections, and the CPN-M was waiting on the sidelines, ready to fill the space voluntarily vacated by a deeply fragmented and politically delirious state (Gersony 2003).

Whereas non-Maoist political parties in West Bengal responded to the Naxalite challenge by fighting tooth and claw to hold on to political and physical space across the entire state, Nepali political parties slowly, surely and permanently ceded the countryside to the armed Maoists as the "People's War" unfolded. The Communist Party of Nepal (United Marxist Leninist) – CPN-UML – was the ideological and political counterpart of the reformist West Bengal CPM, but it was unable to stop the steady migration of its cadre to the Maoist camp, and it was unable to reenter the hinterlands with proposals or campaigns for reforms that might re-energize its base and cut into the expanding bases of the Maoists. And Nepali political parties made no use of the government or the parliament to institute long-term reforms in Nepali society, economy, and polity, thereby bolstering

Maoist propaganda claims that nothing in Nepal would change without a total revolution.

Finally, limited ethnic representation in of the post-1990 Nepali state and political parties – in some ways more limited than the during the Panchayat period (Lawoti 2005, this volume) – became a serious liability at a time when the Maoists were building a united front composed of a plethora of ethnicity- and identity-based groups with legitimate and unaddressed grievances against generations of Nepali ruling classes and castes. Successful counter-mobilization was not forthcoming from political parties encumbered by such a mixed record of incorporating and reflecting Nepali society's heterogeneity within their own ranks. The Maoist movement had its own share of contradictions, but lack of ethnic/regional diversity and representation in its ranks was not one of them. In short, the post-1990 Nepali state paid a hefty price for its exclusionary character and practices, and for not pursuing even a modicum of meaningful reforms.

With the legitimacy of the entire state edifice almost on its last legs, former King Gyanendra made a dubious attempt to suspend the ineffectual rule of the political parties, and to mobilize the state's political and military resources against the "People's War." Delhi's direct rule in West Bengal was both constitutional and actually yielded results in terms of reasserting the state's legitimacy and hegemony in the face of the chaos and violence brought on by the Naxalite "People's War." Former King Gyanendra's last-minute unconstitutional resort to direct rule had the opposite effect. It completely eroded the political elite's stake and interest in continuing to defend the 1990 Constitution, and prompted them instead (with India's help), to form a political alliance with the Maoists and to embrace the latter's key goals (republic, new constitution via elections to a constituent assembly, and a new federal state structure). Thus, the Nepali Maoists have become the first political party in the post-cold war world to successfully use the "People's War" model not only to end a political regime, but also to bring about a change in the entire state structure.

India's neo-Naxalites

While the neo-Naxalite insurgencies raging in India today are far more sophisticated in terms of party and military organization, and have cultivated a strong base among tribal and other marginal populations, they continue to face the same multilayered state structures possessed with the same capacity for counter-mobilization as faced by the original West Bengal Naxalites. There is mounting evidence that the neo-Naxalites have advanced quite a bit beyond the rudimentary "People's War" conducted by the early Bengali Maoists; yet, there is also evidence that the Indian state structures, at the regional as well as federal levels, remain powerful and effective enough to confine the neo-Naxalite "People's War" within definite and delimited geographic, social, political and tactical territory. Unlike the CPM in West Bengal, the major political parties in the affected regions have not countermobilized to the same extent to politically neutralize the Maoists with radical reform programs. But, at the same time, unlike in Nepal, they are not prepared to completely cede ground to the armed rebels, even if it means forming and funding controversial groups like the anti-Maoist tribal vigilante units such as the Salwa Judum (Guha 2007b). Although the Maoists have managed to create small but strong "base areas" in states like Chattisgarh and Jharkhand, the sheer size, complexity, and political and constitutional stability of the Indian state will likely ensure that the newest waves of "People's War" in India will be prevented from achieving the tactical and strategic success achieved by the Maoist "People's War" in Nepal.

Finally, after 2005, India's central government decided to intervene in Nepal's conflict more actively, in a pre-emptive bid to "mainstream" the Maoists, and to get them engaged fully in the political process of Nepal, rather than traversing India's "red zones" as ambassadors of the most successful Maoist insurgency in the subcontinent. The Indian Government's extremely proactive guidance and monitoring of the events in Nepal after 2005 has been interpreted by top Indian left leaders as partially aimed towards Indian neo-Naxalite groups to persuade them to re-enter the political mainstream as the Nepali Maoists did in April 2006 (Cherian 2006). However, it remains to be seen what lessons the Indian neo-Naxalites will take from the case of Nepal – to continue to use arms until a political victory is in sight, or, as the Indian Government prefers, to pursue the potential rewards of an early migration back to the mainstream (Bakshi 2008; Majumder 2008).

Conclusion

Several generations of Maoist parties in the Indian subcontinent have opted out of parliamentary politics, and pursued the "People's War" in the hope of capturing state power. This chapter examined the two extreme outcomes among them, represented first, by the failed West Bengal Naxalite movement, and second, by the unexpectedly successful Nepali Maoist "People's War." The neo-Naxalite movements currently flaring across central and eastern India were juxtaposed against these extreme cases as representing the intermediate manifestations of Mao-inspired violent politics in the subcontinent. There is a strong bias among analysts to explain Maoist successes in Nepal by evoking factors such as poverty, inequality, and discrimination at multiple levels. This chapter is a reminder that such factors are not necessarily causally conclusive in the rise and success of an attempted "People's War." In levels of poverty, exploitation, landlessness, discrimination and marginality (by any measure), West Bengal of the 1960s and 1970s, Nepal of the 1990s, and the Indian states currently facing the vortex of neo-Naxalite armed insurgencies can hardly be shown to be conclusively and uniformly different from one another. Yet, "People's War" in these three contexts evolved along different trajectories. In the context of relative homogeneity between the three cases on factors typically proposed as "causes" behind the "People's War," this chapter has offered a more disaggregated and discerning perspective on why, how and when Maoist armed insurgencies succeed, fail, or become relatively entrenched. Factors governing rebel mobilization and state counter-mobilization ultimately help determine whether a given "People's War" will have the potential to cause systemic failure or whether it will be absorbed into the existing socio-political system without causing systemic collapse.

Notes

1 The United People's Front Nepal actually won nine seats on its own. However, it controlled 11 votes in Parliament, including two seats won by the Nepal Peasants and Workers Party, a tiny Maoist faction that usually voted with the Maoists.
2 See the Introduction and Conclusion in this volume for a more detailed review of the origins, course and impact of the Maoist insurgency in Nepal.
3 Few rebel groups in the world, and certainly none in South Asia, can match Sri Lanka's LTTE in resources and commitment brought to the cause. Yet, the LTTE appears to be fighting for survival as the Sri Lankan government unleashes its latest surge of counter-mobilization against the battle-hardened Tamil rebels.
4 The Maoists knowingly and successfully tapped into a deep-seated cultural preference for military service among young men in the hills, including what the British rulers of India used to refer to as the "Gurkha" tribes such as the Magar and Gurung of populations of central and western Nepal, and Rai and Limbu communities of eastern Nepal.
5 The actual number of Maoist combatants is difficult to calculate in part because after 2006 a sizeable number of former combatants migrated to the cities and towns to form the Young Communist League (YCL).
6 The attack on the Pilli road building crew was a good example of this strategy.
7 India declared the Nepali Maoists a terrorist entity even before Nepal did.
8 This in part explains the CPI-ML's retreat to urban guerilla terror tactics after the failure of the rural campaigns.
9 Sneiderman and Turin report that both class and ethnicity were considerations for villagers joining the Maoists, but that the Maoists did not promise ethnic autonomy in their initial campaigns among the Tamang and Thangmi ethnic community in Dokhala district (Sneiderman and Turin 2004: 102–3). But eventually, the Tamang ethnic leadership did push for, and the Maoists did accept, the idea of a "Tamang Salling Autonomous Region."
10 The major ethnic fronts created by the Maoists along with the proposed "Autonomous Regions" include, but are not limited to: Magarat National Liberation Front, Tharuwan National Liberation Front, Tamuwan National Liberation Front, Tamang National Liberation Front, Madheshi National Liberation Front, Limbuwan National Liberation Front.
11 A one time advantage for the Maoists may now be turning into a series of liabilities, as radical ethnic activists across the country begin to peel away from the mother Maoist party in frustration and disappointment with the priority given by the Maoists to 'class' politics over ethnic agendas. For the latest analyses on this issue, see: http://www.nepalitimes.com.np/issue/2009/02/14/ConstitutionSupplement/15668; http://www.nepalitimes.com.np/issue/2009/02/14/Nation/15670; http://www.nepalitimes.com.np/issue/2009/02/14/Nation/15671; http://www.nepalitimes.com/np/issue/2009/02/14/Editorial/15657
12 The latest development in the Sri Lankan civil war, with the Tamil Tigers (possibly the best-equipped and organized armed rebel groups in the world) on the verge of a comprehensive military defeat, is testament to this.
13 President's Rule was a constitutional means available to the central government to bypass the politics of the states and deal in an unhindered way with short-term regional crises.
14 The Naxalites misjudged the power of Bengali nationalism when senior leaders chose to toe Peking's line and characterize India as the aggressor.

15 The second UF Government led by the CPM continued to pursue a series of aggressive and significant land and agrarian reform programs aimed at drawing the rural poor into its electoral constituency and thereby undercutting the social and political base of the CPN(ML). In the one year that it was in power, the second UF Government redistributed 300,000 acres of land among landless peasants (Dasgupta 1974: 24).
16 Prime Minister Girija Koirala resigned on July 19, 2001, after King Gynandra allegedly refused consent to deploy the national army against the Moists in the village of Holleri, Rukum (see Timeline in this volume).

Bibliography

Bakshi, G. D. 2008. The Tribal Dimension of Internal Security in South Asia. *Journal of Defense Studies*, Winter 2008. http://www.idsa.in/publications/JDS/2.2/article4.pdf (accessed January 16, 2008).

Banerjee, S. 2008. Mercury Rising: India's Looming Red Corridor. Johns Hopkins University, Center for Strategic and International Studies, *South Asia Monitor* No. 123, October 3, 2008. http://www.csis.org/media/csis/pubs/sam_oct08_naxalite.pdf (accessed on February 26, 2009).

Banerji, Sumanta. 1984. *India's Simmering Revolution: The Naxalite Uprising*. London: Zed Books.

——. 1980. *In the Wake of Naxalbari: A History of the Naxalite Movement in India*. Calcutta: Subarnarekha.

Basu, Amrita. 2002. Parliamentary Communism as a Historical Phenomenon: The CPM in West Bengal. In *Parties and Party Politics in India*, edited by Zoya Hasan. New Delhi: Oxford University Press.

Cherian, John. 2006. Indian Flip-Flop. *Frontline*, Volume 23(9), May 06–19, 2006. http://www.hindu.com/fline/fl2309/stories/20060519004801000.htm (accessed January 22, 2009).

Chakma, S. 2007. India's War with Itself. *Open Democracy*, April 2, 2007. http://www.opendemocracy.net/terrorism/articles/naxalites020407 (accessed January 27, 2009).

Chakrabarti, Shreemati. 1990. *China and the Naxalites*. New Delhi: Radiant Publishers.

Dasgupta, Biplab. 1974. *Naxalite Movement*. India: Allied Publishers.

Dash, S. P. 2006. *Naxal Movement and State Power: With Special Reference of Orissa*. New Delhi: Sarup and Sons.

de Sales, A. 2000. The Kham Magar country, Nepal: between ethnic claims and Maoism. *European Bulletin of Himalayan Studies*. Autumn.

Duyker, E. 1987. *Tribal Guerrillas: The Santals of West Bengal and the Naxalite Movement*. New Delhi: Oxford University Press.

Franda, M. F. 1971. *Radical Politics in West Bengal*. Cambridge, MA: The M.I.T. Press.

——. 1973. "Radical Politics in West Bengal." In *Radical politics in South Asia*. Edited by Paul R. Brass and Marcus F. Franda. Cambridge, MA: The M.I.T. Press.

Guha, R. 2007a. A War in the Heart of India. *The Nation*, July 16.

——. 2007b. Adivasis, Naxalites, and Indian Democracy. *Economic Weekly* August 11, 2007: 3305–12 (Special Article). http://www.karainet.org/files/Adivasi,%20naxalites%20and%20indian%20Democracy-16-08-2007.pdf (accessed January 19, 2009).

Gersony, Robert. 2003. *Sowing the Wind: History and Dynamics of the Maoist Revolt in Nepal's Rapti Hills*. Mercy Corps International.

Jawaid, S. 1979. *The Naxalite Movement in India: Origin and Failure of the Maoist*

Revolutionary Strategy in West Bengal, 1967–1971. New Delhi: Associated Publishing House.

Karki, A.K. 2002. *Movements from Below: Land Rights Movement in Nepal*. New Inter-Asia Cultural Studies, Volume 3, Number 2. London: Taylor and Francis.

Kohli, A. 1990. *Democracy and Discontent: India's Growing Crisis of Governability*. Cambridge: Cambridge University Press.

Kumar, D. 2006. Military Dimension of The Maoist Insurgency. In *Nepal: Facets of Insurgency*, edited by Lok Raj Baral. New Delhi: Adroit.

Lawoti, M. 2005. *Towards a Democratic Nepal: Inclusive Political Institutions for a Multicultural Society*. New Delhi: Sage Publications.

Majumdar, S. 2008. India Worries over Nepal's Future. BBC News, New Delhi, April 14, 2008. http://news.bbc.co.uk/2/hi/south_asia/7347227.stm (accessed February 20, 2009).

Nayak, N. 2007. The Maoist Movement in Nepal and Its Tactical Digressions: A Study of Strategic Revolutionary Phases, and Future Implications. *Strategic Analysis*, Volume 31(6).

Ogura, Kiyoko. 2008a. *Seeking State Power: The Communist Party of Nepal (Maoist)*. Berghof Transitions Series No. 3. Berlin: Berghof Research Center for Constructive Conflict Management.

——. 2008b. Maoist People's Governments, 2001–5: The Power in Wartime. In *Local Democracy in South Asia: Microprocesses of Democratization in Nepal and its Neighbors*, edited by David N. Gellner, Krishna Hachhethu. New Delhi: Sage Publications.

Pandey, S. 1985. *Naxal Violence: A Socio-Political Study*. New Delhi: Chanakya Publishers.

Philipson, L. 2002. *Conflict in Nepal: Perspectives on the Maoist Movement*. DFID Nepal. Final Report.

Ramana, P.V. 2007. The Maoist Movement in India. *Defense and Security Analysis* 22(4): 435–49.

Samanta, A. K. 1984. *Left Extremist Movement in West Bengal*. Calcutta: Firma Publishers.

Sen, S. 2002. *Tryst with Law Enforcement and Human Rights: Four Decades in Indian Police*. New Delhi: APH Pub. Corporation.

Sengupta, S. 2006. In India Maoist Guerillas Widen 'People's War.' The *New York Times* (New York), April 13.

Sharma, S. 2004. The Maoist Movement: An Evolutionary Perspective. *In Himalayan People's War: Nepal's Maoist Rebellion*, edited by Michael Hutt. Bloomington: Indiana University Press.

Sneidernam, S. and Mark Turin. 2004. The Path to Jan Sarkar in Dolakha District. In *Himalayan People's War: Nepal's Maoist Rebellion*, edited by Michael Hutt. Bloomington: Indiana University Press.

Thapa, Deepak, and Bandita Sijapati. 2003. A *Kingdom Under Siege: Nepal's Maoist Insurgency, 1996 to 2003*. Kathmandu: The Printhouse.

Part VI
External dimension

11 External engagement in Nepal's armed conflict

Bishnu Raj Upreti

Introduction

International actors and factors influenced the dynamics and outcome of the Maoist insurgency significantly. The objective of this chapter is to analyze the dynamics of external engagement in Nepal's armed conflict and draw general conclusions that provide lessons for the future. There is extensive documentation of internal coordinates and determinants of the armed conflict in Nepal (see Introduction to this volume) but analyses on external engagement are rare. This chapter will analyze the external dimension of the Maoist armed conflict. The chapter attempts to answer the following questions:

- What was the nature and extent of external engagement during Nepal's armed conflict?
- What approaches did the external actors adopt while engaging in the armed conflict?
- What were the major areas of engagement by external actors; and what particular factors guided their actions in dealing with the armed conflict?
- How did the role of international actors change over time with the changing conflict dynamics?

Experience from around the world clearly demonstrates that the interests of powerful nations are among the main reasons for external involvement in intra- and inter-state armed conflict and civil wars (McCartney 1999; Armon and Carl 1996; Armon and Philipson 1998; Barnes 2002; Hendrickson 1998; Lucima 2002; Misra 2002; Tate 2004). Nepal is not an exception (Lohani 2005; Pandey 2005; Bhattarai 2004; Upreti 2006). In the subsequent sections the issue of external engagement in Nepal's armed conflict will be discussed in detail.

Interests of external actors in Nepal's conflict

Certain external actors were overtly or covertly engaged since the very beginning of the armed conflict initiated by the Communist Party of Nepal (CPN-M). The main interests of international powers in Nepal's armed conflict are (i) political – political influence and ideological differences with the Maoists; (ii) developmental

– commitment to address poverty and inequality, and maintaining influence through development: (iii) strategic – security issues, natural resources use, balance of power at regional strategic context; (iv) commercial; and (v) commitment on human rights and humanitarian areas. In South Asia ambitions of two powerful countries in recent decades – India and China – has not only brought profound changes in the geo-strategic interests of other powerful nations but has also led to the creation of new power equations (Dixit 2003). Continuing conflict and instability in South Asia is manifested in the hostile relations between India and Pakistan, armed conflicts within Indian states, Sri Lanka and Nepal, and internal political tensions in all South Asian countries.

As recently as 2000, many in the international community adopted a strategy of avoidance in dealing with Nepal's armed conflict. In other words, they operated in a business-as-usual fashion and more or less ignored the armed conflict. However, they shifted their strategy towards a multi-track approach after 2000 once the insurgents began to target their interests and to threaten the continuity of their development programs and the safety of their local staff. The multi-track approach recognizes that dealing with armed conflict and restoring peace requires the involvement of many different actors of society (Lederach 1999; Louise and McDonald 1996). Accordingly, the international community engaged with the palace, political leaders, military officials, human rights activists, civil society mediators and representatives of various communities. Nevertheless, because of inter-state relation, legitimacy and so on, powerful external actors focused more on a Track I approach (engagement at the level of official state).

International actors: disguised escalators and mediators

The international engagement with Nepal's internal armed conflict contributed to both the escalation and the resolution of the armed conflict. Some of the external actors were very actively engaged in informal mediation of the armed conflict whereas others were directly engaged in its escalation. As mediation is a process of intervention in a conflict situation by an acceptable, impartial and neutral third party to assist contending parties to reach an acceptable settlement (Bush and Folger 1994), powerful bilateral countries were not able to mediate because of their biased position against the Maoists. The Maoists did not accept diplomats and envoys of the powerful nations like India and the USA as neutral third parties because of their vehement public opposition to the CPN-M. Ambassadors from the USA and India publicly criticized the Maoists, visited military barracks and supported the Nepal army against the Maoists. They were working to strengthen the "twin pillar theory" – constitutional monarchy and multi-party democracy as necessary elements in defeating the Maoists (see Box 11.1). Hence, their actions often further complicated the political situation and exacerbated the conflict. They, nevertheless, remained highly influential actors in Nepal's decade-long armed conflict.

Some neutral countries like Switzerland and Norway were engaged as informal mediators. Their special advisors and diplomats acted neutrally, and engaged and assisted the warring parties in identifying common issues and developed proposals for negotiation. They held unofficial confidential meetings with the Maoists and government authorities to build confidence and create conducive environment, developing and projecting a greater sense of their own efficacy and potential to resolve conflict.

Box 11.1 Commitment of major powers on twin pillar theory

"Monarchy can still be a constructive force, and a unifying symbol in Nepal, if it so chooses," Shyam Sharan, Foreign Secretary of India in a book release function in New Delhi. Source: www.nepalnews.com 17 November 2005

"India has consistently supported multiparty democracy and constitutional monarchy enshrined in Nepal's Constitution as the two pillars of political stability in Nepal," press release of the External Affairs Ministry of India on February 1, 2005.

"We strongly support constitutional monarchy and multi-party democracy in Nepal, and want to see a sustainable peace-process," Jack Straw, Foreign Secretary of the UK on February, 14, 2005.

"We remain deeply troubled by developments in Nepal. King Gyanendra's dismissal of the government, declaration of a state of emergency . . . and the suspension of fundamental constitutional rights is a step away from Nepal's path toward democracy. The King needs to . . . move quickly toward the restoration of civil liberties and multi-party democratic institutions under a constitutional monarchy," press statement by Richard Boucher, spokesman in Washington, DC, on February 14, 2005.

In addition, a number of actors from international NGOs, academic institutions, and religious and philanthropic agencies such as Action Aid International Nepal, Care International Nepal, Mercy Corps, Lutheran World Federations, Médecins Sans Frontières (MSF), International Alert and Search for Common Ground were mainly engaged in small activities such as documenting cases, helping communities and study causes of the conflict, and their influence was minimal. The United Nations and European Union constantly offered their support to Nepal to resolve the armed conflict. However, the state did not pay attention, whereas the Maoists were relatively positive. India was not ready to allow any of them to engage and mediate directly. This Indian resistance might have been the reason behind the unwillingness of the Nepali government to engage with the United Nations or European Union in the mediation process.

India

Among international powers, India is the most extensively engaged external actor in Nepal's armed conflict. Mishra (2004) found the trajectory of the insurgency was heavily influenced by cross-border links and by the past history of Indo-Nepal relations. Sanjaya Upadhaya (2008) has extensively documented the Indian interest-based influence in Nepal using historical, geographical, religious, cultural, economic and political advantages (Upadhaya 2008). Shah (2004: 211) has argued that the Maoists continuously "received patronage from Delhi."

There are two reasons for India's extensive engagement in Nepal. First, Nepali ruling elites rely excessively on India. For example, training and orientation of many senior Nepali Congress leaders occurred in India. They lived in India for considerable periods and developed a strong network with Indian leaders and officials. Some of the communist leaders were also trained in India or used India as shelter during their political life. Therefore, many older-generation Nepali political leaders are heavily influenced by India and have come to accept India's decisive role in Nepal since the 1950s.

Second, India's perception of being a regional power based on geography, economic development, technological advancement, nuclear strength and military capability psychologically facilitated it to influence South Asia in general and Nepal's politics in particular. While India's responses are shaped by its strategic interests of expanding influences, its behavior towards Nepal is subject to profound contradictions and complications. This observation is supported by the writing of K.V. Rajan, who was the Indian Ambassador to Nepal from 1995 to 2000: "the past five decades of India–Nepal relations have witnessed many lost opportunities, costly judgments and avoidable misunderstandings. It is remarkable that successive governments in both countries have so comprehensively failed to establish a stable, mature relation based on mutual trust and a long term vision of cooperation" (Rajan 2003: 97).

The following were some of major concerns of India:

1   Strategic interests in Nepal: India wants to continue keeping Nepal in its security umbrella, which was designed by Prime Minister Nehru in the 1960s. Indian response was generated from that strategic interest (Rajan 2003; Bhattarai 2004; Dixit 2003).
2   More than 1,800 km of the porous border between Nepal and India was another concern for India, particularly after the establishment of Coordination Committee of Maoist Parties and Organizations of South Asia (CCOMPOSA), where several communist groups active in India including People's War Group and CPN-M of Nepal talked about expanding their influence across South Asia (Upreti 2006). South Asian Maoist parties and organizations were encouraged by the success of CPN-M in Nepal and wanted to replicate the success of Nepali Maoists. They formed CCOMPOSA to pursue this goal. This was a source of serious worry for India.
3   India is in need of a huge amount energy/power for sustaining and expanding its economic growth, and Nepal's water resource is one of the best available options. India is constantly interested in Nepal's water resource, and its engagement in the political process paves the way towards achieving this end (Bhattarai 2004).
4   Psychological dimension: the vast majority of Nepalis perceive that India is overtly and covertly interfering in Nepal's internal affairs. Even in the case of

Nepal's armed conflict the Indian role was severely questioned and criticized by large sections of Nepali society, in particular the dual approach India took in the course of the armed conflict (by supporting both the warring parties). The Nepali public attitude towards the behavior of Indian rulers is by and large negative and India wanted to minimize the growing anti-Indian feeling among Nepali people (Pandey 2005).

Indian engagement in Nepal's armed conflict evolved through the different phases of the insurgency. Before the royal massacre of June 1 in Nepal and the September 11, 2001, terrorist attack in the USA, India was less concerned with the Nepali conflict. After these two events India became more active. After the formation of CCOMPOSA on July 1, 2001, and the escalation of Maoist insurgency in different Indian states, India adopted a more aggressive position against the Nepali Maoists and provided greater military and other support to the government to suppress the Maoists. After the royal takeover of February 1, 2005, India's role changed drastically and led to their support for collaboration between the Maoists and democratic political forces of Nepal to topple the king.

Though India had declared Nepali Maoists as "terrorists" after the September 11, 2001, Al Qaeda attack in the USA, it maintained a dual approach vis-à-vis the Maoists. The Nepali Maoists were using the Indian territory for shelter, meetings, and for importing arms and ammunition. However, the Indian government was not active in controlling this. Even though, the Indian government was the major supplier of arms to the Nepali government, Indian territory was also the main source of arms and weapons for the Nepali Maoists (Upreti and Nepali 2006). At times the Indian authorities handed over Nepali Maoists arrested in India to the Nepal government (e.g. Suresh Ale Magar and Matrika Yadav), while at other times they did not (e.g. C. P. Gajurel arrested in Chennai and Kiran Baidya in Silguri were kept in Indian jails). The then government of Nepal had expressed dismay with the Indian government for non-cooperation on exchange of information about the activities of Nepali Maoists in India (Bhattarai 2004).

However, the role of various power centers within India was different and sometime contradicted the official Indian policy. The Communist Party of India-Marxist and its leaders Sitaram Yachuri and Prakash Karat supported the Nepali Maoists whereas the Bharatiya Janata Party was against the Maoists and supported the king. The Indian military was in favor of supporting the Nepali army and suppressing the Maoists whereas the Indian bureaucracy, particularly the Ministry of External Affairs, took a different stand from the Indian army (Bhattarai 2004).

Between October 2002 and January 2005 when the king ruled indirectly, India tried to develop consensus between the monarchy and political parties. However, this approach did not work. The king worked with his own roadmap, undermining the political parties, and finally staged a complete takeover on February 1, 2005. After the royal takeover the Indian position gradually shifted in favor of collaboration between the political parties and the Maoists to end the king's direct rule. Immediately after the royal takeover, India issued a statement from New Delhi on February 1, 2005, which reads:

The King of Nepal has dissolved the multiparty government led by Prime Minister Deuba, and has decided to constitute a Council of Ministers under his own Chairmanship. An emergency has been declared and fundamental rights have been suspended. These developments constitute a serious setback to the cause of democracy in Nepal . . . India has consistently supported multiparty democracy and constitutional monarchy enshrined in Nepal's Constitution as the two pillars of political stability in Nepal. This principle has now been violated with the King forming a government under his chairmanship . . . We will continue to support the restoration of political stability and economic prosperity in Nepal, a process which requires reliance on the forces of democracy and the support of the people of Nepal.

The thirteenth South Asian Association for Regional Cooperation (SAARC) Summit planned at Dhaka in February 2005 was cancelled because India refused to attend the Summit, citing the royal takeover in Nepal. But later, without any substantial change in the political situation in Nepal, India attended the summit. At the Summit the king not only defended his takeover but also openly criticized the "double standard" of some of the powerful nations, hinting at India. He said:

My country has been the victim of senseless terrorism for nearly a decade now. The agents of terror are bent on overthrowing a constitutional order and replacing it with a rejected ideology of a one-party communist dictatorship. We would like to emphasize that, as terrorism knows no geographical boundary, terrorism in Nepal is certain to affect the whole of South Asia. Nepal condemns terrorism in all its forms and manifestations, committed by whomever, whatsoever and for whatever reasons. We expect a similar attitude on the part of the international community . . . The February First step in Nepal was necessitated by ground realities, mainly the failure of successive governments to contain ever-emboldening terrorists and maintain law and order. It has not come at the cost of democracy, as some tend to project it.[1]

Indian rulers took this statement by the king as a challenge to them. What is more, when India proposed that Afghanistan be included in SAARC as the eighth member, the king tabled a proposal to include China in the SAARC with an "observer" status. India did not anticipate such a proposal from Nepal. This event made India further unhappy and wary about the king's strategy of using the "China card." Following the Dhaka SAARC summit, India partly suspended military aid to Nepal.

Before the royal takeover, India said repeatedly that it had full commitment to multiparty democracy, constitutional monarchy and the fight against the insurgency in Nepal. India felt that failure to contain the insurgency in Nepal would embolden Indian Maoists and would pose a national security threat for India. Therefore Indian direct engagement was thought to be essential in the Nepali conflict. Indian engagement in Nepal was fundamentally guided and shaped by its security concerns and strategic interests. Indian diplomat K.V. Rajan writes, "As in the past, India's security concerns and Nepal's inability to satisfy them became the driving force in the relationship" (Rajan 2003: 112). Unlike the USA, India had adopted a dual approach in Nepal's armed conflict. The approach of the UK and India was similar. On one side, it provided military aid, arms and ammunition to suppress the insurgency. At the same time, it was also advocating the line that the conflict was political and could not be resolved militarily. India also showed support for the social agenda of Maoists (Bhattarai 2004). However, after the royal takeover India changed its approach.

After the royal takeover, India established direct communications with the Maoists. The international community accepted the leadership of India to deal with Nepal's armed conflict, especially after the royal takeover of the February 2005. The 12-point understanding signed between the Seven Party Alliance (SPA) and the Maoists in New Delhi on November 21, 2005, was the clearest sign of India's lead role in the Nepali conflict. The king's takeover, his refusal to agree to go along with the Indian road-map, the king's strategy to play the China card, and consequent repeated tensions during the Afro-Asian Summit in Jakarta in the fourth week of April 2005 and during the SAARC Submit in Dhaka (November 2005) between the king and Indian leaders in contrast to the willingness of the Maoists and SPA leaders to follow the Indian roadmap resulted in the Delhi Pact of November 2005. The India-sponsored 12-point agreement between the Nepali constitutional parties and the Maoists virtually ended the ten years of armed conflict and eventually the direct rule of the king.

China

Until the success of the April 2006 people's movement, China adopted a silent vigilance approach in Nepal's armed conflict. China was quite concerned over Nepal's armed conflict but its approach was entirely different from that of other major international players active in Nepal. It was highly vigilant but remained quite silent in the public sphere. China has traditionally supported the monarchy on the belief that it represented a stable and reliable force in Nepal. China did not believe that Nepali communist parties were reliable domestic forces for safeguarding Chinese interests, and even expressed dismay at the use of the name of Chairman Mao by the CPN-M. However, after the failure of the king, China became more vocal and active in Nepali affairs. The following seem to be China's main concerns in Nepal:

1 Preventing anti-Chinese Tibetan activities in Nepal: China perceives that Nepal is one of the main centers of anti-Chinese Tibetan activities sponsored by the USA and other western powers. Indian and American engagement in Nepal's armed conflict would help anti-Chinese activities. China became more alert and gradually vocal at the later stages of the conflict.
2 Influence of India in Nepal's internal affairs: China was also closely watching Indian activities in Nepal's affairs. China does not want to see Nepal being used by India for its strategic interests.
3 Indian–US alliance on Nepal: China was also vigilant on the Indian–US alliance on Nepal that could jeopardize Chinese interests.

High-level visits of Chinese delegates to Nepal and invitations to Maoists leaders Barsaman Pun alias "Ananta" and Krishna Bahadur Mahara to visit China, periodic public statements from the Chinese Embassy on the political issues of peace process, and active engagement in the Security Council of the UN while setting up the UNMIN are some of the examples of China's more active engagement in Nepal's peace process after the political change of April 2006.

The USA

From the very beginning, the USA had a clear position on Nepal's armed conflict. Unlike India, USA was not in favor of bringing the Maoists and political parties together against the 2005 royal takeover. The USA tried its best to prevent collaboration between the SPA and the Maoists against the royal takeover. The then US Ambassador J. F. Moriarty worked hard to prevent the SPA and the Maoists from reaching the 12-point understanding. He visited Delhi before and at the time of the culmination of that understanding. The United States was hesitant to openly criticize the king even after the February 2005 takeover. On February 25, 2005, Richard Boucher, Spokesperson of the US Department of State said, "[W]e think that the king needs to move quickly to reinstate and protect civil and human rights, to release those who are detained under the state of emergency, and to begin a dialogue with the political parties intended to restore multiparty democratic institutions under a constitutional monarchy." The US referred frequently to its sole commitment on twin pillar theory, or multi-party democracy and constitutional monarchy. The USA, however, failed to reconcile king and the political parties and prevent the 12-point understanding between the SPA and the Maoists.

Because of its clear stand against the Maoists, conflict transformation specialists, critical analysts and political scientists considered the USA as the leader of external escalators of the conflict (Bhattarai 2004; Karki and Seddon 2003; ICG 2007; Onesto 2005). The USA supplied arms and ammunition to the government, trained security forces in counter-insurgency, and provided intelligence and financial resources to strengthen security forces. It had organized military-to-military exchanges and visits. As the Nepali state was a party in the conflict, such engagements with the state to suppress the insurgency added fuel to the conflict. However, after the king's takeover, the USA reduced its support for the government but did not change its approach towards the Maoists. During the entire period of the armed conflict, the US used its leverage to put pressure on the Maoists. It wanted to defeat the Maoists through the use of force and therefore opted for a coercive military approach. Some scholars believe that "actually the US believed that the Maoists would not negotiate without being cornered in the battle field. Hence putting pressure militarily was a tactic to get the Maoists to the talking table. The US did not want to fight the Maoists just for the sake of fighting, but to force them to come on the negotiating table."[2] However, the way the USA handled the armed conflict in Nepal had contributed to escalate the conflict. The following were reasons for USA's confrontational approach:[3]

1   The USA did not want to see the expansion of radical communists like the Maoists.
2   The perceived fear of terrorism – the USA is sensitive to terrorist activities and the US administration has equated the Maoists with al Qaeda, Abu Sayyaf, and Lebanon's Hezbollah. The US government feared that the civil war would make Nepal a haven for international terrorists and therefore placed the Maoists on their "terrorist list."
3   The USA wanted to expand its influence in the Nepal army by providing military resources.
4   The geo-strategic interest of US – Nepal is situated between India and China and close to Pakistan, where tremendous strategic interests of the US lie.

The strategic interests of the USA in Nepal did not mean that the US was not closely working with India. The US closely works with the South Block of India on some Nepal-related issues to maintain or strengthen its strategic interests in the region and Nepal, and as a result it sometimes had to accept unwanted outcomes such as the India-sponsored 12-point agreement.

United Kingdom

The United Kingdom was another major visible external actor in Nepal's armed conflict. The UK continued to follow a twin-pillars theory even after the king's takeover. Following the royal takeover, the UK government called its ambassador to London for consultations, saying: "[W]e strongly support constitutional monarchy and multi-party democracy in Nepal, and want to see a sustainable peace-process. We continue to call upon the Maoists to end their violence and for both sides to return to the negotiating table. But we were very clear, when the king dismissed his Prime Minister, that we regarded this as a backward step which undermined Nepal's democratic institutions and risked further instability. In this serious moment, it is appropriate for us to recall our ambassador so that we may reflect with him, and with our international partners, on the way forward." Foreign Secretary Jack Straw in a statement said, "The British government has decided to suspend a planned package of military assistance to Nepal in the light of the disturbing situation there." He urged the king to restore democratic government immediately. The king ignored the reactions of the UK and moved ahead unilaterally on his own road map.

Because of the UK's dual position, the main domestic actors of Nepal's conflict were confused. The establishment (mainly the palace) believed it enjoyed the positive support of the UK because both countries were monarchies. Political parties expected the UK's support mainly because of its democratic history and practices. However, the Maoists were suspicious of the UK on account of its close alliance with the USA in global and regional issues. The UK supplied helicopters and military equipment to the Nepal government. Although the UK government claimed it was for humanitarian purposes, the Maoists were opposed to it. The UK was largely seen by neutral people and certainly by Maoists as another external escalator of the conflict despite the efforts of British diplomats to present it as neutral.

Clearly, the UK had a dual policy in dealing with Nepal's armed conflict. On the one hand, it provided military aid to the Nepal Army, and on the other hand, it provided development aid to address the root causes of conflict and attempted to engage with local Maoists. However, after the king's takeover, the UK changed its approach in dealing with Nepal. The UK government suspended its planned package of military aid (a £1.3 million package of equipments including vehicles, nightflying helicopters, communications improvements and bomb-disposal equipment). The close relation between the monarchies of the two nations, a historical association in Nepal with the Gurkhas, and its interests to engage in global conflict were some of the reasons for UK engagement in Nepal.

United Nations

The United Nations was another active if less influential actor during Nepal's armed conflict. During the time of the armed conflict in Nepal, the UN was quite concerned and UN Secretary General Kofi Anan repeatedly highlighted the worsening security situation of Nepal. He also appointed a special political officer who frequently visited Nepal with messages from the Secretary General. After the Beni attack by the Maoists, Kofi Anan once again expressed his deep concern about the deteriorating situation and offered UN assistance should the warring parties want it. The CPN-M immediately welcomed the UN offer. However, the Nepali government repeatedly rejected these offers for fear of possible problems with its big neighbors, India and China. After the February royal takeover, the Secretary General of the UN sent his senior political advisor, Mr. Lakder Brahimi (one of the most experienced senior negotiators, who was also involved in Afghanistan and Iraq conflicts), to assess the situation in Nepal. After his intensive meeting with political parties, civil society, military officers, the government officials and the king, he came to conclusion that though the conflict was serious, it was manageable if the major political forces wanted to resolve it. Brahimi repeated the UN offer of help but the government stuck to its original position of not accepting any UN involvement in Nepal's conflict.

National and international pressure on the Nepal government was mounted on the grounds of human rights abuses, and member states of the UN High Commission for Human Rights passed resolution and pressured the Nepal government to establish OHCHR (Office for the High Commissioner of Human Rights of the United Nations). Similarly the UNMIN came to Nepal after the political change of April 2006 when the Maoists, who strongly demanded the UN involvement earlier, emerged as a key power. It was pragmatic to have some credible external actors to engage in monitoring of arms and armies. UNMIN came, even though in a relatively small body, despite the reluctance of earlier governments and India to have the UN involved in Nepal's peace process.

Box 11.2 outlines the main operations of OHCHR in Nepal – the largest operation of its kind in the world.

Box 11.2 Main involvement of OHCHR

- Based on the information collected by the Nepal office, the High Commissioner for Human Rights will submit periodic analytic reports on human rights violations committed by either side of the conflict to the Commission on Human Rights, the General Assembly, and the Secretary-General.
- The OHCHR Nepal office will also advise His Majesty's Government on matters related to the promotion and protection of human rights in Nepal and will provide advisory services and human rights support to representatives of civil society, human rights non-governmental organizations and individuals.
- The human rights monitors employed by OHCHR will investigate and report all human rights violations from both the security forces and the CPN-Maoists.
- OHCHR Office will maintain "impartiality, independence, objectivity and transparency" in all its work.
- OHCHR Nepal office will work closely with local human rights defenders, including the press, in carrying out its investigations.

On April 22, 2005, King Gyanendra and United Nations Secretary-General Kofi Annan discussed the political situation in Jakarta during the Afro-Asian Summit. Kofi Annan emphasized the need to restore multiparty democracy in Nepal. A week after his discussion with the king in Jakarta, UN Secretary General Kofi Annan on April 28 in New Delhi said that he wanted to see the restoration of constitutional democracy in Nepal as soon as possible. In a press conference in New Delhi he said, "We have been in touch with the king, and we discussed the issues." He further told to the audience, "I think it's important that political parties are allowed to resume their activities as we have agreed during our discussions." For two main reasons, the UN was seen by many Nepali as one of the most suitable external actors (the other one was the European Union) to mediate. The first was its global experience in negotiating armed conflict and civil war. The other reason was the willingness of the Maoists to accept the UN.

Other European countries

Though less influential compared to other powerful external actors, the European Union (EU) was active in helping to resolve Nepal's conflict. It sent high-level delegations of "Troika" – a special mission of the European Union composed of three member countries. One EU press statement said, "The EU calls upon all constitutional forces in Nepal to work closely together in support of a common strategy for achieving a comprehensive and inclusive settlement in the country, based upon multiparty democracy and constitutional monarchy" (December 13–15, 2004). Again, after the royal takeover, the Troika visited Nepal and discussed the political situation and said, "We believe there may be a role for third party support for brokering and monitoring the arrangements for a formal ceasefire agreement" (October 6, 2005). However, the EU's influence was not very effective in transforming the conflict dynamics of Nepal.

Switzerland, Norway, Germany, Denmark, the Netherlands, and other European countries were largely pursuing a collaborative approach of engagement – a pattern and structure of interaction among the directly related actors to facilitate the process that leads to resolving conflict in a positive way. Their responses during the time of armed conflict were focused on compromise and accommodation. Once the king took over power, Denmark, Switzerland and other European countries strongly opposed it and suspended their aid to Nepal.

European countries were quite active in preventing human rights violations, particularly after the breakdown of the 2001 ceasefire when civil liberties were severely curtailed. Establishment of OHCHR, the largest UN operation of its kind at the time, was the outcome of concern among the international community about the deteriorating situation.

International non-governmental organizations (INGOs)

Some INGOs such as the International Committee of the Red Crosss (ICRC), Amnesty International, the International Crisis Group (ICG), Human Rights Watch (HRW), and the International Commission of Jurists (ICJ) were actively engaged in Nepal's armed conflict.

Amnesty International was very active in Nepal during the time of conflict and had called upon the warring parties to sign a Human Rights Accord to give the National Human Rights Commission (NHRC) a mandate to monitor human rights. It played an instrumental role by influencing 52 members of UN Human Rights Commission to pass Agenda 19 in 2004 that forced the government of Nepal to sign the agreement to open OHCHR in Nepal. Amnesty Interational made forceful demands that the conflicting parties abide by the principles of the Geneva Conventions of 1949 and it vehemently opposed the state of emergency.

ICG was quite active in in-depth analysis of the conflict since 2004 and contributed to making the Nepal crisis understood at an international level, mainly through its critical analysis and periodic reports. The Government of Nepal was quite unhappy with the ICG's analyses of Nepal's armed conflict and exposing the reality in the international arena.[4]

ICJ was another active international stakeholder. ICJ teams regularly visited Nepal and urged the warring parties to respect the human rights of the people. On November 30, 2004, Nicholas Howen, ICJ Secretary-General, said:

> We are deeply concerned about the escalating and gross human rights abuses being committed by both sides of the conflict in Nepal . . . urgent steps can and must be taken to protect non-combatants, halt the spiraling descent into lawlessness and build the confidence for a political process . . . It is tragic that so many of the abuses and the failure to obey the Nepali Constitution and laws, which the ICJ observed when it visited in 2003, persist or have worsened.

The ICJ delegation expressed its dissatisfaction with the armed forces saying;

It saddens us that the Royal Nepali Army (RNA), which has a reputation for professionalism and discipline in United Nations peacekeeping operations, must now face up to daily reports of unprofessional and undisciplined behaviour of soldiers in their own country.

The ICJ claimed that both parties had heavily committed secret, unlawful and arbitrary detention, extra-judicial killings, enforced disappearances, torture and gross violations of international humanitarian law.

The HRW was involved actively in monitoring the human rights situation in Nepal's armed conflict. The decision of the US Congress to tie its military assistance to Nepal with human rights was a result of the lobbying of the HRW. The HRW played a crucial role in informing and sensitizing the US about the violation of human rights in Nepal. It regularly monitored the human rights situation and lobbied internationally for protecting human rights in Nepal. For example, through a statement on October 28, 2005, HRW said, "The Nepali government should immediately reverse its decision to close the popular radio station Kantipur FM and end censorship of the media." The Asia Director of Human Rights Watch also denounced the new media ordinance imposed by the king's government on October 9, 2005.

Other international non-governmental organizations active in Nepal's armed conflict were the Carter Centre, Médecins Sans Frontières (MSF), Search for Common Ground, International Alert, and SaferWorld.

International actors supporting Maoists

The Revolutionary Internationalist Movement (RIM) formed in 1984 in London by the second international conference of the hardliner Maoist parties from around the world supported the Maoists armed conflict in Nepal. Close ideological links between Maoists and RIM was the prime factor behind the latter's support for CPN-M's armed struggle in Nepal. ICG (2007: 8) states: "RIM played an important role in encouraging the Maoists to go ahead with their people's war strategy." When the Maoists started their armed struggle in February 1996, RIM issued a press statement entitled "From the Andes to the Himalayas, People's War is the only way to liberation," and praised the start of armed conflict in Nepal. In an interview given to Lee Onesto of the Revolutionary Worker, Prachanda revealed that there was a constant international involvement in finalizing the launching of the peoples war (Onesto 2000). Ideological and political exchange was main form of international support of RIM to the Nepali Maoists.

Similarly, the World People's Resistance Movement (WPRM) supported the Maoists in their armed campaign. WPRM organized meetings, discussions and interactions in Europe and other parts of the world to get support for Nepal's Maoists. ICG (2007) also points out that during the later part of the armed conflict (November 2005 onwards) WPRM also sent three groups of volunteers to work on the Maoist road building project in Rolpa District.

Considerable support for Nepal's Maoists was obtained from within South Asia.

South Asian communist parties and organizations were encouraged by the success of the Maoists in Nepal and expected this momentum to help expand revolution in the entire South Asian region. They formed CCOMPOSA, whose members were (Upreti 2006):

1 Communist Party of Nepal (Maoist)
2 Communist Party of India (Marxist-Leninist) (People's War Group) →
3 Communist Party of India (Maoist)
4 Maoist Communist Centre (MCC)
5 Revolutionary Communist Centre of India (MLM)
6 Revolutionary Communist Centre of India (Maoist)
7 Communist Party of India (ML) (Nakshalbari)
8 Purba Bangla Sarbahara Party (CC)
9 Purba Bangla Sarbahara Party (Maoist Punarghathan Kendra)
10 Bangladesh Samyabadi Party (ML)
11 Communist Party of Ceylon (Maoist)

The CCOMPOSA became an important support base for Nepali Maoists physically, morally, and ideologically. The CCOMPOSA provided an organizational platform and links in South Asia. CPN-M was a major actor and developed strategies and tactics based on the experiences of CCOMPOSA members. Furthermore, outside of the CCOPMOSA, the Maoists of Nepal received moral, physical and intellectual support from Indian communist parties and leftist outfits throughout the insurgency.

Post April 2006 dynamics and international actors

The nature, pattern and issues/content of international engagement drastically changed after the successful people's movement of April 2006. The CPN-M became the main focus of international actors and the king was sidelined. The twin pillars theory (constitutional monarchy and multi-party democracy) advocated for a long time by international actors as essential for Nepal's democracy and prosperity was abandoned. Those who were not ready to compromise on constitutional monarchy and multiparty democracy had started to acknowledge that the Nepali people themselves should decide the future of the monarchy. The CPN-M joined the interim government in a power-sharing arrangement. With these changes instituted, the functions of the king were completely superseded and the Prime Minister acted as the head of the state. The formal links of the king to the international community were broken.

Following the success of the April movement that came at the heels of the 12-point understanding orchestrated with the help of India, the international community accepted the leading role of India in the subsequent peace process in Nepal. Nepal's peace process initially operated largely according to the Indian roadmap. India wanted to bring the Maoists into mainstream politics, hoping to give a positive message to the Indian Maoists who were waging a "people's war" in more than

14 states of India. India wanted to manage Nepal's peace process according to its strategic interests and practical needs. India did not want to see Maoists being established as the largest force in Nepal, but wanted to bring them into the mainstream as a weak player to keep in check. India suspected the Maoists' role in fomenting anti-India activities. The Maoists had inconsistently yet repeatedly criticized India, and at times had gone as far as digging trenches (bunkers) to prepare for a possible war against India. However, the Maoists also relied on India to make the peace process successful. In January 2008, Prachanda publicly acknowledge that on seven occasions he had held confidential meetings inside the Indian Embassy but journalists were able to catch him just once. The Nepali Congress, by its proven track record, relies on India for political support. India also has strong influence in the CPN-UML and the Rastrya Janasakti Party. All emerging regional parties of the Tarai have close relations with India.

Nepal's peace process became one of the major contested issues within Indian domestic politics. As the peace process in Nepal was largely facilitated by the coalition government of India, a derailed peace process would have been a serious setback to it. The opposition Bharatiaya Janata Party (BJP) was against some elements of the peace process, such as the declaration of Nepal as a secular state and the suspension of the king. The BJP formally stands for Nepal as a Hindu State with a constitutional monarchy and it objected to the ruling Indian coalition government about its acceptance of the secular Nepali state and suspension of the king in the Interim Constitution. The failure of Nepal's peace process may have very negative effect on the coalition government in the forthcoming Indian election. The coalition government of India has a high stake in the success of the peace process in Nepal. Not surprisingly, a series of high-level diplomatic and political visits from India have occurred since the signing of the Comprehensive Peace Agreement (CPA) in November 2006. The High Command of the Indian Congress sent its General Secretary Digvijaya Singh to Kathmandu to meet Prime Minister Koirala on February 14, 2008. Earlier, officials from the Research and Analysis Wing (RAW), an intelligence agency, visited Nepal to discuss the Madeshi issues.

The international community played an important role in reaching the CPA on November 22, 2006, and later the Agreement on Management of Arms and Army between the Government of Nepal and the CPN-M on November 29, 2006. The 5622nd Meeting of the Security Council had established UNMIN by unanimously adopting resolution 1740 on January 23, 2007, as per the request of the Government of Nepal and the CPN-M. The resolution was presented by the United Kingdom and after some informal negotiation with India and China it was presented to the Security Council. Its mandate was to monitor the ceasefire, assist in the election of a Constituent Assembly, and monitor the management of arms and armed personnel of both sides through a Joint Monitoring Coordinating Committee.[5] However, the trade-off between European countries on one side and India and China on the other was intense at the time of the establishment of UNMIN and later during its extension hearings. The European countries led by the United Kingdom were interested to expand UNMIN's role but India and China did not agree and UNMIN has been limited to its original role/mission.

The peace process faced challenges because of competition among the powerful international actors based on their strategic interests (security umbrella, political influence, economic investment, etc.). During the later stages, Nepal became almost entirely dependent upon India to manage the peace process. The Tarai uprising, failure to conduct the Constituent Assembly elections on two separate occasions, blatant competition among the coalition partners to control state power and resources (e.g. constant bargaining and consequent long delays in the appointment of vice-chancellors of universities and ambassadors, tussles while allocating Home, Defense, and Finance ministries, to name but a few cases) have demonstrated that politicians were largely incompetent to effectively manage the political transition and peace process.

External engagement in the economic sector was largely related to economic development assistance such as economic policy reforms, trade promotion, and investment in basic services such as education, health, drinking water, rural infrastructures development, and the promotion of private investment. International financial institutions such as the World Bank, the International Monetary Fund and the Asian Development Bank were the architects of economic engagement during Nepal's armed conflict. However, their economic intervention largely failed to positively impact Nepal's armed conflict.

Powerful external actors were actively working with Nepali civil society activists. Media support was one of their priority engagements. They sent a large numbers of journalists abroad or to their respective countries for study tours, workshops and training related to human rights, conflict resolution and political issues related to armed conflict. They have sponsored several media houses and programs. Some diplomats such as the American and Indian ambassadors frequently appeared on television and delivered what many regarded as political speeches. Besides the media, international actors extensively supported NGOs in the areas of civic education, peace campaigning, and organizing exchange visits for civil society leaders, politicians and business leaders for conflict transformation and peace building.

Conclusion

International actors were actively engaged during Nepal's armed conflict. The main cited objective of their engagement was to help Nepal resolve its armed insurgency, and to restore and strengthen democracy and lasting peace. Initially, they worked hard to defend the twin pillar concept (i.e. constitutional monarchy and multi-party democracy) and therefore concentrated on ensuring power-sharing among politicians and the palace. However, after the royal takeover they were unable to pursue the twin-pillar concept. International engagement with the government of Nepal proceeded along two fronts: (a) war diplomacy – supplying arms and weapons, military assistances, building coercive alliances, restricting travel of rebel leaders in their countries, sharing intelligence information about rebel activities; and (b) peace diplomacy – diplomatic efforts devoted to achieving and implementing peace.

The degree and intensity of external involvement in Nepal was mainly shaped by strategic interests, political orientation and the humanitarian commitment of external actors. International actors used both confrontational and cooperative approaches of engagement in dealing with the armed conflict of Nepal. Inconsistency and duplicity were the main characteristics of international engagements. For example, they were quite ambiguous on several issues such as approach towards the Maoists (terrorist vs political force), the 12-point understanding, and the issue of supplying arms to the government of Nepal.

The engagement of powerful external actors in Nepal's armed conflict largely became a catalyst for confrontation. The international actors like the USA, operating in the framework of confrontation, took very extreme positions in dealing with the conflict of Nepal. Dual role was observed from India. On the one hand, India supplied the largest amount of arms and weapons and arrested some of the Maoists leaders and cadres. On the other hand, the Maoists used Indian territories more freely for managing their insurgency in Nepal.

International actors who supported a cooperative approach focused on state transformation and pushed for a change in Nepal's feudal, centralized unitary and exclusionary state. They emphasized the creation of a new political and social infrastructure for empowerment and the recognition of underprivileged groups, Dalit, and ethnic minorities as a way to enable and foster social justice, address structural inequalities and ensure human security. These actors, including many European countries, emphasized negotiation, compromise and collective responsibility.

Although different countries opted for different approaches during specific phases of the armed conflict, external engagement in general largely employed a multi-track approach in dealing with the Maoist insurgency. They used the Track I approach where political and military leaders were brought on a Nepal visit several times as mediators and/or representatives of their respective governments. They engaged mainly with the Nepal government. In the Track II approach they were engaged with academics, professionals, religious leaders and international and non-governmental organizations. In the Track III approach, they were mainly engaged with local grassroots activists and organizations dealing with development issues, human rights and humanitarian agencies.

Notes

1 King Gyanendra's address at the Thirteenth SAARC Summit, Dhaka, Bangladesh, November 12, 2005.
2 For example Dr. Anup Pahari shared his opinion in this line with this author on July 22, 2008.
3 Bhattarai (2004), Upreti (2006), Onesto (2005) and Pandey (2005) are the basis for the confrontational approach of the US on Nepal's armed conflict.
4 The open dismay of the government towards ICG was so great that it did not allow the ICG to open an office in Nepal in 2004.
5 See the decision (SC/8942) of the 5622nd Meeting (PM) of the Security Council of the UN for details.

Bibliography

Armon, J. and A. Carl, eds. 1996. *The Liberian Peace Process 1990–1996*. Accord issue 1/1996. London: Conciliation Resources.

Armon, J. and L. Philipson, eds. 1998. *Demanding Sacrifice: War and Negotiation in Sri Lanka*. Accord Issue 4/1998. London: Conciliation Resources.

Barnes, C., ed. 2002. *Owning the Process. Public Participation in Peace Making. Featuring South Africa, Guatemala & Mali*. Accord issue 3/2002. London: Conciliation Resources.

Bhattarai, R. 2004. *Geopolitical Specialties of Nepal and a Regional Approach to Conflict Transformation*. Kathmandu: Friends for Peace.

Bush, R. A. B. and J. P. Folger 1994. *The Promise of Mediation: Responding to Conflict through Empowerment and Recognition*. San Francisco: Jossey-Bass Publishers.

Dixit, K. N., ed. 2003. *External Affairs: Cross Border Relations*. New Delhi: Lotus Collection Roli Books.

Fisher, R. J. 1997. *Interactive Conflict Resolution*. Syracuse, NY: Syracuse University Press.

Hendrickson D., ed. 1998. *Safe Guarding Peace: Cambodia's Constitutional Change*. Accord issue 5, Nov. 1998. London: Conciliation Resources.

ICG 2007. *Nepal's Maoists: Purists or Pragmatists*. Asia Report No 132. Brussels: International Crisis Group (ICG).

Jackson, R. and G. Sorensen 2003. *Introduction to International Relations: Theories and Approaches*. New York: Oxford University Press.

Jandt, F. E. and P. B. Pedersen, eds. 1996. *Constructive Conflict Management: Asia Pacific Cases*. London: Sage Publications.

Karki, A, and D. Seddon, eds. 2003. *The People's War in Nepal: Left Perspectives*. Delhi: Adroit Publishers.

Lederach, J. P. 1999. Justpeace: The Challenges of the 21st Century. In *People Building Peace: 35 Inspiring Stories from around the World*, ed. European Centre for Conflict Prevention (in co-operation with the International Fellowship of Reconciliation (IFOR) and the Coexistence Initiative of State of the World Forum). Utrecht: European Centre for Conflict Prevention, pp.27–36.

Lohani, P. C. 2005. What Vision for South Asian Regional Cooperation. In: D. Dahal and N. N Pandey (eds.), New Life within SAARC. Kathmandu: Institute of Foreign Affairs and Fedrich-Ebet-Stiftung, pp. 55–66.

Louise, D. and J. McDonald 1996. *Multi-Track Diplomacy*. Connecticut: Kumarian Press.

Lucima, O., ed. 2002. Protractive Conflict, Elusive Peace: Initiatives to End the Violence in Northern Uganda. Accord issue 11/2002. London: Conciliation Resources.

Lund, M. 1996. *Preventing Violent Conflict: A Strategy for Preventive Diplomacy*. Washington: United States Peace Institute.

Mathew R. and B. Upreti 2005. *Nepal: Environmental Stress, Demographic Changes and the Maoists*. Environmental Change and Security Programme Report, Issue 11. Woodrow Wilson International Centre for Scholars, pp. 29–39.

McCartney, C. 1999. *Striking a Balance: The Northern Ireland Peace Process*. Accord issue 8/1999. London: Conciliation Resources.

Mehrotra, L. 2003. The Role of United Nations: The Case of Cambodia. In: D. D. Khanna and Gert Kueck (eds.) *Conflict Resolution, Human Rights and Democracy*. Delhi: Shipra Publications, pp. 156–74.

Misra, A. 2002. Afghanistan: The Politics of Post War Reconstruction. *Journal of Conflict Security and Development*. 2:3, pp. 5–57.

Mishra, R. 2004. India's Role in Nepal's Maoist Insurgency. *Asian Survey*, September/October 2004, Vol. 44, No. 5, pp. 627–46

Onesto, L. 2000. Red Flag Flying on the Roof of the World (Interview with Prachanda). *Revolutionary Worker*, 20 February 2000.

Onesto, L. 2005. *Dispatches from the People's War in Nepal.* London: Pluto Press and Chicago: Insight Press.

Pandey, N. N. 2005. *Nepal's Maoist Movement and Implications for India and China.* Regional Centre for Strategic Studies (RCSS) Policy Studies, no. 27, RCCS (Colombo). New Delhi: Manohar Publishers and Distributors.

Rajan, K. V. 2003. Nepal In: K. N. Dixit (ed.), *External Affairs: Cross Border Relations.* New Delhi: Lotus Collection Roli Books, pp. 97–120.

Shah, S. 2004 A Himalayan Red Herring: Maoist Revolution in the Shadow of the Legacy of Raj. In: M. Hutt (ed.), *Himalayan 'People's War': Nepal's Maoist Rebellion.* London: Hurst and Company, pp. 192–224.

Susskind, L. and J. Cruikshank 1987. *Breaking the Impasse: Consensual Approaches to Resolving Public Disputes.* New York: Basic Books.

Tate, W. 2004. No Room for Peace: United State's Policy in Columbia, In: Mauricio Garcia-Duran (ed.) *Alternatives to War: Columbia's Peace Process.* London: Conciliations Resources, pp. 70–73.

Upadhaya, S. 2008. *The Raj Lives: India in Nepal.* New Delhi: Vitasta.

Upreti, B. R. 2004. *The Price of Neglect: From Resource Conflict to Maoist Insurgency in the Himalayan Kingdom.* Kathmandu: Bhrikuti Academic Publications.

———. 2006. *Armed Conflict and Peace Process in Nepal: The Maoist Insurgency, Past Negotiation and Opportunities for Conflict Transformation.* New Delhi: Adroit Publishers.

Upreti, B. R. and R. Nepali, eds. 2006. *Nepal at Barrel of Gun: Proliferation of Small Arms and Light Weapons and their Impacts.* Kathmandu: South Asia Small Arms Network-Nepal.

Ury, W., J. Brett and S. Goldberg 1989. *Getting Disputes Resolved.* San Francisco: Jossey-Bass Publishers.

Ury, W. 1991. *Getting Past "No": Negotiating with Difficult People.* New York: Bantam Books.

———. 1999. *Getting to Peace: Transforming Conflict at Home, at Work, and in the World.* New York: Viking.

Vayrynen, R., ed. 1991. *New Directions in Conflict Theory.* London: Sage Publications.

Zartman, I. W. 1987. *Positive Sum: Improving North-South Negotiations.* New York: Transaction Publishers.

Part VII
Identifying the causes

12 An assessment of the causes of conflict in Nepal

Bishwa Nath Tiwari[1]

Introduction

The 1990 constitution of Nepal has been regarded as superior to the previous constitutions on several counts, but because of weak implementation it could not properly address the issue of social exclusion and inequalities, among others (see appendix 12.1). Dissatisfied with the state provisions and practices, the Maoists launched a People's War in February 1996, which lasted until the signing of the comprehensive peace accord on November 21, 2006.

The number of people killed in the decade-long violent conflict was 13, 347. The Mid-Western Development Region is the area most affected by the conflict; however, even in this region, the incidence of conflict varies widely across the districts, implying that there are a number of factors that influence conflict or insecurity at the sub-national level. The intensity of conflict increased after the mobilization of the army in late 2001. The number of casualties increased after 2002, with the state responsible for a greater share of the killings than the Maoists. Political workers topped the list of those killed, followed by agricultural workers and peasants. This signified that, apart from other reasons, the conflict was political in nature, and additionally that it had a rural character as most of the conflict victims were from rural areas.

Apart from the loss of human lives, the violent conflict has had wide-ranging consequences, relegating human development, and therefore any relapse has to be prevented by properly addressing the root causes of conflict. It is against this backdrop that this chapter looks into the reasons for violent conflict in Nepal during 1996–2006.

Brief review of literature

Conflict is inherent in all societies and arises when two or more societal groups pursue incompatible objectives. It is a dynamic process that can lead to positive or negative changes. Violent conflicts occur when institutions that manage conflict in society are no longer able to accommodate different interest groups through negotiation, compromise and grievance resolution.

The contemporary literature offers two possible motivations for the origin of conflict: greed and grievance. The concept of 'greed' emphasizes the role of rents, which are occasionally lootable, in producing inter-group rivalry for their control – a competitive process of rent-seeking that can descend into outright war. The 'grievance' approach is based on a sense of injustice where some social groups are discriminated against, and their grievances could provide a basis for violent conflict (Tiwari 2008).

In practice both motivations co-exist simultaneously; it is difficult to motivate groups to fight one another without historical grievances even when valuable resource rents are at stake. Similarly, wars motivated mainly by grievances can also degenerate into greed, once war produces new avenues for profit. Thus, greed and grievance are inextricably intertwined.

Most contemporary civil wars in poor developing countries have ethnic dimensions, where the different caste and ethnic groups fight each other. Empirical works by Easterly (2001) and Easterly and Levine (1997) have concluded that ethnic fractionalization is one of the major causes of civil wars, while Collier and Hoeffler (1998) have arrived at a different finding which holds that the underlying cause of civil wars is economic and not ethnicity.

Collier and Hoeffler (2004b) and Fearon and Laitin (2003) found that poorer countries face greater risk of conflict; however, they interpret this differently. Collier and Hoeffler have advanced the low opportunity cost of rebels and large stock of easily expropriated natural resources or primary commodities in an area as the motivating factors for conflict. On the other hand, Fearon and Laitin argue that conflict occurs because poor countries lack adequate capacity to govern. In poor developing countries security is generally poor in rural and remote areas compared to city and more accessible areas. This suggests that the cause for conflict is weak governance due to lack of resources. This view is shared by Deng (2004), who maintains that violent conflict is largely associated with bad governance.[2]

Cross-country analyses conducted in the past have established that poor countries have higher conflict intensity than richer countries. While such a finding highlights the significance of economic factors including poverty, one should not forget the root causes of poverty that ultimately affect human security. Cross-country studies cannot provide in-depth analysis of conflict and they ignore the specificity of particular countries. In fact, as advanced by the Human Development Report 1994, security has two dimensions: freedom from fear and freedom from want. The causes of fear and want could be different across countries of the world.

The literature on the causes of conflict first starts out with a cross-country comparison and then moves towards a within-country analysis of conflict. Some early studies favored justice as the reason; later studies focused on economic factors to explain conflict. In recent years, primarily based on the theory of relative deprivation developed by Gurr (1968, 1970), Stewart and researchers at Oxford University have advanced horizontal inequality and social exclusion as the chief reasons for conflict (Stewart et al. 2005, 2007). This approach further broadens the grievance approach. According to this school of thought, conflict entrepreneurs mobilize the socially excluded social groups (different caste and ethnicity or races) for violent conflict because such groups have grievances due to political and socio-economic inequalities and inequities resulting from deep-rooted cultural and historical discrimination, among other factors.

Causes of Maoist conflict in Nepal

A number of studies have already been conducted on the conflict in Nepal. There is some diversity in their findings regarding the causes of conflict. However, the reasons advanced by most of them broadly fall under the grievance and greed approaches as mentioned above. Some studies have suggested that Maoist conflict has found support from oppressed lower castes, portraying the insurgency as stemming from rage against a long legacy of oppression based on caste and ethnicity. Other studies report economic factors, such as inequality, landlessness, and a general lack of opportunity reinforced by complex systems of caste and related discriminatory patterns, which have provided sufficient motivation and support for the Maoist cause (Bray et al. 2003; Do and Iyer 2007). Some researchers found a significant correlation between landlessness and number of fatalities in the conflict. Some others attribute conflict mostly to poverty and the underdevelopment of the country, and find that caste and ethnic divisions are not a major contributor to conflict (Thapa and Sijapati 2004; Gersony 2003; Do and Iyer 2007). There is also the possibility that government repression might have generated further grievances, leading to greater support for Maoist rebels (Do and Iyer 2007).

Mahat (2005) acknowledges the relevance of grievance theory as the explanatory framework for the Maoist People's War in Nepal. According to Pandey (2005) political instability, corruption, unemployment and bad governance helped foster a wider dissatisfaction with the democratic political class at the centre. The socio-economic marginalization of the population of the mid-west coupled with the fighting spirit of local ethnic communities – especially the Magar – triggered the armed uprising. He holds that ethnicity is an important element of the Maoist movement, and that the 1990 change enabled indigenous nationalities to grow a new sense of identity and legal grounds to appeal for their rights. The pro-poor approach of the Maoist has also been a magnet for deprived groups (Pandey 2005).

Karki and Bhattarai (2004) observe that conflict in Nepal is a manifestation of complex social and economic demands, intertwined with ideology and a history of discrimination on which the Maoists were able to capitalize. According to them, democracy and subsequent unfulfilled aspirations are believed to be an important factor behind the outbreak of insurgency. Besides these, they also identify poverty, unemployment, ethnic discrimination and illiteracy as primary causes of Maoist conflict.

Murshed and Gates (2005) analyze the relationship between spatial horizontal inequalities and the intensity of Maoist insurgency. Their analysis does not consider ethnic and caste groups per se, but rather focuses on regional differences. Using a 'gap' measure of human development they find strong econometric support for a relationship between regional deprivation and the intensity of the rebellion, as measured by the number of conflict fatalities by district. A subsequent econometric analysis by Do and Iyer (2007) replicates this finding of regional deprivation, measured by the regional poverty rate and literacy rate.

In their earlier studies, however, Murshed and Gates (2003) suggest that grievance rather than greed is the main motivating force behind the conflict. In particular, they maintain that horizontal and inter-group inequality is central in explaining the Nepali strife. This has both caste and ethnic dimension. Besides, they also found spatial inequality as the cause of conflict because mid- and far-western development regions have significantly low levels of human development, and have a larger proportion of landlessness compared to other development regions of the country.

According to Murshed and Gates (2003), ethnicity mobilizes groups to fight each other, and that ethnicity, whether based on language, religion or some other factor, is a powerful organizing principle and superior to social class. The authors argue that grievance is rooted in deep inter-group disparities encompassing: (i) asset inequality; (ii) unequal access to public employment and public services; (iii) over-taxation; and (iv) economic mismanagement. Thus, they inferred that development strategies failed to meet the challenges of reducing poverty and horizontal inequality.

While Murshed and Gates (2003) found that grievance is the motivating factor for conflict, and that Nepal's conflict has ethnic and caste dimensions, Gurung (2005) concluded that no correlation exists between density of socially excluded population and intensity of insurgency, but that there is correspondence between area of insurgency and level of poverty.

Zartman (2005) has argued that while initiation of conflicts requires the presence of a political entrepreneur, the continuation of conflict requires successful mobilization of a population subgroup. His paper advanced that difference in welfare among socio-economic groups, that is to say relative deprivation rather than absolute deprivation, can help explain the seemingly puzzling coinciding trends of poverty reduction and conflict persistence during the 1990s.

Parwez (2006) made an attempt to investigate the determinants of conflict using a logit regression model, where the dependent variable is a binary one showing presence or absence of conflict in a district. The independent variables are generally the sub-components of human development and its related indices. The study found a negative effect of three variables including life expectancy index, income index and road density, whereas there was a positive effect of the human poverty index on conflict. Moreover, the effect of educational attainment has been found positive, pointing to an increase in level of education also increasing conflict. However, this does not exactly match with the study of Do and Iyer (2007) which found a negative effect of literacy. But a DFID (2003) study indicated that higher levels of education with high unemployment, and increased political awareness with the introduction of democracy, contributed to the conflict in Nepal.

Do and Iyer (2007) investigated proximate correlates of Maoist conflict in Nepal by running a linear regression with intensity of conflict in a district as the dependent variable. In their analysis geographical factors, including elevation and presence of forest areas, explained the variation in intensity of conflict. The coefficient of poverty rate was always found to be significant and fairly stable across the specifications. Areas with higher literacy rates were associated with low intensity of conflict. Moreover, caste polarization was found statistically significant, whereas proportion of advantaged castes was found marginally significant. The relationship with caste polarization disappeared when the authors controlled for poverty measures. One reason for this, as explained by the authors, may be that the effect of social divisions works through poverty, that is to say all other things being equal, an area with greater social divisions has greater poverty. The authors found that economic factors such as poverty or lack of economic opportunity were significantly correlated with intensity of conflict, and that the relationship of conflict intensity with measure of social diversity was much less significant and robust.

Caveats of the past studies and conceptual framework

Most of the studies are not conclusive as to whether the main causes behind the conflict are political and social or economic. Stewart et al. (2005) point out that the reason that cross-country studies do not find grievance to be a significant cause for conflict has to do mainly with their methodology. Cross-country studies accommodate limited data, generally focusing on economic variables available at the cross-country level, and thus tend to ignore the rich array of reasons for conflict found within each country.

Stewart et al. maintain that it is grievance rather than greed that explains conflict in Nepal. Indeed, within a country there are multiple dimensions underlying conflict which can vary significantly from country to country. In some resource-rich countries, the greed approach could better explain conflict, whereas in resource-poor countries the grievance approach has greater explanatory power.

However, single-country econometric studies have also identified different variables as factors responsible for conflict, as shown in two empirical studies by Parwez (2006) and Do and Iyer (2007). While the Parwez study found a positive effect of education on conflict, Do and Iyer's study found a negative effect.

This difference can be attributed to their methodologies, including specification of models and variables and the use of data from different sources. There are differences in the dependent variables used in the two studies. Do and Iyer use the *number of persons killed in the district*, whereas Prawez uses *security phases of districts*[3] (see appendix 12.2); one uses logistic regression and the other uses simple and probabilistic regression models. Moreover, while Do and Iyer (2007) used literacy rate based on the 1991 population census, Parwez (2006) used educational attainment data based on the 2001 population census. The other data used by Parwez generally comes from standard sources such as the Nepal Human Development Report, whereas the Do and Iyer study mainly uses data from district profiles. Besides these factors, the differences in findings may be due to the fact that: (i) literacy is a component of educational attainment; and (ii) use of a continuous conflict variable (number of killed persons per thousand) by Do and Iyer, in contrast to the use of a dummy dependent variable (phases of insecurity) by Parwez. This study, therefore, makes an attempt to understand reasons for different results of regression models.

The major conclusions of the review that provides the conceptual framework of the study are as follows:

(i) Whether greed or grievance explains conflict depends on methodology of study.
(ii) Use of sophisticated statistical tools and cross-country regression models limits the possibility of using qualitative data. Moreover, the data generated in different countries may not be compatible because of the differences in methodology of data collection. This together with the lack of in-depth investigation at times gives spurious results and implications.
(iii) Reasons for conflict differ from country to country; therefore an in-depth within-country study is necessary for deriving the right policy implications.
(iv) The grievance approach is more applicable in countries with caste and ethnic divisions and exclusion in different spheres including in the sphere of state/politics. The greed approach, on the other hand, is more applicable in resource-rich countries where rebels are interested in looting resources.

In view of the above, the author undertakes a within-country analysis. The author believes that the reasons for conflict are diverse, mutually interacting and interdependent, and are related to all the four dimensions of people's life – political, economic, social and cultural – rather than only to one dimension as some studies have found. Therefore, this study is an improvement over the earlier studies in the following aspects:

(i) inclusion of several variables in the regression models for explaining the conflict;
(ii) specification of dependent variable of the regression models, in two ways:

(a) level of insecurity as defined by the security phases,
(b) intensity of conflict as defined by the number of people killed in a district; and

(iii) comparison of the results of the two variants (dependent variables) of the models for explaining the reasons for conflict.

Methodology

Specification of model

Based on the experience of past studies, a linear regression model is fit for estimating the effect of different variables on the likelihood and intensity of conflict. In order to observe effect, examine the robustness of estimates, and explain the differences in the findings of past studies, two forms of dependent variables have been used alternatively in the regression model: *level of insecurity* as a dummy dependent variable and *proportion of population killed* in a district as a continuous dependent variable. The model with the dummy dependent variable primarily helps in finding out factors causing likelihood of conflict; the other model, with proportion of killed people as dependent variable, helps in explaining the intensity of conflict. Moreover, the estimates of two sets of regression models with two different dependent variables will help to look into differences of results relating to the level and intensity of conflict and to look into robustness of estimates. In the case of a dummy dependent variable a logistic regression model has been used, whereas for the other dependent variable a simple regression model has been employed.

In order to estimate the two models, I have used the data of the 2001 population census, 2003/04 Nepal Living Standard Survey (NLSS). I have also used the 2004 United Nations security phase data to look into the reasons for the intensification of the conflict after 2001. To deal with outlier problems, both of the models were estimated using the data of only 72 out of 75 districts of the country (1999).[4]

The inclusion of independent variables is guided by the framework of justice and loot-seeking behavior, results of past studies and, more importantly, availability of data. Both social and economic factors have been taken as independent variables. The variables included in the models are explained below.

Dependent variables and their measurement

Level of insecurity: The United Nations classifies districts according to security condition. Level of insecurity has been converted to a dummy dependent variable along the following lines: security phase 'three' assigned a value of 'one,' and security phases 'one and two' assigned a value of 'zero,' implying that there is insecurity when a district is declared as phase three by the United Nations. As of December 2, 2004, the United Nations classified 75 districts of Nepal as follows: 38 districts in phase one; one district in phase two; and 36 districts in phase three. The details of the security phases and their implications are given in appendix 12.2.

Number of people killed per thousand: The number people killed either by the Maoists or by security personnel was normalized by dividing by total district population. However, it has been expressed in terms of thousands as the number of people killed varies highly across districts. The source of data is the Informal Sector Service Centre (INSEC), Kathmandu.

Independent variables and their measurement

Altogether 21 independent variables have been used. They are broadly categorized into the following groups/themes: development index and infrastructures, economic factors, literacy and education, health and nutrition, and social and natural factors. These independent variables by sources of information are given in table 12.1. Their detail specifications and/or definitions are given in appendix 12.2.

Table 12.1 Sources of information by variables

CBS, ICIMOD & SNV (2003) – 6	UNDP/Nepal (2004) – 5	CBS, WFP and World Bank (2006a) – 5	Gurung, ed., (2006) – 3	CBS (2006) – 2
Overall Composite index Infrastructure development index Road density Overall literacy rate Share of females in non-agricultural occupation Broad occupational structure	Life expectancy index Educational attainment index (EAI) Income index (II) Human poverty index (HPI) Human empowerment index (HEI)	Stunting Wasting Underweight Caloric intake prevalence Poverty incidence	Proportion of Dalit population Proportion of Indigenous nationalities population Proportion of Hindu population	Proportion of forest area District elevation

Estimation of the model

A zero order correlation has been computed for all the dependent and independent variables. A high correlation (0.80 and over) exists between following variables:

- overall composite index and overall literacy rate/educational attainment index/human poverty index/underweight of children
- road density and occupational structure
- overall literacy and educational attainment index/human poverty index
- stunting of children and HPI/HEI
- underweight and proportion of indigenous nationalities population
- educational attainment index and HPI
- HPI and HEI
- proportion of Hindu and proportion of indigenous nationalities population.

Therefore, first a model with all variables has been estimated for the two dependent variables: *level of insecurity* and *number of persons killed* in a district. Later, these models have been estimated excluding the following variables, which have high correlation of the order of +/–0.8 or more:

- overall composite index
- occupational structure
- stunting of children
- underweight of children
- human poverty index
- educational attainment index
- proportion of Hindu population.

The causes and/or correlates of conflict have been observed by estimating the following logistics regression model:

$$Y_i = a + bX_i + e_i \tag{1}$$

Where:

Y_i = a dummy variable for level of insecurity in district i (high insecurity = 1; low or no insecurity = 0)
X_i = a vector of characteristics which influence conflict or insecurity
e_i = error term
i = 1 to 72 districts.

In order to add richness in the analysis of the above model, another model was estimated with a continuous dependent variable, the number of people killed per thousand of a district population. As dependent variables use data for the year 2004 (level of insecurity) and 2006 (number of persons killed by 2006), and the independent variables are measured for the year 2001 and 2003 from 2001 population census and NLSS 2003, this analysis mainly explains the intensity and spread of conflict.

The two models, each with a separate dependent variable, were estimated with SPSS package version 12. In view of the objective of the study and the findings of the past studies, and in order to understand the dynamics of exclusion of insignificant variables step by step, the estimates of backward estimation method were chosen.

The results of the models with a limited number of variables (excluding the correlated variables mentioned above) are not much different from those of the models that included all variables. Moreover, sensitivity of coefficients has also been examined as the backward estimation method eliminates insignificant variables one by one. There was no change in sign or significant difference in the magnitude of coefficients in such a process of computation, suggesting robustness of the estimated coefficients.[5] Therefore, it was decided to estimate the models including all variables.

Interpretation of results

Results of logistic regression model with security level as dependent variable

Out of the 21 variables included in the model, eight are found statistically significant at five or fewer percentage levels of significance. The overall explanatory power of the model (adjusted R^2) is 0.505. The model as a whole is statistically significant in explaining variation in the level of conflict or insecurity.

According to the estimates of the coefficients, an increase in poverty incidence and the proportion of the population below a minimum level of dietary energy consumption (caloric intake prevalence) increases the likelihood of a level of insecurity. On the other hand, an increase in females' share in non-agricultural occupation and income decreases the level of insecurity. Moreover, as expected, an increase in the overall composite index of development also decreases the level of insecurity in a district (table 12.2).

250   *Bishwa Nath Tiwari*

Table 12.2 Estimation of regression models with level of insecurity as dependent variable

	Unstandardized coefficients		Standardized coefficients	t-statistic	Level of significance
	B	Std. error	Beta		
(Constant)	3.572	1.018		3.509	.001
Composite index	−.011	.005	−.469	−2.274	.026
Female in non-agricultural occupation (%)	−.028	.014	−.386	−2.069	.043
Poverty incidence	1.557	.572	.380	2.725	.008
Caloric intake prevalence	1.957	1.007	.279	1.944	.056
Wasting of children	−13.132	3.639	−1.044	−3.608	.001
Income index	−3.625	1.494	−.375	−2.426	.018
Proportion of indigenous nationalities population (%)	−.012	.003	−.556	−3.456	.001
District dummy	−.805	.250	−.724	−3.217	.002

The negative coefficient of a dummy dependent variable for district ecology or altitude suggests that the level of insecurity is low in hills and mountains compared to Tarai in the latter half of the decade-long conflict. This adds to the fact that while the onset was high in the hills in the beginning, the conflict spread faster in Tarai district in the latter half of the conflict.

Results from linear regression with intensity of conflict as dependent variable

When the dependent variable is the number of killed persons, the independent variables that are found statistically significant at less than 5 percent level of significance are the following: overall literacy rate, proportion of females in non-agricultural operations, caloric intake prevalence, proportion of indigenous nationalities population, and proportion of forest area (table 12.3).

Table 12.3 Estimation of regression models with population killed (per thousand) as dependent variable

	Unstandardized coefficients		Standardized coefficients	t-statistic	Significance level
	B	Std. error	Beta		
(Constant)	−.466	.502		−.929	.356
Literacy rate (%)	−.022	.006	−.475	−3.911	.000
Female in non-agricultural occupation (%)	.055	.012	.698	4.473	.000
Caloric intake prevalence	2.761	.787	.366	3.509	.001
Proportion of indigenous nationalities population (%)	−.010	.003	−.424	−2.847	.006
Forest area (%)	.009	.003	.277	2.851	.006

The number of people killed per thousand of population in a district decreases with the increase in literacy rate, and the proportion of indigenous nationalities. On the other hand, it increases with the increase in the proportion of population below a minimum level of dietary energy consumption, female's share in non-agricultural occupation and proportion of area under forest in a district. When this is compared with the results of a regression model with the level of insecurity as the dependent variable, the following notable points emerge for discussion:

(i)   Both models have the following three variables statistically significant: share of females in non-agricultural operation, caloric intake prevalence and proportion of indigenous nationalities population. However, there is one critical difference in the result: the sign of the coefficient of the share of females in non-agricultural operations is negative in the case of the model with level of security as the dependent variable, whereas it is positive in respect of the model with the number of people killed as the dependent variable. This needs further exploration unless the level of insecurity as defined by the United Nations is questioned.

(ii) Unlike in the model with level of insecurity as the dependent variable, literacy rate and proportion of forest area have been found statistically significant when the dependent variable is the number of people killed.

(iii) The model with the level of insecurity as dependent variable comes up with economic indices such as poverty incidence and income index as the variables for explaining the variation, whereas such economic factors disappear in the case of the model with number of people killed. The only economic-related variable that appears significant in this variant of the model is the proportion of females in non-agricultural operations. The implication of this finding is that while economic factors explain the level of insecurity, the intensity of conflict depends more on other non-economic factors like literacy rate and proportion of forest area. This also hints that it was primarily the economic inequality and the consequent dissatisfaction that created an opportune moment for the Maoists to mobilize the people for violent conflict, and that the intensity of conflict increases with the differences in social and other natural characteristics. This result corroborates the finding of cross-country level studies by Collier and Hoeffler, among others.

One important value addition of this chapter is that it has found an inverse relationship between the proportion of indigenous nationalities and level of insecurity, which implies that as the proportion of indigenous nationalities increases, the level of insecurity or the number of people killed decreases. The finding is in conformity with the finding of Gurung (2005), who found an inverse relation between the proportion of indigenous nationalities population and number of insurgency-related deaths. In particular, he found that Western Hill, with the highest insurgency-related deaths had the second lowest proportion of indigenous nationalities, while Central Mountain, with lowest insurgency-related deaths, had the highest proportion of indigenous nationalities.

The inverse relation between the proportion of indigenous nationalities population and number of insurgency deaths is also partially corroborated by the data that the proportion of indigenous nationalities killed is less than the proportion of their share in the total population, whereas the proportion of people killed from Brahmin and Chhetri castes is closer to their share in the total population.

However, such a clear negative relation does not appear in case of the Dalit population. While exploring the relation between Dalit and insurgency, Gurung (2005) found three geographic regions showing convergence and another three near convergence out of the 13 regions in his analysis. The rest do not have much relation. Central Tarai has low insurgency deaths and low Dalit population. The regions with near convergence were Eastern Tarai, Central Tarai and Central Mountain. Out of 13 regions, six appear to have a relation between Dalit population and number of people killed, whereas the other seven do not have such a relation. Thus, as one half has relation and the other half does not, the relation gets blurred on the average at national level. In other words, the proportion of Dalit population does not appear to have an independent effect on conflict intensity.

Comparison of results with previous studies

Comparison with Do and Iyer (2007)

Only three variables were found significant by Do and Iyer in a study that used number of people killed as the dependent variable. These are elevation, proportion of forest area and literacy rate. Out of the three variables, proportion of forest area and literacy rate appear statistically significant in the model, with the number of people killed as the dependent variable of the present study. Elevation by itself has not been included in this study, but a dummy of the three ecological regions has been included with Tarai district as zero and hills and mountain district with a value of one.[6] Besides, three other variables are also statistically significant in this study: proportion of indigenous nationalities population, proportion of female in non-agriculture operation and caloric intake prevalence. Out of these, only the caste polarization variable was included in Do and Iyer, which was found significant when poverty incidence, proportion of advantaged castes and literacy rate were included. As a measure of caste polarization, proportion of indigenous nationalities population was included in the current study, which is statistically significant. Thus, the results of this study are in conformity with those of Do and Iyer. However, the conclusion of Do and Iyer that caste factor does not have a critical role in conflict is not fully supported by the result of the current study. If we support Do and Iyer's findings then even an economic variable like poverty rate also does not appear significant when all the variables are included in the model. It appears significant when only four variables are included.

Comparison with Parwez (2006)

Of the six variables included in the model with dummy dependent variables by Parwez, the following five were reported statistically significant: life expectancy index, educational attainment index, income index, road density and human poverty index. The human empowerment index did not appear significant. In case of the current study with dummy dependent variable, eight out of 21 variables were found statistically significant. The variable that is common to both studies is income index. It is the overall composite index rather than road density that appears significant in the present study. As road density forms part of the overall composite index, which is found significant in the present study, it can be inferred that there is only a little similarity in the results of the two studies. The discrepancies between the results of Parwez and this study could be due to the following: (i) lack of proper consideration of multi-colinearity problem; and (ii) the inclusion of outliers in the Parwez study.

The regression results of the past studies and those of this study could not unambiguously establish the reasons for the conflict. The main reasons for this anomaly are differences in methodology and lack of detailed data for looking into the reasons for differences in the results of regression models. In fact, the model is specified based largely on the availability of data.

Summary of the results and policy implications

The key findings from the cross-district regression results hint that the probability of insecurity or conflict in a district is low when: (i) its level of overall development is high, income is high, or women are involved in non-agricultural occupations at higher rates; (ii) the proportion of indigenous nationalities in the district is high; (iii) a district falls in the mountain and hill belt rather than in the Tarai. On the other hand, the probability of conflict is high when level of poverty and malnutrition is high.

The results of the study are comparable with those of previous studies. Moreover, this study has additional value in terms of the following two aspects:

(i) Conflict is not only due to economic reasons but also due to social and ethnic reasons. This is evident from the negative relationship of level of insecurity and proportion of indigenous nationalities. When the proportion of indigenous nationalities population increases, the level of insecurity decreases.

(ii) The results of studies using regression models depend on how the conflict variable is defined or specified. Despite the fact that the same set of independent variables has been used in both the models of the present study, the results of the two models are quite different, with economic reasons appearing as the significant variables with *level of security,* whereas social and educational variables appear significant with *intensity of conflict* as the dependent variable.

The conclusion regarding the difference in results of the models is that inequalities in the level of development and poverty increase the likelihood of conflict, and once the conflict is initiated with political leaders or conflict entrepreneurs, the intensity of conflict is guided more by the social variables than by the economic variables.

The above findings have significant policy implications, in terms of improving the service delivery, and providing employment and income earning opportunities, and more importantly addressing social exclusion in the provision of services and opportunities to the people of different regions and of different social groups. Thus, discrimination by region and by social group needs to be reduced for long-lasting peace in the country. The causes for these two forms of discrimination must be identified, and addressed by devising policies and programs.

The first step in addressing exclusion is to implement inclusive policies and programs; however, their honest implementation requires a great change in the mind-set of leaders who are ruling the country. Thus, the overall conclusion of the present study is that there is a need for promoting both the spatial and social inclusion in all the four dimensions – political, economic, social and cultural – which is the main message of the comprehensive peace agreement and many other subsequent understanding and agreements, including the Interim Constitution of Nepal. This can come only through improvement in the policies, including removal of the policy barriers, and change in the values and institutions of society.

Notes

1 An earlier version of the chapter was presented at the second Annual Himalayan Policy Research Conference, organized by Nepal Study Center, at Madison, USA, October 11, 2007.
2 A comprehensive definition of governance is given by Kaufmann et al. (2003): the traditions and institutions by which authority in a country is exercised. This includes (1) the process by which governments are selected, monitored and replaced, (2) the capacity of the government to effectively formulate and implement sound policies, and (3) the respect of citizens and the state for the institutions that govern economic and social interactions among them.
3 Based on security situation, the United Nations classifies districts/areas into five phases – phase one with lowest insecurity and phase five as a phase of evacuation (see appendix 12.2).
4 Three districts, viz. Rukum, Rolpa and Kalikot, out of 75 have been excluded because the number of people killed per thousand of district population of the three districts has been found to be more than three standard deviations from the mean. This was initially identified by plotting a scattergram of number of people killed across the 75 districts. They were treated as outliers in this paper. Do and Iyer (2007) excluded only two districts, Rukum and Rolpa.
5 However, on one occasion, the coefficient of literacy rate appears positive rather than negative when the overall composite index is excluded.
6 This dummy variable was not found statistically significant in the model with number of people killed as the dependent variable; however, it appeared significant in the model with level of insecurity as the dependent variable.

Bibliography

Bohara, Alok, Neil Mitchell, and Mani Nepal. 2006. 'Opportunity, Democracy and the Exchange of Political Violence: a Sub National Analysis of Conflict in Nepal', *Journal of Conflict Resolution*, Vol. 50, No. 1, pp. 108–28
Bray, John, Leiv Lunde, and S. Mansoob Murshed. 2003. 'Nepal: Economic Drivers of the

Maoist Insurgency.' In *The Political Economy of Armed Conflict: Beyond Greed and Grievance,* ed. Karen Ballentine and Jake Sherman, Lynne Rienner Publishers, Boulder, Colorado.

Bennet, Lynn, and Dilli Ram Dahal. 2007. *Preliminary Exploration of Caste/Ethnic and Regional Identity Dimensions of the Nepal Demographic and Health Survey*, draft version, 15 February 2008.

CBS. 2006. *Environmental Compendium of Nepal*, Central Bureau of Statistics, Thapathali, Kathmandu.

CBS. 2005. *Poverty Trends in Nepal (1995–96 and 2003–04)*, Central Bureau of Statistics, Kathmandu, Nepal.

CBS. 2003. *District Level Indicators of Nepal for Monitoring Overall Development* (based on selected socio-economic indicators), His Majesty's Government, National Planning Commission Secretariat, Central Bureau of Statistics, Kathmandu, Nepal, 2003.

CBS, ICIMOD/MENRIS and SNV-Nepal. 2003. *Districts of Nepal: Indicators of Development*, update 2003, Kathmandu, December 2003.

CBS, WFP and the World Bank. 2006. *Small Area Estimation of Poverty, Caloric Intake and Malnutrition in Nepal*, Central Bureau of Statistics, Government of Nepal, United Nations World Food Programme and the World Bank, Kathmandu, Nepal.

CBS, World Bank, DFID and ADB. 2006. *Resilience Amidst Conflict: An Assessment of Poverty in Nepal, 1995–96 and 2003–05*, Central Bureau of Statistics, National Planning Commission, Government of Nepal, Kathmandu.

Collier, Paul. 2006. *Post-Conflict Economic Recovery*, A paper for the International Peace Academy, Department of Economics, Oxford University, Revised, April 2006.

Collier, Paul, and Anke Hoeffler. 1998. 'On economic causes of civil war', *Oxford Economic Papers,* Vol. 50, pp. 563–573.

Collier, Paul, and Anke Hoeffler. 2004a. 'Conflict', in B. Lomborg (ed.), *Global Crises, Global Solutions*, Cambridge University Press, Cambridge.

Collier, Paul, and Anke Hoeffler. 2004b. 'Greed and grievance in civil war', Oxford *Economic Papers*, Vol. 56, pp. 563–595.

Deng, Lual A. 2004. *The Challenges of Post Conflict Economic Recovery and Reconstruction in Sudan*, A Paper prepared for presentation at the Woodrow Wilson Center, Washington DC, September 2004.

DFID. 2003. *Economic Aspects of Insurgency in Nepal,* Report 57/02, Department for International Development, United Kingdom.

Do, Quy-Toan, and Lakshmi Iyer. 2007. *Poverty, Social Divisions and Conflict in Nepal*, World Bank Policy Research Working Paper – 4228, May 2007

Easterly, William. 2001. 'Can Institutions Resolve Ethnic Conflict', *Economic Development and Cultural Change*, Vol. 49, No. 4, pp. 687–706.

Easterly, William, and Ross Levine. 1997. 'Africa's Growth Tragedy: Policies and ethnic divisions.' *Quarterly Journal of Economics,* Vol. 112, No. 4, pp. 1203–1250.

Fearon, James, and David Laitin. 2003. 'Ethnicity, Insurgency, and Civil War', *American Political Science Review*, Vol. 97, pp. 75–90.

Gersony, Robert. 2003. 'Sowing the Wind: History and Dynamics of the Maoist Revolt in Nepal's Rapti Hills', *Mercy Corps International Report.*

Gurr, Ted. 1968. 'A Causal Model of Civil Strife: A Comparative Analysis Using New Indices', *American Political Science Review*, Vol. 62, No. 4, pp. 1104–1124.

——. 1970. Why *Men Rebel.* Princeton, Princeton University Press, New Jersey.

Gurung, Harka. 2005. *Social Exclusion and Maoist Insurgency*, Paper presented at National Dialogue on the ILO Convention 169 on Indigenous and Tribal People, Kathmandu, Nepal, 19–20 January 2005.

Gurung, Harka, ed. 2006. *Nepal Atlas and Statistics*, Himal Books for Toni Hagen Foundation, Nepal.

Human Rights Watch. 2004) 'Discrimination against Dalits in Nepal.' http://hrw.org/english/docs/2004/02/09nepal7322.htm

INSEC. 2007. *Human Rights Yearbook*, (various issues), Informal Sector Service Centre, Kathmandu, Nepal. www.inseconline.com

Karki, Arjun and Binod Bhattarai (eds). 2004. *Whose War?: Economic and Socio-Cultural Impacts of Nepal's Maoist-Government Conflict*, NGO Federation of Nepal, Kathmandu, 2004.

Kaufmann, Daniel, Aart Kraay, and Massimo Mastruzzi. 2003. *Governance Matters III: Governance Indicators for 1996 – 2002*, The World Bank, World Bank Institute, Global Governance Department and Development Research Group, Macroeconomics and Growth. August 2003. [http://siteresources.worldbank.org/INTTHAILAND/Resources/May3_Kaufmann_Governance_Matter_III.pdf].

Macours, Karen. 2005. *Relative Deprivation and Civil Conflicts in Nepal*, SAIS, John Hopkins University, 15 March 2005.

Mahat, Ram Sharan. 2005. *In Defense of Democracy: Dynamics, and Fault Lines of Nepal's Political Economy*, Adroit Publishers, 2005.

MOHP, New ERA and Macro International Inc. 2007. *Nepal Demographic and Health Survey 2006,* Ministry of Health and Population, New ERA, Kathmandu, Nepal, and Macro International Inc.

MOPR. 2007. *Administrative Records of ministry of Peace and Reconstruction,* Government of Nepal, Singh Durbar, Kathmandu.

Murshed, S.M., and S. Gates. 2003. *Spatial-Horizontal Inequality and the Maoist Insurgency in Nepal*, World Bank, Washington, DC, February 2003.

——s. 2005. 'Spatial-Horizontal Inequality and the Maoist Insurgency in Nepal', *Review of Development Economics,* Vol. 9, No. 1, pp. 121–134.

National Planning Commission. 2007. *Approach Paper of Three Year Interim Plan (2007/08 – 2009/10)* – in Nepali, Government of Nepal, National Planning Commission, July 2007.

Pandey, Nishchal Nath. 2005. *Nepal's Maoist Movement and Implications for India and China*, RCSS Policy Studies No. 27, Manohar Publishers, Colombo.

Parwez, Shahid Md. 2006. *An Empirical Analysis of the Conflict in Nepal*, NRM Working Paper Series No. 7, Asian Development Bank, July 2006.

Sambanis, Nicholas. 2001) 'Do Ethnic and Non-ethnic Civil Wars have the Same Causes?' *Journal of Conflict Resolution,* Vol. 45, No. 3, pp. 259–282.

Stewart, Frances et al. 2005. *Social Exclusion and Conflict: Analysis and Policy Implications*, CRISE Policy Paper, Centre for Research on Inequality, Human Security and Ethnicity, CRISE, Department of International Development, University of Oxford, Oxford.

——. 2007. 'Major Findings and Conclusions on the Relationship between Horizontal Inequalities and Conflict' in Stewart, Frances (ed), *Horizontal Inequalities and Conflict: Understanding Group Violence in Multi-Ethnic Societies*, Centre for Research on Inequality, Human Security and Ethnicity, CRISE, Department of International Development, University of Oxford, Oxford.

Thapa, Deepak, and Bandira Sijapati. 2004) *A Kingdom under Siege: Nepal's Maoist Insurgency, 1996 to 2003, The Print House,* Kathmandu.

Tiwari, Bishwa Nath. 2006. *Readings in the Millennium Development Goals: Challenges for Attaining the MDGs in Nepal*, Central Department of Economics, Tribhuvan University, Kathmandu, Nepal.

——. 2008. Horizontal Inequality and Violent Conflict in Nepal, a paper presented at a regional conference on Pluralism in South Asia, held at Colombo, Sri Lanka, 23–25 March 2008, organized by National Peace Council and DFID, Sri Lanka.

UNDP. 1994. *Human Development Report, 1994,* Oxford University Press, New Delhi.

UNDP. 2006. *Human Development Report 2006: Beyond Scarcity – Power, Poverty and the Global Water Crisis*, Published for the UNDP, Palgrave Macmillan, New York.

UNDP/Nepal. 2004. *Nepal Human Development Report 2004: Empowerment and Poverty Reduction*, United Nations Development Programme, Nepal. www.unnepal.org.np

Zartman, William I. 2005. *Cowardly Lions: Missed Opportunities to Prevent Deadly Conflict and State Collapse,* Lynne Rienner Publishers, Boulder, Colorado.

Appendix 12.1

Table 12.4 Poverty incidence by caste and ethnicity, Nepal, 1995/96 and 2003/04

	Poverty headcount rate			Distribution of the poor			Distribution of population		
	1995/96	2003/04	Change in %	1995/96	2003/04	Change in %	1995/96	2003/04	Change in %
Brahmin/Chhetri	34.1	18.4	-46	26.7	15.7	-41	32.7	26.3	-20
Tarai middle caste	28.7	21.3	-26	2.9	1.9	-33	4.2	2.8	-34
Dalits	57.8	45.5	-21	10.6	10.9	3	7.7	7.4	-4
Newar	19.3	14	-28	2.5	3.4	35	5.5	7.5	38
Hill Janajati	48.7	44	-10	19.7	27.8	41	16.9	19.5	16
Tarai Janajati	53.4	35.4	-34	10.4	9.2	-12	8.2	8.1	-1
Muslims	43.7	41.3	-6	5.7	8.7	53	5.4	6.5	19
Other	46.1	31.3	-32	21.4	22.3	4	19.4	21.9	13
Total	41.8	30.8	-26	100	100	–	100	100	–

Source: CBS (2005)

Note: The trends in poverty rates across caste-ethnic groups should be treated with caution because the NLSS sampling design was based on geographical unit rather than caste and ethnic groups.

Table 12.5 Major occupations by caste and ethnicity, 2001

Ethnic / caste group	Total economically active	Prof / technical	Legislative / admin	Clerical	Sales / service	Forestry / farm / fishery	Production labor	Of which elementary
Upper castes	35.4	62.2	58.3	53.6	42.2	37.1	21.2	19.1
Middle castes (Tarai only)	10.0	6.6	5.1	7.2	12.8	8.8	8.8	14.9
Dalit	11.9	1.6	1.3	3.9	4.0	10.9	20.3	22.6
Indigenous nationalities	38.7	27.6	33.2	33.3	35.5	40.5	38.1	36.1
– Hill indigenous nationalities	23.6	10.7	10.3	14.4	14.3	28.6	18.1	16.5
– Newar/Thakali	7.5	13.8	20.8	12.7	16.8	5.0	8.7	4.8
– Tarai Indigenous nationalities	7.5	3.1	2.1	6.2	4.4	6.9	11.4	14.9
Muslim/Sikh	3.1	1.2	1.1	1.1	4.5	2.0	6.0	5.7
Others	0.9	0.8	1.1	0.9	1.1	0.7	1.3	1.5
All	100.0	100.0	100.0	100.0	100.0	100.0	100.0	100.0

Source: Gurung, Harka (2005), *Social Exclusion and Maoist Insurgency*, Paper presented at National Dialogue on the ILO Convention 169 on Indigenous and Tribal People, Kathmandu, Nepal, January 19–20, 2005

Appendix 12.2: Specification of variables

B1. Classification of districts by security phases

The United Nations classifies 75 districts of Nepal according to security situation. There are five phases of security, starting with phase one with the lowest insecurity and five with the highest insecurity. Security phase five implies a situation of evacuation. As of December 2, 2004, the UN classified the districts only into the first three of the five phases – 38 districts in phase one; one district in phase two; and 36 districts in phase three – meaning that Nepal's districts had not reached a state of emergency operations (phase four) and evacuation (phase five). The level of security is being updated by the United Nations.

Security phase implications:

Security phase one

Warning (operations continue but staff require a security clearance prior to moving into a phase one; area, homes and offices have emergency supplies ready, wardens brief staff regarding evacuation procedures, all international staff have VHF walkie-talkies, a central radio room running on 24/7 basis to communicate with all agencies) FSO approves travel for phase one.

Security phase two

Restricted Movement (clearance required to travel for essential business, and communications between traveler and agency security focal point required when traveling to notify of safe arrival, delays, etc.; field offices must have radio room, vehicles must have radio communications) FSO approves travel for phase two.

Security phase three

Relocation (staff may be relocated out of the area, non-essential staff and dependants are relocated) Travel clearance required to be approved by the Resident Coordinator.

Security phase four – Emergency Operations

Security phase five – Evacuation

Source: www.unnepal.org.np

B2. Specification of independent variables

Composite development index and infrastructures

Overall composite index: This is an aggregate of five sets of indices: child deprivation index, gender discrimination index, health development index, primary sector development index, and infrastructure development index. These five sets of indices have been computed based on 29 indicators.

Infrastructure development index: As a sub-set of overall composite index, this index has been computed including eight indictors: density of roads, banks, cooperatives, health institutions, and post offices; percentage of forest user households; and per capita regular and development budget expenditure.

Road density: This is the sum of different categories of road, and is expressed in per 100 square km of total surface area of a district.

Economic factors

Broad occupational structure: Ratio of labor force (economically active population aged 15+ years) engaged in non-agricultural occupations to those engaged in agriculture as a major occupation.

Share of females in non-agricultural occupation: Defined as the female population aged 15 years and above engaged in non-agricultural occupations as a percentage of total population in the same age group engaged in the same activities.

Poverty incidence: The proportion of population below the national poverty line of Rs 7,696 per year in average 2003 Nepalese rupees.

Life expectancy index: One of the three components of the human development index, computed using standard methodology.

Income index: Also one of the three components of the human development index of Nepal.

Human poverty index:Computed using standard methodology as given in the *Nepal Human Development Report* (NHDR) 2004.

Literacy and education

Overall literacy rate:The literate population aged six years and above as a percentage of total population of the same age group.

Educational attainment index: One of the three components of the human development index, computed using standard methodology. It comprises both adult literacy and school enrolment of children. However, NHDR 2004 has used the adult literacy rate and mean years of schooling instead of enrolment rate because enrolment is over-inflated whereas mean years of schooling also takes into account quality of education.

Human empowerment index: Computed using standard methodology as given in NHDR 2004.

Health- and nutrition-related factors

Caloric intake prevalence: Estimates of prevalence of caloric intake below the threshold predicted on the basis of Small Area Estimation (SAE) methodology (for details see CBS, WFP and World Bank 2006).

Proportion of stunted children: The proportion of children between 6 and 59 months who with short height against their age.

Proportion of wasted children: The proportion of children between 6 and 59 months who are light in weight against their age.

Proportion of underweight children: The proportion of children between 6 and 59 months who are light in weight against their height.

Social factors

Proportion of Dalit population: The total hill Dalit population as a ratio of total population of a district. It consists of three castes: Kami (blacksmith), Damai (tailor) and Sarki (cobbler).

Proportion of indigenous nationalities population: The total indigenous nationalities population as a ratio of total population. The indigenous nationalities consist of about 59 groups.

Proportion of Hindu population: Total Hindu population divided by total population of a district.

Natural factors

Proportion of forest: Area under forest divided by total area of a district.

District dummy: Used for approximating the effect of elevation or topography, and expressed as a dummy variable with the values as follows: Tarai district = 0; hills and mountain district = 1 at the increasing order of altitude.

13 The Maoist insurgency and the political economy of violence

Avidit Acharya*

Introduction

What were the causes of insurgency in Nepal? There have been two approaches to answering this question. In one line of research, studies such as Murshed and Gates (2005) and Bohara et al. (2006) have used cross-sectional regression techniques to predict the effect of poverty, inequality, rough terrain, and ethno-linguistic divisions on the intensity of political violence. In the other approach, historical analyses have highlighted the incentives of rebel leaders and the failed policies of the Nepali government to suggest that politics has also played a crucial role. Typical studies of this kind include Thapa (2002, 2003) and Whelpton (2005).

Both approaches have their advantages and shortcomings. While the cross-sectional studies have focused on reasons why individuals may choose to commit acts of political violence, they have ignored the important role that political parties and leaders play in organizing and instigating conflict. The qualitative studies, on the other hand, treat the insurgency as if it was the outcome of a number of possible causes, none of which are disproved to be explanatory.

This chapter combines insights gained from the two approaches to evaluate the causes of the Maoist insurgency in Nepal. I use basic multiple regression analysis to test hypotheses that are motivated both by observations specific to Nepali politics and by general findings related to civil conflict. Specifically, I take a cross-sectional approach where the unit of analysis is the district, and the dependent variable is total killings by the state and Maoists divided by district population.[1]

There is a considerable degree of sub-national heterogeneity that may account for the variation in conflict intensity across districts. In line with existing theories of conflict, I hypothesize that less prosperous districts show greater conflict intensity because recruiting guerillas is less costly in poorer economic conditions; that districts with rougher terrain are more conducive to fighting because insurgents can hide from government forces better; that leftist ideology is associated with greater conflict intensity owing to the adversarial relationship between a centrist state and more extreme citizens; and that districts that have been neglected by the state and where economic inequality is high will be propitious to insurgency because rebellion is one of the few ways by which the politically and economically downtrodden can respond to what they perceive as the injustices of state and society.

264   *Avidit Acharya*

I also test hypotheses that emerge from a literature that is more specific to Nepal. I hypothesize that districts where polarization between the Bahun-Chhetri caste group and other castes is greater exhibit greater conflict intensity; that if not caste, then linguistic polarization is associated with higher conflict intensity; and that areas where leftist leaders developed operations over half a century ago were more propitious to conflict.[2]

To measure leftist ideology, I construct a variable as follows. A district receives one point for each seat won in a neighboring district by the United People's Front (UPF) in the 1991 general elections, and three points for each seat won in that district itself.[3] Because this variable takes into consideration the possibility of regional spillovers, it serves as a better measure of the political activity of the left than simply a dummy variable indicating UPF success. The districts where leftist leaders successfully developed operations lie mostly in the Midwestern development region, particularly the hills (see figure 13.1). Although there is some positive correlation between the ideology score and a dummy variable indicating whether or not a district falls in the Midwest, the relationship is not statistically convincing. Thus, there is no reason to be concerned that the ideology score actually captures the political entrepreneurship of leftist leaders, or that the Midwestern dummy captures leftist ideology, even though this possibility has been hinted at by previous authors (see Thapa 2003).

Neither the electoral success of the UPF nor the constructed measure of leftist ideology appear to be correlated with measures of economic prosperity, grievances or caste and ethnic polarization. In particular, the left was not necessarily more successful in poorer districts, those with greater land inequality, those that received fewer funds for development, or those where polarization between Nepali-

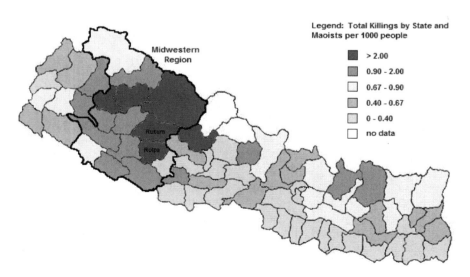

Figure 13.1 Map of Nepal showing the intensity of conflict

speaking Bahun-Chhetris and non-Nepali-speaking ethnic groups was higher. This in itself is an interesting finding, but a more important consequence of the observation is that it casts doubt over the hypothesis that party ideology is derived from the social class of its members. Whatever the intentions of the leftist leaders of Nepal, their emergence does not seem to be a natural outcome of the grievances of the poor and neglected.

The results show only weak evidence that ideology is correlated with conflict intensity once other factors are taken into account. They also show no evidence of a causal relationship between measures of political and economic grievance (such as land inequality and development budget allocation) and the frequency of violence. Further, there is no evidence that after controlling for politics and geography, districts that may have had high caste and ethnic cleavages saw more conflict.

The only robust significant variables are those associated with political activism and geography. First, districts in the Midwestern development region witnessed more violence than other districts even after controlling for a host of other factors. Second, fighting was more intense in districts that were less penetrated by roads and those that were more forested. Third, after controlling for road density, economic prosperity is not a significant predictor of conflict intensity. Since road density and economic conditions are correlated, it is evident that rebel leaders had access to areas where operating an insurgency had low costs in terms of both the technology of conflict and the recruitment of soldiers. Nevertheless, the important cost variables seem to be geography and remoteness, less so guerilla wages.

I take these results as evidence against the claim that class, caste or ethnic grievances were at the root of the Maoist conflict. Rather, the data seem to favor the hypothesis that many of the villagers who joined the insurgency probably did so out of a necessity associated with their own security (i.e. they would have a greater probability of being killed if they did not join) or for personal economic reasons such as the desire for food, shelter and clothing – things that were promised by the rebel leaders to their soldiers, and which these recruits may not otherwise have had in their lives as peasants.

Historical background

The history of left-wing politics in Nepal dates back to 1949, the year that the Communist Party of Nepal (CPN) was formed by Pushpa Lal Shrestha with four of his associates in Calcutta (Shaha 1990: 2: 239). The party's platform in the decade of the 1950s preceding the general elections of 1959 included radical land reforms, the abrogation of the 1950 Treaty with India and opposition to the United States (Whelpton 2005: 94). Campaigning on this platform, the party was rather unsuccessful in the 1959 elections, securing only four of the 109 seats in parliament (Joshi and Rose 1966: 296). After the ideological split of the Chinese and Russians in the 1950s, the CPN correspondingly split into two factions with the pro-Russia faction, led by Keshar Jung Rayamajhi, declaring its support for King Mahendra's coup of 1960. The pro-China faction was still led by Shrestha and opposed the royal coup.

Throughout much of the 1960s, Nepali politics reflected little more than a power struggle between a few prominent Bahun and Newar leaders and King Mahendra. However, while the politics of that era continued to become increasingly concentrated at the center, a young Communist Party cadre by the name of Mohan Bikram Singh was working hard in developing a base of left-wing activists in the Midwestern hill districts of Rolpa, Rukum and Pyuthan. Singh's strategy was to take advantage of "local grievances, particularly the decline in living standards, which the inhabitants [of these districts] reportedly ascribed to the government's suppression of hashish production in the 1970s" (Whelpton 2005: 203). He was extremely successful as, for example, in the village of Thawang where he campaigned, 700 out of 703 voters voted against the Panchayat-with-reforms championed by the monarchy in the referendum of 1980.

In 1974, Singh and his protégé, Nirmal Lama, orchestrated a second split from the pro-China CPN faction to form the CPN (Fourth Convention). The split came as a result of disagreements between radicals and moderates on whether tactical allegiance with the Nepali Congress against King Mahendra was in the interest of the party. The Singh-Lama faction, representing the more radical group, demanded a constituent assembly instead of the mere restoration of parliamentary democracy, which Congress had been pressing for.

In the mid 1980s the Singh-Lama faction again split into three smaller groups – the CPN (Masal) led by Singh, the CPN (Mashal) led by Pushpa Kamal Dahal (aka Prachanda), and another that retained the original party name. It was then that the Fourth Convention lost its place at the forefront of leftist politics in Nepal. Rather, in the People's Movement of 1990 it was a coalition of seven other parties – all descended from the original CPN – that represented the left in efforts to overthrow absolute monarchy. After the restoration of democracy, this coalition ran under the banner of the CPN-United Marxist-Leninist (CPN-UML) and emerged as the second largest party in the 1991 general elections (the largest being the Nepali Congress). Singh's men, having been sidelined, re-united to form the Unity Centre, a subversive revolutionary organization, and participated in the elections under the umbrella of the UPF. The Unity Centre was led by Prachanda, while the UPF was governed by Nirmal Lama and Baburam Bhattarai, the inheritor of Singh's legacy and leader of what was formerly the Masal faction.

Notwithstanding one final split in 1994 when Nirmal Lama usurped control of the UPF, it was the Unity Center that first represented insurgent communism in Nepal. Since the election commission officially recognized Lama's faction as the legitimate UPF, the Prachanda-Bhattarai faction announced that it would not take part in the general elections of 1994. It was this militant group that was christened the Communist Party of Nepal (Maoist).

Of the nine seats won by the UPF in the 1991 general elections, two were from the district of Rolpa and one from neighboring Rukum. After the split of 1994, only the three MPs from these districts allied with the Prachanda-Bhattarai faction. The others remained loyal to Lama's UPF, which chose to remain involved in parliamentary politics and took part in the general elections of 1994 and 1999. It is, therefore, not surprising that the geographical base for Maoist operations lay in the

Midwestern hills. What was also in favor of the Maoists in that region was the fact that the districts of Rolpa and Rukum were both well-suited for a guerilla uprising. For example, Whelpton (2005: 205) notes that:

> the Maoists' task of extending their influence in these parts was made easier because these areas were not of crucial economic importance and were only weakly penetrated by the Nepalese state. Neither Rolpa nor Rukum had any motorable roads until those to the district headquarters were completed by the army in 2002 and 2003 respectively. In the past the government had relied on a small number of local 'big men,' who owed their status partly to state patronage but were also chosen partly because they were already influential. Social control was maintained by these individuals and also through the self-regulating mechanisms of village communities. In western Nepal, such people had generally worked within the Panchayat system but switched allegiance in 1990 to Congress. Their role as (relatively) large landowners and often also money-lenders meant that many of their poorest neighbors feared opposing them openly but might welcome their removal by a *force outside of the village* [emphasis added].

There is also evidence that the state had been conducting exercises to suppress the activities of the left in the Midwestern hills. The Sija movement (named for Sisne peak and Jaljala mandir) was the first organized campaign launched by the Maoists in 1995, and was developed in response to atrocities described in grim reports of politically motivated human rights violations commissioned by the Nepali Congress government in 1992 and 1993 (cited in Thapa 2002: 84). Conscious of the well-rootedness of leftist leaders in these districts and the popularity of Sija, the government responded in 1995 with a structured campaign of state-terror known as Operation Romeo, the precursor to the equally ruthless but more widespread Operation Kilo Sierra Two. It would take less than a year for the Maoists to respond with their armed struggle known as "the People's War" that over the next ten years grew into one of the most intense civil conflicts in the world (see Gersony 2003).

That the Maoist insurgency in Nepal was born from a combination of political and economic factors is historically undeniable. But while the local grievances of marginalized populations, ethnic tensions, and poverty may all be important contributors, they are inadequate to explain the rise of insurgency in Nepal. The political animosity between the ultra-left and those occupying the seats of power in Kathmandu – be they the royalists, the Nepali Congress, or the CPN-UML – seems to be of paramount importance. Additionally, the success of revolutionary leaders such as Prachanda and Baburam Bhattarai in mobilizing the inhabitants of the Midwestern districts against the state in the last 15 years owes much to the long history of leftist activism in these parts – a history that dates back to Mohan Bikram Singh's campaigns of the 1950s and 1960s.

Was the left successful only because the Midwesterners, owing to their marginalization, had a natural hostility towards parties that at least in their eyes represented the interest of only the elite? If that was the case, then why did we not witness leaders like Mohan Bikram Singh springing naturally from the communities of the downtrodden Tharus in the western Tarai, the marginalized Satars and Yadavs of the eastern Tarai, or the neglected Limbus of the eastern Himalayas? While it is true that the Kham Magars of the Midwestern hills are an oppressed community, they are not the only ones, and perhaps not the most oppressed either.[4] Whelpton (2005: 206) is correct in pointing out that in the Kham Magar areas of Rolpa, where the conflict was most intense, "there were no really big landlords and inequality was less than in many other parts of the western hills." A more complete explanation of the Maoist conflict will necessarily look to the political entrepreneurship of radical leaders and the history of leftist activism in Nepal.

Theory, data and past literature

The political economy approach

The formal analysis of conflict as an economic activity dates back to the pioneering work of Hirshleifer (1991). Relevant insights from the subsequent literature are summarized as follows.[5] Insurgency, as a form of conflict, typically involves three sets of actors: the rebel leaders, their guerilla recruits, and the government.[6] It is when the insurgency is profitable, given the economic and political circumstances, to both rebel leaders and potential recruits that it can pose a serious threat to central and local authorities. Further, the insurgency can be successful only if the insurgents are able to use geographical conditions and infrastructure (or its absence) to their benefit. For example, it is easier to hide from the police or army in more rugged terrain, forested areas, and in regions that are ill-penetrated by roads. This political-economy approach to the understanding of conflict broadly highlights three sets of variables – economic conditions, geography, and political activity – all of which are discussed in detail below.

Economic conditions: Whether or not a potential recruit joins the insurgency depends on her economic circumstance. Perhaps the choice is simply an occupational one, as by joining the cause a poor villager is able to attain a certain degree of economic stability that she did not have in her previous occupation. Of course, participating may be costly because of the non-negligible probability of death. But there is an equally good chance that an individual will be killed even if she chooses not to participate. Once a certain number of guerillas have been recruited, their presence in the countryside threatens the lives of others, who are more easily persuaded to take a side for security-related reasons (Kalyvas 2006). Thus, it may be that only a handful of extremely poor recruits are needed to get the conflict going.

The negative relationship between conflict and economic prosperity was empirically uncovered by Fearon and Laitin (2003: 80), who claim that poor economic conditions increase the probability of civil war onset because "recruiting young men to the life of a guerrilla is easier when economic alternatives are worse." Other authors such as Collier and Hoeffler (2004) have also stressed the importance of

Table 13.1 Descriptive statistics

	Min.	Max.	Ave.	St. dev.
Total killings per 1,000 people	0897	4.786	.8108	.8301
GDP per capita	125	631	227.1	85.12
Unemployment rate	.1175	.5840	.3681	.1234
GDP per worker	292.9	2882	678.5	384.1
HDI	.304	.652	.455	.067
Land Gini	.381	.700	.484	.064
Dev. budget	187	7153	679	958.1
Post offices	.10	.46	.22	.077
Roads	0	93.78	6.84	14.55
Slopes	0	92.68	51.49	25.74
Forests	0.01	2.99	0.53	0.59
UPF	0	7	0.88	1.4
Fraction of Nepali speakers	.0526	.9958	.5931	.2918
Bahun-Chhetri fraction	.0233	.7940	.3412	.1848

Note: The table shows the minimum, maximum, average, and standard deviation over districts. Total killings by state and Maoists was taken from the Informal Sector Service Centre (INSEC; http://www.inseconline.org/hrvdata.php) and normalized by population data from the *Nepal Human Development Report* (NHDR) 2004. GDP per capita in US dollars and HDI are 1996 figures taken from NHDR 1998. The unemployment rate is defined here as the fraction of individuals above the age of ten who are not economically active (which is why it is unusually high). The data on economic activity are 1991 figures taken from the *Statistical Yearbook of Nepal*, 2001. The implicit assumption here, of course, is that unemployment did not show differential trends by district in the early 1990s. GDP per worker is a proxy for the wage rate, calculated by dividing total district GDP by the economically active population. The Gini coefficient for land ownership was taken from NHDR 2004. Development budget allocation per capita, post offices per capita, road density, slopes (percentage of total land area inclined greater than 30 degrees) and forests per capita were all taken from *Districts of Nepal: Indicators of Development*, published by the International Centre for Integrated Mountain Development (ICIMOD) in 1997. UPF was calculated based on election results data in Whelpton (2005). The percentage of Nepali speakers and the percentage of Bahuns and Chhetris in the population were calculated for each district from linguistic and caste data from the 1991 census, reported in the *Statistical Yearbook of Nepal*, 2001. The number of Bahuns does not include Tarai Brahmins (hence Bahun, for Hill Brahmin). All data were available for all 75 districts, except killings data, which was not available for the districts of Mustang and Manang.

economic conditions. Although several of these studies investigate economic conditions at the national level, it is still reasonable to hypothesize that lower levels of GDP are associated with greater conflict intensity even at the sub-national level. In particular, since the theory stresses economic alternatives and prosperity, I take GDP per worker, effectively a proxy for the wage rate, as the key explanatory variable.[7] The significant negative correlation between GDP per worker and conflict intensity shown in column (1) of table 13.2 is promising for this aspect of the theory. We will soon see whether or not this relationship is robust when we account for other factors.

Geography and infrastructure: As mentioned before, an insurgency can only be successful if the insurgents are able to take advantage of opportunities in their favor (Collier and Sambanis 2002). In the previous literature on the Maoist insurgency, Bohara et al. (2006) highlight the importance of opportunities for violence; and in a wider-ranging study, Fearon and Laitin (2003) focus specifically on opportunities

Table 13.2 Upper panel: univariate regressions, where dependent variable is total killings per 1,000 people

	all districts except Mustang and Manang					without Rolpa and Rukum in (6)–(9) and Kathmandu Valley districts in (10)					core sample		
	(1)	(2)	(3)	(4)	(5)	(6)	(7)	(8)	(9)	(10)	(11)	(12)	(13)
GDP pw	−.8544* (.2066)					−.6785* (.1487)							
Land Gini		−5.014* (1.410)					−3.512* (1.050)				−3.504* (1.061)		
Dev budget pc			.0954 (.3647)					.2314 (.2650)					
Caste				2.162* (.7470)					1.660* (.5431)			.9225* (.3386)	
Roads					−.0166* (.0064)					−.1191* (.0226)			−.0950* (.0159)
R^2	.194	.151	.001	.101	.087	.232	.139	.011	.119	.289	.142	.101	.352

Lower panel: correlation coefficients for ideology and other variables

	HDI	Unemp.	Dev. Budget	Land Gini	Forests	Slopes	Post offices	Roads	Nepali sp	Bahun-Chhetri
UPF	−.0468	−.1480	.0392	−.1293	.0644	.1855	.0571	.0620	.1977	.0615

Note: GDP per worker and development budget allocation per capita have been logged. Core sample refers to all districts for which the data were available, except the Kathmandu Valley districts and Rolpa and Rukum.

relating to geography and infrastructure. They note that the number of insurgents is usually much smaller than the number of government soldiers, and the insurgents would be much weaker were it not for the fact that forests and rugged terrain make hiding from government soldiers easier. They also suggest that "terrain more 'disciplined' by roads" (p. 80) is less conducive to insurgent activity because it increases the ability of the government to monitor activities in rural parts and because it facilitates communication between local administrators and central authorities. In view of this argument, it is worth testing whether terrain factors such as percentage of land area inclined more than 30 degrees, total area of forest cover per person, and road density, which is defined as the total length of roads in kilometers as a percentage of 100 square kilometers of surface area, are associated with conflict intensity.[8]

Political activism: The ideas developed so far stress the collaborative nature of insurgency. Insurgency is a joint effort between rebel leaders and members of their rank and file, whose personal objectives in joining the rebel army may be different from those of their commanders. Knowing that the left was active in the Midwestern region, and that this region exhibits much higher levels of conflict intensity than other regions, it is important to test the effect of leftist activism on conflict intensity.[9] In consideration of the history summarized in the previous section, I do this by testing the significance of a dummy variable for the Midwestern development region. I argue that the Midwestern dummy serves largely as a proxy for political activity. As table 13.3 indicates, the Midwestern region differs from the rest of Nepal in a plausibly significant way only in terms of prosperity and geography, both of which we control for directly.[10] It receives more attention from the central government in terms of budget allocation, has a linguistically less polarized population, and has lower land inequality.

Table 13.3 Average statistics for the Midwestern districts, Kathmandu valley and rest of Nepal

	MW districts	Kathmandu valley	Rest of Nepal
Killings per 1,000 people	1.78	.126	.583
	(1.25)	(.040)	(.414)
GDP per worker	494.1	1768	670.0
	(203.8)	(970.3)	(279.7)
Land Gini	.452	.500	.492
	(.047)	(.053)	(.066)
Dev. budget pc	639	3766	527
	(355.7)	(3106)	(549.8)
Roads	1.784	72.25	4.734
	(2.332)	(25.25)	(3.867)
Nepali speakers pc	.823	.428	.541
	(.221)	(.087)	(.286)

All figures are averages over the sample indicated in the column. Standard deviations for the averages are included in brackets.

Social factors and ideology

Moving beyond the political economy approach, there is obvious reason to suspect that social and economic grievances, group divisions and political ideology have a significant causal impact on conflict intensity. Reynal-Querol (2002), for instance, has stressed the importance of ethnic and other social divisions, and Collier and Hoeffler (2004) discuss the theory of grievances in competition with the theory of greed in explaining civil wars. It is, therefore, appropriate to also test the idea that grievances and ethnic polarization are related to the intensity of conflict. In the case of the Maoist insurgency, these hypotheses already receive some support from Macours (2006), who finds that increases in land inequality have exacerbating effects on the number of abductions related to the Maoist insurgency in Nepal. In addition, nearly all of the existing literature on the Maoist insurgency has, to varying extents, highlighted the importance of grievances, caste and ethnic divisions, and ideology in explaining the Maoist conflict.[11]

Grievances: The idea that local grievances, exploitation and injustice may raise the intensity of conflict by inducing locally disadvantaged populations to join an insurgent movement is not at odds with the political economy approach to insurgency (see e.g. Berdal and Malone 2000). In countries like Nepal, where the rural population is highly estranged from the activities of the state, one would suspect that if grievances were to matter then it is local grievances that are most salient. In 1991, just a few years before the start of the insurgency, approximately 80 percent of Nepal's population was engaged in agricultural activities (*Statistical Yearbook of Nepal*, 2001). Therefore, intra-district land inequality is perhaps the best available indicator of economic inequality and grievances. It is an especially good indicator of local grievances, as in largely agrarian societies, landholdings "give their owner special social status or political power in a lumpy way" (Bardhan and Udry 1999: 60–74).[12]

On the other hand, although the land Gini nicely captures intra-district inequality, it does not capture the possible effect of inter-district inequality, or what I would interpret as district-level grievances. To capture the effect of such grievances, we cannot appeal to the variation in GDP or HDI across districts because these variables would more likely reflect district-wise economic conditions.

Instead, I measure district-level grievances by using indicators of government absence and neglect. Of course, the level of government absence not only indicates neglect, it also reflects the level of state capacity (see e.g. Migdal 1988), and thus partially reflects the ease in waging an effective campaign against the state. Either way, we should observe a negative relationship between government presence and intensity of conflict. I use the number of post offices per capita as a proxy for government presence, and to measure government neglect I use district-wise development budget allocation per capita.[13] If these variables emerge as significant, then we could conclude that grievances are perhaps explanatory. If not, then the evidence that grievances matter is only weak, since one would be hard pressed to make the case that the economic variables discussed in the previous subsection reflect district-level economic grievances as much as they do economic conditions.[14]

As the regressions in table 13.2 show, both the Gini coefficient for land owner-ship and development budget allocation per capita are related to conflict intensity in ways opposite to what we expect.[15] Nevertheless, whether this relationship con-tinues to hold in the multivariate setting should be tested, and I do this with the underlying assumption that land inequality and development budget allocation reflect local and district-level grievances respectively.

Caste and ethnicity: That places more ethnically divided are at greater risk of political violence is an idea that several scholars have suggested and tested (Olson 1965; Horowitz 1985; Fearon and Laitin 2003). Bohara et al. (2006) cite theoreti-cal research to justify testing the effect of social capital on intensity of conflict. However, owing to the inherent endogeneity of the measures of social capital, it is difficult to draw any causal inferences even though we may observe strong correlations.

Therefore, instead of focusing on social capital, I test the hypothesis that inten-sity of conflict is increasing in polarization between the Bahun-Chhetri caste group and other castes.[16] To measure caste divisions, I use the probability that of any two randomly chosen individuals in a district, one will be a member of either the Bahun or Chhetri caste group, and the other will not. This is a less fine version of the usual Herfindahl-type index, used by Do and Iyer (2006), which gives the prob-ability that any two randomly chosen individuals will be of different castes. Because several authors have argued that it is the social and economic disparity between the hill-based Bahun-Chhetri caste groups and more marginalized castes that is at the heart of social tension in Nepal, I find this less fine measure of polar-ization to be more appealing than the full index.[17] Table 13.2 shows that at least in the univariate case, caste polarization is strongly and positively associated with conflict intensity.

In addition to caste polarization, I also test the effect of linguistic polarization by calculating the probability that of two randomly chosen individuals, Nepali will be the mother tongue of only one individual.[18] In the context of Nepal, I find it more compelling to use this modification of the ethno-linguistic fractionalization index (ELF) for reasons similar to those discussed in the case of caste.[19]

Ideology: There does not seem to be any relationship between socio-economic conditions (grievance variables) and leftist political ideology. If such a relationship did exist, then one would expect the distribution of parliamentary seats for the ten least developed districts (ranked by HDI) to be more skewed to the left than the overall distribution for the entire country. But as table 13.4 indicates, this is not the case. Even among those districts in which the UPF won seats in the 1991 general elections, there is no convincing relationship between leftist ideology and eco-nomic prosperity or inequality (table 13.5). In fact, Rolpa and Rukum, where the intensity of conflict was greatest, are among the top ten districts with the lowest inequality in landownership. Further, the history of leftist activism in Nepal pro-vides no clues as to why the last five districts listed in table 13.5 are districts where the UPF achieved electoral success. If anything, one would have expected more seats for the UPF in the Midwestern region or perhaps in the far eastern districts rather than the ones listed.

Table 13.4 Parliamentary seats in the 1991 elections for ten districts with the lowest HDI

	UPF	NWPP	CPN-UML	NC	NDP
Mugu				X	
Bajura				X	
Kalikot				X	
Bajhang				XX	
Jajarkot			X	X	
Dolpa				X	
Jumla		X			
Achham				XXX	
Humla	X				
Dailekh				XX	
Share in Sample	.067	.067	.067	.800	.000
Share in Nepal	.044	.010	.337	.537	.020

The parties are the United People's Front (UPF), Nepal Workers and Peasants Party (NWPP), the Communist Party of Nepal (United Marxist Leninist – UML), the Nepal Congress (NC), and the National Democratic Party (NDP). They have been ordered from political left to political right. The Nepal Goodwill Party, the Communist Party of Nepal (Democratic) and the Independents are not included, as it is difficult to place them in this ordering of political ideology.

Table 13.5 Economic and social indicators for districts where UPF won in the 1991 elections

	Seats	GDP pc	Land Gini	Dev. budget	Nepali sp.	Bahun-Chhetri
Humla	1	186	.481	967	.824	.497
Rolpa	2	161	.423	309	.850	.335
Rukum	1	184	.410	405	.916	.440
Chitwan	1	315	.508	558	.690	.400
Kavrepalanchok	1	288	.430	391	.530	.367
Lalitpur	1	378	.588	3094	.425	.305
Ramechhap	1	185	.434	343	.587	.333
Siraha	1	161	.427	358	.052	.023
Sample average		232	.471	803	.609	.337
Standard deviation		83	.054	950	.282	.142
Average over all districts		227	.484	679	.593	.341

The indicators are GDP per capita in US dollars, the Gini coefficient for landownership, development budget allocation per capita by the central government in Nepali rupees, fraction of individuals whose mother tongue is Nepali, and fraction of Bahun and Chhetri caste groups in the population. A more detailed description of the data is given in the note below table 13.1.

These observations suggest that it is insufficient to control only for grievances, since leftist ideology can emerge for reasons other than those associated with class. In particular, the success of the UPF in the 1991 elections was likely due to aspects of ideology uncorrelated with socio-economic variables. The electoral success of the UPF thus offers a natural measure of non-grievance-based leftist ideology. As mentioned in the introduction, I construct the ideology variable (named UPF) by giving a district one point for each seat that the UPF won in the 1991 general elections in a neighboring district, and three points for each seat that the UPF won in that district itself. According to this measure, the district of Rukum, for example, receives a total of five points: three because the UPF won one seat there and two because it borders on Rolpa, where the UPF won two seats.[20] Correlations reported in the lower panel of table 13.2 reveal that ideology is not much related to prosperity, inequality or social cleavages – a finding that supports the characterization of political entrepreneurs as independent actors in accord with the ideas developed in the political economy approach. Figure 13.2 shows the expected, albeit not entirely convincing, positive relationship between ideology and conflict.[21]

Results

The theory outlined in the previous section naturally divides the independent variables into two broad groups and six categories within these groups. The first group consists of political economy variables, namely those associated with economic conditions, geography and political activism. Given the intuitive and empirical strength of GDP per worker as a proxy for the wage rate, and road density as a proxy for remoteness and infrastructure, I estimate models that include these two variables and the Midwestern dummy as the core control variables. Table 13.6 reports the findings. The results are revealing.

First, it is evident from the table that geography, infrastructure and the opportunities created by the remoteness of a district are significant in determining conflict intensity. The road density variable is significant in all the regressions, and its effect on conflict is robust to the inclusion of a host of controls. On average, a 10 percent increase in road density is associated with a reduction of 0.5 to 1 death per 1,000 people. For a district like Dolakha, for example, which ranked twentieth according

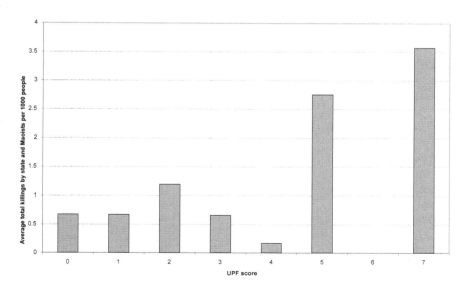

Figure 13.2 Average total killings by UPF score

to conflict intensity, a 10 percent increase in road density would be associated with almost no conflict whatsoever. Although the effects of forests per capita and land inclination are not as robust, these variables, unlike road density, do not capture remoteness and infrastructure in addition to geography.

Second, the table also indicates that being a Midwestern district is associated with higher conflict intensity. In particular, being a Midwestern district is associated with a significant increase of almost 1 death per 1,000 people in samples that include Rolpa and Rukum. Even for Kalikot, the district that saw the most violence among those where the UPF had no influence, this would translate to a difference of 33 percent in conflict intensity.

Third, it appears that local and district-level grievances, caste and ethnic polarization, and ideology are not linked in any causal way to conflict intensity. Land Gini is significant but the coefficient has the wrong sign, implying that lower levels of land inequality are associated with higher levels of conflict. Ideology, on the other hand, is significant even after roads, income and political activity are taken into account. But unlike the dummy variable for Midwestern districts, its effect is not significant when we exclude the districts of Rolpa and Rukum.

Fourth, and somewhat striking, is the result that GDP per worker does not have a significant effect on conflict intensity after we account for road density. Its effect is, however, significant and substantial when we leave out the roads variable, as reported in columns (12) and (13) of table 13.6 and columns (1) and (2) of table 13.7. Given the high correlation between wages and remoteness, this is not really a surprising result. In addition, both roads and GDP per worker represent cost variables, and the relative importance of one over the other simply indicates which of the two kinds of costs was more important in determining the success of the insurgents. Therefore, issuing skepticism toward the political economy approach based on this result for GDP per worker may be unwarranted. I conjecture that in a country as poor as Nepal, every district has individuals sufficiently poor that they are willing to participate in conflict for lack of reasonable alternatives. If the story described in the beginning of the previous section is right, then the average economic condition may not be a complete metric for analyzing the effect of economic conditions on conflict intensity.[22] On the other hand, the insignificance of even GDP per worker, GDP per capita and HDI, as reported in table 13.7, puts another nail in the coffin of any hypothesis that inter-district inequality (district level grievances) had robust causal effects on conflict intensity.

Table 13.7 reports various additional robustness checks. In their analysis, Murshed and Gates (2005) found a nonlinear relationship between land inclination and intensity of conflict in Nepal. However, there is no evidence of such a relationship here. There is also no evidence for a nonlinear relationship between caste or linguistic fractionalization and conflict intensity. Therefore, not only is it unlikely that caste and ethnicity matter at all, but it is also unlikely that there is either a positive or a negative relationship between these variables and conflict below some threshold, and then the opposite effect above the threshold. Finally, there is no evidence that caste divisions and grievances have any significant interaction. In other words, the insignificance of the interaction terms in columns (8) and (9) casts doubt

Table 13.6 Multivariate regressions, where dependent variable is total killings per 1,000 people

	without Kathmandu Valley									core	w/o Val	all	w/o RR
	(1)	(2)	(3)	(4)	(5)	(6)	(7)	(8)	(9)	(10)	(11)	(12)	(13)
GDP pw	-.1360	-.1561	-.0714	-.1218	-.0884	-.1322	-.1297	.0655	-.0895	-.1198	-.1280	-.5034*	-.4043*
	(.2653)	(.3004)	(.2736)	(.2826)	(.2746)	(.2740)	(.2661)	(.2875)	(.2460)	(.1908)	(.2683)	(.1904)	(.1350)
Roads	-.0756*	-.0752*	-.0634*	-.0749*	-.0731*	-.0756*	-.0792*	-.0776*	-.0709*	-.0679*	-.0795*		
	(.0266)	(.0269)	(.0294)	(.0271)	(.0269)	(.0278)	(.0270)	(.0263)	(.0247)	(.0191)	(.0296)		
MW	.9249*	.9137*	.9097*	.9235*	.9059*	.9224*	.9639*	.8804*	.7656*	.6005*	.9552*	.9459*	.4756*
	(.1920)	(.2080)	(.1927)	(.1936)	(.1946)	(.1977)	(.1988)	(.1912)	(.1837)	(.1442)	(.2163)	(.2212)	(.1662)
Post offices		-.1880											
		(1.284)											
Slopes			.0039										
			(.0040)										
Bahun-Chhetri				.0738									
				(.4780)									
Caste div.					.4716								
					(.6667)								
Ling div.						-.0275							
						(.4384)							
Dev. budget pc							-.3058						
							(.3880)						
Land Gini								-2.243*					
								(1.327)					
UPF									.1812*	.0001			
									(.0524)	(.0513)			
Forests											-.0584	.1588	.3296*
											(.1872)	(.1735)	(.1247)
R^2	.48	.48	.49	.45	.48	.45	.49	.50	.56	.50	.48	.44	.47

The usual monetary variables have been logged. *Core* refers to the sample for which the data was available, excluding Rolpa, Rukum and the Kathmandu Valley districts. Star indicates significance at 5 percent.

Table 13.7 Further robustness checks, where dependent variable is again total killings per 1,000 people

	Core	without Kathmandu Valley							
	(1)	(2)	(3)	(4)	(5)	(6)	(7)	(8)	(9)
GDP pw	-.5394* (.1616)	-.6021* (.2192)			-.0471 (.2892)	-.1118 (.2887)	-.1438 (.2887)	-.0657 (.2777)	.0904 (.2963)
Roads			-.0902* (.0218)	-.0840* (.0233)	-.0653* (.0303)	-.0713* (.0279)	-.0757* (.0270)	-.0766* (.0274)	-.0857* (.0273)
MW	1.033* (.1523)	-.6920* (.1979)	.9778* (.1948)	.9355* (.2067)	.9148* (.1949)	.9170* (.1998)	.9193* (.2004)	.9586* (.2037)	.8577* (.2029)
GDP pc			.3303 (.3434)						
HDI				-.0072 (1.570)					
Slopes					.0073 (.0128)				
Slopes^2					-3.7E-5 (.0001)				
Caste div						1.278 (2.934)	2.982 (7.897)	3.352 (7.894)	
Caste^2						-1.400 (4.955)			
Ling div							.2989 (2.415)		
Ling^2							-.5969 (4.342)		
Dev budget pc								-.0001 (3.147)	
Caste × Budget								-.9470 (3.147)	

Land Gini								.0436
								(5.820)
Caste × Gini								−6.503
								(14.27)
R^2	.40	.42	.49	.48	.49	.49	.48	.49	.50

The usual monetary variables have been logged. *Core* refers to the sample for which the data was available, excluding Rolpa, Rukum and the Kathmandu Valley districts. Star indicates significance at 5 percent.

as to whether inequality between the Bahun-Chhetri and other ethnic/caste groups may have been an important driving force behind the Maoist conflict.

There is one remaining issue, and that has to do with the validity of the Midwestern dummy as a proxy for ultra-leftist political activism. Since we observed that the Midwestern region is poorer and more isolated than the rest of Nepal, it is obvious that the Midwestern dummy partially reflects prosperity and remoteness. However, several of the remoteness and prosperity variables such as GDP, HDI, roads, forests, and slopes have been included in the tests. While these variables appear to be insignificant themselves, the coefficient on the Midwestern dummy is hardly affected by their inclusion (generally lying around 0.9). Therefore, it is more likely that the part of the variation in the dummy that is significant in predicting conflict intensity is due to factors not associated with remoteness or income. The only other plausible candidate is political history – in particular, the history of ultra-leftist activism.

Conclusion

In the political economy approach to insurgency that served as the guide to this empirical investigation, the relationship between rebel leaders and their recruits is analogous to that of employers to employees. While the objectives of the two parties may not necessarily coincide, a contract of exchange may be profitable for each. The insurgency survives, as a firm does, as long as costs are low, that is to say as long as the wage needed to provide soldiers is low and as long as operating costs are low. Wages are low when alternative employment options are limited, and operating costs are low when physical geography and the absence of infrastructure aid in preventing the government from being able to suppress the rebels.

I restate the logic of the political economy approach with reference to the variables used in the regressions. First, we can think of GDP per worker, GDP per capita or HDI as proxies for guerilla wages. Second, the geography and infrastructure variables, particularly roads, act as proxies for operating costs. And third, the Midwestern dummy is mostly a proxy for leftist activity, indicating districts where rebel leaders chose to invest their efforts. Two of these three sets of variables were found to be significant in explaining conflict intensity. Although the proxy for wages was not found to be significant, it, like the proxies for geography and infrastructure, captures costs. We can conclude that wages were not as important as infrastructure in determining the profitability of conflict. This is not a particularly surprising result when viewed with the fact that this study of insurgency was restricted to a single conflict in a developing country. In short, the findings justify the political economy approach.

On the other hand, the insignificance of the remaining variables – grievances, caste and ethnic divisions and ideology – solidly rejects the proposition that the Maoist conflict in Nepal emerged from anything but a rational calculus on the part of the insurgents. This result is in harmony with the findings of the cross-country studies discussed in the literature review section. In short, the ten-year-long Maoist insurgency in Nepal does not appear to be linked in any causal way to grievances, social factors or even ideology. What seem to have mattered most are incentives.

Notes

* I would like to thank Jayaraj Acharya, José Azar, Nicholas Sambanis, Swarnim Waglé, an anonymous referee, and the editors of this volume for valuable comments and discussions.

1 This is also the dependent variable of choice in a working paper by Do and Iyer (2006). On the other hand, Bohara et al. (2006) analyze killings by Maoists and killings by the state separately, and Murshed and Gates (2005) study total killings by the state and Maoists in relation to the Maoist insurgency but they do not normalize these figures by district population. Since Tiwari (this volume) finds that the choice of dependent variable appears to be important, I choose one that I think best reflects the frequency of violence.

2 Throughout this paper the terms "left" or "leftist" as political characterizations refer exclusively to the ultra-left and its ideology. The ultra-left includes the Communist Party of Nepal-Maoist (CPN-M), the United People's Front, and other descendants of Mohan Bikram Singh's faction of the Communist Party of Nepal (CPN) that were not mainstream constitutional parties throughout the 1990s (see next section for more on this). Of course, one may object by arguing that the Jhapali communists were just as extreme, if not more extreme, than the ideologues of the Singh faction. However, the political descendants of the Jhapali faction did accept the Constitution of 1990 and were represented by the CPN-United Marxist Leninist (CPN-UML) and the CPN (Marxist Leninist) – both constitutional parties. Therefore, for the purposes of this paper I consider them less extreme than the descendants of the Singh faction.

3 The UPF was the political front for the underground CPN-M.

4 The districts of both Rolpa and Rukum, where the frequency of violence was greatest, are among the top ten districts with the lowest Gini coefficient of land ownership. The districts with the highest levels of inequality in land ownership actually happen to be in the Tarai (see Nepal Human Development Report-NHDR-2004).

5 The literature following Hirshleifer's contribution is too large to summarize here. Some prominent contributions are Collier and Hoeffler (1998), Grossman (1995), Fearon (2007) and Skaperdas (2008). See Garfinkel and Skaperdas (2007) for a good overview.

6 A fourth group is of course the noncombatants. Although Kalyvas (2006) argues that this group plays an important and active role in the creation of violence, we take their presence as given and focus instead on explaining the rise of leaders and armies. The role of noncombatants is difficult to incorporate into a model that intends to use frequency of violence to explain the origins of conflict. Nevertheless, I try to incorporate the role of this group and arguments by Kalyvas in explaining the hypotheses outlined in this section.

7 The variable is constructed by dividing total district GDP for the year 1996 by economically active population above the age of ten. It is also worth noting here that Sharma (2006) and Deraniyagala (2005) find that the economy was on the rise before and even during the insurgency in districts where the conflict was concentrated. But in a cross-sectional model that focuses on initial conditions, we should not be concerned with temporal changes in GDP. I use figures from around 1995 so as to avoid reverse causality and other indirect feedback. Descriptive statistics for GDP and other data, along with details of their sources and construction, are provided in table 13.1 and the note below it.

8 As table 13.2 indicates, the Kathmandu Valley districts seem to be serious outliers in the regression of conflict on road density. This is also corroborated by findings in the multivariate setting. Whereas road density is less than 15 percent for every other district, road densities in Kathmandu, Bhaktapur and Lalitpur are 93.8 percent, 78.5 percent and 44.5 percent respectively. With these three districts included, the average road density is 6.84 percent, as opposed to a 4.12 percent average for the other 72 districts; this is a significant difference of 2.72 percentage points. Therefore, in all regressions that include the road density variable, I exclude the three districts.

9   Since we want to focus here on the kind of activism that leads to insurgency, it is necessary to work with a more restrictive notion of political activism than the one that is common in the political science literature. I am specifically interested in anti-establishment activism rather than political activism within the framework of constitutional politics. Therefore, identifying the Midwestern region as the historical center of leftist activism seems natural. I thank the editors for pointing out this abuse of terminology, and seeking a clarification.

10 I discuss whether the Midwestern dummy reflects remoteness or prosperity rather than politics in the last paragraph of next section.

11 See Bohara et al. (2006), Thapa (2002, 2003), Whelpton (2005), and Do and Iyer (2006) among others.

12 Although district level Gini coefficients for land ownership are 2001 data taken from the NHDR 2004, land markets are relatively inactive (Bardhan and Udry 1999: 60) so it is unlikely that the insurgency has had a significant effect on the land Gini since the start of the conflict in 1996.

13 I use development budget allocation rather than total budget allocation because total budget allocation may include expenditure by the state in suppressing political activity.

14 Murshed and Gates (2005) argue that the prosperity variables (GDP per capita and HDI) actually capture the effect of grievances associated with spatial inequalities, more so than economic conditions. From a theoretical standpoint it is not clear why GDP and HDI should be taken to be more likely indicators of grievances than intra-district economic conditions.

15 Higher land inequality seems to be associated with lower levels of conflict intensity, while higher levels of development budget allocation appear to be associated with higher levels of conflict intensity.

16 I use Bahun to refer to Hill Brahmin, which does not include the Tarai Brahmins.

17 In the literature on Nepal, Gurung (2007) and Lawoti (2005) provide detailed arguments. Gurung identifies cleavage along linguistic and caste lines, highlighting the exclusion of the indigenous nationalities and Dalit communities. Lawoti argues that the fault lines of social and political tension are between the Bahun-Chhetri group and other groups. In the broad literature on civil conflict, Montalvo and Reynal-Querol (2005) find that polarization fares better than fractionalization as an explanatory variable.

18 According to these modified measures, conflict should be greatest in districts where a caste or ethnic group forms exactly 50 percent of the population. This is consistent with findings by Bates (1973) in the case of ethnic conflict in Africa, and what Dion (1997) has suggested more formally. Esteban and Ray (1994) provide a more detailed approach not dissimilar in spirit to the one taken here.

19 I test for nonlinear relationships in the case of both caste and linguistic polarization. For robustness, I also interact them with the grievance variables.

20 These assignments seem arbitrary, but the objective is only to construct an ordinal measure of ideology that might be correlated with the dependent variable. The implicit assumption of the assignments is that the effect of having a UPF candidate win one seat in the home district is roughly equivalent to having three seats won in neighboring districts. Importantly, the constructed measure of ideology accounts for the fact that ideology may have regional components, if not origins. Although the tables do not report the results of alternative specifications, such as one and two points, or one and four, they are qualitatively identical to the specification used above.

21 One political variable that is included by Bohara et al. (2006) but which I choose not to include here is the voter participation rate in the 1999 general elections. The authors find that this variable is significantly related to conflict, and conclude that districts where democracy has flourished have seen less intense fighting. But including this variable could potentially cause a serious reverse-causality problem since the 1999 elections took place three years well into the conflict.

22 One may look to Do and Iyer (2006) to find the argument that poverty does indeed have a robust effect on conflict intensity.

Bibliography

Bardhan, Pranab and Christopher Udry. 1999). *Development Microeconomics*, New York: Oxford University Press.

Bates, Robert. 1973). *Ethnicity in Contemporary Africa: Eastern African Studies* XIV. Syracuse University Maxwell School of Citizenship and Public Affairs.

Berdal, Mats and David Malone (eds.). 2000). *Greed and Grievance: Economic Agendas in Civil Wars*, Boulder, CO: Lynne Rienner Publishers.

Bohara, Alok, Neil Mitchell and Mani Nepal. 2006). "Opportunity, Democracy and the Exchange of Political Violence: A Subnational Analysis of Conflict in Nepal," *Journal of Conflict Resolution*, 50: 108–28.

Central Bureau of Statistics (CBS) (1996). *Nepal Living Standards Survey Report, 1996: Main Findings*. Vol. 1, Kathmandu: Central Bureau of Statistics.

Collier, Paul and Anke Hoeffler (2004). "Greed and Grievance in Civil War," *Oxford Economic Papers*, 56: 563–95.

——. (1998). "On Economic Causes of Civil War," *Oxford Economic Papers*, 50: 563–73.

Collier, Paul and Nicholas Sambanis (2002). "Understanding Civil War: A New Agenda," *Journal of Conflict Resolution*, 46: 3–12.

Deraniyagala, Sonali (2005). "The Political Economy of Civil Conflict in Nepal", *Oxford Development Studies*, 33: 47–62.

Dion, Douglas (1997). "Competition and Ethnic conflict: Artifactual?" *Journal of Conflict Resolution*, 41, 5: 638–48.

Do, Quy-Toan and Lakshmi Iyer (2006). "An Empirical Analysis of Civil Conflict in Nepal", Institute of Government Studies Working Paper 2006–14.

Esteban, Joan and Debraj Ray (1994). "On the Measurement of Polarization," *Econometrica*, 62, 4: 819–51.

Fearon, James (2007). "Economic Development, Insurgency and Civil War," in Elhanan Helpman (ed.) *Institutions and Economic Performance*, Cambridge, MA: Harvard University Press.

Fearon, James and David Laitin (2003). "Ethnicity, Insurgency and Civil War," *American Political Science Review*, 97: 75–90.

Garfinkel, Michelle and Stergios Skaperdas (2007). "Economics of Conflict: An Overview," in T. Sandler and K. Hartley (eds.) *Handbook of Defense Economics, Vol. 2*, Amsterdam: Elsevier.

Gersony, Robert (2003). "Sowing the Wind . . .: History and Dynamics of the Maoist Revolt in Nepal's Rapti Hills," Mercy Corps International.

Grossman, H.I. (1995). "Insurrections," in K. Hartley and T. Sandler (eds.) *Handbook of Defense Economics, Vol. 1*, Amsterdam: Elsevier.

Gurung, Harka (2007). "Social Exclusion and Maoist Insurgency," in A. Aditya (ed.) *The Inclusive State: Reflections on Reinventing Nepal*, Kathmandu: SAP Nepal.

Hirshleifer, Jack (1991). "The Technology of Conflict as an Economic Activity," *American Economic Review*, 81: 130–34.

Horowitz, Donald (1985). *Ethnic Groups in Conflict*, Berkeley, CA: University of California Press.

International Centre for Integrated Mountain Development (ICIMOD) (1997). *Districts of Nepal: Indicators of Development*, Kathmandu: International Centre for Integrated Mountain Development.

Joshi, Bhuwan Lal and Leo Rose (1966). *Democratic Innovations in Nepal: A Case Study of Political Acculturation*, Berkeley, CA: University of California Press.

Kalyvas, Stathis (2006). *The Logic of Violence in Civil War*, Cambridge: Cambridge University Press.

Lawoti, Mahendra (2005). *Towards a Democratic Nepal: Inclusive Political Institutions for a Multicultural Society*. New Delhi: Sage Publications.

Macours, Karen (2006). "Relative Deprivation and Civil Conflict in Nepal," Working Paper, School of Advanced International Studies, Johns Hopkins University.

Migdal, Joel (1988). *Strong Societies and Weak States: State-Society Relations and State Capabilities in the Third World*, Princeton, NJ: Princeton University Press.

Montalvo, Jose and Marta Reynal-Querol (2005). "Ethnic Polarization, Potential Conflict and Civil Wars," *American Economic Review*, 95, 3: 796–816.

Murshed, S. Mansoob and Scott Gates (2005). "Spatial-Horizontal Inequality and the Maoist Insurgency in Nepal," *Review of Development Economics*, 9: 121–43.

Olson, Mancur (1965). *The Logic of Collective Action*, Cambridge, MA: Harvard University Press.

Reynal-Querol, Marta (2002). "Ethnicity, Political Systems and Civil Wars," *Journal of Conflict Resolution*, 46: 29–54

de Sales, Anne (2003). "The Kham Magar Country, Nepal Between Ethnic Claims and Maoism," in Thapa, Deepak (ed.) *Understanding the Maoist Movement of Nepal*. Kathmandu: Martin Chautari.

Shaha, Rishikesh (1990). *Modern Nepal*, New Delhi: Manohar.

Sharma, Kishor (2006). "The Political Economy of Civil War in Nepal," *World Development*, 34: 1237–53.

Skaperdas, Stergios (2008). "An Economic Approach to Analyzing Civil Wars," *Economics of Governance*, 9: 25–54.

National Planning Commission (2001). *Statistical Year book of Nepal 2001*, Central Bureau of Statistics, Ramshah Path, Thapathali, Kathmandu.

Thapa, Dipak (2002). "The Maobadi of Nepal," in Dixit, Kanak Mani and Shastri Ramachandaran (eds.) *State of Nepal*, Lalitpur, Nepal: Himal Books.

Thapa, Dipak (ed.) (2003). *Understanding the Maoist Movement of Nepal*, Kathmandu: Martin Chautari.

Tiwari, Bishwa Nath (2008). "An Assessment of the Causes of Conflict in Nepal," in M. Lawoti and A. Pahari (eds.) *The Maoist Insurgency in Nepal: Revolution in the Twenty-First Century*, London: Routledge.

Whelpton, John (2005). *A History of Nepal*, Cambridge: Cambridge University Press.

United Nations Development Programme (UNDP) (2004). *Nepal Human Development Report 2004*, Kathmandu: United Nations Development Programme.

———. (1998). *Nepal Human Development Report 1998*, Kathmandu: United Nations Development Programme.

Part VIII
After the war

14 Bullets, ballots, and bounty

Maoist electoral victory in Nepal

Mahendra Lawoti[1]

Introduction

The Maoist electoral victory in Nepal in April 2008 surprised and shocked not only the competing political parties but also national and international commentators and the Maoists as well. The Communist Party of Nepal-Maoist (CPN-M), which had waged a decade-long violent rebellion, received two times more seats than their nearest rival in the election for the 601-member Constituent Assembly.[2] Under the first past the post (FPTP) election for 240 members, the Maoists won 120 seats – more seats than the rest of the 53 competing parties in total. The distribution of 335 seats under the proportional representation method closed the gap between the Maoists and other parties and prevented the Maoists from gaining a majority in the Constituent Assembly (see table 14.1). I will examine different factors behind the Maoist victory in this chapter.

Elections in post conflict environment

Holding elections in a post-conflict environment is challenging because of the fragile conditions. Competitive politics and hard-fought elections could aggravate existing social and political tensions and conflicts (Kumar 1998; Jarstad and Sisk 2008). A necessary condition for any election is that it should be free and fair. These minimum institutional guarantees are necessary so that people can raise issues, competing parties can campaign without fear, and citizens can get the opportunity to hear alternative positions and policies and make informed decisions (Dahl 1971). A free and fair election would also make it acceptable to the losing side as they would think that they would have a fair chance the next time.

However, what constitutes a free and fair election in post-conflict situations? Elklit and Svensson operationalize freedom in the context of post-conflict elections by contrasting it with coercion: "Freedom entails the right and opportunity to choose one thing over another. Coercion implies the absence of choice, either formally or in reality" (1997: 35). Challenges increase in post-war societies because the environment is fragile, the rule of law is often yet to be established, the legitimacy of the process is weak, and warring parties distrust each other and are capable of employing coercive force (weapons and organizations maybe yet to be

Table 14.1 Seats in the Constituent Assembly, 2008

Party name	FPTP	PR votes, %	PR	Total
Communist parties				
Communist Party of Nepal-Maoist (CPN-M)	120	29.28	100	220
Communist Party of Nepal-United Marxist Leninist (CPN-UML)	33	20.33	70	103
Communist Party of Nepal-Marxist Leninist (CPN-ML)	0	2.27	8	8
People's Front Nepal (PFN)	2	1.53	5	7
Communist Party of Nepal-Joint (CPN-J)	0	1.44	5	5
National People's Front (NPF)	1	0.99	3	4
Nepal Worker's Peasant Party (NWPP)	2	0.69	2	4
Communist Party of Nepal-United (CPN-U)	0	0.45	2	2
Sub-total	158		195	353
Identity parties				
Madhesi Peoples Right Forum (MPRF)	30	6.32	22	52
Tarai Madhesh Democratic Party (TMDP)	9	3.12	11	20
Nepal Goodwill Party (NGP)	4	1.56	5	9
National People's Liberation Party (NPLP)	0	0.5	2	2
Nepal Goodwill Party –Anandi (NGP-A)	0	0.52	2	2
Federal Democratic National Forum (FDNF)	0	0.67	2	2
Dalit Nationalities Party (DNP)	0	0.38	1	1
Nepa: National Party (NNP)	0	0.35	1	1
Chure Bhawar National Unity Party Nepal (CBNUPN)	0	0.25	1	1
Sub-total	43		47	90
Other parties				
Nepali Congress	37	21.14	73	110
National Democratic Party (NDP)	0	2.45	8	8
National Democratic Party – Nepal (NDP-N)	0	1.03	4	4
National People Power Party (NPPP)	0	0.95	3	3
Nepal Peoples Party (NPP)	0	0.46	2	2
Nepal Family Party (NFP)	0	0.22	1	1
Nepal Democratic Socialist Party (NDSP)	0	0.23	1	1
Independents	2		0	2
Sub-total	39		92	131
Total	240		335	575

Source: Election Commission (2008).

Note: PR stands for proportional representation.

demobilized) against opponents. Wars have erupted again after elections in some post-war societies. Angola's 1992 election and Liberia's 1997 election created more problems than they solved.[3]

Elklit and Svensson (1997: 35) define fairness in terms of impartiality: "the opposite of fairness is unequal treatment of equals, whereby some people (or groups) are given unreasonable advantages." Control of state resources in war-torn societies could advantage groups in power. Incumbents can deploy state resources and power to influence elections. The incumbents may also have name recognition and well-oiled electoral machines. In many developing countries elections have been influenced by the blatant use of money and muscle. For instance, the military ruler J. J. Rawlings in Ghana used control over the state to influence the first post-conflict election. The election was announced at short notice, the government unilaterally appointed the Interim National Electoral Commission, and the opposition alleged rampant fraud, including intimidation by security personnel and "revolutionary" organs, ballot dumping, and pre-stuffed ballot boxes. The election result triggered a spate of violence and the boycott of the parliamentary election (Gyimah-Boadi 1999).

Oppositions also attempt to reduce their disadvantages. In the case of war-torn societies, the rebels could deploy their fire power. Further, incumbency may act in opposite directions as well. For example, if the ruling group has either irked some groups or failed to please others, such parties may not support the incumbent. Over time, such groups may grow and reach a critical mass to tilt the majority against the incumbent. On the other hand, people in war-torn societies may feel that the rebels have to be mainstreamed and hence may vote for them.

Contributing factors in the Maoist victory

Vote for change

The victory of the rebel Maoists at face value suggests that the people voted for change. However, because opposition parties and election observers have accused the Maoists of violence and intimidation, it is necessary to verify both claims. The change thesis can be demonstrated by the fact that the Maoists won seats in urban districts like Kathmandu and Lalitpur where the elections were held in a relatively free and fair environment. Further, they also won in districts that were considered the bastion of the CPN-UML and the Nepali Congress (such as Kathmandu, Lalitpur, Jhapa, Dang, Tanahun etc.). Only a strong yearning for change among traditional supporters of established parties would have made the people vote for a new party.

The fact that the Maoists stole votes away from different ideological parties also suggests that people across the board were not happy with the established parties. Many commentators have often assumed that the Maoists won by stealing the communist votes away from the CPN-UML. Table 14.2, however, shows that the Maoists took votes away from the centrist Nepali Congress as well as from the rightist NDP factions. While the CPN-UML lost 10 percent of votes,[4] the Nepali Congress lost 15 percent and the rightist parties lost 9 percent of votes from their 1999 tally. The Madhesi parties gained 8 percent of votes. Even if all the gain of the Madhesi parties is attributed to the votes they took away from the Nepali Congress (which is not true), 7 percent of the Nepali Congress's vote from 1999 goes unaccounted for. This means that the Nepali Congress lost votes to the Maoists because no other major political parties gained votes (the indigenous nationalities' parties gained less than 1 percent of votes).

The people's vote for change during the Constituent Assembly election is clear not only because of the Maoist win but also because of votes received by Madhesi and indigenous nationalities' parties that were fighting for major changes. Table 14.2 demonstrates that parties that advocated for major changes in the society and polity increased their vote share in 2008 compared to parliamentary elections in the 1990s. The change-seeking CPN-M and Madhesi and indigenous nationalities' parties increased their vote share while the older parties (NC, CPN-UML and NDPs) that were either conservative or status quoist lost votes. The sound defeat of the rightist parties reinforces this thesis since they were the least change-seeking parties.

Among the Madhesi parties, the MPRF, which led the most vigorous movement and which was perceived as the most change-deliverable agent got more seats than other Madhesi parties including the older NGP. Likewise, within the indigenous nationalities' parties, the FDNF, which launched a movement that was reasonably effective in the far Eastern districts, received more votes than its parent party NPLP, from which the FDNF had split, that supported the royal intervention in 2002 and 2005 as well as another older party, the Mongol National Organization (MNO).[5]

The change dimension is supported by other indirect indicators as well. The rapid growth of the Maoists after 1996 showed that a large segment of the population was not happy with the old parties. Similarly, the low popular support for established parties in the opinion polls prior to the election suggested that people were not happy with the status quo (Sharma and Sen 2008).[6] The support for the Maoists was also low but it does not indicate that they were losing support. It was a growing party, and having a similar support level to established parties indicates its growth.

Table 14.2 Popular votes received by parties during the 1990s and 2008, %

Parties	1991 FPTP	1994 FPTP	1999 FPTP	2008 PR	Gain/ loss, 99–08	Proportion of gain/loss in 99–08, %
CPN-M (extreme left)	4.83[1]	Boycott	Boycott	29.28	Gain	Gain
Nepali Congress (center)	37.75	33.38	36.14	21.14	−15	−41.51
CPN-UML (left)	27.75	30.85	30.74[2]	20.33	−10.41	−33.86
NDParty factions (right)	11.94	17.93	13.47	4.43	−9.04	−67.11
Madhesi Parties (identity)[3]	4.10	3.49	3.13	11.55	+8.42	+269.01
Indigenous Nationalities Parties (identity)[4]	0.47	1.05	1.07	1.86	+0.79	+73.83

Source: Election Commission (2008) and Lawoti (2005).

Notes
1 The CPN-M's predecessor fought the 1991 election under the banner of the United People's Front Nepal. The vote assigned to CPN-M for 1991 is that received by the front, from which the CPN-M split in 1994.
2 CPN-ML, a breakaway faction of CPN-UML, received 6 percent of popular votes. I have not added this vote in this calculation. A large number of leaders and cadres returned to the mother party but a significant number continued to operate as CPN-ML and received 2.27 percent of popular votes in 2008.
3 The votes for the 1990s are those received by NGP.
4 These are votes received by the NPLP in 1991, 1994 and 1999. The MNO had also fielded candidates as independents but the Election Commission publications do not tabulate them separately.

The Maoists' image as agents of change was helped by their activities. They were responsible for mainstreaming the agendas of the republic and the Constituent Assembly. They presented the most inclusive candidate list for the FPTP election with substantial Dalit, indigenous nationalities, Madhesi, women and youth candidates. The lack of senior leaders meant that the Maoist had to recruit many young candidates, especially from rural areas as well as from marginalized groups. The Maoists fielded 52.5 percent of candidates from the 18–35 age group that comprised of 51 percent of voters, while the Nepali Congress and CPN-UML fielded 8 and 12 percent respectively. This resonated well with the young voters (Pathak 2008).

The Maoists were the most vigorous champions of the marginalized groups among the mainstream political parties. They actively worked against caste and gender discrimination and supported the right to self-determination and autonomy (de Sales 2003; Hutt 2004; Thapa and Sijapati 2003). The Maoist promises also appeared more plausible compared to older parties' because the established parties were discredited by their previous misgovernance characterized by corruption, a culture of impunity, the inability to provide security, and so on (Dhruba Kumar 2000; Baral 2005). The Maoists successfully projected themselves as a clean party and discredited others by, among other means, catchy campaign slogans, such as "arulai mauka dheria patak, maobadilai mauka ek patak" (others have received opportunity many times; give the Maoists an opportunity this time).

The perception of the party as a winner also helped the Maoists. Adoption of many Maoist agendas, such as republic and Constituent Assembly elections, by other parties helped to create and reinforce this image. After the political transformation Nepalis tend to change their support to the winning side. After the 1990 political changes, the Panchayat groups lost large-scale support. The Nepali Congress and CPN-UML transformed into strong parties in the 1991 election, even in districts where their organizations and activities were limited before 1990. The Maoists benefited from this phenomenon after 2006.

Vote for peace and stability

The Maoists, however, did not get all the votes from change seekers. Ironically, they might have received considerable votes from independents and conservatives, who were yearning for order and stability. Many people perceived that the Maoists might engage in street protests or even return to the insurgency if they fared badly in the election. The former perception was based on the frequent street protests the Maoists engaged in, not only during the insurgency but even after they had joined the coalition government. The latter fear was based on the widespread media discussion that the Maoists could lose badly. Some prominent Maoist leaders also publicly warned that they might revert to the insurgency if they did not win. Voting for rebels to enhance peace is not unusual in post-conflict elections. In Liberia in 1997 people said to Charles Taylor's party, "You killed my mother, you killed my father, I will give you my vote." The people were desperate for peace and were ready to vote even for former enemies to attain it.[7]

It is difficult to ascertain to what extent this factor played a role in the Nepali election. This explanation, however, should not be lightly discounted because a significant segment of people supported King Gyanendra in 2005 when he took over the reins of government, citing the past government's inability to establish peace and order in the society. The yearning for peace was quite strong among the people after more than a decade of violent insurgency and many were ready to support or vote for anyone if they could deliver peace.

Violence and intimidation

How free and fair was the election considering the post-conflict context in which it was held? Did intimidation and fear affect the electoral outcomes as charged by some? I will employ a two-step process to determine whether fear and intimidation also affected the electoral result. First, I will assess intimidation and violence during the campaign and on election day, and the actors responsible for them. Second, I will trace whether these activities had an effect on the election result.

Elections and influence in Nepal over the years

All parties attempt to influence the outcome of elections but it should be done fairly. Free and fair elections mean that, among other necessary conditions, people in power should not abuse state power to influence elections. Democratic elections in Nepal, however, have always been influenced by state power to a considerable extent (Lawoti 2007). The most glaring examples are the two local elections held in the 1990s: the parties that controlled the government – Nepali Congress in 1992 and CPN-UML in 1997 – won the elections with big margins. A cabinet minister quit the coalition government in 1997 charging the home minister from another party of directing gross fraudulent activities. Even the parliamentary elections were influenced by power, but the influence was less owing to a higher uncertainty of the winners.[8]

Power has influenced elections in Nepal in several ways. First, the party and leaders in power can distribute resources, development projects and jobs to get votes. Such promises also look more plausible when made by the ruling party candidates in a clientelistic society. Second, the government can manipulate the administration to influence elections. For example, in a competitive election, polling staffs with certain ideological predilections could be deployed to a certain constituency with the complicity of district election officers. As polling staff vote where they are deputed, they can add a few hundred votes in a constituency, determining the election outcome in a stiff competition. This is just an example of how electoral outcomes can be subtly influenced. Power and influence were deployed brazenly as well during the 1990s. For instance government-owned media (print, radio, TV) were blatantly abused by the government to propagate partisan issues while the government-appointed election commissioners did not or were unable to stop such abuses. Third, people also vote for parties and candidates they think will win because they would like to increase the possibility of receiving resources and services from the winners. This voting behaviour usually favors ruling parties in societies where ruling parties abuse state resources to influence electoral outcomes.

Violence during the Constituent Assembly[9]

If one were to compare elections in Nepal, the 2008 election was the most violent.[10] Eighty persons were killed after the code of conduct was implemented on January 15, 2008, up until the election-day whereas ten people were killed in the 1991 election (DEAN 2008; INSEC 2008). Nepal had never encountered such large-scale killings, intimidation, and disturbances during previous elections.

DEAN reported that violent incidents occurred in 81 percent of the districts (61 out of 75) between November 26, 2007, and April 30, 2008. DEAN reported 485 incidents of political and election-related violence in the pre-election (November 26, 2007–April 9, 2008), election (April 10, 2008) and post election (April 11–30, 2008) periods. According to DEAN, 50 people were killed, 1,286 people were wounded and 116 people were kidnapped all together.[11] Other forms of violence included torture, intimidation and psychological abuse, verbal harassment and threats of physical harm, destruction of property, attacks on the homes of party cadres and candidates, destruction of election materials, and attacks on government offices (DEAN 2008: 6). Several candidates were killed during the election campaign and a number of others were kidnapped, while many were obstructed from campaigning. Even top party functionaries of major political parties, such as the party president, were restricted from campaigning freely, mostly by the Maoists. The INSEC webpage listed around a dozen acts of violence and disturbances almost every day during the last few weeks of the campaign.

The DEAN data probably under-represented violence and intimidation because it required the data to be twice verified by its 480 locally based monitors. The case of Gorkha district is an example of this. DEAN lists only one pre-election incident for Gorkha whereas INSEC and Kantipuronline reported around a dozen incidents of violations from March 10 to April 9, 2008. The data may also not have measured numerous low-level conflicts. However, since DEAN employed a methodology used internationally, the level of violence can be compared with that in other countries. The violence in Nepal was higher than in Nigeria but lower than in Timor-Leste based on numbers of registered voters.[12] Even if undercounted, the DEAN data shows that political and electoral violence was widespread in the CA election.

The violence occurred as a result of electoral competition between political parties and as a result of ongoing ethnic movements by the Madhesi and indigenous nationalities. Major Madhesi and indigenous nationalities' organizations participated in the election after reaching a settlement with the government before the election but others boycotted the election and some resisted it violently as well.

Political party cadres, supporters and leaders, and others affiliated with political parties' perpetrated 62 percent of the violence.[13] This shows that most violence was related to electoral competition. The Maoists were the highest perpetrators of violence. The Maoist cadres and youth front, the Young Communist League (YCL), perpetrated 51 percent of the violence. The CPN-UML (16 percent), Nepali

Table 14.3 Percentage perpetrator or victim among political parties, 2008

Parties	Incidents perpetrated, %	Victim incidents, %
CPN-M	51	19
Nepali Congress	16	32
CPN-UML	16	29
MPRF	6	5
TMDP	3	–
NPF	2	–
NDP	–	3
SPA	–	2
Others	4 (less than 1 % for many parties)	10 (less than 1% for many parties)

Source: DEAN (2008); data provided for groups when incidents reached 1 % or above.

Congress (16 percent), MPRF (6 percent), TMDP (3 percent) and NPF (2 percent) also perpetrated political and electoral violence but less frequently.

The Nepali Congress (32 percent) and CPN-UML (29 percent) were the top two victims of violence among the political parties and affiliated groups. The Maoists were victim 19 percent of the time while MPRF, NDP and others were victim 5 percent, 3 percent, 2 percent respectively (DEAN 2008: 5). The perpetrator and victim analysis shows that the Maoists and the MPRF perpetrated violence in a higher proportion than they were victims (see table 14.3). On the other hand, the Nepali Congress and CPN-UML were victims more often than perpetrators of violence. This shows that the Nepali Congress and CPN-UML were at the receiving end while the Maoists and the MPRF were on the offending side.

Violence and its effect on electoral outcome

CPN-M and MPRF, who perpetrated more violence than they were at the receiving end of, won decisively (see table 14.3). This indicates that violence affected electoral outcome. Margins of victory can help to further establish the role of intimidation and fear. If incidences of violence and a wide margin wins exist, one can argue that the environment of intimidation and fear affected the election. On the other hand, if candidates from many parties won with landslide victories, it can be argued that the election was reasonably competitive despite violence because no party enjoyed hegemonic domination.

Based on the 1994 and 1999 elections, a winning margin of at least three times (a ratio obtained from dividing votes received by the winning candidates to votes received by the runner up) can be established as a criterion to gauge the uncompetitive environment. This criterion was established based on the history of power influencing Nepali elections. The three times criterion was established because the influence of power can be ascertained more definitively with the three times threshold: it was met only by the ruling party members, whereas opposition candidates also won with double margins. The assumption behind the criterion is not that the leaders win just because of power abuse but that power plays a role in widening the margin. Likewise, the argument is not that one has to win with a triple margin ratio for power to influence electoral outcomes but that such wide-margin wins help to

Table 14.4 Candidates winning with more than three times votes, 1994, 1999 and 2008

Name	Party	Vote ratio	Ratio	Constituency	Region
		1994			
Ram Chandra Paudel	NC	22639/6493	3.49	Tanahu-2	Hill
Palten Gurung	NC	2315/721	3.21	Manang	Mountain
		1999			
Sher Bahadur Deuba	NC	28651/7840	3.65	Dadeldhura	Hill
Khum Bahadur Khadka	NC	27865/9159	3.04	Dang-1	Tarai
		2008			
Jun Kumari Roka (Oli)	Maoist	31410/4015	7.82	Rukum-1	Hill
Baburam Bhattarai	Maoist	46272/6143	7.53	Gorkha-2	Hill
Puspa Kamal Dahal (Prachanda)	Maoist	34220/6029	5.68	Rolpa-2	Hill
Jaypuri Gharti	Maoist	26505/4946	5.36	Rolpa-1	Hill
Parbati Thapa Shrestha	Maoist	40606/9142	4.44	Gorkha-1	Hill
Mohammad Estiyak Rai	MPRF	19396/4565	4.43	Banke-2	Tarai
Dilliman Tamang	Maoist	31121/7010	4.44	Ramechap-2	Hill
Amar Bahadur Gurung	Maoist	28969/7442	3.89	Gorkha-3	Hill
Krishna Kumar Chaudhari	Maoist	27547/8367	3.29	Kailali-4	Tarai
Janardan Sharma	Maoist	30270/9250	3.27	Rukum-2	Hill
Suryaman Dong Tamang	Maoist	27471/8407	3.27	Kavrepalanchowk-2	Hill
Bir Man Chaudhari	Maoist	19739/6126	3.22	Kailali-3	Tarai
Ram Chandra Chaudhari Tharu	Maoist	24444/7611	3.21	Bardiya-4	Tarai
Renu Chand (Bhatt)	Maoist	20021/6366	3.14	Baitadi-2	Hill
Kali Bahadur Malla	Maoist	19009/6223	3.05	Jajarkot-1	Hill
Brijesh Kumar Gupta	TMDP	18126/5944	3.05	Kapilvastu-3	Tarai
Agni Prasad Sapkota	Maoist	30175/10063	3.00	Sindhupalchowk-2	Hill

Source: Election Commission (2008).

establish influence of power more definitively. In fact, the influence of power/intimidation could be more significant in competitive elections.

Table 14.4 shows that two candidates each won with a ratio of three and higher in 1994 and 1999. All four candidates belonged to the party that controlled the government. Wins by a very large margin only by the ruling party candidates suggest that being a member of a ruling party mattered in the electoral outcome. Three of the four winners were very powerful leaders who occupied senior cabinet positions for very long time whereas Manang, the fourth constituency, is a district where power and money had been historically influential owing to the district's very small population.

The three times threshold clearly establishes that the 2008 election was influenced by power dynamics. Seventeen candidates won elections by a ratio of three times or higher in 2008.[14] Except for one candidate each from MPRF and TMDP, the rest of the 15 winners belonged to the Maoists. Further, close inspection of the large-margin win data indicates several things. One, the win ratios increased sharply from around three and a half in the 1990s to nearly eight in 2008. This suggests that the election had become far less competitive. Two, the frequency of such wide-margin wins also increased. In 2008 there were eight times more uncompetitive wins (17/240 in 2008 compared to 2/205 each in 1994 and 1999). Three, unlike earlier elections, when the Nepali Congress had not won all constituencies in districts with two or more constituencies, 2008 saw the Maoists win all constituencies in three districts (Gorkha, Rukum and Rolpa) and two constituencies in another district (Kailali). These trends point to domination of one party at a much higher level across wider regions during the 2008 election. Lastly, the data also shows that the Maoists completely monopolized the wide-margin wins in the hills. All 13 large-margin winners in the hills were Maoists. If different parties had won with large margins, one could argue that the effect would have balanced out to some degree. In the Tarai, the Madhesi parties competed with the Maoists for domination in some regions. The Maoists won three large-margin wins in western Tarai, whereas TMDP and MPRF won large-margin win each in the central and western Tarai respectively. The domination in the Tarai was not as bad as in the hills because no party monopolized wide-margin wins and the depth of domination was also less (the highest ratio was 4.43).

It will be instructive to discuss a case to understand the phenomenon of intimidation and its influence. In Gorkha district, where all the three Maoist candidates won with a more than three times margin, media and human rights organizations reported that non-Maoist candidates and cadres were restricted from campaigning freely by the Maoists. According to INSEC and *Kantipuronline* reports, candidates of the Nepali Congress (March 28 and 15), NDP (March 26) and CPN-UML (April 6 and March 15) were obstructed from campaigning by the Maoists. In some cases they also barred central committee members of other parties from campaigning (CPN-UML leader on April 6). On April 3, the Maoists obstructed election observers of the Asian Network for Free Election, whose team member consisted of the district chairperson of the Federation of Nepal Journalist, while they also obstructed representatives of the National Human Rights Commission and INSEC for some time in another incident (INSEC 2008).

Ten different incidents of obstructions and conflicts from March 10 to April 9 were recorded by INSEC (7) and *Kantipuronline* (3). Apart from a violent confrontation involving Nepali Congress and Maoist cadres on April 5 when a Maoist cadre was seriously injured and two cases involving election observers and human rights activist, the rest of the incidents involved election candidates. This suggests that perhaps other incidents involving local cadres and low-level conflicts and intimidation that could have been more widespread and effective in affecting voting behaviour in villages may not have come to the attention of election-monitoring observers.

Even the Maoist ideologue Dr. Bhattarai, who himself was a candidate from Gorkha, accepted that "some" violence by the Young Communist League (YCL) had occurred during the election. The CPN-UML and Nepali Congress boycotted the vote counting, alleging that their poll agents were not allowed in some polling stations by the Maoists.

An election where candidates and parties leaders are barred from freely campaigning cannot be considered fair. When candidates of different parties are barred by one particular party, the message to the voters is quite clear: the state and other parties cannot provide protection and security and the hegemonic party may do anything, including deploying violence, to "win" the election. The people may not have been left with much free choice.

In the absence of violent conflict on election day, the Election Commission did not conduct re-polling in any polling stations in Gorkha. The case of Gorkha points out that the absence of violent conflict on the voting day does not mean that the voting took place in a free and fair manner. Violent conflicts on election day occurred where two or more sides were competitive. Where one party dominated the region through pre-election violence and/or the threat of it, overt conflict might not occur on election day because opposing parties might be unable to challenge the hegemony. In many districts where the Maoists had hegemonic domination, as in Gorkha, the party "peacefully" and significantly violated the free and fair electoral norms. This might be the reason why many respected international observers based in urban areas or road heads did not observe the real pre-election coercive activities that eventually influenced electoral outcomes.

Previous discussion of vote transfer of centrist and rightist parties to the Maoists also supports the intimidation hypothesis to some degree. Normally people vote for political parties that are close to their policy preferences. A relatively small percentage of independent voters change their support to competing parties, determining the winners. Even when the voters change parties, they usually shift to one ideologically close or one that may provide them with goods and services in return. The Maoists received a considerable amount of votes from people who previously voted for rightist and centrist parties. This is unusual electoral behaviour. It suggests that the transfer of votes must have occurred through an unnatural process. The Maoists did not have resources to distribute to attract votes so patronage is not a plausible reason. However, they had an aggressive cadre base that was associated with violence previously. Some voters may have voted for the Maoist aspiring for changes, but it is hard to believe that all voters, especially conservative voters to whom the Maoist agendas and rapid socio-political changes were anathema, voted willingly for the Maoists. If that were the case, then the Maoists should have won with large margins even in urban areas and the Tarai, where elections occurred in a relatively free, fair, and competitive environment.

It can be argued that perhaps the Maoists won with very big margins because of their popularity. The argument here is not that the Maoist did not have popular support. They would have probably won in many hill areas with competitive margins. The wide-margin wins demonstrate that they "received" far more votes in many regions of domination than any popular party usually gets. As mentioned above, the historical record demonstrates that this year's level of vote distribution was highly skewed. Obtaining more than 80 percent of votes in a constituency (in Gorkha and other districts) does not indicate competition, especially when 30 percent of votes could be enough to win in multi-party competition under FPTP. The fact that the Maoists did not win with a three-point ratio and higher in any urban constituency where the election was held in a reasonably free environment also supports the argument that such wins were possible in rural areas because the elections in those areas were marred by intimidation and fear. The argument is that the extremely wide-margin wins demonstrate the role of intimidation, violence and one-sided campaigns. Intimidation may have affected election outcomes in many other districts even if the effect was less.

It can be argued that the Maoists did not control the government in Kathmandu and hence could not have abused power. The home and finance ministry, which were more instrumental in influencing the previous elections, were under the control of the Nepali Congress. The Nepali Congress, which took those ministries despite clear public displeasure of coalition partners, may have become smug because of it. However, this strategy did not work during this election for the Nepali Congress because the formal state no longer enjoyed a similar level of influence in the rural areas. The Maoists not only challenged but had undermined or replaced the state in large parts of the country, especially in the hills. In many parts of the country, the Maoists were the effective state as they dictated political life and campaign terms to leaders and cadres of other political parties. In some Tarai areas, the MPRF and other Madhesi forces were the effective alternative power sources (though not as hegemonic as the Maoists). The power wielders not only constrained the activities of opposition groups but the voters also understood which party was powerful and hence many may have voted accordingly to be on the winning side. In the absence of protection by the government and other parties, some may have voted for the Maoists to reduce risk of future Maoist wrath. The Maoists had widely spread stories of owning binoculars that enabled them to see how people voted. Such stories may have scared many straightforward people. Thus, power still influenced the 2008 elections, but it was not the "old" state which was effective but the "new" regime that prevailed. The raw coercive power of the mobilized parties was more effective this time than the traditional clientelistic distribution of resources and subtle manipulations of electoral mechanisms through the government agencies.

The Maoist intimidation was effective because a few Maoists could threaten dozens of cadres of other political parties. The perception among the non-Maoists that the Maoists could employ violence, which was fuelled by their past violent history and continuing occasional violence, helped to create fear among supporters and cadres of other parties as well as the common citizens. The Maoists cadres were also emboldened because of psychological support they received from the Peoples Liberation Army (PLA). In fact many PLA personnel left their cantonment to campaign during the election (INSEC 2008).

The Maoists employed violence strategically and selectively. The highly partisan ruling political parties did not complain when the Maoists attacked other groups, parties and common people. When the Maoists began to attack cadres of the ruling parties, individual parties tried to negotiate with the Maoists to address the "problems" its cadres were facing. When the political parties realized that bipartisan requests and pressures did not work and realized that they had to deal with the Maoists collectively, the election was too close to negotiate an effective agreement and enforce it. The only alternative would have been to postpone the election, which could have created more problems as they would have been blamed for the third postponement.

A relevant question about violent activities is why they did not backfire. After all, the Maoists were engaged in widespread extortions, took free food and shelter, assaulted people, and forced people to contribute labor for weeks for different activities, such as road construction. Many people were not happy with these activities and they could have voted against the Maoists. However, such voting did not occur at a significant level. One explanation could be that such "victims" were small in number. This does not seem plausible as forced labor was almost universal in many areas. Further, fear affects people even if they have not been direct victims. People could become anxious that they could be victims in the future. A more plausible explanation in the context of large-scale intimidation discussed earlier is that people may not have voted against the Maoist because the environment to do so did not exist. The widespread violence and intimidation on the one hand and the failure of the state and other political parties to provide security and protection to voters on the other reduced effective choices for the people. Practically, the Maoists may have been the only available "choice" for many.

Innovative strategies and mobilization

The Maoists were successful in their movement, including the election, because of brilliant strategies, such as adopting and raising ethnic issues, forming and deploying the YCL as a strong-arm agency for the election and other work once the PLA was confined to the cantonments, preventing monopoly of the state by older parties by insisting on a broad coalition government that included them, and so on. These strategies facilitated mobilization of large numbers of people from hitherto untapped groups in society, such as the indigenous nationalities, Dalit, women, the poor and youth, to their cause in a much higher level than other mainstream political parties.

As insurgents, the dynamics of being rebels made them take new initiatives to expand their base and dismantle the political forces occupying the state. Every rebel and opponent would attempt that, but the Maoists were successful. For instance, the Maoists forced the postponement of the November 2007 election by resigning from the coalition government because they perceived that popular support towards them had declined. What made them confident enough to take part in the election after six months? They developed a strategy for overcoming the problem by deploying hundreds of YCL and party cadres in the campaign and the polling stations. It was a strategy to win elections by supplementing popular support with votes through the show and use of force. The violence and intimidation generated a demonstration effect and installed fear widely in cadres, supporters and leaders of other parties.

The Maoist win was also helped by their liberal promises. They promised different things to different groups facing discrimination and inequality. In a society of severe inequality and scarcity, hope and promises may have been better than no promises or hope. In the earlier elections, the CPN-UML benefited from this 'promising the sky' factor but the party's failure to fulfill earlier promises put it at a receiving end – its slogans and promises appeared not only unreliable but too little as well, especially in comparison to the Maoists' more radical promises.

The Maoists had already addressed the potential monopolization of state forces and resources by the parliamentary parties by insisting on a broad coalitional government that included them for conducting the election. As one of the three major partner of the coalition government, they not only abused government resources for partisan purposes such as monopoly propaganda by the state media under the communication ministry they controlled but also had a say in the deployment of the security forces.

The mobilization of the hill ethnic/caste groups, ironically even by a class-based insurgency, paid rich dividends not only during the insurgency by providing recruits for the PLA, militia, and party but also in the election. The Maoists also fielded the most inclusive candidates in the election and, not surprisingly, they won decisively in the regions of Magars, Tharus, Tamangs and Rais.[15]

Power, privilege and organizational decay

The Maoists also benefited from the actions, inactions, omissions, and mistakes of competing parties. A major weakness of the older parties was their defunct organizations. First, as mentioned above, the non-Maoist parties had not operated regularly in the rural regions during the insurgency in particular and thereafter as well owing to Maoist threat and intimidation. The obstructions and disturbances prevented the non-Maoist parties from re-establishing party organization and re-connecting with the people. The party organizations, as a result, were in a shambles, because of which the Maoists could easily sweep the parties aside. The lethargic attitude of the central leadership was also a major factor in the poor performance of older parties, especially in the hills. In retrospect, it appears that the major non-Maoist party leadership were not fully aware of the dire straits of their party organizations outside the Kathmandu Valley, where most resided.

The weakened party organizations were also the result of the absence of intra-party democracy, because of which competent leaders and cadres were sidelined, cadres and leaders did not have a significant role in formulating party policies and activities, and the top leadership did not receive genuine popular feedback. The undemocratic intra-party culture was responsible for disconnecting the leadership from the needs and aspirations of cadres and the common people. The Maoists may not have had intra-party democracy either, but as a rebelling party they were flexible and sensitive toward the people because they had to mobilize them.

The Nepali Congress and CPN-UML's culture of distributing tickets to cadres who hung around the supreme leaders in the center may have undermined their ability to gauge the needs, mood, and aspirations of rural people. Candidacy distribution based on loyalty to different factions rather than to popular and competent persons lowered the Nepali Congress's competitiveness. Excessive reliance on student leaders by the Nepali Congress and CPN-UML undermined grassroots leaders who understood the people's pulses better. A good example of the Nepali Congress and CPN-UML's failure to understand and capture the sentiments of the people is their failure to cash in on the rising aspirations of marginalized groups. The established parties, in fact, resisted or ignored ethnic and nationalist aspirations, and they continued to favor the exclusionary nationalism and domination of the caste hill Hindu elite males in practice despite the rhetoric of inclusion. The continued domination of Bahun males in the CPN-UML organization and candidate list and its ambivalent attitude towards ethnic issues chipped away its support from the marginalized groups. A lesser number of tickets to the youth and marginalized groups in the FPTP election demonstrated CPN-UML's lack of commitment towards inclusion. On the other hand, YCL and the Maoists mobilized the disgruntled youth and marginalized groups.

Being part of the establishment brought perks and privileges but eroded the older parties' ability to be inventive, flexible and alert. With its long tenure in government, the Nepali Congress increasingly relied on the bureaucracy and police to help influence the elections. As mentioned above, the government agencies could not deliver this time. In the case of the CPN-UML, the party also enjoyed the perks and privileges bestowed upon its supporters by the international donors. The party relied heavily upon its vast network of human rights and development NGOs. This time the NGOs were less effective and in fact may have indirectly harmed the party's prospect by holding up cadres in the NGOs.

Conclusion

Many people yearned for change while others voted for the Maoists for peace and stability. The Maoists were successful in mobilizing hitherto neglected groups by raising their issues and fielding candidates from the groups. By forcing the established parties to accept the Maoist agenda, they projected an image of being a vigorous agent for change. On the other hand, the Maoists also created an environment where other parties could not freely and fairly seek votes. The parliamentary parties could not re-establish connection with the people owing to Maoist violence and intimidation, real as well as perceived, while the established parties' organizations weakened not only because of Maoist obstruction and intimidation during the insurgency and afterwards but also because of the undemocratic intra-party culture and inertia that resulted from enjoying power and privilege. Meanwhile the Maoists continued to be innovative. As a result, in many cases people did not have effective "choice" in the election. All these factors helped to create momentum for the Maoists.

The Maoists would have probably become the largest party without intimidation and violence because a large number of people aspired for change and other factors also favoured them. The intimidation strategy nevertheless paid a rich dividend to the Maoists by increasing their vote and seat share, leaving the nearest party far behind. The long-term effect of the success of this strategy could be that the Maoists would employ it again because it delivered a win. Democracy, freedom, and the Nepali people will become the victims if that strategy is employed again in future elections.

Notes

1 An earlier version of the paper was presented at the Himalayan Policy Conference, Annual South Asia Conference (October 16, 2008). I would like to thank Anup K. Pahari and Dikhsya Thapa for commenting on an earlier version.

2 575 members were elected and 26 were nominated.

3 Elections in Namibia in 1989, El Salvador in 1994, and Mozambiquie in 1994, however, contributed positively to peace-building and democratization (Reilly 2008: 158).

4 If votes received in 1999 by CPN-ML, a faction that split from CPN-UML, are included in the count, the moderate communist factions lost 16 percent of votes.

5 The indigenous nationalities parties received nearly 2 percent of popular votes and the three parties that emerged out of the split of the National People's Liberation Party (NPLP) received 1.2 percent of votes, which is higher than NPLP had received in 1999 (1.07 percent).

6 Less than 15 percent supported the Nepali Congress and CPN-UML in surveys conducted after the 2006 change.

7 I thank Fodei Batty for sharing the Liberian example.

8 The 1991 and 1999 general elections were won by the party that controlled the government. The 1994 election was an exception because of widespread intra-party factionalism that resulted into loss by the Nepali Congress, the incumbent.

9 This section is based on the final report of DEAN (Democracy and Election Alliance Nepal), an election-monitoring network.

10 The 1999 election was held amidst an insurgency and was conducted on two days for security reasons. INSEC does not list major violence on the election campaigns and election day (INSEC 2000).

11 The death toll reported by DEAN is lower than that reported by INSEC.

12 Three deaths per one million voters occurred in Nepal while there were 2 per million and 2 per half a million in Timor-Leste. Thirty-one, three and two violent incidents occurred per 100,000 registered voters in Timor-Leste, Nepal and Nigeria respectively. The methodology was developed by International Foundation for Electoral Systems (DEAN 2008: 2).

13 Armed/unarmed groups perpetrated 18 percent of violence while the state and public were responsible for 5 percent. The local election monitors of the DEAN could not identify 15 percent of violence perpetrators.

14 Thirty-seven candidates won by double margins in 2008 whereas ten and seven candidates had won in 1994 and 1999 respectively. In the 1990s 205 seats were elected by FPTP.

15 The Maoists, however, were not able to capture all the rising ethnic sentiments. In fact, the Madhesi and indigenous nationalities' parties played a significant role in halting the Maoist momentum in the central and eastern Tarai and in the far-eastern hills respectively. The groups mobilized because their demands conflicted not only with the state but with the Maoist positions as well. For instance, the hill-dominated Maoists were also influenced by hill nationalism. Some issues in the Maoists' 40-points demand given to the government prior to launching the insurgency were against the interests of the Madhesi. On the other hand, the proposal of a Kirat autonomous region went against the aspirations of the Limbus who wanted their own autonomous region. The ethnic indigenous nationalities' parties, even though not performing as well as the Madhesi parties, nevertheless, blunted the Maoist win by diverting towards them the disgruntled votes that could have gone to the Maoists.

Bibliography

Baral, Lok Raj, ed. 2005. *Election and Governance in Nepal*. New Delhi: Manohar.
Dahl, Robert A. 1971. *Polyarchy*. New Haven: Yale University Press.

de Sales, Anne. 2003. The Kham Magar Country: Between Ethnic Claims and Maoism. In *Resistance and the Nepalese State*, edited by D. N. Gellner. New Delhi: Social Science Press.

DEAN. 2008. *Election and Political Violence in Nepal.* Kathmandu: Democracy and Election Alliance Nepal.

Dhruba Kumar, ed. 2000. *Domestic Conflict and Crises of Governability in Nepal.* Kathmandu: CNAS.

Election Commission, Nepal. 2008. *Constituent Assembly Election 2064.* Election Commision, Nepal 2008 [cited April 2008 2008]. Available from http://www.election. gov.np/EN/.

Elklit, Jorgen, and Palle Svensson. 1997. What Makes Election Free and Fair. *Journal of Democracy* 8 (3):32–46.

Gyimah-Boadi, Emmanuel. 1999. Institutionalizing Credible Elections in Ghana. In *The Self-Restraining State: Power and Accountability in New Democracies*, edited by A. Schedler and L. Diamond. Boulder, CO: Lynne Rienner Publisher.

Hutt, Michael, ed. 2004. *Himalayan People's War: Nepal's Maoist Rebellion.* Bloomington: Indiana University Press.

INSEC. 2000. *Human Rights Year Book 2000.* Kathmandu: INSEC.

——. 2008. *Documentation and Dissemination Department, INSEC.* INSEC 2008 [accessed October 2008].

——. 2008. *Violation of CA Code of Conduct, Daily Report, April 4.* INSEC 2008 [accessed May 29 2008].

Jarstad, Anna K, and Timothy D Sisk, eds. 2008. *From War to Democracy: Dilemmas of Peacebuilding.* Cambridge: Cambridge University Press.

Kumar, Krishna, ed. 1998. *Postconflict Elections, Democratization, and International Assistance.* Boulder, CO: Lynne Rienner Publisher.

Lawoti, Mahendra. 2005. *Towards a Democratic Nepal: Inclusive Political Institutions for a Multicultural Society.* New Delhi, London, and Thousand Oaks: Sage Publications.

——. 2007. *Looking Back, Looking Forward: Centralization, Multiple Conflicts and Democratic State Building in Nepal.* Washington, D.C.: East-West Center.

Pathak, Bishnu. 2008. Nepal's 2008 Constituent Assembly Election: Converting Bullets into Ballots. Review of Reviewed Item. *Asia Pacific Bulletin, East-West Center* (15).

Sharma, Sudhindra, and Pawan Kumar Sen. 2008. Nepal Contemporary Political Situation V: Nationwide Opinion Survey. Lalitpur: Interdisciplinary Analysts.

Thapa, Deepak, and Bandita Sijapati. 2003. *A Kingdom Under Siege: Nepal's Maoist Insurgency, 1996 to 2003.* Kathmandu: The Printhouse.

15 Violent conflict and change

Costs and benefits of the Maoist rebellion in Nepal

Mahendra Lawoti and Anup K. Pahari[1]

Introduction

The violent Maoist movement has brought major changes in the Nepali polity and society, both positive and negative. Some of the changes are clear while others are not – changes are, in fact, still going on and others are being institutionalized. The Constitution is being drafted and many important issues like the federal and executive model are being contested and debated; the Maoists participated in the election to the Constituent Assembly but have not renounced violence and the party still declares its end goal as communism. On the other hand, the possibility of counterrevolution cannot be ruled out. In the meantime, ethnic movements have become more assertive – Madhesi have emerged as a strong force after their 2007 Movement, while some indigenous and Tarai groups have declared independence and/or are engaged in armed conflict and others have established armies in preparation for a longer struggle.

What will be the final outcome of the change processes started by the armed conflict? How did the conflict affect the society, polity and economy? Will democracy consolidate in new Nepal? Will it be inclusive and peaceful? These are important questions that many are interested to know more about, but the answers are not yet clear. We believe that an analysis of transformations to date and ongoing political processes and activism in the context of existing social, political and economic structure can provide clues to the answers. That will be our attempt in this chapter. Before that, however, we will briefly discuss the events and processes that led to the settlement of the armed conflict.

Peace settlement

The first peace talks

Peace settlements are said to come out of "hurting stalemates" (Arnson 1999: 8) but it is safe to conclude that the Maoists neither felt stalemated nor were they particularly hurting when they arrived for the first peace talks with the government in August 2001.[2] After three rounds of talks, Prachanda called off the talks and unilaterally broke the four-month-long ceasefire on November 21, 2001. On November

23, 2001, the People's Liberation Army (PLA) for the first time attacked the Royal Nepal Army (RNA) barracks in Dang, and captured the largest ever single cache of arms.

Fundamentally, the talks failed because the two sides approached them with fixed agendas, and were unwilling to reach a compromise in the course of the talks. Going into the negotiations, the Maoists wanted, at the very least, a promise of writing a new constitution. The state negotiators had no mandate to offer that to the Maoists. In the end, the state and the Maoists both used the talks to try to gain advantages over the other side. The Maoists in particular made little effort to hide the fact that the peace talks were a "strategic pause" in their campaign to advance the insurgency to the next level (Karki and Seddon 2003: 35; Ogura 2008: 16–18; Thapa and Sijapati 2003: 114).

The second peace talks

Several things had changed in the period between the first and the second talks between the Nepali state and the CPN-M. First, people's faith in the Nepali monarchy was badly shaken by the Royal Massacre of June 2001. Second, the new King Gyanendra dissolved the Parliament in 2002, thereby widening division in the establishment side and increasing the legitimacy crisis that progressively engulfed the state. Third, the Maoists had neutralized most of the rural police presence, and effectively downsized the presence and personnel of rival political parties. The state was weaker, politically more fragmented and still in search of a cohesive counter-insurgency strategy. The constitutional political parties had no stake in the peace process advanced by the King's appointed Government, and the Maoists were well aware of the Government's precarious position (Ogura 2008).

However, the Maoists were also facing tough challenges. The RNA had joined in the fray at the end of 2001. Even though the RNA had not been able to repress the Maoists (despite widespread expectation among the mainstream society), it had hurt the Maoists (see Mehta and Lawoti, this volume). The RNA had captured and killed a larger number of Maoist cadres, leaders, and sympathizers than the police had before. This had indirect fallout as well – it increased the cost of joining the Maoists, and the rebels faced challenges in recruitment for the PLA. The repeated call by the Maoist leadership for negotiations after less than a year of RNA mobilization suggests that the Maoists were encountering challenges.[3]

The second talks begun in April 2003 failed after three rounds.[4] The third round of talks was conducted in the Maoist stronghold of western Nepal on August 17 and 18. Responding to the written 24-point Maoist agenda submitted at the first peace talks in 2001, the Government negotiators read out a proposal that purported to offer a framework for addressing the core Maoist agendas with the single exception of the Maoist demand for elections to a constituent assembly.[5] A week later, Maoist supreme Prachanda ended the ongoing ceasefire and talks, citing the "Doramba" incident as part of his reason for withdrawing from the talks.[6]

A peace settlement with a Royal Government could not have met many of the radical ideals important to the CPN-M leadership and supporters. And certainly, it would have fallen far short of allowing the Maoists to claim that they had brought revolutionary change to the country. Just as in the first talks, it appears that the chief goal of the Maoists during the second talks was to buy time. Maoist ideologue Baburam Bhattarai claimed that the talks helped achieve a vital tactical goal, namely to isolate the monarchy (Bhattarai 2003).

Royal activism, political polarization and the transition to Republic

In 2005 the nature of the conflict in Nepal reverted to a two-way confrontation between the monarchy and the political parties, including the Maoists, from the previous three way conflict since 2002 among the monarchy, Maoists and parliamentary parties. This political realignment catalyzed by King Gyanendra's takeover of the Government, ironically, managed to help accomplish what previous attempts had failed to do – namely to convince the Maoists to give up armed rebellion.

On November 22, 2005 the Seven Party Alliance (SPA) and the Maoists signed the 12-Point Understanding (TPU) after secret negotiations in New Delhi, the crux of which was an agreement to resist and fight royal rule in Nepal, and end the armed conflict. On April 24, 2006, following 19 days of escalating nationwide mass protests, King Gyanendra was forced to revive the House of Representatives (HOR) before stepping down. Girija Prasad Koirala, the new Prime Minister, promptly announced the Government's commitment to hold elections to a constituent assembly and formally invited the CPN-M to sit for peace talks with the new Government.

By the time of the start of the third formal peace talks (May 26, 2006), most of the sticking points that plagued the two previous peace talks were more or less settled by the TPU. In short, events starting with the signing of the TPU and ending with the restoration of the HOR had already set the environment for a successful peace settlement between the CPN-M and the reconstituted Government of Nepal.

Despite lingering mutual animosities, the SPA and the CPN-M moved relatively quickly to end armed conflict and establish a new political order – chief mandates of the mass uprising. On January 15, 2007, the sitting Parliament approved the Interim Constitution and proceeded to dissolve itself to make room for a new Interim Legislature-Parliament. Eighty three CPN-M-nominated lawmakers entered the Interim Legislature-Parliament, bringing its total strength to 330. Eventually the Maoists joined the Interim Government.

The constituent assembly election and political realignment

Mainstreaming the Maoists hinged on holding elections for a Constituent Assembly, but the polls were postponed twice – from to June 20 to November 22, 2007, and finally to April 10, 2008. The April 10 Constituent Assembly elections proceeded as scheduled, despite widespread doubts, primarily because the major political stakeholders agreed that more things would go wrong in the country if the polls were postponed than if they were held. Defying all pre-poll predictions, the CPN-M emerged victorious (see chapter 14). In a nutshell, the Maoists won because their candidates and their agenda struck a chord with an overwhelmingly young electorate of which a full 22 percent were first-time voters with little or no history of loyalty to the traditional parties. Intimidation and threats by the Maoists also helped them to enlarge their vote and seat share. Furthermore, on most param-eters that influence voting, fair or foul, the Maoists were cautious and well-pre-pared while their major opponents were complacent and underprepared. And lastly, many Nepali voters believed that a vote for the Maoists was their only leverage to keep the party with a violent past from returning to rebellion.

Twelve years after the CPN-M opted out of multiparty electoral democracy, the radical communist party is now not only back in the parliamentary fold but has managed to shift the Nepali political mainstream considerably leftward. The elec-toral victory of the Maoists verified the tectonic shift in Nepali politics. For the first time in Nepal's electoral history (see figure 15.1), the communist parties collec-tively polled a majority of popular votes and seats: more than 57 percent of popular votes and 61 percent of seats in the Constituent Assembly.[7] Nepal transformed into a country where a majority voted for the communist parties in the twenty-first cen-tury, perhaps the only one of its kind. The 2008 tally is a huge improvement for a movement that received a paltry 7.2 percent of popular votes and 3.7 percent of seats in the 1959 general election, especially in the context of the global decline of the communist movement. The two largest communist parties alone would have mustered a majority of votes and seats in 2008 if they had united or formed a joint front.

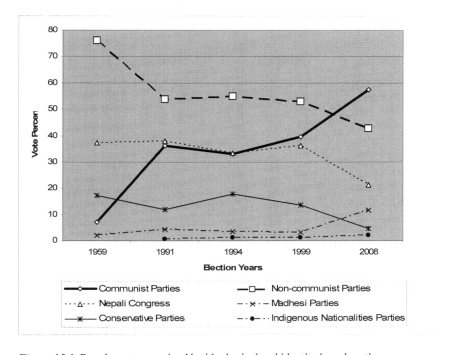

Figure 15.1 Popular votes received by ideological and identity based parties

The Maoists played a major role in this substantial expansion of the communist influence. During the three parliamentary elections in the 1990s (the Maoists boycotted the 1994 and 1999 elections), the communist parties polled more than 30 percent of votes but never reached 40 percent. The Maoists expanded communist votes by 18 percent in 2008 from the 1999 tally. The Maoists peeled votes away from the centrist Nepali Congress and conservative NDPs, in addition to stealing votes away from other communist parties such as the CPN-UML (see chapter 14).

It has been ironic for the non-communists that the communists for the first time won a majority of votes and seats in the Constituent Assembly election. This means that the communists will set the agenda for a new Constitution and could incorporate major extreme leftist agendas in the Constitution, which will guide the country for decades if not generations – a Constitution crafted by a Constituent Assembly would probably have higher legitimacy than the previous documents.

The Communist Party of Nepal–United Marxist Leninist (CPN-UML), a bitter rival of the Maoists for the left votes, may end up supporting many Maoist agendas so as to not appear a lesser communist or a traitor to the cause, especially if the party believes that such perception among communist voters may have caused its electoral loss. In fact, it may engage in a bidding war to project itself as a hardcore communist party in some realms and the process may contribute in further radicalizing the agenda of the Constituent Assembly. Nevertheless, conflicting organizational interests and personal ambitions and personality conflicts among the leaders of the CPN-M and CPN-UML, despite a similar name and ideology, may create hiccups in building a smooth alliance. However, even if the CPN-UML does not go along, with 38 percent of seats the Maoists have a veto power – other parties do not have the two-thirds votes required to pass the Constitution articles and hence Maoist approval is necessary for anything in the Constitution to be adopted. The Maoists will therefore greatly influence the outcome.[8]

The emergence of an effective multiparty system in place of the two- or three-party system of the 1990s in the Constituent Assembly, however, may help to moderate the Maoists. The election has produced at least four significant political parties with more than 50 seats. The adoption of a mixed electoral system, the increase in the FPTP constituencies in the Tarai, and the rise of new political forces, especially the Madhesi parties, contributed to the change.[9] The multiparty competition helped the Maoist to emerge as the largest party with two times more seats than the second largest party but will probably force the Maoists to moderate their agenda as they will have to build a coalition to form a government and adopt and implement policies.[10] The multiparty system may contribute in developing consensus politics but could invite governmental instability if not handled properly.

One consequence of the Maoist victory in the Constituent Assembly would be more reforms because they have the most radical agenda for change and they have been the most vigorous change agent compared to other large parties. Changes would have come even if other parties had emerged as the largest party because the second people's movement had mandated major reforms, but it is plausible to assume that the Maoists will initiate more changes than the Nepali Congress and CPN-UML. The chances of ethnic federalism, proportional or mixed electoral method, some sort of land reforms, and other more egalitarian and inclusive policies being adopted is higher with the Maoists at the helm.

Consequences of armed rebellion

The consequences of the insurgency, including the 2006 political transformation and the Constituent Assembly election discussed above, have been profound, positively as well as negatively, heralding perhaps the most rapid political, social, and cultural transformation affecting a large proportion of citizens after the conquest of Nepal. The discussion of varied consequences may help to provide pointers on future direction of the Maoist movement and the Nepali polity.

Human rights violations

A major cost of the civil war was the gross violation of human rights by both state and insurgents. The Maoists openly espoused and employed violence to kill opponents, security personnel and innocent people in their decade-long insurgency and, in principle, have still not renounced violence. The security forces, on the other hand, killed many Maoist cadres as well as people suspected of being Maoists, in their attempt to repress the insurgency. From February 13, 1996, to the end of 2006, the state was responsible for 63 percent of those killed in the insurgency (see figure 15.2),[11] while the Maoists killed nearly 5,000 people or 37 percent (INSEC 2007). The Maoists sometimes employed very cruel methods and engaged in demonstration killings to terrorize opponents and other villagers into submission.

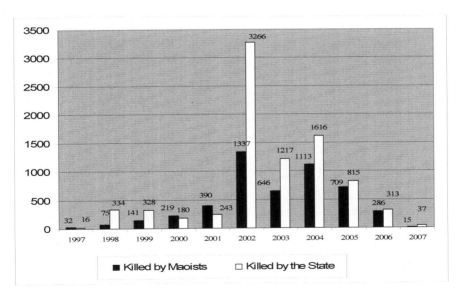

Figure 15.2 People killed by the Maoist and the state during the insurgency and afterward

Beyond killings, the state and the Maoists employed many different forms of violent methods. The Maoists threatened and beat up people they considered as enemies. The Maoists also employed public shaming tactics, especially in the villages. They often smeared black soot on the faces of political opponents and shaved their heads, garlanded them with shoes and took them around the villages and towns. INSEC recorded 116, 117 and 89 such incidents in 2004, 2005 and 2006 respectively. They would also beat people with sticks as a form of public shaming. Such "stick actions" often were employed for less important people or "lesser crimes." The security forces, on the other hand, harassed common people during checks along roads, patrol forays into the hinterlands, and counter insurgency operations.

The Maoist abducted and kidnapped a large number of people during the insurgency. INSEC records 85,185 cases of known abductions from 1996 to 2006. The real number could be higher because many instances of abductions in villages went unrecorded. School children, village opposition leaders and sometimes whole villages were abducted in groups and taken to the Maoist workshop and public meetings in different villages, and sometimes kept there for weeks. Some years witnessed extremely high numbers of abductions of school children. INSEC recorded abductions of 33,160 students from schools in 2005. Many of the abductees were subsequently released but some were killed while others joined the movement voluntarily or under pressure.

The state and the Maoists disappeared people as well. According to INSEC, the state disappeared 828 and the Maoists disappeared 105 persons during the insurgency. The disappeared people were often taken into custody but their whereabouts were not revealed. The security forces often kept the disappeared people in army barracks. Some of the disappeared are suspected to have been tortured, killed and buried in mass graves.

Due process rights were abused before and during the insurgency by both the state and the Maoists. The state levelled false charges against the Maoists, their sympathizers and the common people, beginning with the security operations in the mid-western hill districts conducted prior to the start of the insurgency. Some of the imprisoned were forced to spend longer periods of time in jail without trial than their crimes would have warranted even if they were found guilty. Likewise, the government also disobeyed court rulings. The security forces would re-arrest Maoist cadres and leaders outside the court immediately after the courts released them. The due process rights were more widely violated by the state during the state of emergency when the security forces acted with impunity.

The Maoists confiscated the property of opponents and better-off people in many parts of the country. In other instances, people out-migrated because of Maoist threats. Tens of thousands of people left their homes in the villages. Between 2002 and 2004, 50,365 people were displaced: 3,837 and 21,320 people by the state and the Maoists respectively, whereas 25,199 persons emigrated from fear and terror (INSEC 2008). The impacts of many of these human rights violations, such as war-related trauma, have not been fully recorded, but the effects will continue to be felt for a long time into the future. A long-term consequence of the insurgency has been the socialization of a violent political culture, owing to which human rights abuses have continued, by the Maoists and their fronts as well as other groups with various grievances.

Attack and support of liberal democracy

The Maoists launched the insurgency against a fledgling parliamentary democracy. Political rights and civil liberties of a growing segment of Nepalis were constrained as the insurgency spread nationwide and human rights violations, discussed earlier, became routine, reflecting severe restrictions of political and civil liberties. The Maoists curtailed free movement of people in their areas of control. Sometimes they would not allow villagers to travel to the district headquarters, while outsiders had to get permission to visit their base areas. The Maoists also restricted free expression and forbade political opponents to organize and mobilize in their area of influence. They expelled many local leaders of non-Maoist parties, government officials, and family members of security personnel from villages. The situation had deteriorated so much that by 2002 the government could not hold local and parliamentary elections owing to Maoist obstructions and threat.

The government also restricted the Maoists' right to freely express, publish and disseminate their policies and positions. Eighteen journalists were killed during the insurgency by both the state and the Maoists. As discussed earlier, the state and the Maoists did not recognize due process rights. During the state of emergency, the state curtailed press freedom and political mobilization. Not only Maoists but also the common people suffered from the unrestrained activities of the security forces.

The relationship of the Maoists with liberal democracy, however, has been complex. As discussed above, initially they undermined the fledgling democracy by frontally attacking it. However, once the king took over in 2005, they actively participated in the movement that forced the king to give up power in April 2006. Their intolerant attitudes and violence against citizens and members of other parties even after the peace settlement, though limited, does throw into question their commitment to democratic norms and practices.

Socio-political transformation

Large scale socio-political transformations have resulted directly and indirectly from the Maoist movement. The two-and-half-century-old monarchy was uprooted. The state has been declared secular in place of a Hindu state. Likewise, the Interim Constitution 2006 has committed to establish a federal system in the country, ending a two-and-half-century-old unitary system. The Constituent Assembly election was held with a mixed electoral method. The identity movements – particularly the Madhesi but the indigenous nationalities and Dalit movements as well – forced the ruling interim coalition to end the unitary system and previous electoral method. But the Maoists' contribution towards these changes was significant because they not only backed the demands but had mainstreamed the agendas of federalism and proportional electoral method in the country. These institutional reforms have changed the rules of the game and as a result hitherto marginalized sectors and groups will probably have more presence and influence in the governance of the country. These institutional changes are significant, especially because institutional inertia normally restrains major reforms (Lijphart 1999; Rothstein 1996).

The Maoist rebellion catalyzed indirect political ramifications as well. Citizenship certificates were distributed to more than two million Nepalis after the April 2006 changes. Mostly Madhesi but also Dalit and indigenous nationalities and the offspring of Nepali women married to foreigners were denied citizen certificates until then despite petitions and movements demanding it.

With the end of monarchy,[12] formal dynastic politics has weakened. Among the political parties, the Constituent Assembly election outcome may have undermined the control of the Nepali Congress by the Koirala clan with the loss of most stalwarts from the family. However, political nepotism seems to be persistent. Many Maoist ministers, including the prime minister, have appointed family members to public offices.[13]

Ethnic, caste and gender inclusion

Post-insurgency politics has become more inclusive. For instance, the Constituent Assembly is more inclusive than previous Parliaments. The president, vice president and chairperson of the Constituent Assembly hail from the marginalized groups even though these are largely symbolic positions. With a total of 52 seats, the MPRF of the Madhesi emerged from the Constituent Assembly elections as the country's newest and unsuspected power broker. The Constituent Assembly has 50 Dalit members. This is a significant improvement compared to 1994 and 1999 when no Dalit were elected to HOR and only a single Dalit was elected in 1991. The representation of women (33 percent), indigenous nationalities and Madhesi also increased significantly.[14] The rise of the nationalist parties, election of large numbers of marginalized groups under FPTP from the Maoist party, and quotas for Dalit, indigenous nationalities, Madhesi and women in the 60 percent of proportionally elected seats helped to increase the representation of marginalized groups. However, the major mainstream political parties, including the Maoists, are still led by the CHHEM. An important question is whether ethnic/caste and women representatives elected from the mainstream political parties can effectively represent the marginalized groups' issues because while some may not identify with the issues others may be constrained from the parties' primary emphasis on class and the antipathy of top leadership towards ethnic/caste issues.

Exclusion, however, still remains very high in many other important sectors. Exclusion of women, Dalit, indigenous nationalities, and Madhesi in the bureaucracy, judiciary, security sector, constitutional councils, cabinet, political parties, economy, academia, media, and other civil society organizations is still high. Past post-movement recruitment history is not inspiring either. Domination of CHHEM increased in Parliament and bureaucracy at the cost of marginalized groups in later years compared to immediately after the 1990 transformation (Lawoti 2008). A section of the dominant group is also fiercely resisting autonomy for ethnic groups – they are arguing for models that they claim are "non-ethnic" but in which the CHHE will dominate not only the center but also most or all regions as well (Lawoti 2009).

The formal structural and policy reforms could also be hindered by informal institutions and practices such as the caste system, ethnic prejudice, sexism, hill nationalism and so on that are widespread among the elite power wielders of the society. The formal structural political reforms, thus, may not necessarily lead to desirable societal transformations. Social movements might be necessary to enforce the implementation of announced reforms and to counter the resistance for the status quo.

Social transformation

The insurgency also introduced some social changes. It increased social and political awareness in rural Nepal and mobilized large numbers of people as never before; and it changed existing power relations in many areas by attacking traditional norms, practices and sources of discrimination. This often reduced traditional oppression faced by the powerless, the poor and marginalized groups. The punitive public actions against the village elite often conveyed a message to the poor people that things were no longer firmly in the control of the traditional elite while the traditional elite also may have felt unsure of their position with the rise of a new source of power that challenged them and their base of privilege and power. The fear among the rural elite of being targeted by the Maoists and the possibility of resistance by the recently empowered commoners may have cautioned the unscrupulous elements to continue with repressive practices; or even if they attempted, they often faced resistance or non-compliance. The patron–client networks that had sustained oppression eroded and the socioeconomic oppression decreased with the undermining of the traditional power base. Hence, one can make a case that the situation became less oppressive for many poor people if they did not oppose the Maoists. However, as discussed earlier, people had to supply the Maoists with food and resources, and many became victims of new forms of human rights violations, which were sometimes very cruel.

The Maoist policy of attacking and undermining traditional practices and norms such as caste hierarchy, religious and social practices, sexism, and ethnic prejudice weakened male-biased norms, untouchability, and ethnic domination. Human rights activists and Dalit activists acknowledge that untouchability was reduced in Maoist-controlled areas during the insurgency because they forcefully implemented the ban on it. Dalit were encouraged to enter homes of the "high" caste and eat with them while the "high" caste members who resisted were often punished (see Lecomete-Tiloune, this volume).

Likewise, the Maoists punished men engaged in polygamous marriages and other sexist practices. Women also became empowered with the blurring of the traditional role of men and women as women participated in the public domain – rather than being limited to the private sphere as earlier – including as members of the fighting force. The indigenous nationalities became more empowered by recognition of their demands for ethnic equality and autonomy, establishment of ethnic/caste fronts, and the formation of autonomous regions.

Many Dalit, indigenous nationalities, and women faced negative consequences as well. The Maoists killed many Dalit, indigenous nationalities, and women who supported the government or other political parties while the state killed members of the groups on suspicion of being Maoists. The rebels often forced the Dalit to repair or manufacture weapons and sew and repair uniforms, with or without compensation. The security forces, on the other hand, suspected the Dalit of being Maoist sympathizers because of the services they had to render to the Maoists. Many Dalit abandoned the profession or migrated to escape from cross-fire (Biswakorma 2004). In the case of the indigenous nationalities, many became "cannon fodder" in the civil war as they were the fighting force on both sides. The war increased the burden of many women as men were killed or migrated to escape forced recruitment by the Maoists or joined the Maoist ranks (Manchanda 2004). The vulnerability of women and children, especially families of Maoist victims who could no longer live in the villages, increased as they had to migrate to new places, often leaving behind whatever resources they had. Likewise, the insurgency also restricted the work of NGOs, including those providing services for women, because of which women were deprived of useful services (Crawford et al. 2007).

Overall, the impact on Dalit, indigenous nationalities and women, however, might have been positive because of the erosion of sexism, ethnic prejudice and discrimination, and the weakening of the caste system and the practice of untouchability. Crimes involving women victims – such as rape and trafficking – showed a declining trend as the insurgency spread (see figures 15.3 and 15.4). Activists of INSEC, a leading human rights organization, point out that the Maoist campaign against such crimes contributed to the decline.

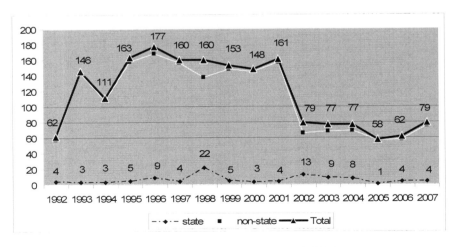

Figure 15.3 Rape incidents recorded by INSEC (2008), 1992–2007

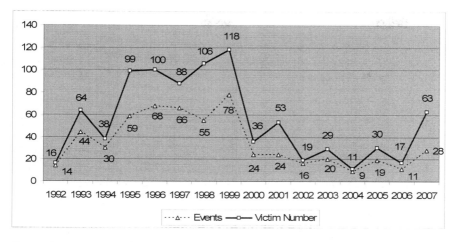

Figure 15.4 Women trafficked recorded by INSEC (2008), 1992–2007

Economic transformation or decline

The major drive behind the growth of the insurgency was economic transformation but, ironically, the immediate impact on the economy has been negative. The insurgency, in fact, stunted economic growth. During 1987–88 to 1994–95 the real GDP growth (%) was 4.1 while it declined to 3.8 from 1995–96 to 2001–2 (Sharma 2006: 1242). The real GDP growth declined to 2.7 percent in 2001–2, when the war escalated, while it had been 5 percent from 1995 to 2000 (Deraniyagala 2005: 54). Many factors contributed to the decline. Tourist arrival declined because of insecurity and negative publicity. Investment in manufacturing and service industries diminished owing to the poor law and order situation. Capital of many small traders in the hills dried up as the Maoists did not pay for a long period for goods taken on credit. Existing industries and service sectors suffered from militant trade unionism, closures and extortions by the Maoists. Many banks were looted and industries destroyed (Dhruba Kumar 2003; Sapkota 2004; Pyakuryal and Sainju 2007; Dhakal et al. 2004). The economy could further stagnate if the Maoist-led government constrains competition in the market. Because of trade union militancy and extortion, many industries have closed down while Maoist near-monopoly over contracts in the construction industry and the collection of commission in land transaction, vehicle registration and so on has negatively affected the economy and consumers.

The economic stagnation affected rural regions acutely where food production declined and food supply was insufficient because of periodic disruptions of food sale by the state to deprive the insurgents. The forced extortion of food, grain and money by the Maoists decreased food security of rural people as they had to part with already meagre incomes and produce. The situation was aggravated because the rural Maoist strongholds already faced food shortages because of barren lands or neglected farms as able men and women either participated in the insurgency or migrated to escape Maoist threats and forced recruitment.

Social services also suffered indirectly from the escalation of the war. The increase in defence spending by the government meant reduced investment in the social sectors. By 2001–2, spending on the police and army had more than doubled since 1997–98 while spending on social services fell below the levels of 1997–98 (Pyakurel and Sainju 2007: 12).

The destruction of infrastructure by the Maoists also pushed the country backwards. The Maoists had destroyed 1,683 or 43 per cent of Village Development Committee (VDC) office buildings by July 2003 (Dhakal et al. 2004). They also destroyed many government office buildings, police posts, airports, electricity power stations and substations, telecommunication towers and bridges.[15] The Maoists vandalized many schools and forced them to close down during the frequent general strikes. They also chased away many INGO and NGO development programs from rural areas. The provision of services and development projects also suffered from the unwillingness of staff to work in the Maoist-affected areas. The rural people were deprived of even the occasional services they received, such as agricultural extension and credit.

Poor peasants, however, could benefit in the long run if the land-based patron–client network, which was undermined by Maoist activities, is effectively dismantled and the poor and powerless gain more autonomy in socio-economic-political matters. An alternative source of employment, however, is necessary if this is to happen. A genuine land reform that provides land to the poor peasants could help complete and consolidate this possibility. Large scale collectivization of land, the communist ideal, if implemented, however, could spell disaster, as in former USSR, China and Vietnam.[16] Despite highlighting land reform to mobilize peasants, the Maoists have not pushed it forcefully, unlike other political issues such as republicanism and the proportional electoral method which had direct consequences and bearing for the Maoist leadership. Land reforms could stimulate agricultural production as small landholder farmers have been found to increase productivity per unit of land by investing surplus time and resources in the land they have (Binswanger and Elgin 1998). To date, however, the Maoists have grabbed land haphazardly and on an ad hoc basis and distributed it to their cadres and supporters while the victims were often their political opponents. In some cases, the victims became the new landless.

Peace-building and democracy

A peace settlement is a welcome respite after a long and brutal civil war but it does not guarantee a lasting peace or democracy. Some countries like Namibia (1989), Mozambique (1992), and El Salvador (1992) established peace and democracy after peace settlements,[17] but others like Angola (1991) and Liberia (1990) reverted back to civil war while some like Cambodia (1991) and Eritrea (1991) attained a level of peace but became non-democratic after a few years. Fortna (2008: 74), in fact, found that "peacekeeping has no clear or strong positive effect on democratization" after a comprehensive study of all conflicts that reached ceasefires since 1989. Even though peace-building and democratization are desired goals after ending a civil war, they may not go together. Sometimes compromises necessary for peace restrict democratization while at other times advances in democratization could threaten peace. For instance, electoral competition immediately after peace settlement could exacerbate tensions and could threaten the peace (Hoglund 2008). In this context, the salient question for Nepal is whether the peace settlement of 2006 will lead to a lasting peace and functioning democracy.

The electoral victory of the Maoists may have contributed to peace-building by reducing the possibility of the Maoists returning to armed rebellion – there is less reason to revert back to insurgency when you head the government. However, several challenges still remain. Ambivalent pronouncements and attitudes of the Maoist leadership towards violence have fostered lingering doubts about their commitment towards peace and democracy. For reasons that are not clear, the Maoists have refused to renounce violence even after heading the government. This is in contrast to other post-war cases like Northern Ireland where pledges to non-violence were used as means to regulate violence after peace settlements (Hoglund 2008: 97).

A split within the Maoist party, which cannot be completely ruled out, could also threaten the peace process. A sharp division within the Maoists between the hard-liners, who want to establish a People's Republic immediately, and pragmatists, who want to operate within a multiparty democracy, became clear when despite various attempts, instead of presenting a single official document as is usually done, the chairman Prachanda and dissident leader Kiran presented two reports at the national cadre conference on November 21–26, 2008. As the leadership moves away from the core principle of Maoism after joining mainstream electoral politics, the resulting ambivalence in ideology could widen the schism in the party. If the Maoists split up, there is always the possibility that one faction could revert to insurgency.

The integration and/or disbanding of the PLA is emerging as another major challenge for the peace process. The existence of two armies in the country even after more than two years of peace settlement points to serious work still left to complete the peace process. The Maoists want to integrate the PLA into the Nepal Army, preferably collectively, but other parties and the Nepal Army resist this formula. The failure to settle the issue properly earlier on in the peace agreement has resulted in the two sides interpreting the ambivalent clauses differently.[18]

Another major challenge is governance and rule of law. In the course of the past decade's massive political upheavals, Nepal has also become more anarchic and ungovernable. The continuing violence, extortions, and excesses by the Young Communist League (YCL) and other Maoist cadres have undermined law and order in the country. Some violence may continue in post-war societies (Hoglund 2008) but establishment of paramilitary forces like YCL does not help to subdue it. Unable to force the Maoists into disbanding the YCL, which the Maoist established after the PLA was to be cantoned under UNMIN (United Nations Mission in Nepal) supervision, other political forces have formed similar outfits. The frequent confrontations between the Youth Force of the CPN-UML and YCL has increased tension and undermined the rule of law.[19] The criminalization of politics and the politicization of crime, therefore, are both on their way to becoming major barriers to governance and rule of law.[20]

Rapid and massive political changes have unleashed an avalanche of public aspirations. The state's organizational, fiscal, and security resources and infrastructure, however, remain at or even below pre-insurgency levels. The CPN-M is perhaps fast realizing, as indicated by Prachanda's public admissions a number of times, that an armed rebellion was more easily managed than a fractious, haphazard, and as some would say, a failed state of 27 million (Riaz and Basu 2007).

A major "unexpected" threat for the peace-building process is the rising ethnic assertion and mobilization. Ironically, settlement with an insurgent group itself granted legitimacy to violent methods and the government's approach of negotiating with groups only after they disrupt life through strikes and closers is not sending a good signal. Disgruntled ethnic groups, who mistrust the CHHEM leadership's commitment towards ethnic equality, have perceived that violence bears fruits. A number of armed Madhesi groups in the Tarai and indigenous groups in the eastern hills are waging insurgencies for ethnic autonomy or secession. Media has reported that other groups like Tharus and Tamangs have also established armies. Some of these groups govern local areas with militia and army, collect taxes, adjudicate local conflicts, maintain labor camps, and run communication outlets like newspapers and FM radios. A few rebel ethnic groups responded to the government call for negotiations in late 2008 and at the beginning of 2009, while others seem disinclined to sit for talks. The government has shown maturity by continuously negotiating with various agitating groups. However, the lack of implementation of previous agreements by the government and holding of the Constituent Assembly without reaching settlements with armed ethnic outfits could haunt the peace process later if some of the groups broaden their organizations and influence. The ethnic grievances, if not accommodated in time, could unleash large-scale violent conflicts. Scholars have pointed out that ethnic mobilization during transition in new democracies could turn violent (Snyder 2000) and even transform into secessionist movements if autonomy is not provided (Gurr 1993, 2000). The challenge for Nepal is to simultaneously address positively the class and ethnic cleavages the country has inherited for peace and democracy to be durable.

Finally and crucially, it is well to remember that political mobilization does not automatically translate into economic and resource mobilization. While the CPN-M, and others inspired by its success, have mobilized sizeable masses and stirred their aspirations, the profile of economic assets and possibilities in Nepal remains unchanged. In fact, excessive partisan mobilization of trade unions by the Maoists may have further eroded the viability of the national economy.[21] The Maoists have promised to raise Nepali per capita income to $3,000 per year from its current level of $350.00 per year (Mehta 2008), arguably based on exploiting the country's tourism and hydro-power potentials.[22] However, whether and how soon the CPN-M delivers on such lofty promises will determine whether a New Nepal actually emerges out of the political transformations that the CPN-M has engineered, or whether, as in regimes past, economic underachievement, among other things, ends up acting as the proverbial albatross around the neck of the CPN-M and the New Nepal.

Future political regime

Politicians and civil society leaders have coined the phrase "New Nepal" as a metaphor for their common hope and vision for a democratic state but there is no more than a skeletal consensus on what a "New Nepal" means in practical terms, or how to get there. With the abolishment of the common enemy – the monarchy – the mistrust and rift between the Maoists and other political parties has widened. At the political level, Nepal is being pulled simultaneously in a number of directions, at times at variance with one another. While non-Maoist parties are pushing for a liberal, plural democratic republic, the CPN-M has made it clear that it seeks a transitional political framework – a stepping stone of sorts towards a true Peoples' Republic. As a result of the often mutually conflicting political goals of the major stakeholders, the constitution-making process in Nepal has been delayed and is liable to be deeply contentious till the very end.

If the Maoists do not revert back to the insurgency, the question is which type of political regime will emerge from the Constituent Assembly dominated by the Maoists and the polity with the current political actors? Three scenarios are possible: the Maoists establish a People's Republic; the polity opts for liberal democracy and democracy consolidates; or a liberal democratic framework is adopted but political actors govern with semi-democratic norms.

The ideal preference of the Maoists is to establish a People's Republic or one-party communist state with token opposition parties. Even if some pragmatic leaders may not be enthusiastic for a People's Republic right away, the hardliners could push for it. Prachanda makes radical speeches when he addresses party cadres and PLA soldiers. This suggests that the cadre base is radical, and he spouts radicalism to assuage the cadre base. He may not always succeed, however, because the highly indoctrinated cadres may still favor the dream of a communist republic, especially if the government stumbles and fails to meet their expectations and the hardliners exploit the situation to push for a People's Republic. The hardliners could accuse the pragmatists of deviating from party ideology and principles as the leadership compromises on various issues, such as return of confiscated properties or integration of the PLA. If the party base pushes to establish a People's Republic, Prachanda's operating style of going with the majority to remain the party chief suggests that the Maoist could attempt to establish a People's Republic, through force or otherwise. If the Maoists are successful in neutralizing the Nepal Army, the fractious political parties may be hard pressed to mount an immediate and effective resistance against the Maoist juggernaut.

The national, regional, and international context, however, may prevent the Maoists from pursuing the People's Republic option. Even if the Maoists establish the People's Republic, the recent Nepali experience suggests that the non-democratic haul may not be a long one. The last non-democratic interregnum lasted less than four years (2002–6). The fact that the top Maoist leadership have repeatedly reached settlements on various issues with other political actors suggests that unless they are pushed in the People's Republic direction by the hardliners, they may gradually give up that objective.

The second possibility is that the Maoists agree to some form of liberal democratic framework, even if that term is not used to describe it. The Maoists may agree to this regime type because it has rewarded them and they see benefits in sticking with it. National and international actors and contexts will pressure the Maoist to go along with some form of liberal democracy. More importantly, as the Maoists govern and strike deals with different political actors to remain in power, the liberal democratic system may suck them deeper into it.

It is questionable, however, whether the polity with the Maoists at the helm will transform into a true liberal democracy where full political rights and civil liberties of citizens, especially of opponents, are respected and protected. Toleration of activities that one dislikes is a necessary element of liberal democracy but the Maoists are very intolerant of criticism and opponents they deem enemies. Even though such activities of the Maoists have declined compared to the war years, they still harass, thrash, and sometimes even kill their opponents. They also continue to infringe upon property rights of individuals despite repeated pledges by the leadership to not repeat such activities. For instance, Maoist cadres and trade unions have attacked or disrupted all major media houses since entering the peace process.

Thus a good possibility, at least in the short run, is that the New Nepal would be some form of illiberal democracy. On the one hand, the Maoists may initiate major reforms and obtain crucial support from various sections of the society, but on the other hand they may continue with coercion and intimidation, which has served them well to date. Periodic elections could be held but the Maoists may continue to employ coercive means and methods to win elections and sustain their rule. The Maoists would have access to state resources in addition to their paramilitary organizations and cadres to influence electoral outcomes. The regime may resemble some sort of semi-democracy, and the Maoists may head and support this type of regime for the medium run unless they implode internally from the ideological contradictions resulting from entering into a competitive multiparty system.

Even if the Maoists follow a liberal democratic path, the belief in centralization among major political parties, especially by the Maoists, could create problems for the future polity. The Maoists and other communists may in fact push for centralization even within a federal set-up owing to ideological imperatives and a belief in central planning and vanguard leadership. The Maoist espousal of the presidential system appears not to be based on a belief in separation of power but their desire for an extremely powerful president. One major problem that undermined democracy in the 1990s was the weak accountability system owing to centralization that was unable to check power abuse and corruption (Lawoti 2007b). Actors who abused power, including the Maoists, have not been held accountable even after the peace settlement. The discussion and debates on state restructuring have not focused seriously on accountability mechanisms to date. Political leaders accuse opponents of corruption and power abuse but are collectively reluctant to establish effective accountability mechanisms because it might come to haunt them in the future. Thus preference for centralization among political leaders may prevent the establishment of an effective accountability mechanism, because of which the problems of power abuse and corruption witnessed in the 1990s may continue in "New" Nepal.

If the country adopts a liberal democratic framework and the Maoists support it by renouncing coercive methods regarding political and civil rights of citizens, then there is a possibility for democracy to consolidate. If the Maoists head the government through subsequent elections, there is a very good likelihood that they will introduce major reforms to address class, ethnic/caste, regional, and gender inequalities. Such reforms are necessary to prevent other violent conflicts and to consolidate democracy. However, effective pressure from the media, human rights organizations, political parties and international actors is necessary to make the Maoists shed coercive methods, become tolerant of criticism and dissenting views, and develop a democratic culture.

A second pathway toward the consolidation of democracy could be that the Maoists win the next election but govern without regard for people's rights and democratic values despite introducing major reforms. The excesses reach a critical level and the people deliver them a blow during the subsequent election. This bitter lesson will teach them to develop a democratic culture to win the hearts of the people. The emergent multiparty system, because of which no party, including the Maoists, dominates the polity, may facilitate the process. Federalism that effectively divides power between the centre and regions and proportional representative electoral method could facilitate the process through promoting power-sharing among multiple parties, even though superficially the process may look messy.

Conclusion: where is the revolution?

The rise of the Maoists in Nepal has shown that violent communist rebellions are possible even after the end of the Cold War, though they might have to be ultra strategic, co-opt ethnic issues and change track along the way. It has also shown that if substantive reforms are not conducted incrementally in polities, major transformations could occur through violent rebellion, the cost of which was heavy, resulting in large-scale death, destruction, and displacement.

If social revolution is defined as social, political, and economic transformation, has social revolution occurred in Nepal? Will the changes to date lead to other changes? It is too early to tell because ramifications of the rebellion are still being manifest but we can point to changes or their absence in various sectors. The attempt is not to judge whether the changes are good or bad but to recognize ruptures from the past.

One could plausibly argue that Nepal is on its way to a political revolution – the 240-year-old monarchy is no more; the Interim Constitution has committed to establish a federal system; the Constituent Assembly election was held with a mixed electoral system and political awareness and mobilization increased significantly. Whether a People's Republic is established or liberal democracy is consolidated, the changed political structure and culture will impact a large number of people.

The verdict is not clear with regard to social transformation. The Maoists did bring about major changes in relations among different caste and ethnic groups, and men and women, by violently pursuing the cause of the disadvantaged groups, but how significant and lasting the changes have been is not clear. Dalit activists point out that caste practices were reverted after the Maoists reached a peace settlement and halted violent methods to enforce those reforms (see Lecomte-Tilouine, this volume). The informal institutions such as the caste system, ethnic and religious prejudice, sexism, and hill nationalism are very deeply ingrained in the society, and they continue to obstruct social transformation. For groups like the indigenous nationalities, Madhesi, and Muslims, real social transformation will not come without the provision of autonomy for self-governance.

Perhaps the Maoist rebellion's least impact to date has been on the economic front. Ironically, the Maoist leadership has not placed much importance on economic transformation despite primarily being a class-based insurgency. For instance, as discussed earlier, they never insisted on launching land reform right away, unlike their insistence for the immediate abolition of the monarchy. However, the political transformation could lead to changes in the economic sector. The Maoists might change the distribution system for the benefit of the poor but the challenge is to generate resources as well. How the economy will perform under Maoist watch, if they return to power, will depend upon the type of economic policies they adopt. Successful land reform, a focus on agriculture, and certain industrial policies may increase production and reduce poverty, but obstructing the private sector and constraining competition could become counter-productive.

Nepal is undergoing major political changes but the challenge is to prevent the changes from going overboard. Will the Maoists attempt to transform Nepal into a communist state? The debate among the Maoists over a Federal Democratic Republic versus a People's Republic seriously questions the Maoist commitment towards democracy. For the Maoists, however, an inability to establish communism could be better in the long run. They will still probably introduce major reforms even without establishing communism if they win elections, thus contributing to the country's development, whereas pushing to establish communism would invite disaster and discredit them in the long run. Attempts at the consolidation of communism after its establishment led to millions of deaths in the USSR and China. In China, Mao's Great Leap Forward and collectivization killed around 30 million peasants while Stalin's collectivization killed around 14 million.

Whether the ongoing changes will have positive or negative impacts – or in what combination – in the society it is too early to tell. The communists have a zeal for reforms but they also demonstrate questionable democratic attitudes and behaviors. The rise of the Maoists in Nepal is thus going to result in major changes, but whether a new Nepal will be democratic, and the political rights and civil liberties of groups with different ideologies and worldviews will be respected and tolerated, remains to be seen.

Notes

1 A few sections draw liberally from Lawoti (forthcoming, 2009; 2005).
2 The first round of first-ever official peace negotiations between the Nepali State and the Communist Party of Nepal-Maoist (CPN-M) was conducted on August 30, 2001, in Godavari Resort (Kathmandu outskirts). The second round of talks was held at a jungle resort in Thakurdwar (Bardia district) between the same teams from September 13 to 14, 2001. The final round of talks was terminated without agreement at Godavari Resort on November 13, 2001.
3 Prachanda and Baburam Bhattarai called for a truce and dialogue more than half a dozen times in the six months prior to the ceasefire on January 29, 2003. According to the South Asia Terrorism Portal's (2008) time line, some of the calls were made on August 11, September 16, September 22, October 25, November 13 and December 3, 2002.
4 The first round of the second Peace Talks was held in Kathmandu on April 27, 2003. A 22-point code of conduct was signed by the State and Maoist representatives. The second round was also held in Kathmandu, on May 9, 2003, where the negotiators agreed on some goodwill gestures.
5 See Pathak (2005: 360–61) for an English translation of the government's proposal.
6 On August 16, a day before the third round of talks was to start, the RNA apprehended 19 unarmed Maoists from a meeting in the village of Doramba (Ramechhap district), and shot, killed and buried them on the way back to army barracks. Dr. Prakash Chandra Lohani, a government negotiator, however, says that the Maoists already had plans to break off the talk – they were reluctant to sit for the last round of talks but the government side persuaded them to hear the government's response to their demands. (Personal communication.)
7 The highest vote and seat obtained earlier by the communist parties collectively was around 40 percent of votes in 1999 and 42 percent of seats in 1994.
8 The Maoists unified with the CPN-Unity Center on January 12, 2009, and renamed the party Unified CPN-M. The unification added seven seats to the Maoist fold.
9 The party system may continue to change after the state is restructured along federal lines. This suggests that Nepal will probably encounter a coalitional politics at the center in the future. If the Constituent Assembly does not craft a political structure that complements coalitional politics, the incongruence between the structure and political dynamics may foster instability in the polity.
10 With a similar percentage of popular votes, the CPN-UML had not become the undisputed largest party in the 1990s. In 1999, the CPN-UML had become only the second largest party with 30.74 percent of votes.
11 The state killed more during the nine months of state of emergency: 2,580 persons from November 26, 2001, to August 31, 2002. The state had killed only 991 persons in the previous six years.
12 See Lecomte-Tilouine (2004) for an interesting analysis of Prachanda's actions, which reflected that of a warrior king.
13 Since December 2008, to the author's knowledge, a list containing Prachanda's nine and Baburam Bhattarai's six family members appointed to various public offices did the rounds in online forums and through emails. Maoist intellectuals have also accused Prachanda of appointing family members to public offices (Khanal 2008).
14 ICG (2008) mentions that 192 and 204 indigenous nationalities and Madhesi respectively were elected (out of 575) but Darnal (2009) gives the number of indigenous nationalities and Madhesi as 216 and 196 respectively in the full Constitution Assembly of 601.
15 A weekly magazine, *Samaya* (August 12–18, 2005: 38, cited in Upreti 2006: 277–78), listed the following damages to infrastructure by the Maoists (units inside parenthesis): police posts (579); district police posts (35); airports (14); jails (7); courts (18); post offices (641); health posts (85); forest office and range posts (290); telecom towers

(128); powerhouses and electricity offices (96); irrigation infrastructure (30); district education offices (34); agricultural offices (149); livestock offices (24); social conservation offices (8); land revenue offices (43); land reform offices (9); women's development offices (18); revenue offices/units (22); radio station (2); national parks and reserves (8); bridges (44); dairy development units (9); municipalities and wards (77); VDCs (1621); drinking water systems (22); food depots/stores (25); schools (159); treasury offices (5); financial institutions (222); land measurement offices (15); family planning offices/units (38); Sajha transport (7); roads (45) – a total of 5,138.

16 The few 'communes' established by the Maoists in the base areas did not produce enough food for commune members, despite propaganda (Lecome-Tilouine, this volume).

17 Ceasefire dates, inside parentheses, are from Fortna (2008).

18 The debate revolves around integrating the PLA into the Nepal Army, collectively or based on individual qualification, as well as on the question of whether to integrate into the Nepal Army or into other security forces.

19 Many other parties have established similar youth fronts (see Punmagar 2008).

20 Ian Martin, the Special Representative of the United Nation's General Secretary, told the United Nation's Security Council in mid January that "Not a single perpetrator of major human rights violations, whether committed during the armed conflict or since its end, has been properly brought to justice" (Post Report 2009).

21 Escalating labour union militancy by the Maoist union has already made Nepal less attractive to business and investment (*Wall Street Journal*, 2008).

22 While the CPN-M pegs its hopes on a future made prosperous by hydro-energy exports, there is great irony in the fact that as of December 2008, the Government of Nepal put into place a 16-hours-per-day electrical load-shedding in the country.

Bibliography

Arnson, Cynthia J., ed. 1999. *Comparative Peace Processes in Latin America*. Washington DC: Woodrow Wilson Center Press.

Bhattarai, Baburam. 2003. Dr. Baburam Bhattarai on the Failure of the Peace Talks in Nepal *Monthly Review*, September 7, available at http://www.monthlyreview.org/0903bhattarai.htm.

Binswanger, Hans P., and Miranda Elgin. 1998. Reflections on Land Reform and Farm Size. In *International Agricultural Development*, edited by K. K. Eicher and J. M. Staatz. Baltimore: Johns Hopkins University Press.

Biswakorma, Baburam. 2004. Daundale Khoshyo Dalitko Pesa (Conflict took away Dalit's Profession). In *Bandukko Boj (Gun's Burden)*, edited by R. Dahal and M. Mainali. Kathmandu: Himal Books.

Crawford, Mary, Michelle R. Kaufman, and Alka Gurung. 2007. Women and Children Last: The Effects of the Maoist Insurgency on Gender-based Violence. In *Contentious Politics and Democratization in Nepal*, edited by M. Lawoti. Los Angeles, London and Delhi: Sage.

Darnal, Suvash. 2009. Sambidhan Sabhama Dalit: Aasha ra Apeksha (Dalit in the Constituent Assembly: Hope and Expectation): Jagaran Media Center.

Deraniyagala, Sonali. 2005. The Political Economy of Civil Conflict in Nepal. *Oxford Development Studies* 33 (1):47–62.

Dhakal, Suresh, Khagendra Sangroula, Govind Bartaman, Arjun Karki, and Binod Bhattarai. 2004. *Whose War? Economic and Socio-cultural Impacts of Nepal's Maoist-Government Conflict*. Kathmandu: NGO Federation of Nepal.

Dhruba Kumar. 2003. Consequences of the Militarized Conflict and the Cost of Violence in Nepal. *Contributions to Nepalese Studies* 30 (2):167–216.

Election Commission, Nepal. 2008. *Constituent Assembly Election 2064*. Election Commision, Nepal 2008 [cited April 2008 2008]. Available from http://www.election.gov.np/EN/.

Fortna, Virginia Page. 2008. Peacekeeping and Democratization. In *From War to Democracy*, edited by A. K. Jarstad and T. D. Sisk. Cambridge: Cambridge University Press.

Gurr, Ted Robert. 1993. *Minorities at Risk? A Global View of Ethnopolitical Conflicts*. Washington, D.C.: United States Institute of Peace Press.

———. 2000. *Peoples Versus States: Minorities at Risk in the New Century*. Washington, D.C.: United Institute of Peace Press.

Hoglund, Kristine. 2008. Violence in war-to-democracy transitions. In *From War to Democracy: Dilemmas of Peacebuilding*, edited by A. K. Jarstad and T. D. Sisk. Cambridge: Cambridge University Press.

ICG. 2008. Nepal's Election: A Peaceful Revolution? Asia Report 155. Brussels and Kathmandu: International Crises Group.

INSEC. 2007. *Human Rights Year Book 2007*. Kathmandu: INSEC.

INSEC. 2008. *Human Rights Year Book 2008*. Kathmandu: INSEC.

International Crisis Group. 2008. Nepal's Election: A Peaceful Revolution?.

Karki, Arjun and David Seddon. 2003. *The People's War in Nepal: Left Perspectives*. Delhi: Adroit

Khanal, Mumaram. 2008. Sai Dinmai Oralo (On the Way Down within a Hundred Days). *Nepal: National Weekly*, December 18.

Lawoti, Mahendra. 2005. *Towards a Democratic Nepal: Inclusive Political Institutions for a Multicultural Society*. New Delhi, London, and Thousand Oaks: Sage Publications.

———. 2007. *Looking Back, Looking Forward: Centralization, Multiple Conflicts and Democratic State Building in Nepal*. Washington, D.C.: East-West Center.

———. 2008. Exclusionary Democratization in Nepal, 1990–2002. *Democratization* 15 (2):363–85.

———. 2009. The Myth of Non-ethnic Federalism. *The Kathmandu Post* February 18, 8.

———. Forthcoming, 2009. Nepal. In *Encyclopedia of Human Rights*, edited by D. P. Forsythe. New York: Oxford University Press.

Lecomte-Tilouine, Marie. 2004. Regicide and Maoist revolutionary warfare in Nepal: Modern incarnations of a warrior kingdom. *Anthropology Today* 20 (1):13–19.

Lijphart, Arend. 1999. *Patterns of Democracy: Government Forms and Performance in Thirty-Six Countries*. New Haven and London: Yale University Press.

Manchanda, Rita. 2004. Maoist Insurgency in Nepal: Radicalizing Gendered Narratives *Cultural Dynamics* 16 (2/3):237–58.

Mehta, Ashok K. 2008. Nepal's Wounded Democracy. *Far Eastern Economic Review*, April 8.

Ogura, Kiyoko. 2008. *Seeking State Power – The Communist Party of Nepal (Maoist)*, *Berghof Transitions Series No. 3*: Berghof Research Center for Constructive Conflict Management.

Pathak, Bishnu. 2005. *Politics of People's War and Human Rights in Nepal*. Kathmandu: BIMIPA Publications.

Post Report. 2009. Peace still in rough weather, says Martin. *The Kathmandu Post*.

Punmagar, J. B. 2008. Gundaraj Tira (Towards Holigoonism) *Himal Khabarpatrika*.

Pyakuryal, Bishwambher, and Rabi Shankher Sainju. 2007. *Nepal's Conflict: A Micro Impact Analaysis on Economy*. Kathmandu: Pyakuryal and Sainju.

Riaz, Ali, and Subho Basu. 2007. *Paradise Lost? State Failure in Nepal*. Lanham, MD: Lexington Books.

Rothstein, Bo. 1996. Political Institutions: An Overview. In *A New Handbook of Political Science*, edited by R. E. Goodin and H.-D. Klingemann. Oxford: Oxford University Press.

Sapkota, Bishnu, ed. 2004. *The Costs of War in Nepal: A Research Study*. Kathmandu: National Peace Campaign.

SATP. 2008. *Nepal Time Line*. South Asia Terrorism Portal 2008 [cited November 26 2008]. Available from http://www.satp.org/satporgtp/countries/nepal/timeline/index.html.

Sharma, Kishor. 2006. The Political Economy of Civil War in Nepal. *World Development* 34 (7):1237–1253.

Snyder, Jack L. 2000. *From Voting to Violence: Democratization and Nationalist Conflict*. New York: W.W. Norton and Company.

Thapa, Deepak, and Bandita Sijapati. 2003. *A Kingdom Under Siege: Nepal's Maoist Insurgency, 1996 to 2003*. Kathmandu: The Printhouse.

The Wall Street Journal. 2008. Maoist Rule in Nepal: Their style of governance so far suggests little improvement. *The Wall Street Journal*.

Whelpton, John. 2005. *A History of Nepal*. Cambridge: Cambridge University Press.

Annex A: 40-point Maoist demand, February 1996

Nationalism (7)	Political (13)	Economic (13)	Socio-cultural (7)
1. Abrogation of 1950 Treaty	10. Republican constitution	6. End capital aggrandizement	18. Secular state
2. Abrogation of Mahakali Treaty	11. End royal privileges	7. Self-reliant economy	19. Equality to women
3. Border regulation	12. Civil authority over army	27. Land to the tiller	20. End ethnic oppression
4. Discontinue Gurkha Recruitment	13. Repeal repressive regulations	28. Nationalization of dubious property	21. Abolish untouchability
5. Introduce work permit system	14. Release prisoners	29. Employment generation	22. Equality of languages
6. End cultural invasion	15. End state terrorism	30. Set minimum wage	35. Access to education and health services
7. Stop imperial elements (INGO)	16. Enquiry on actions against Maoists	31. Resettle squatters	40. Protection of the disabled
	17. Recognition on martyrs and penalty to perpetrator	32. Debt relief, credit provision	
	20. Ethnic autonomy	33. Cheap inputs, fair price for agriculture products	
	23. Freedom of speech	36. Control price	
	24. Freedom of thought	37. Provide road, electricity, water supply to rural areas	
	25. Regional devolution	38. Promote cottage industries	
	26. Local governance	39. Control corruption	

Source: Gurung, Harka. *Social Exclusion and Maoist Insurgency*. Paper presented at National Dialogue on the ILO Convention 169 on Indigenous and Tribal People, Kathmandu, Nepal, 19–20 January 2005.

Annex B: Nepal Maoist insurgency timeline

Year/date	Event description
1947	First union-led industrial strike in Nepal shuts down the Biratnagar Jute and Cotton Mills. Communist leader Manmohan Adhikari and Nepali Congress leader Girija Prasad Koirala both claimed to have led the strikes.
1949	
April	Communist leader Pushpa Lal translates the *Communist Manifesto* into Nepali.
September	Communist Party of Nepal (CPN) is officially launched in Calcutta. Seeks to achieve people's sovereignty, but does not fully support the armed anti-Rana movement started by the Nepali Congress.
1951	
February 7	India helps to cobble together the 'Dehli Compromise' whereby the monarchy, Rana Prime Minister, and the Nepali Congress reach an agreement on forming a post-Rana Government in Nepal. The CPN denounces the Delhi Compromise.
November	CPN forms the National People's United Front. It identifies the Nepali Congress as stooges of Nehru and India, and defines its main goals in opposition to what it sees as the Nepali Congress–India/Nehru designs on Nepal.
1952 January	The CPN is banned after allegations that it fomented violence against the Government by associating with an armed group called the Raksha Dal.
1954 January	CPN holds its first convention in secret in the city of Patan. Manmohan Adhikari is recognized as official party General Secretary. The CPN affirms to continue to oppose feudalism, to push for a Constituent Assembly to establish a republican state.

1955

March 13   King Tribhuvan dies and King Mahendra ascends the throne.

1956

April   Tanka Prasad Acharya's Government lifts the ban on the CPN after the latter accepts constitutional monarchy. This sows the seeds of party division along ideological lines.

August   Keshar Jung Rayamajhi takes over as acting party General Secretary in the absence of Manhohan Adhikari. Rayamahji pushes the pro-monarchy line aggressively within the CPN; Pushpa Lal leads the 'radical' opposition. Intense intra-party struggles begin.

1957

June   CPN holds its second National Convention in Kathmandu as intra-party ideological dissension peaks. Beginnings of pro-China and pro-Russia factions in the party. Rayamajhi is elected General Secretary.

1958

February 1   King Mahendra announces parliamentary elections for February 1959. CPN decides to participate even as it continues to demand elections for a Constituent Assembly.

1959

February 12   King Mahendra proclaims the 1959 Constitution with provision for two Houses of Parliament and an elected Government to be headed by a Prime Minister.

May 10   Election results announced. Nepali Congress wins majority (79 out of 105 seats). B.P. Koirala becomes first elected PM of Nepal. CPN has a dismal showing at the polls, winning only four seats.

1960

December 15   King Mahendra stages a coup, disbands the Parliament, ousts the Koirala Government, and illegalizes political parties. CPN General Secretary Rayamajhi issues statement supporting King Mahendra's move while on Moscow visit. Puhpa Lal faction opposes the King's takeover.

1961

March   CPN holds its 'Darbhanga Plenum' which adopts the Rayamajhi line of working with the monarchy while pressing for the restoration of civil rights.

1962

April   CPN holds its third convention in Beneras (India) and removes Rayamahji as its General Secretary. Party further subdivides between the Rayamajhi, Pushpa Lal and Tulsi Lal camps.

1968	Royal regime releases Manmohan Adhikari from prison on promise of endorsing the King's rule.
1971	Government releases hardliner Mohan Bikram Singh from prison. Singh starts attempt to bring party together, but Pushpa Lal resists.
April–May	The Jhapa District Committee, a Naxalite-inspired cell operating in eastern Nepal, announces its campaign to liquidate 'class enemies'. But the movement fails to gain support of other radicals like Mohan Bikram Singh, Nirmal Lama and Pushpa Lal, who wave the campaign aside as immature and untenable. Government quickly suppresses the Jhapa rebellion after the group assassinates seven individuals.
1972	King Mahendra dies (January 15) and King Birendra succeeds.
1974	Mohan Bikram Singh and Nirmal Lama organize 'Fourth Convention' and establish CPN (Fourth Convention).
1975	
June	Jhapa District Committee forms the All Nepal Communist Coordination Committee (ANCCC), but 'Fourth Convention' CPN leaders stay away.
September	CPN holds its Fourth Convention in India under the leadership of Mohan Bikram Singh. The Convention expresses support for a qualified 'armed struggle', but denounces the Jhapa armed actions. Nirmal Lama heads the post- 'Fourth Convention' militant wing of CPN.
1976	Narayan Man Bijukchhe (aka 'Rohit'), who broke away from Pushpa Lal in 1971, forms the Nepal Peasants and Workers Party. Madan Kumar Bhandari breaks away from Pushpa Lal to form the Mukti Morcha Samuha.
1978	In parallel with the 'Fourth Convention' faction of the CPN, the ANCCC transforms into the CPN (Marxist-Leninist) by bringing together a number of splinter left parties.
July 22	Pushpa Lal Shrestha, founder of the CPN and iconic figure in Nepali communist movement, dies.
1979 May 24	In response to mounting nationwide student unrest King Birendra announces a referendum to decide between continuing with the party-less Panchayat system or opting for a multi-party form of government.
1980 May 2	Referendum. The majority supports retaining a reformed Panchayat system. A special commission amends the

Constitution to allow for direct elections to Parliament, and a Prime Minister elected by the House.

1981
May 9

Direct elections for the Parliament. Nepali Congress boycotts the elections. Rayamajhi faction of the CPN decides to participate in the elections while the more radical factions stay away.

1983
November

Mohan Bikram Singh breaks away from the CPN (Fourth Convention) and forms a separate wing of the communist party called CPN (Masal).

1984

Under Mohan Bikram Singh, CPN (Masal) becomes a founding member of Revolutionary Internationalist Movement (RIM).

1985

CPN (Masal) fragments into two groupings: the original CPN (Masal) headed by Mohan Bikram Singh and the CPN (Mashal) led by Mohan Vaidya (aka 'Kiran'). Baburam Bhattarai stayed with Mohan Bikram Singh until 1991.

1986

Pushpa Kamal Dahal (aka 'Prachanda') replaces Mohan Vaidya as head of the CPN (Mashal).

1987

CPN (Manmohan) merged with CPN (Pushpa Lal) to form the CPN-Marxist.
Nepali Congress and various communist parties field candidates in nationwide elections to fill local bodies.

1989
March 24

The 1950 Nepal-India trade and transit treaty expires, and India blocks all trade transit to Nepal. The trade blockade lasted until the Panchayat regime yielded to a multi-party system in April 1990.

1990
January 10

United Left Front (ULF) formed in preparation of launching a mass movement against the King's Panchayat regime. Sahana Pradhan heads the ULF, a composition of six splinter left factions. The ULF excludes the radical left factions.

January 18–20

Nepali Congress holds a national conference at the residence of its veteran leader Ganesh Man Singh. The conference decides to launch a peaceful movement for the restoration of democracy (MRD) starting February 18.

February

Nepali Congress and ULF decide to establish a 'functional unity' in what they mutually termed the 'National People's Liberation Movement' to oppose the Panchayat Regime. G. M. Singh was nominated as its chief coordinator.

February 18–April 7th

Nepali Congress and ULF chose February 18, Nepal's

'Democracy Day', to launch the MRD. Nationwide demonstrations continue unabated until King Birendra relented and agrees to officially end the Panchayat System.

April 9 — King lifts ban on political parties, and the parties call off the protest movement.

April 19 — NC leader Krishna Prasad Bhattarai is nominated as Prime Minister of the Interim Government.

November 9 — King Birendra promulgates the kingdom's new Constitution.

November 23 — CPN (Fourth Convention), CPN (Mashal) and Bhattarai faction of the CPN (Masal) together with CPN (Peasants' Organization) combine to form the 'Unity Center' and adopt Maoism and 'People's War' as the party's ideology. Prachanda becomes the General Secretary of the Unity Center which brings together radical/Maoist strains of the original CPN.

1991

January — CPN-M and CPN (ML) unite to form the CPN (ML) which becomes the largest left party in Nepal.

January 21 — The CPN (Unity Center) establishes United People's Front Nepal (UPFN) as a front organization to participate in electoral/parliamentary processes. Baburam Bhattarai is its first head.

April 6 — CPN (UC) calls for strikes in Kathmandu valley to protest what it sees as the sell out policies of the NC. Up to a dozen people are killed in police firings.

May 12 — General elections. Nepali Congress wins 110 out of 205 seats followed by UML with 68. Bhattarai's radical outfit UPFN wins 9 seats, making it the third largest in the HOR.

November 25 — CPN (UC) holds its first national convention in Chitwan. Differences emerge between Nirmal Lama and Prachanda over ideology and the need for waging an armed struggle.

1993

May 16 — UML leader Madan Bhandari is killed in a highway accident. UML leaders publicly raise suspicions about possible conspiracy in Bhandari's death.

1994

May 22 — CPN (UC) splits into two groups, one led by Nirmal Lama and the other led by Prachanda. Split is reflected within the UPFN, with Bhattarai aligning with Prachanda and N. G. Vaidya siding with Lama.

August 10 — Bhattarai's faction of the UPFN decides to boycott mid-term elections after the Election Commission

	decides to assign the UPFN election symbol solely to the Lama-Vaidya faction.
December 13	CPN (UC) submits a list of its demands to PM Manmohan Adhikari. It is two short of the well-known 40-point list submitted by the Maoists to PM Deuba in early 1996.

1995

March	CPN (UC) holds its 'Third Plenum' in which the Party decides to change its name to Nepal Communist Party (Maoist), to abandon elections altogether, and to take up arms in order to capture state power. Many leaders go underground.
September	CPN-M formally adopts Mao's prescription of a protracted 'Peoples' War'.
November	Under Deuba's Government and Home Minister Khum Bahadur Khadka, the Nepal Police conducts Operation Romeo in Rolpa and Dang districts to suppress pro-Maoist activists. Dozens of local women are raped, and hundreds of suspected Maoists beaten and arrested.

1996

February 4	Baburam Bhattarai submits the CPN-M's '40-Point Demand' to PM Deuba and gives the Government up to February 17 to meet all the demands.
February 13	CPN-M launches its 'People's War' by attacking seven targets in six districts, including an agricultural office in Gorkha District and police posts in Rukum, Rolpa, Gorkha and Sindhuli.

1997

January 3	Maoists attack police post east of Kathmandu in Bethan (Ramechhap district).
March 10	Nepali Congress's Deuba Government collapses.
March 11	Incoming Lokendra Bahadur Chand Government forms and tasks the 'Dhami Commission' to study the Maoist problem and to propose solutions.
October 7	Surya Bahadur Thapa of NDP becomes PM after a Napali Congress-NDP-NGP coalition takes over power from the Chand Government.

1998

January 8	PM Surya B. Thapa recommends dissolution of the HOR
March 5	The CPN-UML splits into two groups over the signing of the Mahakali Treaty. The rebel faction is called CPN (ML) and is headed by Bam Dev Gautam.
April 12	Girija Prasad Koirala forms a NC minority Government.
May 26	Police start a counter-insurgency operation named Kilo Sierra II in the Maoist heartland of Rukum and Rolpa.

September 8	Top Maoist politburo member Suresh Wagle and commander Bhimsen Pokharel are killed in a police encounter.
November 27	CPN-M announce a campaign to develop 'base areas'.

1999

January 2	For the first time, Maoists attack a police post just outside the Kathmandu Valley.
April 19	Maoists explode bombs in Kathmandu, targeting the offices of the Election Commission and Gorkhapatra, the state-run newspaper.
December 30	A taskforce is formed under Sher Bahadur Deuba to study and propose solutions to resolve the Maoist crisis.

2000

March 20	K. P. Bhattarai is ousted as PM and G. P. Koirala replaces him.
June 8	Maoists attack a police post in Jajarkot district using mortars and bombs. Nine policemen, seven civilians and 21 Maoist rebels are killed.
August 7	Maoists reject talks offer by Government.
September 23	Maoists attack and destroy the district administration building in Dunai, headquarters of remote Dolpo district.
December 27	Fifty-six rebel Nepali Congress members withdraw their support for the Koirala Government, forcing the PM out.

2001

January 22	Government announces formation of the Armed Police Force (AFP) to supplement the Nepal Police's counter-insurgency deployment.
February 4	Maoists attack Supreme Court Chief Justice K. P. Upadhyay in western Nepal (Surkhet). Chief Justice narrowly escapes, but six in his convoy are killed.
March 6	PM Koirala makes overtures to Maoists to sit for talks. Civil society leaders are mobilized to make contacts with the Maoists.
April 1	Maoists attack police post in their stronghold of Rukum, killing 31, injuring 11 and abducting 23 policemen.
April 16	PM Koirala makes public appeal to Maoists to surrender in return for amnesty.
June 1	Royal Palace massacre, in which the Crown Prince kills the King, Queen, and their immediate and extended families gathered for a family weekend dinner.
June 4	Prince Gyanendra is crowned King.
July 12	Maoists attack police post in Holleri (Ropla district) and take 71 policemen prisoners. Girija Koirala alleges that the Royal Nepal Army (RNA) refused his orders to

	mobilize against the Maoist forces and rescue the prisoners.
July 19	PM Koirala resigns over his inability to tackle the Maoist insurgency, and over the alleged failure of the RNA to obey his orders.
July 22	Sher Bahadur Deuba becomes new PM, and immediately proposes peace talks with the Maoists.
July 25	Government and Maoists both declare a ceasefire.
August 30	Round 1 of the peace talks held in Kathmandu.
September 13–14	Round 2 of the peace talks held in Bardiya district.
November 13	Round 3 of the peace talks held in Kathmandu. Maoists insist on CA elections, but drop their demand for an immediate republican state.
November 21	Prachanda indicates that the talks have failed, and announces end of Maoist ceasefire.
November 22	Maoists launch daring night attack on the RNA Barracks in Dang district, and make away with a large cache of arms and ammunitions. Fourteen soldiers are killed and dozens injured.
November 25	Maoists attack RNA station in town of Salleri in Eastern Nepal.
November 26	Government declares a state of emergency. CPN-M is designated as a 'Terrorist' organization and the RNA is officially mobilized. Government promulgates the Terrorism Ordinance 2001.

2002

February 17	Maoists attack Mangalsen (Acham district) and kill 48 army troops and 49 policemen.
May 2–3	State security kills 32 Maoists in Dang and 50 in Rolpa.
May 7	US President Bush pledges American support for Nepal to combat insurgency.
May 15–18	UK and India offer help to combat insurgency.
May 22	PM Deuba dissolves Parliament as it is unlikely to support an extension of emergency. Elections are scheduled for November 3.
July 15	Deuba Government dissolves the elected local bodies and deputes Government officials to carry out local functions.
September 8	Maoists attack the police post in Bhimad (Sindhuli district) and kill 49 police personnel, while injuring 21. Roughly 50 insurgents are killed in the clashes. The same night, Maoists attack the town of Sandhikharka (Argakhachi district headquarters), kill 68 security personnel and loot 90 million rupees from a state bank.

October 3	PM Deuba proposes that elections be delayed by one year.
October 4	King Gyanendra ousts PM Deuba. King mentions Deuba's failure to hold timely elections as reason for his dismissal.
October 11	King appoints Lokendra Bahadur Chand as Prime Minister.
December 3	Maoists issue press release indicating their openness to peace talks. However, they stick to their core political demand of a Constituent Assembly.

2003

January 26	Armed Police Force IGP Krishna Mohan Shrestha and his wife are assassinated by the Maoists.
January 29	Ceasefire. Government removes terrorist tag and Interpol Red Corner notices.
February 17	Chand calls for an all-party meeting between the constitutional parties before talks with the Maoists begin. The parties reject this offer.
April 27	First round of peace talks is held between the Government and the Maoists in Kathmandu. Maoists submit a 35-point agenda.
April 30	US places Maoists on 'other terrorist organization' list.
May 9	Second round of peace talks takes place. Government is said to agree to restrict the RNA to within 5 kilometers of its barracks in the Maoist areas. Five days later Government refutes it agreed to the 5 kilometer clause.
May 11	Maoists open an office in Anamnagar in Kathmandu.
August 17	Round three of the peace talks. Government agrees to meet many items in the Maoist agenda except for holding Constituent Assembly elections.
August 23	Chennai (India) immigration officials arrest Maoist leader C. P. Gajurel as he tries to fly to London on a fake passport.
August 26	Maoists fire at motorcade of PM Deuba.
August 27	Maoists officially announce the end of the ceasefire.
August 28	Maoists shoot two army colonels in Kathmandu. One succumbs to injuries.
November 25	United States commits to give Nepal an additional 20,000 M-16 rifles to ". . . modernize the Royal Nepal Army and for political stability and democracy."
December 17	RNA claims that the RNA has killed at least 1,056 Maoists since the collapse of ceasefire on August 27.
December 20	RNA announces the formation of village security forces in Lamjung, Parsa and Kapilavastu districts.
December 26	Defense Secretary Madan Prasad Aryal survives

repeated attempts on his life by the Maoists at Manahari Village Development Committee (VDC) area in Makwanpur.

2004

February 3	Detention of Maoist Politburo member Chandra Prakash Gajurel (alias Gaurav) in India extended after court hearing to have him released fails.
February 8	Indian authorities arrest two Maoist leaders, Matrika Prasad Yadav and Suresh Ale Magar, from Lucknow and hand them over to Nepali authorities.
March 21	Maoists launch a night attack on Beni Bazaar, headquarters of the Myagdi district. They break into the local jail and destroy every government building.
March 29	Indian police arrest second-ranked Maoist leader and standing committee member Mohan Vaidya (alias Kiran) in Siliguri, West Bengal.
June 2	King Gyanendra appoints Sher Bahadur Deuba the Prime Minister of Nepal.
July 20	Chairman of the CPN-M, Pushpa Kamal Dahal, says there is no chance for an immediate ceasefire or talks unless the Government is prepared to concede to Constituent Assembly and United Nations mediation.
August 12	Government spokesperson Mohammad Mohsin announces the formation of a High-level Peace Committee headed by Prime Minister Deuba with representation of senior leaders of the political parties in the coalition.
October 13	Deuba Government promulgates the Terrorist and Disruptive Activities (Control and Punishment) Ordinance (TADA).
October 14–16	Army launches major campaigns to flush out Maoists from Rukum, Rolpa and Pyuthan districts. Army also goes after Maoist training camps in Argakhanchi, Gulmi, Myagdi and Baglung districts.

2005

January 5	RNA attacks Maoist base in far-western Kailali district and kills many Maoists.
February 1	King Gyanendra dismisses the Government led by Prime Minister Deuba and imposes emergency in the country. Senior party and civil society leaders are imprisoned or placed under house arrest. Communications and media freedoms are curtailed.
February 2	King Gyanendra appoints a ten-member cabinet.
February 22	India and UK suspend military aid to Nepal.

April 7	Maoists launch a major attack on an army barrack in Khara (Rukum district) but RNA repels it, killing many PLA fighters and capturing significant amounts of weapons and bombs.
April 13	King Gyanendra calls on Election Commission to hold municipal elections within the Nepali year.
April 17	UML demands restoration of full democracy before it will agree to participate in the municipal elections.
April 21	Maoist leader and 'central committee' member Muma Ram Khanal quits the CPN-M. King's Government frees from house arrest at least 61 political detainees, including former Deputy Prime Minister Bharat Mohan Adhikary.
April 29	King lifts the state of emergency rule.
May 5	Parties sidelined by King Gyanendra – Nepali Congress (NC), Nepali Congress (Democratic), CPN-UML, People's Front Nepal (PFN), NWPP, Nepal Goodwill Party-Anandi (NGP-A) and United Left Front (ULF) led by CP Mainali – begin talks to form a seven-party alliance (SPA).
May 11	US Assistant Secretary for South Asia makes arms supply to the RNA contingent on the restoration of democracy and release of political prisoners.
June 6	Maoists blow up a passenger bus in Chitwan district killing 36 civilians and injuring 72 others.
June 20	Seven Party Alliance (SPA) call on Maoists to renounce violence and join peaceful democratic movement against Royal rule.
June 30	Former Prime Minister Girija Prasad Koirala says he will open dialogue with the Maoists to bring peace and democracy to the country.
July 11	Maoists Chairman Pushpa Kamal Dahal says that his party is ready to collaborate with political parties to reverse Royal rule.
July 19	Falling out between Prachanda and Baburam Bhattarai is repaired.
August 9	Maoist fighters attack an army road-building crew in Pili (Kalikot district) and kill 43 army personnel.
September 1	CPN-M's Prachanda and Communist Party of India (Maoist) Ganapathy issue simultaneous statements against outsiders who are opposed to revolution in South Asia.
September 3	As rapprochement efforts between SPA and Maoists proceed at informal level, Prachanda announces a three-month unilateral cease fire.
October 12	King Gyanendra in a national address instructs the

	Election Commission to hold elections to the House of Representatives by April 2007. SPA opposes the proposal the very next day.
October 26	China is reported to have agreed to supply military aid to Nepal to the tune of 72 million rupees.
November 4	US warns SPA against a possible alliance with the Maoists.
November 22	With support from the Indian Government, SPA and Maoists sign a 12-point agreement to jointly combat Royal rule in Nepal. The agreement includes a commitment to hold Constituent Assembly elections and for Maoists to renounce violence and join the democratic mainstream.

2006

March 19	SPA and the Maoists (SPA-M) announce an agreement to launch separate movements against Royal rule starting on April 6. Maoists withdraw their proposed blockade the of the Capital city and district headquarters.
April 6–12	On April 6 SPA starts its pro-democracy agitation to roll back Royal rule. Over 400 pro-democracy protesters are arrested in Kathmandu while dozens of others are injured nationwide. There are non-stop street protests and demonstrations across the country.
April 20	Protests continue. King meets with special Indian envoy, Dr. Karan Singh, at the Royal Palace.
April 21	Following Dr. Karan Singh's visit, King Gyanendra announces that he is ready to hand over the reins of Government to the SPA. He invites SPA to forward a name for Prime Ministership of the country.
April 22	SPA and Maoists both reject the King's offer, and resolve to continue the agitation.
April 24	King Gyanendra announces the reinstatement of the HOR. The SPA agrees to withdraw its protest movements. The Maoists reject the King's moves and vow to continue their agitation.
April 25	SPA welcome's the King's move and appoints Girija Prasad Koirala as new Prime Minister.
April 28	The reinstated HOR holds its first meeting, and Koirala proposes elections for a Constituent Assembly as the first order of business.
May 26	The Government and Maoist talks teams meet for the first peace talks after the reinstatement of the HOR. The government team is led by Home Minister Krishna Prasad Sitoula and the Maoist team is led by their spokesman, Krishna Bahadur Mahara.

June 2	Maoists hold their largest open mass political rally in Kathmandu after going underground. Over 200,000 attend the rally. Maoists demand the dissolution of the HOR and the holding of a national round table conference.
June 15	Government and Maoists hold a second round of peace talks. A 31-member Code of Conduct monitoring committee is formed.
June 16	An eight-point Agreement of Peace is signed between the Government and the Maoists at the residence of the Prime Minister in Kathmandu. The agreement includes: drafting an interim constitution within 15 days; forming an interim Government within a month; HOR as well as Maoist local bodies to be dissolved; and UN to manage and monitor arms of both sides. Prachanda holds his first public press conference from the PM's residence.
August 6	PM Koirala says that democracy in Nepal must make room for both extremes, the Maoists as well as the Monarchy. The next day, Maoist ideologue Baburam Bhattarai strongly disagrees with this view from Koirala.
August 9	Government and Maoists reach agreement on inviting the United Nations to Nepal to monitor the peace and manage the arms of the two sides.
November 21	Government, SPA leaders, and the Maoists sign the Comprehensive Peace Agreement (CPA). The CPA brings the armed struggle of the CPN-M to a formal close.
November 30	Government of West Bengal (India) releases two top Maoist leaders, Mohan Vaidya and C. P. Gajurel.
November	CPN-M forms the Young Communist League (YCL).

2007

January 14	Cabinet approves the draft of the Interim Constitution. It will be presented to the HOR for approval on January 15.
January 15	The Interim Constitution is approved. The HOR dissolves itself, opening the way for an Interim Legislature-Parliament and Interim Government. A 330-member new Interim Parliament holds its first session. The CPN-M is represented by 83 members.
January 16	Madhesi activists burn the Interim Constitution in Kathmandu. Twenty-eight activists are arrested by the police.
January 18	Maoists issue orders to dissolve all their 'people's governments' across the nation as well as their 'people's courts.'
January 19	Maoist activist shoot and kills a Madhesi People's Rights Forum (MPRF) activist in Siraha district.

January 23	United Nations Mission in Nepal (UNMIN) officially established.
March 21	Maoists and MPRF supporters have a major face-off in Gaur (Rautahat district). At least 28 Maoist cadres are killed when MPRF supporters retaliate against what they see as provocation by the Maoists.
April 1	An Interim Government headed by Girija Prasad Koirala is formed and includes five CPN-M members. Leaders agree to hold the CA elections on June 20, 2007.
September 4	Maoists decide to revive their kangaroo courts across the country.
September 5	Government and agitating MPRF sign a 22-point deal.
October 5	CA elections scheduled for November 22 are postponed as SPA and Maoists cannot reach agreement on monarchy's future and the specific electoral method to be adopted.
September 17	CPN-M quit the Interim Government over the Koirala Government's refusal to give in to Maoist demands to declare the country a republic prior to CA elections, and the additional demand of using a fully proportional system of voting in the CA elections.
December 15	SPA agree to most Maoist demands to hold the CA elections, including declaring Nepal a republic through the first sitting of the new assembly. The number of seats in the CA is increased to 601 to accommodate the members to be elected through the proportional system.
December 30	Maoists rejoin the Government.
2008	
April 10	Constituent Assembly elections.
April 22	US State Department says although there is no change in the 'terrorist' status of the CPN-M, there is a chance there will be a review in the future if the Maoists adhere to accepted democratic norms and peaceful politics.
April 24	All CA elections votes are counted, giving the CPN-M 120 out of 240 seats in the first-past-the-post portion of the elections, and 100 seats through proportional representation.
May 28	Nepal becomes a republic.
June 26	PM Koirala resigns as Prime Minister, making way for the Maoist Government.
July 21	Ram Baran Yadav of Nepali Congress becomes the first president of Nepal. Parmananda Jha of MPRF is elected Vice-President.
August 15	The Constituent Assembly elects CPN-M's Prachanda as the first Prime Minister of Federal Democratic Republic of Nepal.

August 21	Cabinet positions are shared between CPN-M (9), CPN-UML (6) and MJF (4) and other parties. Maoists keep the defense and finance ministries.
September 21	Prachanda arrives in the US to attend the UN General Assembly meetings. Army Chief says only those who meet army's strict standards will be inducted into the state army.
September 25	NC spokesman Arjun KC issues a stern message that a new round of conflict would begin in the country should the Government integrate the ideologically trained PLA into the Nepali Army.
October 12	US not to remove Maoists from the 'other terrorist groups' list, but open to engaging the Maoists in other ways.
November 23	NC leader Girija Prasad Koirala says that there can be no PLA merger into the Nepali Army as the Maoists had violated most previous agreements.
December 12	Prime Minister Prachanda extols the role that violence has played in bringing positive change in Nepal, and says that people need to become educated about this fact.
December 16	Constituent Assembly special committees start the preliminary work for drafting the new Constitution.

2009

January 1	Nepali Congress ends its boycott of Parliament after a new agreement is reached with the CPN-M: the Maoists are to ensure the return of all seized property within 90 days; the YCL will vacate all public and government space and buildings it occupies (for residence and training) as well as renounce its paramilitary structure within three weeks.
February 2	CPN-M changes its name to United Communist Party of Nepal (Maoist) after merger with Communist Party of Nepal-Ekata Kendra Masal. In a meeting to ratify the party merger statute, Prime Minister Prachanda recommits his party to the goal of communism.
February 8	In the face of strong opposition by the Maoist Defense Minister Ram Bahadur Badal, Nepali Army announces it will go ahead with plans to fill 2,800 vacancies.
February 9	Senior Maoist Matrika Prasad Yadav announces departure from parent party and commits to remake the party in line with its revolutionary goals.
February 24	Jhalnath Khanal is elected General Secretary of the CPN-UML.

Index